Processing Syntax and Morphology

OXFORD SURVEYS IN SYNTAX AND MORPHOLOGY

GENERAL EDITOR: Robert D Van Valin, Jr, Heinrich-Heine Universität Düsseldorf & University at Buffalo, The State University of New York

ADVISORY EDITORS: Guglielmo Cinque, University of Venice; Daniel Everett, Illinois State University; Adele Goldberg, Princeton University; Kees Hengeveld, University of Amsterdam; Caroline Heycock, University of Edinburgh; David Pesetsky, MIT; Ian Roberts, University of Cambridge; Masayoshi Shibatani, Rice University; Andrew Spencer, University of Essex; Tom Wasow, Stanford University

PUBLISHED

IN PREPARATION

Processing Syntax and Morphology: A Neurocognitive Perspective

INA BORNKESSEL-SCHLESEWSKY
AND MATTHIAS SCHLESEWSKY

OXFORD
UNIVERSITY PRESS

OXFORD
UNIVERSITY PRESS

Great Clarendon Street, Oxford OX2 6DP

Oxford University Press is a department of the University of Oxford.
It furthers the University's objective of excellence in research, scholarship,
and education by publishing worldwide in

Oxford New York

Auckland Cape Town Dar es Salaam Hong Kong Karachi
Kuala Lumpur Madrid Melbourne Mexico City Nairobi
New Delhi Shanghai Taipei Toronto

With offices in

Argentina Austria Brazil Chile Czech Republic France Greece
Guatemala Hungary Italy Japan Poland Portugal Singapore
South Korea Switzerland Thailand Turkey Ukraine Vietnam

Oxford is a registered trade mark of Oxford University Press
in the UK and in certain other countries

Published in the United States
by Oxford University Press Inc., New York

© Ina Bornkessel-Schlesewsky, Matthias Schlesewsky 2009

The moral rights of the authors have been asserted
Database right Oxford University Press (maker)

First Published 2009 by Oxford University Press

British Library Cataloguing in Publication Data
Data available

Library of Congress Cataloging in Publication Data
Data available

Typeset by SPI Publisher Services, Pondicherry, India
Printed in Great Britain
on acid-free paper by
CPI Antony Rowe, Chippenham, Wiltshire

ISBN 978–0–19–920781–7 (Hbk.)
      978–0–19–920782–4 (Pbk.)

1 3 5 7 9 10 8 6 4 2

Contents

General Preface

Oxford Surveys in Syntax and Morphology provides overviews of the major approaches to subjects and questions at the center of linguistic research in morphology and syntax. The volumes are accessible, critical, and up-to-date. Individually and collectively they aim to reveal the field's intellectual history and theoretical diversity. Each book published in the series will characteristically contain: (1) a brief historical overview of relevant research in the subject; (2) a critical presentation of approaches from relevant (but usually seen as competing) theoretical perspectives to the phenomena and issues at hand, including an objective evaluation of the strengths and weaknesses of each approach to the central problems and issues; (3) a balanced account of the current issues, problems, and opportunities relating to the topic, showing the degree of consensus or otherwise in each case. The volumes will thus provide researchers and graduate students concerned with syntax, morphology, and related aspects of semantics with a vital source of information and reference.

Dr. Ina Bornkessel-Schlesewsky and Dr. Matthias Schlesewsky's *Processing Syntax and Morphology: A Neurocognitive Perspective* presents a comprehensive overview of work in psycholinguistics and neurolinguistics with regard to how human beings process morphosyntax. The discussion covers both the experimental methods employed in this research as well as the main empirical results, results which have implications for theories of syntax and morphology.

Robert D. Van Valin, Jr
General Editor

Heinrich Heine University,
Düsseldorf

University at Buffalo,
The State University of New York

Preface

This book is the product of many fortunate circumstances. Neither one of us could – or would – have written it alone. Rather, it is the result of countless joint weekends, several prolonged hikes through various mountains and, yes, one or two glasses of wine. Nonetheless, the following sixteen chapters are not solely due to our own efforts.

Our first note of thanks must go to our wonderful teacher and friend Gisbert Fanselow. He taught us what it means to love linguistics without indoctrination – a legacy which we have done our best to honor in this volume.

We are also deeply grateful to Robert Van Valin. He not only gave us the opportunity to write this book but has also supported and inspired our own research for a number of years.

A special thank you goes to Petra "B." Schumacher, who not only provided very helpful comments on previous versions of this manuscript but also showed us that discourse-based influences on the neurocognition of language involve so much more than lovesick peanuts. The book manuscript also benefited greatly from discussions with Brian McElree and Richard Wiese, who have both helped us to broaden our perspectives beyond the domains of syntax, morphology and the brain. We are also deeply thankful to Angela Friederici for her unselfish support over many years, which gave us the luxury of being able to develop our own perspective on the neurocognition of language in a relatively short period of time.

Finally, we would like to thank all of our collaborators and students for putting up with a continuous state of deprival for the last few months. Without their patience, we would never have been able to complete this enterprise. In particular, thanks to Dietmar Roehm for his continuous support and encouragement even in the darkest of hours. But thank you also to all of the others: Katja Brüning, Kamal Kumar Choudhary, Şükrü Barış Demiral, Safiye Genç, Tanja Grewe, Friederike Haupt, Yu-Chen Hung, Sabine Keller, Franziska Kretzsch-mar, Amelie Mahlstedt, R. Muralikrishnan, Markus Philipp, Isabel Plauth; Luming Wang, Susann Wolff.

For artistically non-inclined scientists like ourselves, access to a graphic design department that produces beautifully crafted figures always gives one the feeling of being in "heaven on earth". Yet even by the standards of this very favorable overall situation, we were especially fortunate: in putting together the figures for this book, we had the help of someone who is not only exceptionally capable and who did not utter a single word of complaint when confronted with our long list of desired figures just before Christmas but who is also simply a wonderful person and a joy to work with. So thank you, Kerstin Flake.

To our friends, it will hardly come as a surprise that our final set of acknowledgments is gastronomic in nature. It is difficult to say exactly how many of the following pages were written in places with good food and/or fantastic wine. We would therefore like to thank the following "safe havens" for all of the hours in which they tolerated us, protected us from the outside world, and gave us the opportunity to work in perfect peace and harmony:

- Weinlädele, Marburg. What can we say: it's been "home" for many years now.
- Landhaus Freiberg, Oberstdorf. For the perfect refuge in which to write a book. Did we say "perfect"? Yes: that's exactly what we meant.
- Stillwater/Fresh, Launceston, Tasmania. There are many special places in Tasmania, but the edge of the Tamar River has always been a great place to work. "Ripples" has given rise to two worthy – though very different – successors.
- Alt 168, Oberstdorf. For the ultimate in friendliness and hospitality and because, every once in a while, one needs a restaurant with a chef who has no aversion to cheese.

List of Plates

List of Figures

List of Tables

List of Abbreviations

1	first person
3	third person
a	anterior
ACC	accusative
AUX	auxiliary
BA	Brodmann's area
BOLD	blood oxygenation-level dependent
CC	corpus callosum
CPS	closure positive shift
DAT	dative
DEF	definite
EEG	electroencephalogram
ELAN	early left anterior negativity
ERG	ergative
ERP	event-related brain potential
F	feminine
fMRI	functional magnetic resonance imaging
GEN	genitive
IFG	inferior frontal gyrus
IPFV	imperfective
IPS	intraparietal sulcus
LAN	left anterior negativity
M	masculine
MFG	middle frontal gyrus
MMN	mismatch negativity
MTG	middle temporal gyrus

N400	centro-parietal negativity with a maximum at approximately 400 ms post stimulus onset
NOM	nominative
NP	noun phrase
p	posterior
P300	family of positivities with a maximum at approximately 300 ms post stimulus onset
P600	centro-parietal positivity with a maximum at approximately 600 ms post stimulus onset
PFV	perfective
PL	plural
PP	prepositional phrase
PRS	present
PRT	particle
rCBF	regional cerebral blood flow
ROI	region of interest
RSVP	rapid serial visual presentation
rTMS	repetitive transcranial magnetic stimulation
sLAN	sustained left anterior negativity
SG	singular
STG	superior temporal gyrus
STS	superior temporal sulcus
TMS	transcranial magnetic stimulation
V	verb
VP	verb phrase
S	sentence
SOV	subject–object–verb (basic word order)
SVO	subject–verb–object (basic word order)

1

Introduction

The last ten years of the twentieth century might well be considered the "decade of the brain". With the advent of neuroimaging methods, and particularly of functional magnetic resonance imaging (fMRI), the field of cognitive neuroscience thrived. The study of language posed no exception to this general development: in addition to providing a vehicle for more general goals in neuroscientific research, language soon became one of the major domains of neurocognitive investigation in its own right. On the one hand, the methodological advances suddenly offered a completely new perspective on the tradition of linking language-related functions with particular brain regions, a correlation which has intrigued scientists and non-scientists alike for at least two thousand years. While these insights had previously relied entirely on the study of lesions in patients with particular language (speech) disorders, the possibility of a non-invasive mapping of the neural regions involved in language processing in healthy individuals opened entirely new avenues of investigation. On the other hand, the importance of electrophysiological studies for psycholinguistic investigation also increased dramatically. This method (electroencephalography, EEG), which was first applied to humans at the beginning of the twentieth century and which had been successfully used to examine a variety of dimensions of word processing in the 1980s, became the rising star among the methods employed to investigate sentence processing in the 1990s. In contrast to imaging methods such as fMRI, electrophysiology provides an exquisitely precise temporal resolution, which is of primary importance if the very rapid and complex processes that make up language comprehension and production are to be captured adequately. In this way, by the end of the twentieth century, the field of linguistics had at its disposal the means to examine both the spatial and the temporal characteristics of how language is processed in the brain.

This book provides an overview of the insights gained within the continually growing field of the neurocognition of language, with a special focus on the processing of syntax and morphology. It aims to acquaint the reader with the main questions and developments within this area of research, with the results obtained and with the models that have been formulated to capture the existing data patterns. In addition, it describes the main methods used for the neurocognitive investigation of language and draws some conclusions as to the relative advantages of particular techniques and the factors that constrain them. Furthermore, we attempt to bind the neurocognitive perspective back to the classical, "behavioral" view on language, in which insights on language architecture were gained primarily from an examination of the "output" from the neurocognitive system (e.g. in the form of speakers' judgments over particular constructions). This focus is maintained throughout the volume: while its overall orientation is primarily neurocognitive in nature, each chapter will also consider the way in which non-neurocognitive psycholinguistic findings may inform neurocognitive models and, conversely, how the passage from neurocognitive processing to the behavioral output might be envisioned.

The book is organized as follows. In the second chapter, we provide an overview of the main neurocognitive methods presently in use in the investigation of morphosyntax as well as a short introduction to relevant behavioral methods. In addition, the chapter discusses some major considerations that should be kept in mind with respect to neurocognitive experimental designs and data interpretation. Chapter 2 therefore aims to render the remainder of the volume accessible to readers without the necessary experimental background and should enable them to interpret studies conducted in this area and to recognize their advantages and limitations. Following this initial introductory chapter, the volume is subdivided into four parts, which discuss morphosyntactic processing at the word level, the sentence level, at the interfaces to other linguistic domains such as prosody and pragmatics, and neurocognitive models of morphosyntactic processing, respectively. Parts I–III are independent of one another and thus do not presuppose any knowledge beyond the methodological prerequisites discussed in Chapter 2. Part IV builds upon the empirical insights discussed in the preceding sections and attempts to show how these can be bound together to form coherent characterizations of the processing architecture. Finally, Chapter 16 discusses possible future directions in the neurocognition of syntactic and morphological processing.

2

Methodological prerequisites

Brain responses at the level of higher cognition can essentially be characterized with respect to time and space. The temporal dimension is concerned with the question of "when" particular processes take place, for example with regard to the question of whether different linguistic information types become available at different points in time. In contrast to behavioral methods, which serve to characterize the output of a cognitive process (e.g. in the form of a button-press once an experimental participant has categorized a particular stimulus), neuroscientific methods with a high temporal resolution allow us to track the brain activity engendered by cognitive processes such as language comprehension or production in real time. The spatial dimension seeks to specify "where" specific aspects of cognitive processing take place in the brain. As already mentioned in the introduction, the attempt to associate certain brain regions ("language centers") with language functions has a long tradition in the history of medicine and philosophy. However, the possibility of examining clearly localizable brain activity in the living, healthy brain has only become available during the last decades. This methodological advance, which is still undergoing a continual refinement, has opened up a myriad of new possibilities for the investigation of the brain bases of cognitive processing.

   This chapter aims to provide a short introduction to the neuroscientific methods that have been and are being used to examine language-related processes. In accordance with the categorization undertaken above, we begin by discussing methods with a high temporal resolution, before turning to methods with a high spatial resolution. Finally, in view of the major role that behavioral methods have played in psycholinguistic theorizing over the last decades, the chapter concludes with a brief introduction to the most important of these techniques.

2.1 Methods with a high temporal resolution

2.1.1 *Electroencephalography (EEG)*

Event-related brain potentials (ERPs) are currently the most widely-used electrophysiological technique for the examination of language processing. Like alternative methods, which will be briefly discussed at the end of this section, ERPs are based on the human electroencephalogram (EEG), which provides a measure of changes in the electrical activity of the brain.

2.1.1.1 The human EEG: Some preliminary remarks   The EEG was first recorded in humans by the German psychiatrist Hans Berger (1873–1941). In his 1929 article "Über das Elektrenkephalogramm des Menschen" ("On the human electroencephalogram"), he described a number of observations suggesting that EEG measures correlate with cognitive processing (Berger 1929). In particular, he noted that changes in the rhythmical activity of the EEG depend on changes in cognitive state: the so-called alpha rhythm (prominent oscillations in the range of approximately 8–12 Hz) decreases during problem solving (e.g. mental arithmetic) and increases again during relaxed wakefulness.

The neurophysiological activity measured by the EEG results primarily from the summed postsynaptic activity of parallelly-oriented pyramidal cells perpendicular to the surface of the scalp (cf. Figure 2.1; see also section 2.1.3). It is currently assumed that this activity results from dipole moments between different cortical layers, i.e. from the current flow between a "source" (place of low depolarization) and a "sink" (place of higher depolarization). It is also important to note that the EEG reflects the activity of cell assemblies, rather than of single cells.

EEG measurements can be obtained non-invasively by electrodes applied to the surface of the scalp. This type of measurement has several consequences for the interpretation of the recorded potential changes, of which we would like to note two. The first concerns the possibility that activity may, under certain circumstances, be "invisible" to surface recordings. This is the case, for example, when potential changes in different cortical layers cancel one another out to yield no measurable deflection at the surface of the scalp. (A similar situation results when the cell assemblies yielding the activity are not oriented perpendicularly to the surface of the scalp.) The second point relates to the so-called "inverse problem". This term refers to the well-known phenomenon that, while the distribution of changes in the activity of the surface EEG can be predicted if the source of the activity is known (a "forward solution"), the location of a source cannot be uniquely reconstructed from the surface pattern. For example, while Broca's region in the inferior left frontal cortex (see section 2.2.1.1) is known to be important for language processing, it nevertheless *cannot* be unequivocally concluded that changes in surface EEG activity directly above this region are generated in Broca's area. While such a causal relationship between an underlying brain region of interest and surface EEG activity might of course hold, the fact that there are always multiple solutions to the inverse problem means that the activity could also have been generated elsewhere. One should therefore always be cautious in linking EEG topography to underlying neural regions, even when an association appears attractive. Many software packages for the analysis of EEG data nowadays offer mathematical solutions to the inverse problem. Here too, however, it should be kept in mind that results obtained in this way can only ever be regarded as approximations, since there is no *unique* mathematical solution to the inverse problem.

The interested reader is referred to *Electroencephalography* (Niedermeyer and Lopes da Silva 2005), a volume which provides a wealth of information regarding the underlying assumptions of EEG measurements, technical considerations and techniques for data analysis (see also Handy 2004). In addition, Berger's monograph *Das Elektrenkephalogramm des Menschen* (Berger 1938) is an impressive work and, as such, well worth reading. It reveals that many of the technical considerations and underlying assumptions in state-of-the-art EEG-based research conducted today could already be found in Berger's pioneering approach.

2.1.1.2 Event-related brain potentials (ERPs)   ERPs are potential changes in the EEG that are time-locked to sensory or cognitive events and which may therefore be used to examine the brain's response to critical stimuli (e.g. words or sentences). As these stimulus-induced changes are very small (between approx. 2–8 μV for language) in comparison to the spontaneous electrical activity of the brain (approx. 10–100 μV), they must be isolated from this background activity by means of an averaging procedure. This means that approximately 30–40 items of each stimulus type of interest must be presented in order for the signal-to-noise ratio to reach an acceptable level. For the same reason, single participant ERPs typically cannot be interpreted with respect to psycholinguistic manipulations (though strong effects are sometimes visible in single participant averages). Rather, once averaging has been accomplished for each participant, a "grand average" is computed over these individual averages, which then forms the basis for a functional interpretation. The setup of the ERP method is illustrated schematically in Figure 2.1.

As is evident from Figure 2.1, ERPs consist of a series of negative and positive potential changes relative to critical stimulus onset. They provide a multidimensional measure of electrical brain activity in that they can be classified with respect to a number of parameters: latency, polarity, topography and amplitude. These different dimensions are described in detail in Table 2.1. A typical electrode setup (the so-called "extended 10–20 system") is shown in Figure 2.2.

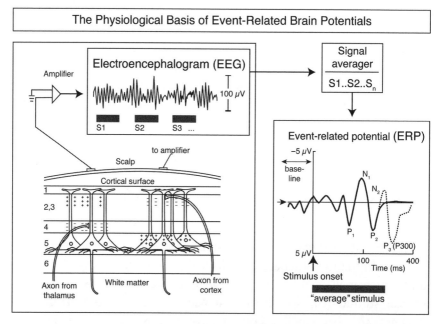

Figure 2.1 Schematic illustration of the physiological basis of the EEG signal (left panel) and the extraction of event-related brain potentials (ERPs) from the background EEG (right panel). The right panel depicts the conventional way of presenting ERPs, namely as voltage changes (y-axis) as a function of time (x-axis). By convention, negative potential changes are plotted upward. ERP components (see text) are often labeled with the letters "N" and "P" for "negativity" and "positivity", respectively.

Source: Adapted from Martin (1991) and Köster (2004).

Table 2.1: Dimensions for the classification of ERP components. All of the dimensions can only be interpreted relative to a control condition (see text for further details).

Dimension	Description
Latency	The time point relative to critical stimulus onset at which the potential change is observable. Latency can be defined either as *peak latency*, which refers to the latency of the amplitude maximum, or as *onset latency*, which refers to the time point at which the critical condition begins to diverge from the control condition. Latency often forms part of the component name and is typically measured in milliseconds (ms).
Polarity	Whether the potential change in the critical condition is positive or negative relative to the control condition. Polarity ("N" for negativity and "P" for positivity) is also often part of a component name.
Topography	The scalp distribution of an effect, i.e. the electrode positions at which the effect is measurable. On account of the fact that the underlying source activity does not lead to punctual changes at the surface of the scalp (i.e. changes are not restricted to single electrodes), topography is usually defined with respect to groups of electrodes, so-called "regions of interest" (ROIs). For an overview of electrode positions and example ROIs, see Figure 2.2. Changes in topography between two effects are usually interpreted as an indication that different neuronal populations are involved in their generation.
Amplitude	The "strength" of an effect (measured in microvolts, μV). Amplitude increases are typically viewed as resulting from higher neural activity in the source population (for an alternative interpretation, see section 2.1.1.3). In contrast to the other three parameters discussed here, amplitude is not a defining factor of ERP components. Rather, it is viewed as reflecting quantitative changes in qualitatively similar activities.

Source: Donchin, Ritter, and McCallum 1978.

The dimensions described in Table 2.1 are used to classify ERP effects into so-called "components". Components are associated with functional interpretations, such that different components may be interpreted as reflecting distinct cognitive processes. In this way, it is important to distinguish between a component and an effect. We will illustrate the difference between the two concepts with reference to one of the classical ERP correlates of language processing, the so-called N400 (i.e. a negativity with a peak latency of approximately 400 ms; see Figure 2.3). The N400, which was first described by Kutas and Hillyard (1980), has long been viewed as a correlate of lexical–semantic processing and, as such, is elicited whenever a content word is processed. In addition, the amplitude

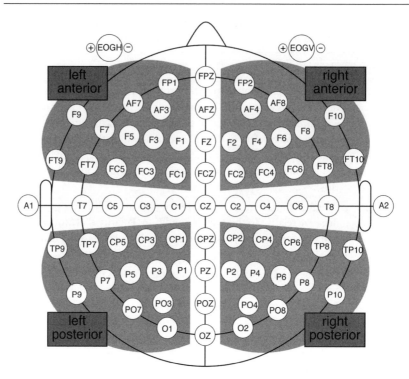

Figure 2.2 Schematic illustration of the electrode positions in the "extended 10–20 system". The figure depicts a top view of the scalp (up = forward; left = left). The electrode labels "EOGH" and "EOGV" refer to the electrodes used to record the horizontal and vertical electro-oculogram, respectively, i.e. to the electrical signals resulting from eye movements (saccades and blinks). This activity leads to artifacts in the EEG, which must either be excluded from the data analysis or corrected. The electrode labels "A1" and "A2" refer to electrodes positioned at the left and right mastoid bones, respectively. These are often used as reference electrodes in language-related EEG experiments (see Handy 2004). Shaded areas indicate sample regions of interest (ROIs) and illustrate the typical nomenclature for the topographical charac-terization of ERP effects. In addition to "anterior" (or "frontal") and "posterior" (or "parietal"), effects may also be characterized as "central".

of the N400 is modulated by a variety of lexical–semantic parameters such as word frequency (see Kutas and Federmeier 2000). For example, words with a low frequency of occurrence (e.g. *oologist*, someone who specializes in birds' eggs) engender a larger N400 than words with a relatively higher frequency (e.g. *pianist*). Thus, while both types of words give rise to an N400, there is a relative amplitude difference between the components arising in the two cases. This difference is referred to as an N400 "effect", i.e. the lower frequency word elicits an effect within a

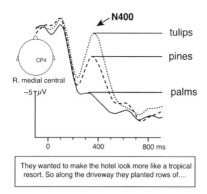

Figure 2.3 Illustration of a typical N400 effect. This example shows one of the best-known characteristics of the N400, namely that its amplitude is inversely correlated with the expectancy of a word in a sentence or discourse context. Moreover, the N400 is modulated by the relationship between different words/concepts in the mental lexicon (or semantic memory) as an unexpected continuation (*pines*) that is closely related to or of the same category as the expected continuation (*palms*) engenders a smaller N400 than a completely unrelated continuation (*tulips*).

Source: Data from Federmeier and Kutas 1999; figure adapted from Kutas and Federmeier 2000.

component relative to the higher frequency word, while the component per se is elicited in both cases.

A final very important consideration that should always be kept in mind when examining ERP data concerns the relative nature of ERP measures. This means that an effect can only be interpreted relative to a control condition but never with respect to the coordinate system (i.e. in absolute terms). For example, a "negativity" is defined as a more negative-going waveform in comparison to the control and may therefore show a positive mean voltage in absolute terms. The absolute voltage may be positive or negative for a number of reasons, all of which result from the fact that the effects of interest in an ERP experiment are elicited in the context of an active overall neurophysiological system. Thus, differences may arise by chance or as a result of other neural processes that are independent of the manipulation of interest (e.g. simply the state of being vigilant).

With respect to language comprehension, a number of ERP components have been described. The classical functional interpretation of these components is summarized in Table 2.2. Note, however, that this classification should be considered preliminary in the sense that, throughout the remainder of this book, we will describe a number of cases in which recent observations are difficult to reconcile with the

Table 2.2: Summary of the main language-related ERP components and their classical interpretation (for a comprehensive overview, see Kutas and Van Petten 1994; Kutas et al. 2006).

Component		Description	Interpretation	Sample references
N400		centro-parietal negativity with a peak latency of approximately 400 ms	lexical-semantic processing; integration into a meaningful context	Kutas and Hillyard (1980); Kutas and Federmeier (2000)
P600 (syntactic positive shift, SPS)		centro-parietal positivity with a peak latency of approximately 600 ms	syntactic processing (e.g. reanalysis, complexity)	Osterhout and Holcomb (1992); Hagoort et al. (1993)
ELAN (N125)		left-anterior negativity with a peak latency of approximately 150 ms	word category-based phrase structure processing	Neville et al. (1991); Friederici (2002)
LAN	focal	left-anterior negativity with a peak latency of approximately 400 ms	morphosyntactic processing	Gunter et al. (1997); Hagoort and Brown (2000)
	sustained	left-anterior negativity with a duration of approximately ≥500 ms	working memory-related processing costs	Kluender and Kutas (1993a); Münte et al. (1998)

classical component interpretations. A revised summary of language-related components will therefore be presented in Chapter 16 (see Table 16.1).

To summarize, ERPs provide a highly sensitive, multidimensional measure of cognitive processing. In combination with the method's very high temporal resolution (in the range of milliseconds), these properties render ERPs extremely well suited to an examination of the rapid and complex nature of language processing.

2.1.1.3 Alternative EEG-based techniques   While the vast majority of EEG-based language research has been based on ERPs, alternative analyses of stimulus-related EEG activity are also available. In the spirit of Berger's original observations, these methods are based on stimulus-induced changes in the frequency characteristics of the EEG (see Plate 1). In essence, two approaches can be distinguished in this regard, which we will refer to as the "complementary" and "integrative" perspectives, respectively.

(a) The "complementary" approach
      It has long been known that ERPs do not capture all of the stimulus-related activity that is present in the human EEG. On the one hand, activity that is stimulus-related but not strictly time-locked (i.e. that may occur with slightly different latencies from trial to trial, "induced activity"; cf. Plate 1) is eliminated by the averaging procedure (see, for example, Basar 1998). On the other hand, stimulus-related activity may occur in frequency bands that are "invisible" to ERP measures. This is the case for activity in frequency ranges higher than approximately 8 Hz. In particular, a substantial amount of research on the word level has focused on the so-called gamma band (> 25–30 Hz), which appears to reflect many of the factors that also modulate the N400 (see Pulvermüller 1999 for an overview).

(b) The "integrative" approach
      More recently, the attempt has been made to integrate frequency-based measures with ERP measures. The basic assumption of this approach is that ERP components may come about by various means. They can either, as described in Table 2.1,

result from increased neuronal activity (increased single trial amplitude) or, alternatively, from a better synchronization of the critical activity across trials (increased phase locking across trials). The second possibility basically results when activity in a frequency band is aligned to a particular phase by the critical stimulus, thus leading to a superposition of the activity across trials and generating an ERP in the averaged output even in the absence of an amplitude increase. The difference between the two possibilities can be illustrated on the basis of the following very simple example. Let us liken the appearance of an ERP component to the collapse of a bridge. There are two ways in which such a collapse can be induced. The most obvious possibility is that the number of people on the bridge exceeds the maximal weight that can be borne by it. However, a similar situation can also be brought about by means of fewer people (amounting to a total weight within the limits) marching across the bridge in perfect synchrony. If the marching rhythm corresponds to the critical frequency of the bridge, it collapses. This is therefore a case in which the mass borne by the bridge (and, by analogy, the neuronal activity) has not reached a critical level, but the bridge collapses nonetheless (an ERP component is observable in the averaged data). By means of suitable frequency-based data analysis techniques, ERP effects induced by an activity increase can be distinguished from phase (rhythm)-based ERP effects. This method therefore allows for a more fine-grained classification of ERP components and may therefore even help to distinguish components that look identical on the surface, but nonetheless result from different mechanisms. For an overview of this type of integrative approach that combines ERPs and frequency-based measures and how it may be used to shed light on the internal structure of classical ERP components, see Roehm, Bornkessel-Schlesewsky, and Schlesewsky (2007b).

In sum, while alternative EEG-based measures appear potentially promising for the study of language processing, the relatively limited number of studies beyond the word-level (or, in the case of the integrative approach, of total studies) currently do not provide for a similar level of explanatory capacity to that offered by the ERP technique. The true potential of these types of studies will therefore be revealed in future research. On account of these considerations, frequency-based analyses will only play a minor role throughout this volume. We will, however, refer to relevant studies whenever appropriate.

2.1.2 Magnetoencephalography (MEG)

Magnetoencephalography (MEG) provides a similarly high temporal resolution as EEG and, at the same time, offers the possibility for an improved spatial resolution. MEG measures the changes in the magnetic fields induced by changes in the electrical activity of the brain. Unlikely electric potentials, magnetic fields are not distorted by the skull, thereby leading to a better spatial resolution in MEG as opposed to EEG. Nonetheless, the reconstruction of the underlying sources still depends on dipole modeling and is therefore also subject to the inverse problem. In addition, as magnetic field strength drops away rapidly with increasing distance from the source, the accuracy of localization is reduced significantly for deeper sources.

Similarly to the frequency-based methods described in section 2.1.2, MEG studies of morphosyntactic processing have currently not reached a state in which they can be considered a true alternative to ERPs (from a temporal perspective) and fMRI (from a spatial perspective). While the reason for this situation is not entirely clear, there are presently astoundingly few MEG studies on morphological or syntactic processing to be found in the literature. (This stands in stark contrast to the many published experiments that have used MEG to examine lexical, semantic, and phonological processing, primarily at the word level.)

As a final note on MEG, it is important to keep in mind that, despite the interdependence of electrical and magnetic fields, EEG and MEG do not measure identical neural activity. Thus, in contrast to EEG, MEG cannot detect activity from sources oriented perpendicularly to the surface of the scalp (radial sources). This difference between the two methods is illustrated in Figure 2.4. As the dipoles giving rise to MEG and EEG signals are therefore not overlapping, this complicates possible conclusions about the correlation between MEG and ERP effects. This is not always reflected in the literature: for example, the so-called M350 MEG-component, which is elicited by typical "N400 manipulations" (see Figure 2.3), is often equated with the N400. While this correlation appears plausible from a functional perspective, it

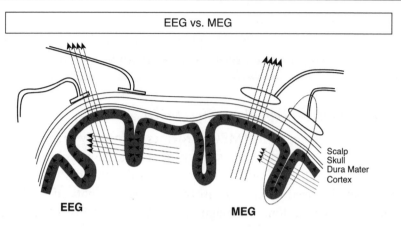

EEG vs. MEG

EEG   MEG

Scalp
Skull
Dura Mater
Cortex

Figure 2.4 Comparison of the neural activity detected by EEG and MEG measures. MEG only captures activity from tangential sources, i.e. sources oriented in parallel to the surface of the scalp (circled region). By contrast, it is blind to radial sources, i.e. sources oriented perpendicularly to the surface of the scalp. EEG, by contrast, primarily picks up on activity from radial sources but, depending on the exact positioning of electrodes, may also include some tangential activity.

should be treated with caution on account of the considerations outlined above.

2.2 Methods with a high spatial resolution

2.2.1 *Functional magnetic resonance imaging (fMRI)*

2.2.1.1 MRI: some historical remarks In view of the very high number of studies now employing fMRI and the scientific interest which they are being afforded, it is deceptively easy to forget that the first study employing functional MRI was published in 1990. The method is thus less than 20 years old. Despite this relatively short period of time, fMRI has been the method of choice for mapping out the functional neuroanatomy of cognitive processing for a number of years. The primary reason for this lies in the method's very precise spatial resolution (currently at approximately 1 mm).

As its name suggests, the basic methodological origins of fMRI lie in nuclear magnetic resonance (NMR), a method that has existed for a little over half a century and that was first developed for the identification of complex chemical substances and structures. The logic of NMR relies on the fact that some atomic nuclei such as hydrogen nuclei ("protons") can be influenced by an external magnetic field. When the field is applied, the protons align in the direction of the field. By means of a radio-frequency impulse, the protons reach a more energetic state, thereby departing from their aligned orientation within the magnetic field. Like all things in life, the protons have an inherent tendency to return to the state of lowest energy. Thus, they attempt to realign to the direction of the magnetic field as quickly as possible, i.e. as quickly as permitted by the properties of the proton itself and of its environment. The MR signal results from the energy that is emitted during this realignment process, i.e. during the transition from a state of high energy to a state of lower energy. As the protons themselves are always associated with similar properties, differences in the MR signal can only arise as a function of the environment in which the protons' realignment process takes place. Environmental differences in this sense include, for example, properties of different tissue types or organs, thereby enabling the NMR-based visualization of anatomical properties of the human body. On the basis of precisely these properties, the first application of MRI in the life sciences consisted in fine-grained anatomical analyses, e.g. for the identification of tumors or attrition/degeneration in the skeletal system.

2.2.1.2 **The bases of functional MRI**   The breakthrough enabling MRI to be utilized for the examination of functional aspects of human cognition came about with the discovery of the so-called "blood oxygenation level dependent" (BOLD) response (Ogawa et al. 1990a; Ogawa et al. 1990b). The basic idea behind the BOLD is that, since the brain offers no storage space for energy, all energy usage must be compensated immediately. This means that active neural regions must be provided with energy carriers via the blood flow. The main carrier of energy in all metabolic cycles is oxygen, which is transported via the blood by means of hemoglobin. Increased activity of a particular brain region thus results in increased blood flow to that region (effectively overcompensating for the need for oxygen). In this way, the distribution of oxygenated and deoxygenated hemoglobin (i.e. the hemoglobin carrying oxygen vs. that stripped of oxygen via energy use) is altered and it is the ratio of these two substances that forms the basis for the BOLD response. Crucially, oxygenated and deoxygenated hemoglobin are associated with different magnetic properties: the former is diamagnetic and therefore has little effect on the magnetic field, while the latter is paramagnetic and thereby leads to a higher degree of inhomogeneity of the magnetic field.

Hence, changes in the ratio of the two types of hemoglobin lead to changes in the magnetic field, effectively amounting to changes in the "environment" of the protons as discussed above. The MR signal measured in fMRI therefore originates from the properties of hydrogen nuclei in the human brain and the differences in their realignment behavior depending on the properties of the magnetic field (as determined by the ratio of oxygenated to deoxygenated hemoglobin). This is depicted in Figure 2.5. For a detailed discussion of the BOLD signal and its relation to neural activity, see Heeger and Ress (2002).

On account of the dependency of the fMRI signal on blood flow, this method is associated with a relatively poor temporal resolution. Thus, the BOLD signal takes approximately six seconds to reach its peak (perhaps a little less in primary sensory areas, e.g. something in the order of four seconds). The consequence of this delay is that fMRI correlates of cognitive processes typically reflect a response to neural activity that has occurred at a substantially earlier point in time. This is

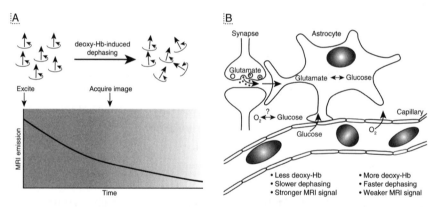

Figure 2.5 The physiological basis of the blood oxygenation level dependent (BOLD) signal in functional magnetic resonance imaging. Neural activity leads to an increased need for oxygen (O_2), which is extracted from the blood (Panel B). This leads to a brief increase of deoxygenated hemoglobin, which is then compensated (more precisely: overcompensated) by incoming oxygenated hemoglobin from the blood flow to the activated region. Deoxygenated hemoglobin (Hb in the figure) leads to inhomogeneities in the magnetic field, thereby leading to a weaker MRI signal (Panel A). The fMRI technique capitalizes upon this effect of the changing concentration of oxygenated and deoxygenated hemoglobin: the signal increase in activated brain regions results from the high concentration of oxygenated hemoglobin that overcompensates for the oxygen that has been consumed. In this regard, the relative ratio of oxygenated and deoxygenated hemoglobin directly correlates with the observed signal strength.

Source: Adapted from Heeger and Ress 2002.

especially relevant for sentence processing, during which multiple processes take place over a period of several seconds. For a comprehensive introduction to the fMRI method, see Jezzard, Matthews, and Smith (2001).

2.2.1.3 Interpreting fMRI data on language   An important point that should be kept in mind when interpreting fMRI data is that the "pretty pictures" resulting from these experiments are very suggestive – even for researchers highly familiar with the method. However, it is important to note that the "activations" displayed in contrast maps never reflect differences in neural activity (between two conditions) per se, but rather provide a statistical likelihood for the assumption that the two conditions differ from one another significantly.

Contrasts follow the "subtraction method" (Donders 1969), according to which activation of interest can be isolated by subtracting the activation in a control condition from that in a critical condition. Depending on the specificity of the question under examination, control conditions may either be rest, a low-level baseline (e.g. a string of Xs in comparison to a word as a control for activation due to the perception of a visual stimulus), or may stem from the domain of interest itself and only differ from the critical stimulus with respect to a single feature/process (e.g. a simple control sentence in comparison to a syntactically complex sentence). Thus, this way of computing contrasts presupposes that activation for a critical condition can be parceled into the activation engendered by the control condition and activation associated with the feature/process dissociating between the two conditions.

A further issue concerns the interpretation of functional imaging results. Thus, in contrast to deficit-lesion correlations gained from patient studies, imaging data are purely correlative in nature. This means that they cannot be interpreted as evidence for the *necessary* involvement of a particular brain region in a specific cognitive process. A case in point concerns the role of the right hemisphere in language processing: while imaging studies consistently reveal right hemispheric activity in response to linguistic stimuli, lesions to these regions do not show the detrimental effect on language performance that left hemispheric lesions do. Thus, in spite of the many advantages that functional neuroimaging has to offer, patient studies still play an important role in supplementing the interpretation of their results. An alternative approach to the issue of causality is provided by transcranial magnetic stimulation (TMS), a method which will be introduced briefly in section 2.2.3.

Finally, the interpretation of fMRI findings presupposes at least a basic knowledge of neuroanatomy. We will therefore briefly introduce the regions known to be relevant for language processing in order to provide the unfamiliar reader with a first orientation. On the basis of the classical deficit-lesion correlations undertaken in the late nineteenth century, language comprehension was long associated primarily with "Wernicke's area", i.e. with the left posterior superior temporal gyrus (STG) and adjoining parietal regions of the cortex, while "Broca's area" in the posterior portion of the left inferior frontal gyrus (IFG) was thought to be the seat of language production (see Plate 2.B). However, subsequent research in both patients (see Zurif 1995 for an overview) and unimpaired individuals showed that this clear-cut dissociation cannot be upheld. Rather, it suggests that both regions are engaged in comprehension as well as production (see Bornkessel-Schlesewsky and Friederici 2007; Indefrey 2007, for overviews of neuroimaging findings on comprehension and production, respectively). Nonetheless, numerous findings within the imaging literature support the idea that language processing indeed crucially engages a network of (primarily left) *fronto-temporal* brain regions in concert with a small number of other areas such as the basal ganglia. Regions of relevance to the discussion in later chapters of this volume are shown in Plate 2.

2.2.2 *Positron emission tomography (PET)*

Before the advent of fMRI, positron emission tomography (PET) was the main neuroimaging method used to examine the functional neuroanatomy of the human brain. Like fMRI, PET is a hemodynamic method, i.e. it relies on the principle that increased neural activity engenders increased blood flow to the active region (see section 2.2.1.2). In contrast to fMRI, however, it is an invasive method as it requires the injection or inhalation of a radionucleid (e.g. the O^{15} isotope). PET cameras detect the density of these isotopes within particular regions of the brain by measuring the radiation caused by their decay. As the isotopes are transported by the blood, active regions will contain a higher number of them, hence allowing for "regional cerebral blood flow" (rCBF) to be measured. For an overview of the PET methodology directed at a psycholinguistic audience, see Caplan (2001).

In recent years, the ratio of fMRI to PET studies in the domain of higher cognition has increased rapidly. This can be attributed to several factors. Firstly, as outlined above, fMRI does not require the use of radioactive isotopes. Secondly, and perhaps more importantly, PET is associated with a somewhat poorer spatial resolution than fMRI and places much more rigid constraints on the types of experimental designs that can be employed. Thus, while event-related designs with randomized stimuli have become standard with fMRI, PET requires the use of block designs, in which multiple stimuli of the same type are presented one after another in separate "blocks".

2.2.3 Transcranial magnetic stimulation (TMS)

As mentioned briefly above, one limitation of all of the methods described in the preceding sections is that they provide purely correlative measures. In other words, while they can demonstrate the involvement of a particular brain region in a certain cognitive processing operation, they cannot show that the involvement of this region is *necessarily* required. A possible way of overcoming this limitation without recourse to patient data (i.e. deficit-lesion correlations) is offered by transcranial magnetic stimulation (TMS). TMS can be used to temporarily disrupt the function of particular cortical regions, thereby leading to a "virtual lesion" and providing information about the causality of that region's involvement in a particular cognitive task (for overviews, see for example Pascual-Leone, Walsh, and Rothwell 2000; Walsh and Cowey 2000).

TMS operates upon the principle of electromagnetic induction: when an electric current is passed through a wire coil, it induces a magnetic field. With TMS, the coil is placed over a particular portion of the scalp such that the magnetic field passes through the skull and stimulates the tissue underneath. The basic idea behind the disruptive effect of TMS is that the magnetic stimulus leads to the rapid synchronous activation of a number of neurons followed by a period of inhibition, which may disrupt information processing for up to 250 ms (see Jahanshahi and Rothwell 2000).

As an example, consider an early study by Cohen et al. (1997), who examined the role of visual cortex in the reading of Braille by blind participants with an early onset of blindness. TMS of primary visual cortex (V1) led to a disruption of tactile letter identification in blind participants, but not in a sighted control group. This result thus demonstrated that primary visual cortex is causally involved in Braille reading by blind individuals with an early onset of blindness, as opposed to V1 activation being simply an epiphenomenon.

TMS can be administered in several different ways. In particular, it can be applied as a single pulse (with a duration of approximately 100–500 μs) or as a train of pulses (repetitive TMS, rTMS). Depending on the frequency of rTMS pulses, they can either lead to increases or decreases in cortical excitability (see Fitzgerald, Fountain, and Daskalakis 2006 for a review of relevant findings from the motor domain). Since rTMS typically leads to a disruption over a longer period, its effects on behavioral output can be used to infer which regions are required for a particular cognitive task. By contrast, single pulses allow for a more precise temporal localization of the disruption (Pascual-Leone et al. 2000). Moreover, a combination of TMS and neuroimaging can be useful in the identification of cortical networks by revealing how TMS impacts upon activation in regions other than the one directly subject to stimulation.

In recent years, the use of TMS for the examination of the functional neuroanatomy of language processing has increased steadily (for a review, see Devlin and Watkins 2007). However, the number of studies directly concerned with syntax and morphology is currently still very small.

2.3 Correlations in neurocognitive data

The boom of cognitive neuroscience has resulted in a great deal of euphoria with respect to the interpretation of neurocognitive data. Almost every week, newspapers and magazines report new "breakthroughs" on cognition and the brain to the general public. Of course, many findings are indeed fascinating and much has been learned on these issues over the last few years. Nevertheless, we believe that a note of caution is in order, especially in view of the high suggestiveness of the data obtained via neurocognitive methods. This section therefore provides a discussion of two general issues that, in our view, place important constraints on the overall picture that can be gleaned from data of this type.

2.3.1 *Correlations between time and space*

The acquisition of data with both a high temporal and a high spatial resolution might be considered the holy grail of cognitive neuroscience.

As we have described above, no single method provides an optimal solution in this regard. While MEG is sometimes described as a way of obtaining a good resolution within both domains, its spatial resolution is far from that offered by fMRI. Most importantly, the inverse problem still applies, hence rendering all source localizations ambiguous. A possible solution to this issue has been sought, for example, in the use of fMRI data to constrain MEG modeling, thereby ensuring that the chosen solution is at least neuroanatomically plausible. Nonetheless, it must be kept in mind that the two methods measure different things and that associations can therefore only be correlative in nature.

A similar problem of course arises with attempts to correlate fMRI and ERPs. An impressive demonstration of this issue was provided by Brázdil et al. (2005), who combined an fMRI study with the recording of intracranial ERPs (i.e. ERPs measured invasively at the surface of the cortex, thereby providing very precise spatial information regarding the source of the electrophysiological response). These authors observed that regions showing an intracranial ERP response did not in all cases also yield an activation in fMRI. This type of scenario appears plausible, for example, in view of the issues discussed in section 2.1.1.3 above, where we illustrated a means by which ERPs can result from a reorganization of the frequency properties of the neurophysiological system, rather than from an increase in activity. More generally, Brázdil and colleagues' findings demonstrate that even concurrent recordings of EEG and fMRI do not provide a solution to the inherent divergence between the nature of the data acquired by the two methods (but see Debener et al. 2005 for a demonstration of the utility of concurrent fMRI/EEG recordings). This indicates that the co-occurrence of an activation in a particular neural region and an ERP component as measured by an identical paradigm should always be considered as correlative.

With respect to the language domain this means, for example, that activations of Broca's region occurring in an experimental paradigm that also engenders a left anterior negativity (LAN) may be viewed as correlating with this ERP effect under particular circumstances, but that this should not be taken to suggest that the neuronal substrate generating the LAN also engenders the increased blood flow to Broca's region or vice versa. Thus, it is neither the case that the occurrence of a LAN predicts increased activation of Broca's region, nor that activation of this region can always be associated with a particular electrophysiological response.

Finally, language processing is a relatively complex phenomenon and many steps are involved in binding individual words together to form sentences. While these different processes can be teased apart within the temporal domain using ERPs, such a dissociation is much more difficult with fMRI. fMRI activations thus always reflect an integrative response to the processing of larger structures (e.g. entire sentences) and this certainly constrains the way in which fMRI and ERP findings may correlate with one another: an activation pattern within fMRI may well correspond to several ERP components.

To conclude, the issues raised in this section should not be taken to mean that all attempts at a correlation between time and space – either in language or elsewhere in higher cognition – are futile or that the correlations obtained are uninformative. We simply wish to stress that the mapping between the two domains is far from trivial. Nonetheless, the correlations obtained while keeping these points in mind provide for a wealth of interpretive possibilities that will certainly continue to increase our knowledge regarding the "big picture" of how the brain functions in time and space.

2.3.2 Correlations between neurocognitive patterns and functions: the one-to-one mapping problem

One of the major hopes in the investigation of language and its neural correlates has always lain in the assumption that specific linguistic subdomains and/or processes can be associated with particular brain regions or neurophysiological responses. Consider, for example, the classical neurological perspective – gleaned from deficit-lesion correlations in the late nineteenth century – that Broca's region is responsible for language production, while Wernicke's region provides the neural basis for language comprehension (see Goodglass and Kaplan 1972). In fact, this view is still found in many medical and neuropsychological textbooks even today. Yet, as briefly discussed in section 2.2.1.3, and as will become clear in subsequent sections of this volume, the standard view in the literature nowadays is that both regions engage in aspects of comprehension as well as production.

While the distinction between Broca's and Wernicke's areas provides a straightforward illustration of what we will refer to as the "one-to-one mapping problem", the overall pattern of how neurocognitive correlates map onto linguistic domains and processes is much more complex. Thus, one might argue that the production vs.

comprehension distinction is, in fact, orthogonal to the distinctions that have been undertaken within linguistics, in which domains such as phonology, morphology, syntax, and semantics play a much more important role in characterizing language and its internal architecture. Perhaps then, the failure to find a precise characterization of the regions in question in relation to this major processing-based divide might simply have resulted from a wrongly posed question? After all, both production and comprehension encompass phonological, morpho-logical, syntactic, and semantic information. It thus appears plausible that posing the mapping question in relation to these well-motivated linguistic subdomains might yield a clearer picture. In this way, much of the research conducted in the decade of the brain – as well as earlier patient studies – focused on precisely this type of question, namely: Can we identify specific neurocognitive correlates of the processing of dis-tinct linguistic subdomains? Indeed, this way of proceeding initially appeared rather successful, as findings from both the neurophysio-logical and the neuroanatomical domains seemed to support the idea that lexical–semantic processes can be clearly dissociated from pro-cesses related to morphosyntax (see, for example, Ullman 2001; Friederici 2002; Hagoort 2003; Kutas, Van Petten, and Kluender 2006).

Unfortunately, recent research has shown that – in spite of indisput-able correlations between particular linguistic subdomains and certain neurocognitive processing signatures – a strict one-to-one mapping currently cannot be upheld. Perhaps the most important immediate consequence of this observation, which will be illustrated by a number of the findings to be discussed at later points in this book, is that the appearance of a particular processing effect cannot provide the basis for concluding that the experimental manipulation leading to this effect must be attributed to a particular linguistic domain. Consider, for example, the case of polarity items such as *ever* in *No politician was ever popular.* Within theoretical linguistics, the nature of the con-straints on the occurrence of these elements has been subject to debate: Should they be considered syntactic (Haegeman 1995), semantic (Horn 1997), pragmatic (Krifka 1995), or semantic–pragmatic (Linebarger 1987)? This question was subsequently addressed using ERPs (Saddy, Drenhaus, and Frisch 2004), leading to the finding that unlicensed negative polarity items engender an N400 followed by a late positivity (P600). Given the classical functional interpretation of language-re-lated ERP components (see Table 2.2), this might lead one to conclude that the processing of negative polarity items involves both semantic and syntactic aspects. However, as will be shown in detail in the following chapters, neither semantics nor syntax can be unequivocally associated with an unambiguous neurophysiological or neuroanatomical processing correlate. Hence, empirical findings pertaining to polarity items cannot be used to prove or falsify any of the competing theoretical positions described above. Yet this should not be taken to mean that neurocognitive findings are uninformative with respect to the internal structure of language. As we will argue in detail throughout the remainder of this book, the one-to-one mapping problem only shows that the absolute interpretation of individual empirical phenomena is not straightforward and should be treated with caution. Thus, rather than assigning absolute functional interpretations to individual components or neural regions, the occurrence of these responses should be compared, contrasted, and interpreted across different phenomena and experimental paradigms. The modulations of the neurophysiological and neuroanatomical responses thus arising provide the information that is crucial to modeling language architecture in neurocognitive terms.

In addition, it presently cannot – and should not – be excluded that the one-to-one mapping problem may be resolved at some point in the future. The most obvious way in which this might happen is by way of advances in data analysis. Consider, for example, the alternative analysis techniques for EEG data that were discussed in section 2.1.2 and particularly the idea that ERP measures can be supplemented by more fine-grained descriptions of their internal frequency characteristics. Initial findings in this regard have already suggested that components that "look the same" on the surface can in fact be dissociated from one another using this type of technique. Whether an approach along these lines will indeed help to overcome the one-to-one mapping problem or whether it will only end up providing an asymptotic approximation to the solution of this problem can only be determined by systematic further research.

2.4 The output: behavioral methods

Methods measuring participants' behavioral responses in a language task long provided the basis for psycholinguistic modeling of language comprehension and production and they remain highly influential. On account of the focus of this book, we will not introduce the behavioral methods used in psycholinguistics in as much detail as was provided for the neurocognitive methods above. We will, however, provide a brief introduction to the methods relevant to the processing of syntax and morphology in order to establish a link between the neurocognitive domain and the "output" of the processing system that is constituted by the behavioral response. In addition, the information given in this section should allow readers not familiar with psycholinguistic methods to effectively interpret the results discussed throughout this book. References to more comprehensive introductions to each of the methods are provided where appropriate.

2.4.1 *Judgments*

Judgments regarding the grammaticality/acceptability of linguistic stimuli (sentences) – and especially time-insensitive (offline) judgment methods – are typically used to provide an empirical basis for linguistic theorizing. Some of the methods used to obtain data of this type completely disregard the time course of language processing (e.g. questionnaire studies, magnitude estimation). Alternatively, theoretical considerations are sometimes informed by judgment techniques employing a moderate amount of time pressure (e.g. speeded grammaticality/acceptability judgments).

In judgment experiments, participants are typically confronted with 3–10 items per critical condition, which are embedded in a relatively large proportion of filler items that are not related to the experimental manipulation (the ratio between critical items and fillers is at least 1:2, but often 1:3 or even higher). When judgments are carried out under time pressure, not only the acceptability rates per condition are evaluated but also the corresponding reaction times. In unspeeded judgments, participants see each sentence as a whole, while speeded judgments typically employ rapid serial visual presentation (RSVP), in which sentences are presented word-by-word (or chunk-by-chunk) at a set rate and participants have no control over the speed of presentation. Alternatively, sentences may be presented auditorily, in which case participants similarly have no control over the presentation rate and cannot backtrack. The judgment itself is most often acquired via a discrete scale, ranging from two up to eight points. Odd-numbered scales are avoided, as these provide participants with a possible strategy in which the middle value can be chosen in the case of uncertainty. In all cases, the way in which participants are instructed plays a major role in determining the results. As a very simple example, consider the difference between acceptability/grammaticality and plausibility judgments. While a sentence such as *My toothbrush is pregnant* is highly implausible, whether it should be considered grammatical depends on the linguistic theory assumed. Similarly, whether a participant judges this sentence as acceptable or not will be highly task-dependent: it would likely be judged as acceptable, for example, when participants are asked to focus not on whether the state of affairs described by the sentence is likely to occur in the real world but rather whether it could be described in this particular way in the language under consideration. This highlights a potential problem with asking participants to judge grammaticality: as this is a theoretical concept, it is very difficult to judge intuitively. Acceptability thus appears to provide a more neutral concept for separating structural knowledge from plausibility, even though participants must nonetheless be instructed with respect to the notion expressed by the term. For a detailed discussion of linguistic judgments, see Schütze (1996).

An alternative approach to obtaining judgment data is provided by the magnitude estimation technique. Originally adopted from psychophysics (where it has been successfully used for the evaluation of lower cognitive functions), this method requires participants to judge the critical stimuli relative to a baseline sentence (the so-called "modulus"). Participants firstly assign the modulus an arbitrary number and then judge the relative grammaticality/acceptability of each subsequent sentence by providing it with a number that stands in relation to that of the modulus. In this way, the relative distance between each critical sentence and the modulus is assessed. One of the basic assumptions of the method is that grammaticality is a graded rather than a categorical concept. Participants are therefore "liberated" from judging sentences to be "good" or "bad" in absolute terms and can rather choose their own scale by way of the relative judgment procedure. A second, somewhat more implicit, assumption is that the relative distance between two critical stimulus types should remain stable independently of the choice of modulus. However, this has not yet been empirically verified. Magnitude estimation experiments are typically conducted without any time pressure. For a detailed discussion of the magnitude estimation method as applied to linguistic stimuli, see Bard, Robertson, and Sorace (1996). A more recent perspective on how this method might be applied to inform linguistic theory is provided by Featherston (2007); see also the commentaries on this article that appear in the same issue.

2.4.2 *Speed–accuracy trade-off (SAT)*

With respect to speeded judgment tasks, it has often been criticized that the dimensions of speech and accuracy are conflated within participants' responses (e.g. Reed 1973; Wickelgren 1977). A very simple example of this phenomenon can be found in the classical "speed–accuracy trade-off", which refers to the situation that, in a reaction time experiment, participants can choose how accurately or how quickly they perform the task. When answers are provided as quickly as possible, errors will increase. Conversely, slower responses will typically serve to minimize errors. Therefore, reaction times cannot be viewed as an "unadulterated" measure of processing speed and accuracy rates are never independent of the point in time at which the response was given.

Transferred to the domain of language processing, these considerations mean that a reaction time difference in a language task can reflect the time needed to compute a particular interpretation, but also the likelihood that readers can compute that interpretation or how plausible readers find the resulting interpretation (e.g. McElree 1993; McElree and Griffith 1995; McElree and Griffith 1998; McElree and Nordlie 1999; McElree, Foraker, and Dyer 2003). A standard solution to this problem is to derive a full time course function that measures how the accuracy of processing varies with processing time (Wickelgren 1977). The speed–accuracy trade-off (SAT) procedure provides the required conjoint measures of processing speed and accuracy.

The SAT task requires participants to make their judgment of acceptability at particular times. This serves to chart the full time course of processing, measuring when discrimination departs from a chance level, the rate at which discrimination grows as a function of processing, and the asymptotic level of discrimination accuracy reached with (functionally) unlimited processing time. There are essentially two ways in which this can be accomplished: (a) by signaling to participants (e.g. via a tone) at which time a response is required on each trial, with the signal varying between a number of different lag times relative to stimulus onset (the response-signal SAT procedure), or (b) by cuing participants to respond at multiple, regularly spaced points within a single trial (the multiple-response SAT procedure). In both cases, responses are collected over the entire time required for processing, thus enabling processing speed and accuracy to be differentiated,

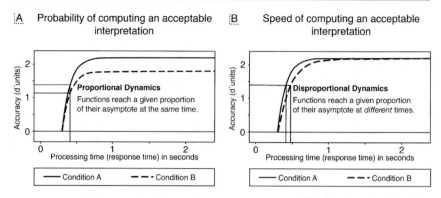

Figure 2.6 Idealized SAT functions illustrating an asymptotic difference (Panel A) and a dynamics difference (Panel B). The accuracy of discriminating acceptable from unacceptable sentences is measured in d′ units (the z-transform of the probability of correctly accepting an acceptable sentence minus the z-transform of the probability of falsely accepting an unacceptable sentence). Typical SAT functions display three distinct phases: a period of chance performance (d′=0), followed by a period of increasing accuracy, followed by an asymptotic period where further processing does not improve performance. In a sentence acceptability task, the SAT asymptote provides a measure of the probability (across trials and materials) that readers arrive at an interpretation sufficient to support an "acceptable" response. If two conditions differ in asymptote, as illustrated in Panel A, it indicates that they differ in the likelihood that a meaningful interpretation can be computed or in overall acceptability/plausibility of the respective interpretation. The point at which accuracy departs from the chance level (the intercept of the function) and the rate at which accuracy grows over processing time are joint measures of the underlying speed of processing. If one type of structure can be interpreted more quickly than another, the SAT functions will differ in rate, intercept, or some combination of the two parameters. This follows from the fact that the SAT rate and intercept are determined by the underlying finishing time distribution for the processes that are necessary to accomplish the task. The time to compute an interpretation will vary across trials and materials, yielding a distribution of finishing times. Intuitively, the SAT intercept corresponds to the minimum of the finishing time distribution, and the SAT rate is determined by the variance of the distribution. Panel B depicts a case where the functions differ in rate of approach to asymptote, leading to disproportional dynamics; the functions reach a given proportion of their asymptote at different times. Dynamics (rate and/or intercept) differences are independent of potential asymptotic variation. Readers may be less likely to compute an interpretation for one structure or may find that interpretation less acceptable (e.g. less plausible) than another; however, they may not require additional time to compute that interpretation.

Source: Adapted from Martin and McElree 2008.

and both methods have been successfully applied to the study of sentence processing (see, for example, McElree and Griffith 1995; McElree and Griffith 1998 for single response; and McElree 1993; Bornkessel et al. 2004b for multiple response SAT). The response-signal procedure is associated with the advantage that sentences can be presented using RSVP, with the response tones occurring relative to the last word of the sentence (which should be the word inducing the critical manipulation). However, as approximately 30–40 items are required per time point and condition in order for the SAT function to be charted accurately, this procedure results in a very high number of critical trials. Multiple-response SAT avoids this problem by collecting responses from each time point each time a critical stimulus is presented. Some studies using this method are associated with the disadvantage that sentences were presented in their entirety in order to allow for the collection of multiple successive responses (Bornkessel et al. 2004b), thereby calling for carefully chosen fillers in order to avoid reading strategies that might affect the results. However, it has also been demonstrated that multiple-response SAT data can be collected successfully relative to the final (critical) segment of sentences that are presented using RSVP (e.g. McElree et al. 2006; Martin and McElree 2008). Furthermore, initial findings suggest that multiple-response SAT can also be used to examine auditory sentence comprehension (Foraker 2007).

The properties of SAT functions and their functional interpretation are illustrated in Figure 2.6.

2.4.3 "Online" methods

With the exception of the SAT methodology, the judgment techniques discussed in the previous sections are generally described as "offline" methods because they collect responses after processing has already been completed (i.e. at the end of the sentence). The data from these methods therefore provide a composite measure of processing difficulty over the entire sentence, but cannot be used to characterize the way in which processing takes place in time. Rather, the examination of these types of processes requires the use of "online" methods. While neurocognitive methods such as ERPs or MEG clearly provide online measures of processing, this section will focus on online measures in the behavioral domain.[1]

2.4.3.1 Eye movement measures   Eye movements have long been used as a sensitive and relatively unobtrusive measure of processing behavior during reading and, more recently, also during listening and in language production. As the measurement of eye movements ("eye-tracking") has been *the* method of choice in psycholinguistic research since the mid 1970s, a full discussion of the wealth of findings and models in this domain would require a monograph in and of itself. Here, we will therefore restrict ourselves to a description of the method's basic underlying assumptions and the types of measures that can be obtained, before turning to some psycholinguistic applications.

Reading is characterized by a series of rapid eye movements ("saccades"), which are separated by fixation pauses. Saccades typically cover approximately 8–9 character spaces and have a duration of approximately 25–40 ms. As visual perception is greatly reduced during a saccade, it is generally assumed that no information can be extracted between fixations. Saccades can be either progressive (i.e. from left to right in languages with a left-to-right writing system) or regressive (i.e. from right to left). Regressive saccades ("regressions") make up approximately 10–20% of saccadic eye movements and are often associated with increased comprehension difficulty or the need for reanalysis. For proficient readers, fixations have an average duration of 200–250 ms. However, fixation durations are associated with a relatively high degree of variability, both within and across individual readers. It is this variability and its systematic modulation by properties of the linguistic stimulus that has led eye movements to be considered a relatively direct measure of the cognitive processes taking place during reading (for a comprehensive overview, see Rayner 1998).

A further advantage of the eye-tracking methodology is that it provides a multidimensional measure of language comprehension. In particular, many researchers assume that "early" measures can be distinguished from "late measures", and that this dissociation can help to shed light on the time course of processing. However, as pointed out by Clifton, Staub, and Rayner (2007), this distinction should not be confused with the difference between theoretically postulated processing stages in hierarchically organized models of sentence comprehension (see Chapter 7, for an introduction to the assumptions underlying these models). The main eye-tracking measures used in reading research are summarized in Table 2.3.

Finally, eye movements have been investigated using a variety of different paradigms. In the reading domain, the use of eye-contingent display techniques can restrict the information that is available to the reader at a particular position in the sentence, thereby allowing potential influencing factors to be carefully controlled. The most widely used display methods are illustrated in Panel A of Figure 2.7. These techniques have allowed researchers to determine the "perceptual

Table 2.3: Summary of the eye movement measures typically used in psycholinguistic investigations of reading. First fixation duration, gaze duration, and first pass time are typically considered "early measures", whereas second pass time and total time are regarded to be "late measures" (see the text for further discussion).

Measure	Description
First fixation	The duration of the first fixation on a word.
Single fixation	The fixation time spent on a word on those trials when the word was fixated only once.
Gaze duration/First pass time	The sum of all fixations on a word before the eyes leave the word for the first time (either to the right or left). The term "first pass time" is often used instead of "gaze duration" when the region of interest encompasses multiple words.
Go-past time/Regression path duration	The time from the first fixation on a word/region until that word/region is left with a saccade to the right. This measure therefore includes time spent rereading previous parts of the sentence.
Second pass time	The time spent rereading a word or region.
Total time	The sum of all fixations on a word or region.
Regression probability	The probability of making a regression out of a particular region (typically during first pass reading) or into a particular region.

Source: Staub and Rayner 2007.

span" in reading, namely the size of the region from which information can be extracted (cf. Rayner 1998). For languages with an alphabetic orthography, this region is typically assumed to extend from the beginning of the currently fixated word (but at most 3–4 characters to the left of the current fixation) up to approximately 14–15 characters to the right of fixation. (Note that, in languages with a right-to-left writing system, the directionality of this span is reversed, i.e. it is asymmetrically larger to the left.) However, the "word identification span" is considerably smaller than the overall perceptual span, extending approximately 7–8 characters to the right of fixation. The extraction of information from the area to the right of fixation is partly due to what is known as "parafoveal preview".[2] This term is used to describe the phenomenon that readers typically spend less time fixating a word if they have had a valid preview of it while fixating the preceding word.

More recently, eye movement measures have also been applied to the study of spoken language by means of the so-called "visual world" paradigm (Tanenhaus et al. 1995). Here, participants view a display with several objects/characters or a complete visual scene and simul-

| A | Eye Movements in Reading | | B | Visual World Display |

during a saccade because the eyes are moving so   *Normal Text*
                              *

XXXXXX X XXXcade because the XXXX XXX XXXXXX XX
                              *
                                                   Moving
                                                   Window
XXXXXX X XXXXXXX XXXXXse the eyes are mXXXXX XX
                                    *

during a saccade because the dogs are moving so
                              *
                                                   Boundary
during a saccade because the eyes are moving so
                              *

Figure 2.7 Presentation techniques for the measurement of language-related eye movements. Panel A shows different types of display techniques that have been employed to examine the extraction of linguistic information during reading. Here, asterisks indicate the current fixation position. In the moving window paradigm, only a certain window of text surrounding the current fixation is shown. In the boundary paradigm, a critical word changes when a saccade crosses an invisible boundary (in the example, the word *the* following *because*). By manipulating the relationship between the word initially displayed and the word that is finally fixated, the depth of parafoveal processing can be determined. Panel B shows a sample visual world display that was used to examine the processing of grammatical function ambiguities in German (see Chapter 9.3.2 for further discussion).

Source: Panel A adapted from Rayner 1998; Panel B adapted from Knoeferle et al. 2005.

taneously hear a sentence. By examining the proportion of fixations on certain objects or parts of a scene as a function of the unfolding auditory stimulus, researchers draw conclusions about which information has been extracted at a particular point in time. A sample visual world display is shown in Panel B of Figure 2.7. For a comprehensive overview of the visual world methodology and its application to the examination of language processing, see Henderson and Ferreira (2004).

Several very detailed models of eye movements during reading have been proposed. From a psycholinguistic perspective, the most well-known of these is the E-Z Reader model (Reichle, Rayner, and Pollatsek 1998; Reichle, Rayner, and Pollatsek 2003). Two prominent alternative proposals which are also concerned with the modeling of psycholinguistically relevant parameters (as opposed to "basic" models of oculomotor control) have been proposed in the form of the SWIFT (Engbert, Longtin, and Kliegl 2002; Engbert et al. 2005) and Glenmore (Reilly and Radach 2003) models. To date, however, all of these approaches are restricted to the modeling of lexical factors such as word frequency, familiarity, and predictability and do not incorporate morphological or syntactic influences. For this reason, a discussion of these models is beyond the scope of the present volume. For further information, the interested reader is therefore referred to the references cited above. A comprehensive overview of eye movement research in psycholinguistics is provided by Rayner (1998). For a recent review of eye movement correlates of syntactic processing, see Clifton et al. (2007).

2.4.3.2 Self-paced reading   Like eye-tracking, self-paced reading provides a measure of the time that it takes to read particular words or regions of a sentence, which can be used as an indication of processing difficulty. The undisputed advantage of the self-paced reading method lies in the fact that, in contrast to eye-tracking, it only requires a computer (of any type) and a (freeware) presentation software. This method therefore provides a very simple and cheap means for the collection of online data anywhere in the world.

In the self-paced reading paradigm, participants view sentences or texts in a segment-by-segment fashion, with segments constituted by words, phrases (e.g. NPs), or larger chunks. The rate of presentation is controlled by the participant him-/herself, i.e. the presentation of the next segment is induced by means of a button-press. Participants therefore read the critical stimuli at their own pace (hence the term "self-paced" reading). Several different presentation modes are employed. The method that is closest to natural reading is the "cumulative" presentation technique, in which the position and length of individual words is first indicated on the screen by means of underscores. Upon the participant's button-press, these underscores are replaced by the actual words or segments until the entire sentence or text is displayed on the screen. Alternatively, a non-cumulative presentation method may be used to prevent regressions to previous parts of the critical sentences. This can be implemented in several different ways. In the "non-cumulative moving window" technique, segments disappear (i.e. are replaced by underscores again) once the participant presses the button to move on. A somewhat more rarely used non-cumulative presentation method is RSVP-like in that words/segments are presented at the center of the computer screen and replaced by the next word/segment upon the participant's button-press.

In contrast to eye-tracking, self-paced reading provides a unidimensional measure of language processing, i.e. for each region of interest, only a single measure (namely "reading time") is available. In addition, participants are in control of the responses that they provide because they can choose when to press the button to move on to the next segment. For this reason, self-paced reading is subject to all of the concerns that apply to standard reaction time measures, e.g. speed–accuracy trade-off (see section 2.4.2 for discussion). Thus, reading times provide a "less direct" measure of the comprehension process in comparison to eye-tracking. This can be seen, for example, in the fact that reading times obtained via self-paced reading are often several hundred milliseconds higher than the corresponding fixation times in eye-tracking measures. In addition, self-paced reading is highly susceptible to so-called "spill-over" effects, i.e. to the phenomenon that processing difficulty sometimes does not become apparent until the post-critical region. While these effects are sometimes also observable in eye movements, they occur most systematically with self-paced reading.

In summary, while self-paced reading has been used in many investigations of online language processing, it is clearly more susceptible to strategic influences than all of the other online methods discussed above.

2.5 Summary

The aim of this chapter was to provide a brief introduction to the experimental methods which underlie the empirical data to be presented throughout the remainder of this volume. As should be apparent from the preceding discussion, there is no single "perfect" method for the examination of psycholinguistic and neurolinguistic questions. Neither are behavioral methods superior to neurocognitive methods because they have been available to the field for a longer period of time, nor do neurocognitive methods provide definitive answers to processing questions simply because they are "closer" to the brain. Rather, all methods are associated with their own particular strengths and weaknesses. For this reason, we believe that true insights into the language processing architecture can only be gained from an integrative perspective, in which a variety of methods are compared and contrasted.

Notes

1. It is interesting to consider the status of fMRI/PET in light of the online/ offline distinction. Whereas these methods are associated with a low temporal resolution, they measure brain responses over the entire course of processing a critical stimulus (word, sentence, dialogue). Thus, in contrast to offline behavioral measures, the data collected using fMRI/PET comprise neural correlates of each processing step as the stimulus in question unfolds over time. These methods – and especially event-related fMRI, in which stimuli are not presented in a blocked fashion – may therefore be considered online methods, albeit with a low temporal resolution.

2. The visual field that is perceived when looking straight ahead can be subdivided into three main regions: the *fovea, parafovea,* and *periphery.* The fovea, which encompasses the central 2° of the visual field (approximately eight letters), has the highest visual acuity (resolution). Acuity is much reduced in the parafoveal region (approximately 5°) and even more so in the periphery (beyond 5°).

Part I
Syntax and Morphology at the Word Level

Overview

Word-level processing in the domains of syntax and morphology provides a microcosm-model of virtually all of the main debates within the cognitive neuroscience of language. For example, do neural representations of words provide evidence for a distinction between rules and non-rule-like representations that must be stored in memory? This question, which has been discussed extensively as part of the so-called "past tense debate", applies both to the domain of inflectional morphology and to that of derivational morphology. A second major issue that has received a lot of attention within the area of word processing concerns the abstractness of the stored neural representations for words. Should these representations be considered specific to language or are they shared with other cognitive/perceptual domains? For example, to what degree do the neural representations of nouns overlap with those of "objects" more generally and to what extent are the representations of verbs similar to those of "actions"? Finally, from a somewhat more general neurocognitive perspective, this section on word processing will be concerned with the question of whether there is empirical evidence for specific neural correlates of combinatorial linguistic processes. Importantly, note that the questions to be addressed within this section are specifically focused on syntactic and morphological properties at the word level and their neurocognitive correlates. The following chapters therefore do not provide an introduction to more general aspects of word recognition (e.g. how is a word's representation in the mental lexicon accessed?). For an introduction to word recognition, see McQueen (2007) and Gaskell (2007).

This section is subdivided into three chapters and a final discussion. Chapter 3 focuses on categorial distinctions at the word level and particularly on possible differences between nouns and verbs. In Chapter 4, we discuss neurocognitive results on the processing of inflectional morphology, i.e. morphology that serves to produce "new forms of the same word" rather than creating new word categories/lexical entries. As most of the research in this domain has been sparked by the past tense debate, this chapter is centered around the question of whether regular and irregular inflectional morphology are represented differently at the neural level. Chapter 5 examines neurocognitive studies of derivational morphology, i.e. morphology that serves to create new categories. In particular, it deals with the issue of morphological decomposition in word recognition as well as possible neurocognitive correlates of such a decomposition process. For an introduction to basic morphological concepts such as the difference between inflectional and derivational morphology, see Haspelmath (2002) and Spencer (1991). Finally, Chapter 6 provides a summary and a critical evaluation of the research discussed in the preceding chapters.

3

Basic categories:
The noun–verb distinction

Within the neuropsychological literature, a great deal of research on word processing and the neural representation of words has focused on issues of categorization. For example, selective impairments observed in particular patient populations (or in single case studies) have been used to argue for distinct representations of categories such as nouns vs. verbs (Daniele et al. 1994; Miceli et al. 1984), content vs. function words (Caplan, Hildebrandt, and Makris 1996; Gardner and Zurif 1975), concrete vs. abstract words (Eviatar, Menn, and Zaidel 1990; Funnell, Corballis, and Gazzaniga 2001; Tyler, Moss, and Jennings 1995; Villardita, Grioli, and Quattropani 1988; Warrington and Shallice 1984), and different semantic categories (e.g. animals vs. tool names; Warrington and McCarthy 1987). Among these many possible dissociations, the proposed distinctions between different word categories appear particularly relevant from the perspective of syntax and morphology at the word level. In the following, we will therefore focus on the question of whether nouns and verbs are represented differently in the brain.[1]

Word category differences are perhaps best known from production deficits in agrammatic aphasia: agrammatic patients often have more difficulty in producing verbs than nouns (Miceli et al. 1984; Myerson and Goodglass 1972) and these differences obtain even when the two types of categories are closely matched with respect to other parameters. Further research suggests, however, that verb-specific deficits need not be linked specifically to agrammatism (Berndt and Haendiges 2000) and that there are also patients who show a selective deficit for the production of nouns (Zingeser and Berndt 1990). Nevertheless, dissociations of this type suggest that verbs and nouns may be represented differently in the brain, thus allowing for a selective impairment that targets either one or the other class.

From the perspective of electrophysiology, differences between nouns and verbs in the brain responses of unimpaired individuals were first observed in the late 1970s (Brown and Lehmann 1979) and subsequently also reported in a number of more recent experiments (Dehaene 1995; Molfese et al. 1996; Preissl et al. 1995; Samar and Berent 1986). These studies, which focused on possible topographical differences in the brain potentials evoked by the two word categories, primarily observed differences over frontal recording sites. These results were taken to suggest that verbs lead to increased activity in frontal brain regions as opposed to nouns. On the basis of a current source density (CSD) analysis,[2] Pulvermüller, Lutzenberger, and Preissl (1999) further argued for a physiological double dissociation between the two word categories: between 200 and 230 ms post word onset, these authors observed more activity for verbs vs. nouns at electrodes close to motor and premotor regions, and for nouns vs. verbs at occipital electrode sites. A similar dissociation was observed in gamma band (30 Hz) responses within a later time window (500–800 ms) (for category-specific differences in high-frequency brain responses, see also Pulvermüller et al. 1996).[3]

The topographical differences observed in these EEG studies appear to fit quite well with previously observed deficit-lesion correlations. Notably, several patient studies have suggested that difficulties in verb processing are more often observed in patients with frontal lesions, whereas noun-related impairments are more closely linked to lesions in temporal or occipital regions (Damasio and Tranel 1993; Daniele et al. 1994; Goodglass et al. 1966; Miceli et al. 1988; Miceli et al. 1984). These observations led to the theoretical assumption that differences in the neural representation of verbs and nouns might be attributable to their "motor-related" vs. "object (vision)-related" meanings (Damasio and Damasio 1992; Pulvermüller 1999; Warrington and McCarthy 1987).[4]

With the increasing availability of neuroimaging methods, a natural extension of these findings from patient populations and electro-physiological studies lay in the exploration of possible differences in the neuroanatomical representation of nouns and verbs in healthy individuals. Indeed, some early imaging studies appeared to support the association between verb processing and frontal brain regions. Perani et al. (1999), for example, observed increased left inferior frontal activation for Italian verbs vs. nouns (e.g. *tagliare*, "to cut" vs. *martello*, "hammer") and speculated that this finding might reflect the automatic activation of syntactic information associated with verb representations. The general applicability of this conclusion, however, is called into question by other neuroimaging studies which failed to find neuroanatomical differences between the two word classes in English (Tyler et al. 2001; Warburton et al. 1996). These discrepancies might be due to a variety of factors. In addition to examining different languages (Italian vs. English), the experiments in question also used different tasks: lexical decision (Perani et al., 1999), verb generation in response to a given noun (Warburton et al. 1996) and a semantic relatedness judgment (Tyler et al. 2001). Furthermore, as pointed out by Tyler et al. (2004a), these studies also differed as to whether they presented inflected or uninflected nouns and verbs. Tyler and colleagues argued that, due to the morphological structure of Italian, the stimuli used in the experiment by Perani and colleagues were inherently inflected (i.e. *tagli-are*, "stem+infinitive", *martell-o* "stem+masculine.gender"; the stems *tagli* and *martell* are not words on their own). By contrast, neither of the two experiments on English used inflected forms.[5]

To test this hypothesis, Tyler et al. (2004a) conducted an event-related fMRI experiment in which they presented healthy participants with word triplets consisting of either three verbs or three nouns (e.g. eating, grazing, DINING vs. sparrows, thrushes, WRENS). All forms were inflected, i.e. they were either present participles for the verbs or plurals for the nouns. Participants were asked to judge whether the capitalized target word was semantically related to the two preceding words or not. Tyler and colleagues observed pronounced activation for verbs vs. nouns within the left inferior frontal gyrus (BA 44, 45, 47; see Plate 2.A), extending into the insula (i.e. a cortical region located deeper than the brain's lateral surface, at the junction between the frontal, temporal, and parietal lobes). By contrast, no regions showed a higher activation for nouns vs. verbs in a direct contrast. Note, however, that it was not the case that the noun condition did not engender any activation within the left inferior frontal gyrus (IFG) whatsoever. Rather, baseline contrasts involving a subtraction of letter sequences from the critical word triplet conditions also revealed IFG activation for the noun stimuli. Nonetheless, the activation within this region was shown to be significantly larger for inflected verbs as opposed to inflected nouns. This finding contrasts nicely with the study by Tyler et al. (2001), which applied the same experimental paradigm to uninflected verb and noun forms and found no differential activation between the two categories (i.e. both showed comparable activation within a left fronto-temporal network).[6]

On the basis of these findings, Tyler et al. (2004a) argue that verbs and nouns per se are not represented differently in the brain. Rather, the differences between these two categories come about when they are processed in their inflected forms. More specifically, Tyler and colleagues suggest that verb inflections differ from noun inflections in that only the former play an important relational role at the level of the sentence. By contrast, the pluralization of a noun is assumed to play a primarily semantic role at the level of the noun phrase itself. The increased IFG activation for inflected verbs therefore reflects the role of these constituents within relational processes during sentence comprehension. Converging evidence for this assumption stems from an fMRI study by Longe et al. (2007) which directly compared stems and inflected forms of English nouns and verbs in an implicit (pleasantness judgment) task. Category and inflection were shown to interact in the left IFG (BA 47) and left middle temporal gyrus, with these regions showing an activation increase exclusively for inflected verbs. Likewise, the selective involvement of left frontal regions in the processing of verbs suggested by studies using repetitive transcranial magnetic stimulation (rTMS; see Chapter 2.2.3) was shown in studies using inflected verb and noun stimuli (Cappelletti et al. 2008; Shapiro et al. 2001). A recent rTMS study on Italian further supports the idea that these results are at least partially due to the complexity of verbal morphology (Finocchiaro et al. 2008). However, in spite of the overall consistency of the imaging and TMS results, some puzzles still remain. Most notably, it is not clear why the TMS studies implicate a verb-specific involvement of the anterior middle frontal gyrus (aMFG) rather than, as suggested by the fMRI studies cited above, of left inferior frontal and mid temporal regions (but see Shapiro, Moo, and Caramazza 2006, for converging fMRI results). In part, this finding may be due to the fact that the left IFG is activated by both inflected nouns and inflected verbs, though to different degrees (e.g. Tyler et al. 2004a).

The notion that apparent categorial differences between nouns and verbs may rather stem from differences in inflection can be extended with reference to cross-linguistic findings. In a PET study on Finnish, Laine et al. (1999) observed increased activation in left BA 44/45 for the encoding of case-marked vs. non-case-marked nouns in a recognition memory task. A later fMRI study which undertook the same comparison in Finnish using a lexical decision task (Lehtonen et al. 2006) also revealed increased left inferior frontal activation (though, in this case, in BA 47) and increased activation in the left posterior superior temporal sulcus for inflected vs. non-inflected nouns. (For a similar finding of BA 47 activation in Japanese, see Inui, Ogawa, and Ohba 2007). As will be discussed in detail in Chapter 9, there is ample experimental evidence to suggest that morphological case marking plays an important *relational* role in language comprehension at the sentence level. It thus appears plausible that this type of inflectional morphology should pattern with verb inflections rather than noun pluralization in terms of functional neuroanatomy.

These results thus indicate that, rather than being due to inherent categorial differences, the neurocognitive distinction between nouns and verbs may be crucially influenced by inflectional morphology and the potential relational role of the individual words being processed. A proposal along these lines also appears compatible with the cross-linguistic observation that the noun–verb distinction is not a basic lexical property of every language (Bisang to appear; Croft 2001; Van Valin 2008). Thus, in languages such as Chinese, many lexemes display "trans-categoriality" in the sense that they can function either as a noun or as a verb depending on the sentential environment in which they occur and/or the inflections that they bear (Bisang 2008).

Notes

1. For reports of electrophysiological differences between content and function words, which might also be considered relevant to the integration of a lexical item into a sentence-level representation, see Neville, Mills, and Lawson (1992), Nobre and McCarthy (1994), and Pulvermüller, Lutzenberger, and Birbaumer (1995).
2. Current source density (CSD) is a topographical analysis method which serves to identify the locations of current sources and sinks and their relative magnitudes. CSD analyses are further used to minimize influences of the reference electrode and emphasize the contribution of local sources to the activity measured at a particular electrode site.
3. Only very few electrophysiological studies have examined possible differences between nouns and verbs during sentence processing. A notable exception is a study by Federmeier et al. (2000) which compared ERP responses to nouns such as *solution* and verbs such as *carve* in sentences like (i) and (ii). Federmeier and colleagues observed a left-lateralized early positivity (P200) for unambiguous verbs in comparison to unambiguous nouns, and a negativity between 250 and 450 ms for nouns in comparison to verbs at fronto-central electrode sites. (For a similar result, see Corey 1999.)

   (i) Jim learned the <u>solution</u> but went blank when it was time for the test.

   (ii) The girl learned to <u>carve</u> but found it was more tedious than she had thought.

4. In more recent research, Pulvermüller and colleagues have taken this dissociation one step further and proposed a "semantic somatotopy of action words". For example, "foot-related" action words such as *kick* activate regions of motor cortex that are involved in foot movements, whereas "finger-related" action words such as *pick* activate finger-related motor regions (Hauk, Johnsrude, and Pulvermüller 2004). For a review of studies on the relationship between word meaning and action, see Pulvermüller (2005).

5. This generalization appears to be supported by the results of a PET study which revealed increased left frontal activation for the production of inflected verbs as opposed to inflected nouns in German (Shapiro et al. 2005). Interestingly, and in contrast to previous findings, this experiment also yielded increased activation for nouns vs. verbs, for example in right superior temporal, left inferior temporal and left subcortical regions. However, a potential problem with this study is that the first person plural form of the verbs used overlaps with the infinitive form. This introduces an ambiguity with respect to whether the verbs were actually processed as inflected or not.

6. Sahin, Pinker, and Halgren (2006) reported an fMRI study on (covert) verb and noun production in English, the results of which appear to contradict Tyler and colleagues' findings. Increased activation was observed in the left IFG for the inflection of both nouns and verbs and this effect was stronger for nouns than for verbs. However, this result was influenced by an additional manipulation of regular vs. irregular inflectional morphology: the increased activation for the inflected nouns was primarily due to the irregular forms (e.g. *feet*). For further details on this experiment, see Table 4.1 in Chapter 4.

4

Inflectional morphology

Recall from Chapter 3 that inflectional morphology appears to play an important role in shaping the neural responses to the processing of different word categories. Thus, the correlation between left inferior frontal regions and verb processing may be crucially mediated by the presence of verbal inflections (Longe et al. 2007; Tyler et al. 2004a). Interestingly, Tyler and colleagues in fact went one step further in their own interpretation of their results: they suggested that the increased left IFG activation for inflected verbs should be attributed to the presence of *regular* verb inflections and that this cortical region may therefore be responsible for the morphological decomposition of regular verb forms (Tyler, Randall, and Marslen-Wilson 2002b).[1] This restriction should be treated with some caution, as other studies have revealed frontal activation differences between both regularly and irregularly inflected verbs and nouns (Shapiro et al. 2006, though these differences were observed in left aMFG rather than IFG; see Chapter 3). Nevertheless, the assumption that neural representations of grammatical categories may be mediated by morphological distinctions can be situated within a long tradition of distinguishing between "regular" and "irregular" morphological forms and the psychological mechanisms associated with them. The question of whether and how these different forms should be distinguished has led to one of the longest and liveliest controversies within empirical linguistic research, the so-called "past-tense debate".

The past-tense debate was sparked by Rumelhart and McClelland's (1986) proposal that the English past tense could be learned by a connectionist model, which performs in a similar way to English-learning children. This claim broke with the long-standing conviction that the stages evident in children's acquisition of the past tense provide strong evidence for rule-based behavior. In particular, the observation that children first correctly produce the past tense form of irregular verbs (e.g. *come – came*), but later overgeneralize the regular (-*ed*) past tense form even to the verbs that they had previously produced correctly (producing *comed* or *camed*; Brown 1973; Ervin 1964; Kuczaj 1977), was viewed as strong evidence for the acquisition of a "past tense rule". This assumption was further supported by the finding that children also apply this rule to novel (non-existing) verbs (e.g. *spow*) that they have never heard before (Berko 1958). By contrast, irregular forms are seldom over-generalized. Several approaches were proposed in order to account for this dissociation between regular and irregular forms. One of these posited that regular forms are derived by a rule, whereas irregular forms are stored in memory (Pinker 1984). Alternatively, the standard approach in generative phonology proposed that, in irregular forms, an abstract morpheme is affixed to the stem and a rule is applied to change its phonological composition (Chomsky and Halle 1968). Independently of the particular approach adopted, however, it was relatively uncontroversial that the derivation of *regular* past tense forms is achieved via the application of a rule. In this context, the surprising – and inherently appealing – contribution of Rumelhart and McClelland's (1986) approach was that it allowed for the derivation of both regular and irregular forms by means of a single, computational mechanism that was not explicitly rule-based. Rather, their network model recognized patterns between input (an infinitive verb form) and output (a past tense verb form), irrespective of whether the verb in question was regular or not. This relatively simple pattern-associator was able to mimic the acquisitional stages shown by English children with a remarkable degree of accuracy.

Together with a critical commentary by Pinker and Prince (1988), Rumelhart and McClelland's model paved the way for a debate that is still ongoing. Specifically, the discussion has come to focus on the issue of whether regular and irregular morphology can be derived by a single mechanism or whether two mechanisms are required.[2] Approaches positing two different types of processes are known as "dual-route" models (Clahsen 1999; Pinker 1991; Prasada and Pinker 1993), and more recently as the "words and rules" theory (Pinker and Ullman 2002b). The neurocognitive extension of this approach, the "declarative/procedural" model (Ullman 2001), assumes that the processing of regular (rule-based) morphology is handled by a network of inferior frontal, premotor, and parietal regions as well as the basal ganglia, whereas irregular morphology is primarily represented in medial temporal regions. In addition to drawing on the broader theoretical distinction between declarative and procedural memory (see Chapter 15.1 for further details), these functional-neuroanatomical hypotheses were based on observations from an influential patient study (Ullman et al. 1997c) which reported a double dissociation between the processing of regular and irregular morphology in different patient groups. On the one hand, (agrammatic) patients with lesions to the anterior perisylvian cortex (including inferior frontal regions) and patients with Parkinson's disease (involving degeneration of the basal ganglia) had more difficulty in producing regular as opposed to irregular verbs and in inflecting novel verbs. By contrast, (anomic) patients with temporal or temporo-parietal lesions and patients with Alzheimer's disease (affecting structures of the medial temporal lobe) showed difficulties in the production of irregular forms and produced regularizations of irregular forms, but did not produce analogies of irregular forms and had little difficulty with novel verb forms.

From the connectionist perspective, it is also no longer the original Rumelhart and McClelland model that is at issue (a number of clear problems with this model were quickly identified and improved; e.g. Plunkett and Marchman 1993), but rather the single mechanism philosophy behind it. In the most recent instantiation of the past tense debate (for a recent review of both positions, see McClelland and Patterson, 2002a; McClelland and Patterson, 2002b; Pinker and Ullman, 2002a; Pinker and Ullman, 2002b), arguments in favor of the connectionist perspective are typically based on a network model by Joanisse and Seidenberg (1999). As will be discussed in more detail below, this model assumes a crucial role for phonological and semantic representations in deriving morphological effects, thereby effectively eliminating the need for a separate level of morphological representation.

As with other debates in the field of psycholinguistics (e.g. the question of whether language comprehension proceeds in a modular or an interactive manner; see Chapter 7), behavioral evidence on the processing of regular vs. irregular morphology was often equivocal in the sense that it could be accommodated by both competing theoretical approaches. New hope was therefore invested in the neuroscientific examination of these issues. In the words of Beretta et al. (2003a: 69): "One way to try to settle the issue has been to ask the brain how many processes *it* thinks it has." In the neurocognitive domain, research has therefore mainly focused on whether the processing of regular and irregular morphology is associated with separable neural processes, i.e. activation in different brain regions or different ERP components.

4.1 The neuroanatomical perspective

The first neuroimaging study to contrast regular and irregular morphology was reported by Jaeger et al. (1996). Using PET, they presented participants with words (English verb stems) and pseudowords (stems of nonce verbs) and asked them to provide a spoken response to each form. In five different blocks, participants thus read English verb stems or English nonce verbs, generated the past tense from stems of regular or irregular verbs, and generated the past tense of nonce verbs. Most generally, Jaeger and colleagues observed higher overall activation for irregular than for regular forms. More precise localization differences were obtained by subtracting the reading conditions from the respective generation conditions. These subtractions revealed activation of the left middle and inferior frontal gyri (including BA 44, 45) for all contrasts (regular, irregular, and nonce verbs). On the basis of this overlapping activation, Jaeger et al. (1996) suggested that Broca's region may be responsible for the processing of past tense as a grammatical feature. Activation for regular and nonce but not for irregular stimuli was observed in the left middle frontal gyrus (BA 46) and in the left anterior cingulate gyrus (BA 24). Jaeger and colleagues therefore speculate that BA 46 might be involved in "actually computing the regular suffixation process" (p. 482). Furthermore, since the generation of irregular past tense forms showed activation in the left middle temporal gyrus, whereas the generation of regular and nonce forms did not, this region was viewed as potentially responsible for the retrieval of irregular verb forms from memory. These differential activation patterns appear quite compatible with a dual-route approach to regular and irregular morphology, though they are only partly consistent with the specific predictions of the declarative/procedural model (which, for example, leads one to expect a selective left inferior frontal activation increase for regular forms). Jaeger et al.'s study also revealed a common activation for irregular and nonce verb generation within the left orbitofrontal cortex (BA 10), a clustering which appears somewhat surprising from the perspective of a dual-route model. The authors interpreted this result in terms of the inhibition of overlearned behavior and, thereby, of default or high-frequency responses (as in regular verb forms).

Unfortunately, rather than clarifying the issues raised by Jaeger et al.'s (1996) experiment, the findings subsequent imaging studies in English (Ullman, Bergida, and O'Craven 1997a) and German (Indefrey et al. 1997) only served to make matters even more complex. Both of these studies, which are only published in abstract form (see Beretta et al. 2003a for a detailed summary), also reported differential activation patterns for regular vs. irregular inflectional morphology.[3] However, the more fine-grained neuroanatomical dissociations obtained are neither straightforwardly comparable to those found by Jaeger et al. (1996) nor to one another. They are also not predicted by the declarative/procedural model. Note, though, that the experiments all used different paradigms (overt generation in Jaeger et al. and Indefrey et al. vs. silent generation in Ullman et al.; word generation in Jaeger et al. and Ullman et al. vs. sentence generation in Indefrey et al.), which may have crucially influenced the pattern of results obtained. Furthermore, all employed blocked designs, which introduce possible confounds in terms of priming, depth of processing, and further factors (for discussion, see Seidenberg and Hoeffner 1998).

This methodological limitation was overcome by Beretta et al. (2003a), who used event-related fMRI to examine noun (plural) and verb (past tense) generation in German. German appears particularly well suited to the examination of theoretical claims about the regular–irregular distinction because, in contrast to English, there is no direct correlation between regularity and frequency (i.e. the regular forms are not at the same time the most frequent; see Marcus et al. 1995). Similarly to the previous findings by Jaeger et al. (1996) and Indefrey et al. (1997), Beretta and colleagues observed greater overall activation for irregular in comparison to regular forms. In addition, irregular forms engendered higher activation than regular forms in a number of frontal and parietal regions, whereas no region showed higher activation for regular vs. irregular forms. Finally, the activation for regular inflections showed a stronger degree of left-lateralization than that for irregular inflections. In summary, while this experiment again revealed activation differences between regular and irregular forms, its results led to a further diversification of the neuroanatomical regions implicated in the processing of the different inflectional categories. In addition, as the authors themselves noted, a caveat with respect to the interpretation of this study is that it averaged over a number of potentially different stimulus categories. In particular, activation patterns for nouns and verbs were not examined separately, which is problematic in view of the possible functional neuroanatomical differences between these two word categories and especially of their differential interaction with inflection (see Chapter 3). Furthermore, different types of irregular verb forms were examined as part of a single "irregular" condition. As this clustering neglects the issue of subregularities within the German morphological system (see the end of section 4.2 for further discussion), it may have obscured more fine-grained differences within the overall activation pattern.

Proponents of a single-mechanism connectionist approach have leveled a number of criticisms against the studies by Beretta, Jaeger, and colleagues (Seidenberg and Hoeffner 1998; Seidenberg and Arnoldussen 2003). One very basic objection was that increased activation for irregular forms might simply lie in the increased difficulty associated with the processing of these forms. However, while it is true that activation differences between two conditions can only be interpreted straightforwardly in terms of the manipulation of interest if they are equated for difficulty, it is not entirely clear how this explanation can account for the specific findings of the studies by Jaeger et al. (1996) and Beretta et al. (2003a) (see also Beretta et al. 2003b; Jaeger, Van Valin, and Lockwood 1998; for the authors' own responses to the critiques). For Jaeger and colleagues' experiment, for example, "increased difficulty" would need to account for the fact that the generation of irregular past tense forms led to activation in the left MTG, whereas the generation of regular and pseudoword forms did not. The implied involvement of a left temporal region during a more difficult language-related task, while no activation is seen in this region in the easier task, appears relatively unprecedented in the neurocognitive literature on language. Furthermore, with regard to Beretta et al.'s findings, it seems much more problematic to argue that irregular forms are inherently more difficult to process than regular forms in a language like German as opposed to English. Recall from above that, in this language, the regular forms – as a class – are actually *less* frequent than their irregular counterparts. Thus, the reinforcement from many "friends" (i.e. similar forms) which, from the perspective of connectionist models, helps to render regular forms easier to process, is not as straightforwardly given in German.

A further, and theoretically more significant point concerns the potential ability of single-mechanism (connectionist) models to explain dissociations in neuroimaging and neuropsychological data. As pointed out by Seidenberg and Arnoldussen (2003: 527), these approaches need not claim that "regular and irregular forms produce the same pattern of results". More specifically, the network model presented by Joanisse and Seidenberg (1999) is capable of deriving neuropsychological dissociations between regular and irregular morphology by assuming that these can be reduced to more basic factors. This multi-layered model assumes a mapping between speech input and speech output (both modeled in terms of distributed phonological representations) as well as semantics (modeled using localist representations of one unit per word as well as a past tense unit). All of these different levels of representation are connected via a layer of hidden units. The distributed phonological representations allow the model to capture phonological similarities between input and output. Within this model, dissociations between regular and irregular past tense forms are explained with reference to these forms' reliance on phonological and semantic processing, respectively. Thus, regular English past tense forms share a greater degree of phonological overlap with their respective verb stems than irregular past tense forms. Semantic representations are therefore less important in the generation of the past tense of these forms (e.g. *close-closed*), since they are entirely predictable in phonological terms. By contrast, the generation of irregular past tense forms (e.g. *bring-brought*) is more heavily reliant upon semantics, because the system must identify the particular verb in question in order to produce the correct inflected form. From this perspective, selective deficits of regular or irregular morphology in different patient populations (or distinct activation patterns in neuroimaging studies) can be accounted for with reference to phonological and semantic processing difficulties, respectively. Consider, for example, the double dissociation reported by Ullman et al. (1997c), which was viewed as strong converging support for the assumption that regular and irregular inflections draw upon separable neural subsystems. Joanisse and Seidenberg (1999) offer a different explanation: as outlined above, their model links deficits in the production of regular inflected forms to a phonological processing problem, whereas increased difficulty in the production of irregular inflected forms is viewed as a result of a semantic problem. They show that "lesioning" of the semantic component of their model (via the arbitrary severing of connections within this component) has a large effect on the model's performance with regard to irregular past tense forms, while its ability to correctly produce the past tense of regular forms and of pseudowords is affected to a much lesser degree. By contrast, lesioning of the phonological output component affects all three types of verb forms, but especially limits the model's ability to deal with pseudowords. Joanisse and Seidenberg (1999: 7594) conclude that the "double dissociation observed across patient groups can be replicated by introducing different types of damage in a system that does not include separate rule and exception mechanisms".

Converging support for this assumption stems from the observation that, in some patients, an apparent impairment of regular past tense morphology disappears when phonological structure is controlled for (Bird et al. 2003). Similarly, a recent fMRI study on past tense generation indicated that the increased bilateral inferior frontal activation which was observable for regular vs. irregular inflected forms could, in fact, be attributed to phonological considerations (Joanisse and Seidenberg 2005). Thus, irregular forms that were phonologically similar to regulars (e.g. *slept, fled, sold*) showed a similar activation pattern to regulars in this region and engendered significantly higher activation than irregulars that were phonologically dissimilar from regulars (e.g. *took, gave*). Notably, however, one could argue that the irregular verbs that are similar to regulars include a (potential) suffix (*-d/t*) whereas the "true irregulars" do not. We shall return to this potentially important issue below.

In a further fMRI study, Desai et al. (2006) even reported increased inferior frontal activation for overt irregular vs. regular past tense generation. This activation, which formed part of a larger frontal–parietal–basal ganglia network encompassing bilateral premotor regions, bilateral intraparietal sulcus (IPS), and the right caudate nucleus (part of the basal ganglia), was also observable when the two types of verbs were matched for phonological complexity. The reverse contrast of regular vs. irregular past tense generation yielded increased activation in the left superior temporal gyrus/planum temporale (i.e. the superior surface of the temporal lobe), close to primary auditory cortex, and the left supramarginal gyrus, but only when phonological complexity was not matched. A similar finding was reported for Spanish (de Diego Balaguer et al. 2006): the covert generation of irregular vs. regular first person present tense forms led to increased left inferior frontal activation (BA 44/45), whereas regular verbs showed increased activation in the left anterior STG.[4] Materials were matched for phonological structure (both regular and irregular verbs are inflected via suffixation in Spanish). Several other regions were also activated (e.g. the left hippocampus for regular vs. irregular inflection; see Table 4.1 for details). Proponents of single mechanism models have

Table 4.1: Summary of neuroimaging findings on the processing of regular vs. irregular inflectional morphology.

Article	Technique	Design	Task	Activation for irregular > regular	Activation for regular > irregular	Language
Jaeger et al. (1996)	PET	blocked	overt generation	more activation overall	not reported	English
Indefrey et al. (1997)	PET	mixed blocked	overt generation	L BA 46, 44/6, 10, 39/40, 5, 37 R BA 47, 46, 9/32, 18	L BA 39	German
Sach et al. (2004)	PET	mixed blocked	overt generation	—	R BA 37	German
Ullman et al. (1997a)	fMRI	blocked	covert generation	L temporal	bilateral frontal, basal ganglia	English
Beretta et al. (2003a)	fMRI	event-related	covert generation	more activation overall	L BA 44, 41, 22, 32	German
Tyler et al. (2005)	fMRI, sparse	auditory, two pairs of the same cond.	same – different judgment	—	R BA 21, 22, 42	English
Desai et al. (2006)	fMRI	mixed blocked	overt generation	L BA 45/47, 6, 9, 40, 37; thalamus R 13, 6, 19; caudate	L BA 41 R BA 40	English
Sahin et al. (2006)	fMRI	event-related	covert generation	anterior cingulate regions, left IFG; more activation overall	not reported	English
de Diego Balaguer et al. (2006)	fMRI	event-related	covert generation	L BA 45/46, 45, 44/45 R BA 46, 44/45	L BA 22, hippocampus	Spanish
Dhond et al. (2003)	MEG	randomized	covert generation	L fusiform gyrus R prefrontal	L inferior frontal gyrus	English

interpreted findings such as these, which implicate a profound involvement of the purported "procedural" network in the generation of
irregular inflections, as evidence for Joanisse and Seidenberg's (1999)
model. By contrast, de Diego Balaguer et al. (2006) argue that their
data support a neurocognitive differentiation between regular and
irregular morphology, albeit with an alternative functional interpretation of the neural networks involved.[5]

Regarding the association of regular and irregular morphology with
phonological and semantic processes, respectively, further patient
findings suggest that this is not as straightforward as some of the
findings cited above would appear to suggest. Tyler et al. (2002a)
showed that patients who are impaired with respect to regular past
tense processing need not necessarily show phonological processing
deficits (for a similar finding with a smaller group of patients, see
Marslen-Wilson and Tyler 1997). This study differed from those previously discussed in this chapter in that it did not employ a generation
task but rather a priming paradigm in which patients and controls
were presented with word pairs. The control group showed priming
effects for both regular (*jumped-jump*) and irregular forms (*brought-
bring*) as well as semantic priming (*cherry-grape*), while there was no
phonological priming effect (*gravy-grave*). One group of patients
showed no priming from regular forms, but priming from irregular
forms, whereas a second group pf patients showed the reverse pattern.
A second study showed that those patients who were impaired on the
regular forms did not display a general phonological deficit (Tyler et al.
2002b). At the same time, this study suggested that the degree of a
patient's phonological impairment did not predict the degree of his/
her processing difficulty with regular inflections. Regarding the correlation between semantic deficits and deficits of irregular morphology,
Tyler et al. (2004b) reported that semantic dementia patients (i.e.
patients with progressive temporal lobe damage and profound semantic impairments) show priming from irregular verb forms and can also
produce these forms without difficulty. Conversely, Miozzo (2003)
reports an anomic patient who showed difficulties with irregular rather
than regular forms, but had no difficulty accessing word forms per se.
In summary, these findings suggest that – while there may often be
correlations between deficits with regular and irregular morphology
and phonological and semantic impairments, respectively – the relation between these is not one-to-one.

4.2 The electrophysiological perspective

The regular–irregular distinction in inflectional morphology has also been examined in a number of ERP studies (see Table 4.2 for an overview). These offer quite a different perspective to the imaging and patient studies discussed in section 4.1, not only due to the specific advantages of the method (e.g. high temporal resolution) but also via the use of different paradigms. Thus, in contrast to the abundance of verb generation studies in the imaging literature, existing ERP findings on the processing of inflectional morphology have focused exclusively on language comprehension.

To date, the main methodological overlap between these electro-physiological investigations and studies from the neuroimaging and deficit-lesion domain lies in the use of priming paradigms. The priming methodology has a relatively long tradition in the investigation of morphological structure, typically resulting in the observation of priming between regular inflected forms and their stems, whereas irregular forms show no or significantly reduced priming (Kempley and Morton 1982; Stanners et al. 1979). In keeping with these earlier behavioral studies, the first ERP examinations of inflectional morphology also employed priming paradigms. The critical stimuli from these studies, which were carried out in German (Weyerts et al. 1996), English (Münte et al. 1999c), and Spanish (Rodriguez-Fornells, Münte, and Clahsen 2002), are exemplified in (4.1).

(4.1) Example stimuli from ERP investigations of regular and irregular inflectional morphology using priming

    a. Infinitive form to regular past participle form in German (Weyerts et al. 1996)
       tanzen – getanzt (control prime: identical target form)
       "dance" – "danced"

    b. Infinitive form to irregular past participle form in German (Weyerts et al. 1996)
       schreiben – geschrieben (control prime: identical target form)
       "write" – "written"

    c. Regular past tense to stem form in English (Münte et al. 1999c)
       stretched – stretch (control prime: unrelated regular past tense form)

Table 4.2: Summary of electrophysiological findings on the processing of regular vs. irregular inflectional morphology.

Article	Manipulation	Task	Modality	LAN	N400	Pos (P600)	Language / Examples
Weyerts et al. (1996)	Priming (verbs) identical rep, IR vs. morph rep, MR	speeded button press for pseudo-words	visual		200–600 reg: IR = MR irreg: IR < MR		German (4.1 a/b)
Münte et al. (1999c)	Priming (verbs) primed vs. un-primed	lexical decision (ortho/phono con-trolled)	visual		reduction for reg. when primed but not for irreg.		English (4.1 c/d)
Rodriguez-Fornells et al. (2002)	Priming (verbs) primed vs. un-primed	lexical decision	visual		reduction for reg. stems when primed but not for irreg.		Spanish (4.1 e/f)
Penke et al. (1997)	Violation (verbs) sentence, story, single word	test sentence, con-tent question, but-ton-press for noun	visual	for irreg. verbs with regular suffix in all three methods	for pseudowords with regular morphology (−t)	epoch ended at 800 ms; positivity apparent via visual inspection	German (4.2a)
Weyerts et al. (1997)	Violation (nouns) sentence	test sentence	visual	for irreg. nouns (masc/fem) with reg. plural suffix	for reg. nouns (loan/names) with irreg. plural suffix	epoch ended at 800 ms; positivity apparent via visual inspection	German (4.2b)
Lück et al. (2006) (aud. version of Weyerts et al. 1997)	Violation (nouns) sentence	test sentence	auditory	for irreg words with reg. endings + (reg.) loan words with irreg. endings	for reg. words (names/loan) with irreg. endings	for incorrect masc/fem (irreg.) and loan (reg.) words	German (4.2b)

Gross et al. (1998)	Violation (verbs) single word	button-press for noun	visual		for regularized irreg. participles		Italian (4.2c)
Rodriguez-Fornells et al. (2001)	Violation (verbs) story	content question	visual	left neg. (not anterior) for stem changes but not for inflection		750–1200 for incorrect conditions*	Catalan (4.2d)
Bartke et al. (2005)	Violation (nouns) sentence	critical item incorrect re. ortho/ending?	visual		for incorrect forms; reduced effect for "–e" (non-fem subrule ending)	epoch ended at 800 ms; positivity apparent via visual inspection	German (4.4)
Morris and Holcomb (2005)	Violations (verbs) sentence, single word	acceptability	visual	for all incorrect cond. independent of the tense form (sentence)**	irreg. > reg. (word) anterior incorrect irreg. more positive than correct irreg. (word)**	sentence: incorr. irreg. = incorrect reg. word: incorrect irreg > incorrect reg.**	English
Allen et al. (2003)	Tense violation (verbs) sentence[+]	acceptability	visual		low vs. high lex. frequency	for all incorrect conditions; latency differences for irreg. verbs (high freq. < low freq.)	English
Newman et al. (2007)	Tense violation (verbs) sentence[+]	acceptability	visual	for violations of regular past tense		for regular as well as for irregulars	English (4.3)

* Only significant in three out of four critical conditions, but apparent in visual inspection in the fourth.

[+] This study presented morphologically correct words in incorrect sentence contexts rather than morphological violations per se.

** LAN statistically not reliable/effect reported based on visual inspection; statistics for the positivity for incorrect regular single words not reported (P300–P560); anterior effect seems to result from the large posterior positivity for incorrect irregular forms.

   d. Irregular past tense to stem form in English (Münte et al. 1999c)
      fought – fight (control prime: unrelated irregular past tense
      form)

   e. Regular 1st person present tense to infinitive form in Spanish
      (Rodriguez-Fornells et al. 2002)
      ando – andar (control prime: unrelated regular 1st person
      present tense form)
      "I walk" – "walk"

   f. Irregular 1st person present tense to infinitive form in Span-
      ish (Rodriguez-Fornells et al. 2002)
      duermo – dormir (control prime: unrelated irregular 1st
      person present tense form)
      "I sleep" – "sleep"

Priming effects in ERP studies are typically reflected in N400 reduc-
tions (see, for example, Bentin, McCarthy, and Wood 1985, for semantic priming; and Rugg 1985, for repetition priming). Morphological
priming was shown to yield a similar result: Weyerts et al. (1996),
Münte et al. (1999c), and Rodriguez-Fornells et al. (2002) all observed
reduced N400 effects for primed forms when either prime or target
(depending on the particular study) was regular as opposed to irregular. These findings were interpreted as evidence for a larger degree of
lexical overlap for regular forms as opposed to irregular forms of the
same verb and, thereby, as converging support for a dual-route model.[6]
   A further set of ERP studies has examined the processing of inflectional morphology by means of violation paradigms. The vast majority
of these experiments compared ERP responses to regularized irregular
words with those to irregularized regulars in order to examine whether
the two types of violations yield differential ERP effects (Penke et al.
1997; Weyerts et al. 1997; Gross et al. 1998; Rodriguez-Fornells et al.
2001; Lück, Hahne, and Clahsen 2006). Example stimuli from these
studies are presented in (4.2). Note that the experiments differed with
respect to the way in the critical stimuli were presented: as isolated
words or embedded in sentences or stories (see Table 4.2 for an
overview of the presentation modalities).

(4.2) Example stimuli from ERP investigations of regular and irregular
       inflectional morphology using violation paradigms

   a. Regular and irregular past participles in German (Penke
      et al. 1997)
      getanz-t – *getanz-en; gelad-en – *gelad-et
      "danced" (regular); "loaded" (irregular)

b. Regular and irregular plural nouns in German (visual modality: Weyerts et al. 1997; auditory modality: Lück et al.
2006)[7]
Wrack-s – *Wrack-en; Dirk-s – *Dirk-en;
"wreck" (regular loan word); "Dirk" (regular name);
Bär-en – *Bär-s; Alge-n – *Alge-s
"bear" (irregular masculine); "algae" (irregular feminine)

c. Regular and irregular participle forms in Italian (Gross et al.
1998)
parlato – *parlito; preso – *prendato
"spoke" (regular); "took" (irregular)

d. Regular and irregular participle forms in Catalan (Rodriguez-Fornells et al. 2001)
cantat – *cantit (infinitive: cantar); temut – *temat (infinitive: témer)
"sung" (regular, no stem change); "taken" (regular, stem
change)
admès – *admetat (infinitive: admetre); dormit – *dormat
(infinitive: dormir)
"admit" (irregular, no stem change); "slept" (irregular, stem
change)

The logic behind the type of manipulation shown in (4.2) is that, if
regular morphology is decomposed via a rule-based process whereas
irregular forms call for a full-form access to the mental lexicon, only
regularized irregular forms should lead to a morphological rule violation. By contrast, irregularized regular forms should engender a lexical
access problem, since these will not be listed in the mental lexicon.
Whereas this prediction appears to be supported by several of the ERP
results, the overall data pattern is somewhat more complex (see
Table 4.2 for a summary).

ERP violation paradigms on morphological processing have yielded
three main types of effects: left anterior negativities (LANs), centro-
parietal negativities (N400s), and late positivities (P600s). The LAN
and N400 effects tend to show a complementary distribution in the
sense that LANs were more often observed in response to regularized
irregular words, whereas there was a higher likelihood of finding an
N400 for regular words bearing irregular morphology. This dissociation was typically taken as evidence for dual-mechanism models, with
the LAN interpreted as a correlate of a morphological rule violation

and the N400 thought to reflect a lexical search (as also observed for phonologically legal pseudowords, e.g. Holcomb and Neville 1990; Bentin et al. 1999).

There are two exceptions to this general pattern: Gross et al.'s (1998) study of Italian and the word level condition in Penke et al.'s (1997) study on German. In both of these experiments, the ERP responses to correct and incorrect regular participles did not differ from one another. As such a pattern was only observed in the two experiments that presented isolated words, it appears likely that it is somehow related to this presentation mode. In addition, both studies employed a "noun detection" task, i.e. participants were required to press a button when the presented word was a noun. This task may have led to relatively shallow processing, as a word's morphological form should provide sufficient information for it to be categorized as a noun or a verb (i.e. lexical access need not necessarily take place). Furthermore, the findings from Italian also present a second exception to the general pattern: regularized irregular participles showed a broadly distributed (N400-like) negativity rather than a LAN (as also observed at the word level by Penke et al. 1997). As argued by Newman et al. (2007: 437), this might be due to "a greater degree of phonological dissimilarity between the correct and incorrect forms in the Italian study [...] which may have led to a more N400-like effect if the Italian violations were treated as non-words". However, if this interpretation were correct, it would clearly speak against models assuming that regular morphology is obligatorily (or at least automatically) decomposed.

A second issue worth discussing with respect to the studies listed in (4.2) concerns the distribution of P600 effects. Such effects are only reported explicitly by Rodriguez-Fornells et al. (2001) and Lück et al. (2006) – a finding which appears somewhat puzzling in view of the fact that late positivities are otherwise robustly observed as correlates of morphosyntactic violations at the sentence level (see Chapter 12 for detailed discussion). In this regard, Rodriguez-Fornells et al. (2001) speculate that the apparent discrepancy between studies on inflectional morphology and studies investigating other issues might be attributable to the fact that the former typically cut off their ERP epochs at 800 ms post critical stimulus onset. This may have obscured P600 effects that were actually present in the data. Indeed, visual inspection of the papers in question indicates that this suggestion may be on the right track: with the exception of the sentence condition in the study by Penke et al. (1997), all sentence- or story-level experiments show an indication of a late positive effect for the violation conditions. In this way, the apparent incompatibility with experiments from other domains appears resolved.

An alternative violation-based approach to the examination of regular and irregular inflections was adopted in an ERP study by Newman et al. (2007). Rather than presenting morphologically incorrect forms, these authors measured ERP responses to infinitive forms of regular and irregular English verbs in sentence contexts requiring a past tense form. Examples are given in (4.3). In order to allow for a comparison of the observed components to a typical morphosyntactic LAN and a typical lexical/semantic N400 effect, Newman and colleagues also included word category violations (4.3c) and sentences containing a semantically inappropriate word (4.3d).

(4.3)   Example stimuli from Newman et al. (2007)

   a. Regular verbs
      Yesterday I whipped/*whip an egg.

   b. Irregular verbs
      Yesterday I wept/*weep for joy.

   c. Word category violation
      Yesterday I drank Lisa's by brandy the fire.

   d. Lexical/semantic violation
      Yesterday Daniel sipped his sarcasm for hours.

Newman and colleagues observed a LAN for tense violations involving regular verbs (4.3a) and for word category violations (4.3c). (Note, however, that the LAN for word category violations reached significance over the entire left hemisphere, rather than just in the left anterior ROI). The lexical/semantic violation condition elicited an N400 and all violation conditions engendered a late positivity (P600). At a first glance, these findings therefore seem to replicate the general pattern observed using the morphological violation paradigms in (4.2): violations involving regular morphology result in a LAN, whereas those involving irregular morphology do not. Accordingly, Newman et al. (2007) interpret these findings as evidence for the declarative/procedural model: they argue for the LAN as a general marker of combinatorial (procedural) linguistic processing, since it is not only observable for incorrect combinations of stem+affix (as in previous studies) but also for the absence of a required regular morpheme (i.e. past tense), and since it is further observable for both morphological and syntactic violations. In accordance with dual route models of morphological processing, the absence of a LAN for irregular forms is argued to result from the blocking of rule application via the lexical association with a fully inflected form. Upon closer consideration, however, this interpretation appears somewhat problematic: visual inspection of the ERP figures presented by Newman et al. (2007) suggests that both irregular verb forms (4.3b) pattern with the regular violation condition at left anterior electrode sites. In other words, both irregular forms appear to elicit a LAN in comparison to the regular non-violation condition. How this pattern might be derived within existing neurocognitive models of morphological processing is not clear. A possible interpretation, however, seems to be that the materials used by Newman and colleagues led to an expectation for a recognizable past tense suffix and that a violation of this expectation was reflected in a LAN. Hence, such an effect was observed for all conditions without a clearly separable past tense morpheme (the regular violation condition and both irregular conditions).

The idea that LAN effects may depend upon morpheme-related expectations is supported by a recent ERP study on Finnish (Lehtonen et al. 2007). This experiment contrasted inflected (case-marked) and non-inflected real nouns as well as different types of pseudowords: monomorphemic pseudowords, real stems with a pseudosuffix, pseudostems with a real suffix, and illegal stem-suffix combinations. In comparison to monomorphemic pseudowords, real stems with a pseudosuffix and illegal stem-suffix combinations engendered a left anterior negativity between 450 and 650 ms. No such effect was observed for the pseudostems with a real suffix, thereby suggesting that expectations with respect to morphological composition are only generated on the basis of an existing stem. The fact that no LAN was observable for inflected vs. non-inflected real words appears to further emphasize the importance of expectations in engendering this response: since the study by Lehtonen and colleagues used single-word presentation, no expectations with respect to the presence of absence of a particular morpheme were generated by the processing system.

A final ERP study on the processing of inflectional morphology exploited the existence of morphological subregularities in German in order to shed light on more fine-grained aspects of the regularity debate (Bartke et al. 2005). As briefly discussed in section 4.1, one of the inherent interests in examining morphological processing in German is that, in contrast to English, the forms that are considered regular (i.e.

the default forms) are not at the same time the most frequent. This is especially apparent in noun pluralization, in which the regular –s form only occurs with approximately 5% of nouns (Marcus et al. 1995). However, German in fact has five plural forms (−ø, −e, −er, −(e)n, and −s), with further differences arising due to an umlaut process (e.g. *Garten* – *Gärten*; "garden" – "gardens"). Crucially, the characterization of the non-s forms as "irregular" (or non-default) should not be taken to imply that the remaining forms show no internal regularities whatsoever. Rather, a number of subregularities can be identified within these plural forms (e.g. Köpcke 1988; Wiese 1999). For example, feminine nouns typically take the plural −(e)n form, whereas non-feminine nouns have a tendency to be marked with the −e form and non-feminine nouns ending in a reduced syllable have a tendency to take a zero plural marking (for a summary, see Bartke et al. 2005). To examine the processing of these subregularities, Bartke et al. (2005) contrasted correct and incorrect −en and −e plurals in an ERP study. Example word stimuli from this experiment, which were presented visually within sentence contexts, are given in (4.4).

(4.4)   Example stimuli from Bartke et al.'s (2005) study of subregularities in German noun plurals[8]

   a. Deiche – *Deichen; Bären – *Bäre
      "dikes" (−e plural, masculine, subregular); "bears" (−en plural, masculine, irregular)

For the general comparison between incorrect and correct forms, Bartke et al. (2005) reported a negativity with a fronto-temporal maximum (410–590 ms), followed by a late positivity (770–830 ms). Furthermore, Bartke et al. (2005) observed several indications of a processing advantage for the subregular −e plural form for the non-feminine nouns employed in their study. These were apparent in a reduced right posterior negativity (N400) for (a) correct −e vs. −en plural forms, and (b) for incorrect −e-marked vs. −en-marked plural forms. This electrophysiological effect was accompanied by higher error rates for non-feminine nouns incorrectly bearing the −e plural form, thereby suggesting a higher tendency of participants to accept the (incorrect) subregular form. On the basis of these findings (and further observations), Bartke et al. (2005) suggest that the dual-mechanism model should be expanded to a tripartite system, in which rules and lexical entries are supplemented by a third, intermediary information type which is rule-like but qualitatively different from the default rules. However, the authors leave open how this third component should be modeled.

From a neurocognitive perspective, the implications of Bartke et al.'s (2005) study are twofold. Firstly, this experiment revealed that LAN-like effects not only occur in response to completely "regularized" irregular forms (i.e. to irregular forms with a suffixed default s-plural) but also in response to the incorrect use of subregular plural forms. Secondly, it showed that the processing of subregular plural forms correlates with an N400 reduction. These observations are interesting because they cut across the typical component interpretations that have been assumed in the electrophysiological literature on inflectional morphology, namely that LAN effects can be linked to rule-based processing mechanisms, whereas N400 effects correlate with activation differences within a lexical/semantic network. Indeed, the functional interpretation of many findings in the literature has closely relied upon this seemingly clear-cut distinction, which has typically been interpreted as evidence for dual-mechanism models. For example, the declarative/procedural model explicitly views LAN effects as correlates of procedural memory/grammatical rules, while N400 effects are thought to reflect declarative memory/lexical information (Ullman 2001; Ullman 2004; see Chapter 15.1). However, the findings by Bartke et al. (2005) provide a first indication that matters may in fact be more complex. As will be shown in detail in subsequent sections of this book, the idea that "rule-like" (or combinatorial) processes may be reflected in N400 effects is also supported by findings from a number of other domains. Possible consequences of this observation will be discussed in Part IV on neurocognitive models. In addition, before drawing any further conclusions with regard to the nature of morphological processing, we will go on to complete the overall picture by discussing derivational morphology.

Notes

1. The exclusion of irregular verb forms from this generalization was partly motivated by the observation of a partial overlap between the verb-specific activation observed in Tyler et al.'s study and the lesion sites of three patients that displayed a selective deficit with respect to the processing of regular verb morphology. The neuroanatomical locus of this overlap was situated in BA47, "extending posteriorly and medially to the insula, and inferiorly to the superior temporal gyrus (BA 38)" (Tyler et al. 2004a: 520). In addition, there was also a small area of overlap in BA 45.

2. A type of single mechanism model that provides an alternative to the connectionist approach assumes that all forms – both regular and irregular – are listed in the lexicon (Bybee 1988; Bybee 1995; Stemberger 1994).

3. As noted by an anonymous reviewer, the reanalysis of the Indefrey et al. (1997) data by Sach, Seitz, and Indefrey (2004) did not reveal any differences between regular and irregular verb forms at strict statistical thresholds.

4. Tyler et al. (2005) reported fMRI evidence for an almost inverted activation pattern. In a same-different judgment task applied to word pairs such as *stayed – stay* or *taught – teach*, they observed increased activation for regular vs. irregular verbs in left inferior frontal and left superior temporal regions as well as in the left anterior cingulate cortex (ACC). By contrast, no regions showed increased activation for irregular as opposed to regular stimuli. As is apparent from the overview in Table 4.1, these findings pose an exception to the dominant pattern of results in the neuroimaging literature. However, the cause of this divergence is difficult to determine as Tyler et al.'s study differed from other experiments in several respects: task, modality (auditory rather than visual) and the use of a sparse sampling technique for fMRI data acquisition. Furthermore, two word pairs from the same condition were always presented within a single trial. Possible effects of this mode of presentation thus also cannot be ruled out.

5. Specifically, de Diego Balaguer and colleagues propose a "data-driven" account based on previous proposals about the function of the brain regions in which activation was observed. They thus assume that the processing of both regular and irregular verbs involves the retrieval of grammatical features and suffixation (BA 44). Regular verbs additionally engage a phonological rehearsal loop for the maintenance of a presented stem (hippocampus and insula). By contrast, irregular verbs (which require the selection of the correct stem) yield activation in a network supporting lexical retrieval, manipulation of information, and selection of a correct response (BA 45/46).

6. At this point, the attentive reader might be wondering why the results discussed here, in which only regular but not irregular forms showed priming effects, differ from the results obtained by Tyler and colleagues (see the discussion at the end of section 4.1), in which both regular and irregular forms were subject to priming. Apart from the difference in methodology (ERPs vs. reaction times as the dependent variable), a further possible reason for this discrepancy lies in the number of items intervening between prime and target. Whereas Tyler et al. (2002a) presented word pairs, all of the electrophysiological studies discussed here embedded primes and targets in a word list such that a number of words intervened between them (approximately 13 in the study by Weyerts et al. 1996; and 5–9 in the experiments by Münte et al. 1999c; and Rodriguez-Fornells et al. 2002).

7. The example stimuli shown here are taken from Weyerts et al. (1997). Lück et al. (2006) presented very similar stimuli, but used surnames rather than first names (e.g. *Lehnerts* vs. **Lehnerten* as correct and incorrect plural variants of *Lehnert*).

8. Note that feminine –e and –en plurals were also included in this study. However, as the feminine –e forms could not be matched to the remaining critical stimuli regarding criteria such as frequency and length, they were not taken into account in the final data analysis.

5

Derivational Morphology

In comparison to the vast number of studies on the processing of inflec-tional morphology, only comparatively few neurocognitive investigations have concerned themselves with derivational morphology. This discrep-ancy appears somewhat surprising in view of the fact that the earliest psycholinguistic discussions on morphological processing were in fact centered around derivational issues. For example, Taft and Forster's influential model of word recognition (Taft and Forster 1975) posited that morphologically complex words undergo obligatory decomposition. This assumption accounted for the observation that pseudowords which were stems of existing words (e.g. *juvenate*, from *rejuvenate*) or composed of existing morphemes (e.g. *dejuvenate*) took longer to classify than pseudowords that were not stems (e.g. *pertoire*, from *repertoire*) or in-volved a non-existing stem (e.g. *depertoire*).[1] One might therefore specu-late that the present imbalance between neurocognitive studies on inflectional and derivational morphology is related to the overwhelming dominance of the past-tense debate.[2] Clearly, however, the theoretical questions at issue in the two domains are interrelated, as both are essen-tially concerned with the representation of complex words in the mental lexicon. Thus, in a similar spirit to the connectionist approach to inflec-tional morphology, it has also been proposed that processing effects traditionally attributed to morphological decomposition of derived forms should rather be explained via a convergence of semantic, phono-logical, and orthographic codes (Seidenberg and Gonnerman 2000). Research within the domain of derivational morphology has therefore also focused on the question of whether there is evidence for an inde-pendent level of morphological combinatorics ("rules"). In this way, a comprehensive neurocognitive perspective on syntax and morphology at the word level must also concern itself with derivational aspects.

The first neurocognitive study on morphological decomposition in non-inflected forms was reported by McKinnon, Allen, and Osterhout

(2003). Using ERPs, they examined a manipulation that was quite similar in spirit to Taft and Forster's (see above). Examples of their critical stimuli are given in (5.1).

(5.1)   Example stimuli from McKinnon et al. (2003), Experiment 1

    a. Real words with prefixes and bound stems
       sub-mit, re-ceive, dis-cern

    b. Pseudowords with prefixes and bound stems
       pro-mit, ex-ceive, in-cern

    c. Morphologically complex real words
       muffler, bookmark

    d. Pseudowords containing no morphemes
       flermuf

McKinnon and colleagues' experimental design capitalized upon the robust observation of increased N400 effects for phonologically legal pseudowords (see Chapter 4.2). Thus, if pseudowords consisting of real morphemes are accessed as a single unit, they should engender this typical electrophysiological response to a non-existing (but phonologically possible) word. By contrast, if morphemes are represented separately in the mental lexicon, these types of pseudowords might instead be expected to elicit an electrophysiological response similar to that engendered by real words. McKinnon et al.'s (2003) findings support the second hypothesis: morphologically empty pseudowords (5.1d) showed an increased N400 in comparison to all other stimulus types (5.1a–c), which did not differ from one another. (Bound stem pseudowords, 5.1b, engendered a larger P200 in comparison to the other stimulus types, but crucially did not show a differential N400 effect.) This result seems to speak in favor of morphological decomposition.

    To rule out possible alternative explanations, McKinnon and colleagues conducted two follow-up experiments. In their Experiment 2, they presented pseudowords which apparently preserved the morphological structure of the bound stem pseudowords but were "morphologically empty" (e.g. *ensuld*, from *insult*). These "orthographic nonwords" engendered a pronounced N400 effect in comparison to real word controls, thereby suggesting that the findings for the bound stem pseudowords were not due to their orthographic similarity to real words. Finally, Experiment 3 was designed to rule out affix priming as a possible explanation for the results of Experiment 1. To this end, prefixed and suffixed words (e.g. *export, boyish*) were altered to a combination of an affix and a nonce stem (e.g. *extorp, yobish*). These types of affixed pseudowords again yielded a significant N400 increase. From these results, which show different electrophysiological processing correlates for pseudowords composed of existing morphemes in comparison to pseudowords that are word-like in other respects, McKinnon et al. (2003: 886) conclude that "morphological decomposition and representation extend to non-productive and semantically impoverished morphemes".

The findings by McKinnon and colleagues thus provide converging support for the assumption of morphological decomposition. Indeed, they suggest that decomposition is such a fundamental property of the mental lexicon that it even applies to bound stems, thereby yielding lexical entries that can never be words in and of themselves. This result is surprising in that it does not offer any indication as to how the combination of stems and affixes can be constrained, i.e. illicit combinations of existing morphemes did not yield differential ERP responses from possible derivational combinations. A natural next step would therefore seem to lie in the investigation of the combinatorial properties of decomposed lexical entries. Precisely this question was addressed by Janssen, Wiese, and Schlesewsky (2005) in an ERP study of derivational morphology in German. This experiment examined the processing of three highly productive German suffixes (*–ung, –heit,* and *–keit*), which differ with respect to the type of base to which they apply.[3] The suffix *–ung* subcategorizes for verbal bases and, from these, derives nouns which typically denote events (e.g. *messen,* "to measure" – *Messung,* "the measurement"). By contrast, *–heit* and *–keit* derive nouns from adjectives and are generally viewed as allomorphs of a single morpheme (e.g. Wiese 1996). The two forms are in complementary distribution and their applicability is governed by phonological properties. Whereas *–heit* combines with monosyllabic base forms or base forms that end in a stressed syllable (e.g. *korrékt,* "correct" – *Korrektheit,* "correctness"), *–keit* applies to base forms that end in an unstressed syllable (e.g. *éinsam* "lonely" – *Einsamkeit,* "loneliness"). To examine the processing of these morphological regularities, Janssen et al. (2005) applied a similar manipulation to the ERP violation paradigms typically used in the domain of inflectional morphology (see section 4.2). Example stimuli from this study, which were presented as single words in a lexical decision paradigm, are shown in (5.2).

(5.2) Example stimuli from Janssen et al. (2005)

      a. Correct and incorrect forms with *–heit* (base of incorrect form requires *–keit*)

Korrekt-heit, *Einsam-heit
"correctness", "*loneliness"

b. Correct and incorrect forms with –*keit* (base of incorrect
form requires –*heit*)
Einsam-keit, *Korrekt-keit
"loneliness", "*correctness"

c. Correct and incorrect forms with –*ung* (incorrect form has
an adjectival base)
Förder$_V$-ung, *Schädlich$_A$-ung
"support", "*damage"

Janssen and colleagues observed broadly distributed negativities (i.e.
N400-like effects) for all morphological violations in comparison to
correct forms. This effect was apparent between 300 and 500 ms post
critical word onset for forms marked with –*ung* and –*heit*, with the –*heit*
forms showing a somewhat smaller violation response. In a later time
window (500–700 ms), an N400-like effect was apparent for all three
types of morphological violations.

The most striking aspect of Janssen et al.'s (2005) findings is that they
did not reveal a LAN for violations of derivational morphology that are
clearly combinatorial in nature. For –*ung*, in particular, the incorrect
combination with an adjectival as opposed to a verbal base form
should have led to a morphological rule violation. However, in contrast to the typical ERP component interpretations suggested by the
literature on inflectional morphology, this violation yielded an N400
rather than a LAN. Like Bartke et al.'s (2005) results on subregularities
in German plural formation (see Chapter 4.2), the findings by Janssen
and colleagues therefore appear to implicate the N400 as an ERP
component that is sensitive to combinatorial linguistic structure. Alternatively, could the N400 effects in these studies be explained as
resulting from the processing of pseudowords, independently of
whether these pseudowords were derived via a combinatorial rule or
not? Even though an explanation along these lines could help to
uphold the standard interpretation of the N400, it faces two major
challenges. Firstly, it cannot explain why pseudowords engendered
LAN effects in other studies (e.g. for regularized irregular forms),
since, if the N400 response to pseudowords is independent of a possible combinatorial structure, it should also be elicited by these forms.
Secondly, if one were to assume that only those pseudowords which
give rise to a LAN are generated via a rule, whereas those that engender

an N400 are not, this would lead to a circularity in argumentation, since the functional interpretation of the LAN as indexing rule-based combinatorial (or procedural) processing and of the N400 as indexing associative (or declarative) memory was, in turn, based on a priori assumptions about which forms are derived via rules and which are not. In this way, the observation of N400 effects for morphological violations which are clearly combinatorial in nature appears highly relevant for the interpretation of the N400 component and, by extension, the interpretation of the LAN. Interestingly, the combinatorial sensitivity of the N400 extends beyond the domain of morphosyntactic (e.g. word category) information (as is apparent in the case of the *–ung* forms in the study by Janssen and colleagues), since it also applies to phonological regularities (in distinguishing between *–heit* and *–keit*).[4]

In contrast to the studies by Janssen et al. (2005) and McKinnon et al. (2003), which sought to shed light on morphological decomposition by examining affixation, Koester, Gunter, and Wagner (2007) investigated the processing of German compound words (i.e. words arising from the combination of other existing words). In a first experiment, they observed that a (temporary) gender incongruency between the first constituent of a compound word (which is irrelevant to determining the gender of the overall compound in German) and a preceding determiner engendered a LAN effect. This finding was taken to suggest that the individual constituents of the compounds were accessed separately by the language processing system. In a second study, Koester and colleagues contrasted ERP responses to transparent (*Milchkanne*, literally: "milk jug", translation: "milk jug") and opaque compounds (*Kohldampf*, literally: "cabbage steam", translation: "hunger") and observed a larger N400 for the former. The authors argue that this effect reflects processes of semantic composition, which may apply in transparent but not in opaque compounds (which must be stored in their entirety in order to preserve the opaque meaning). This interpretation is also compatible with the observation of an increased N400 for novel vs. existing compound words in Dutch (Krott, Baayen, and Hagoort 2006), since novel compounds clearly *require* semantic composition. Hence, these findings lend further support to the observation that N400 effects may reflect combinatorial processes at the word level (for converging evidence from Chinese, see Bai et al. 2008).

An alternative approach to assessing the neural representation of morphologically complex words has been to use priming paradigms. These have been employed extensively and applied to a variety of languages in the behavioral literature (for a recent review, see Marslen-Wilson 2007). In English, for example, studies of this kind revealed priming between semantically transparent derived words and their stems (*happiness* – *happy*), which was interpreted as evidence for decomposition (see also Note 3). In the electrophysiological domain, morphological priming was examined in an experiment on Spanish (Dominguez, de Vega, and Barber 2004). This study used a paired prime-target presentation with a consciously perceivable prime and required participants to perform a lexical decision for the target word, which was presented in capital letters. Example stimuli are given in (5.3).

(5.3)   Example stimuli from Dominguez et al. (2004)

    a. Morphological priming
       hijo – HIJA
       "son" – "daughter"

    b. Stem homograph priming
       foco – FOCA
       "floodlight" – "seal"

    c. Orthographic priming
       rasa – RANA
       "flat" – "frog"

    d. Synonym priming
       cirio – VELA
       "candle" – "candle"

    e. Unrelated control
       pavo – META
       "turkey" – "goal"

Dominguez and colleagues reported consistent effects of morphological priming, as reflected in an N400 reduction in each of their three experiments. In Experiment 1, they observed an N400 reduction for both morphological priming (5.3a) and stem homograph priming (5.3b) in comparison to unrelated word pairs (5.3e), but a larger priming effect in the morphological condition (the two priming conditions did not differ from one another in an early time window between 250 and 350 ms, but the morphological condition showed an N400 reduction relative to the stem homograph condition between 350 and 450 ms). Experiment 2 revealed no effect of orthographic priming, i.e. an N400 reduction was observed for the morphologically related condition (5.3a) in comparison to both the orthographic condition (5.3c) and the unrelated control (5.3e). Finally, Experiment 3 showed a graded N400 reduction: morphologically related (5.3a) < synonyms (5.3d) < unrelated word pairs (5.3e). On the basis of these findings, Dominguez et al. (2004) argue for an initial stage of morphological decomposition in word recognition, which precedes lexical and meaning selection. They suggest that their results are not easily reconcilable with connectionist approaches that do not assume morphemes as separate units of representation (Seidenberg and Gonnerman 2000), as these should have predicted similar priming effects for the stem homograph condition (5.3b) and the orthographic condition (5.3c).

Priming paradigms have also been used to shed light on the functional neuroanatomy of morphological derivations. Like the neuroimaging studies on inflectional morphology (see Chapter 4.1), experiments in this domain have primarily aimed to shed light on the question of whether morphological composition is supported by a separable neural substrate. In keeping with this question, Devlin et al. (2004) systematically manipulated the orthographic and semantic relationship between prime and target in order to examine whether morphological priming arises as a convergence between these two information types. Example stimuli from this study are given in (5.4).

(5.4)   Example stimuli from Devlin et al. (2004)

    a. no relation [−orth, −sem]
       award – MUNCH

    b. orthographic priming [+orth, −sem]
       passive – PASS

    c. semantic priming [−orth, +sem]
       sofa – COUCH

    d. morphological priming [+orth, +sem]
       hunter – HUNT

    e. pseudoword target
       casino – HODER

    f. consonant string as target
       lather – FRLNK

This study employed a visual masked priming paradigm, i.e. trials began with the presentation of a forward mask (500 ms), followed by the prime (33 ms), and the target (200 ms). Due to their short presentation latency, primes were not consciously perceived by participants. The task was a lexical decision regarding the target word. Devlin and colleagues observed morphological priming, as reflected in a reduced

BOLD response, in the posterior angular gyrus (bilaterally), left occipitotemporal cortex, and the mid left middle temporal gyrus (MTG). In the angular gyrus, all three types of priming (orthographic, semantic, and morphological) were observed, thus leading the authors to propose that activation in this region might reflect attentional demands. Two-way overlaps of morphological priming with orthographic and semantic priming were observed in occipitotemporal cortex and the MTG, respectively. Thus, no regions proved exclusively sensitive to morphological priming. Devlin et al. (2004: 14988) interpret this result as evidence that morphological structure "emerges from the convergence of form and meaning".

Very different results were obtained in a recent fMRI study by Bozic et al. (2007), which used a delayed priming paradigm (primes and targets occurred an average of 18 items apart within a word list) and a lexical decision task to examine stimuli such as (5.5).

(5.5)   Example stimuli from Bozic et al. (2007)

a. Morphologically related (transparent)
bravely – brave

b. Morphologically related (opaque)
archer – arch

c. Form only
scandal – scan

d. Meaning only
accuse – blame

e. Identity
mist – mist

Bozic and colleagues point out that the orthographic control condition in Devlin et al.'s (2004) study in fact contained morphologically decomposable items (e.g. *apartment – apart*, *homely – home*). These types of forms have been shown to yield morphological priming effects (e.g. Longtin and Meunier 2005; Rastle et al. 2000). In their experiment, Bozic et al. (2007) therefore included an orthographic control condition (5.5c) with stimuli that were not morphologically decomposable.

For the first (unprimed) presentation of the critical words, Bozic and colleagues observed increased activation in the pars orbitalis of the left IFG (BA 47) for morphologically complex words in comparison to simplex words. In addition, priming effects were obtained in both of the morphologically related conditions (transparent/opaque) in comparison to the two morphologically unrelated conditions (form/ meaning). These were apparent in a cluster of activation in the pars opercularis of the left IFG (BA 44), extending into the deep frontal operculum/insula, and in a similar region (BA 47) to that observed for the first presentation of morphologically complex words. Priming effects did not differ between transparent and opaque forms. Bozic et al. (2007: 1472) propose that the left IFG activation observed in their study "reflects consequences of an early mechanism that isolates potential morphemes whenever the structure of the complex words allows such a procedure". This decompositional process is thought to apply prelexically on the basis of morpho-orthographic information, before lexical/semantic properties are activated in a next step. Bozic and colleagues' conclusions are thus very close to those drawn by Dominguez et al. (2004). Interestingly, a further fMRI study using a similar type of manipulation and task to Bozic et al. (2007) but a masked priming paradigm (Gold and Rastle 2007) also provided evidence for morphological priming that could not be explained via orthographic or semantic priming. However, in contrast to the inferior frontal effects observed by Bozic and colleagues, Gold and Rastle's (2007) study revealed morphological priming in an anterior occipital/inferior temporal region. Taken together, these results suggest that morphological effects can be dissociated from other domains, while the neural correlates of this phenomenon are dependent upon the particular experimental environment in which morphological priming occurs (delayed priming in Bozic et al., 2007, vs. masked priming in Gold and Rastle, 2007). This, in turn, appears to call into question the automaticity of the neural mechanisms involved.

While also arguing in favor of morphological decomposition, Vannest, Polk, and Lewis (2005) assume that only certain affixes are automatically decomposed. This claim was examined in an fMRI study which used stimuli such as (5.6).

(5.6)   Example stimuli from Vannest et al. (2005)

    a. "Decomposable" words
       adaptable, bitterness

    b. "Whole word" words
       curiosity, temptation

    c. Inflected words
       advanced, flowering

    d. Monomorphemic words
       envelope, parsley

The manipulation in (5.6) was motivated by previous behavioral observations that affixes like English *–able* and *–ness* show evidence of morphological decomposition (Bertram, Schreuder, and Baayen 2000; Vannest et al. 2002), whereas affixes such as *–ity* and *–ation* do not (Bradley 1980; Vannest and Boland 1999). The difference between these two classes of suffixes is that only the latter have the ability to change the phonological properties of the base (e.g. *serene – serenity*). Vannest et al. (2005) contrasted these different types of morphologically complex words in a memory-encoding task similar to that employed by Laine et al. (1999) for the examination of inflectional morphology (see Chapter 3). They conducted a ROI analysis restricted to "Broca's area" (left BA 44/45 and contiguous parts of the insula) and the basal ganglia, i.e. to regions predicted to form part of the procedural language system in the declarative/procedural model (Ullman 2001; Ullman 2004). For both of these regions, Vannest and colleagues contrasted the number of above-threshold voxels activated in the "decomposable" (5.6a), "whole word" (5.6b), and inflected (5.6c) conditions relative to monomorphemic words (5.6d) as a common baseline (i.e. they compared differences between the subtractions (5.6a)–(5.6d), (5.6b)–(5.6d), and (5.6c)–(5.6d)). In both ROIs, the "decomposable" words (5.6a) engendered significantly more activation than the "whole words" (5.6b), while the activation increase for inflected words (5.5c) vs. "whole words" was marginally significant. In terms of the purported involvement of the left IFG in morphological decomposition, these results appear compatible with those by Bozic et al. (2007). They further suggest that the decompositional process may vary according to the particular type of morpheme involved, a conclusion which receives additional support from the patient findings by Hagiwara et al. (1999) (see Note 2). However, a potential caveat with respect to this finding concerns the data analysis employed, i.e. the fact that the analysis was restricted to two predefined ROIs and that no direct contrasts were reported.

Finally, there is some initial electrophysiological evidence to suggest that morphological priming also occurs during language production. In a picture-naming paradigm involving delayed priming in Dutch, Koester, and Schiller (2008) observed a reduced N400 (and faster response times) when words were primed by a morphologically related compound (e.g. *jas*, "coat" primed by *jaszak*, "coat pocket"), but not when the prime merely overlapped in form (e.g. *jasmijn*, "jasmine"). Furthermore, the magnitude of priming did not differ between transparent and opaque compound primes (e.g. *ekster*, "magpie" was primed equally by *eksternest*, "magpie nest" and *eksteroog*, lit: "magpie eye", "corn"). These results therefore suggest that morphological priming in language production is at least to some degree independent of semantic and/or phonological processes.

In summary, neurocognitive findings on derivational morphology provide good evidence for combinatorial morphological processes. While it remains controversial how exactly these should be modeled, existing findings suggest that morphological effects cannot be reduced entirely to orthographic, phonological, or semantic factors.

Notes

1. For further early proposals of morphological decomposition, see for example MacKay (1978) and Jarvella and Meijers (1983). Alternative theoretical proposals were of course also put forward. Some assumed a full listing of all words irrespective of their morphological complexity (Henderson, Wallis, and Knight 1984; Lukatela et al. 1980; Manelis and Tharp 1977; Rubin, Becker, and Freeman 1979), whereas others favored a coexistence of both morphologically decomposed and full-form representations (e.g. Burani and Caramazza 1987; Stanners et al. 1979).

2. The asymmetry between studies of inflectional and derivational morphology also extends to the neuropsychological domain. Thus, only very few studies have examined the processing of derivational morphology in patient populations. A notable exception to this general pattern is a study by Hagiwara et al. (1999), who observed a double dissociation in different groups of aphasic patients with regard to the processing of derivational suffixes with a high (*–sa*) vs. low productivity (*–mi*) in Japanese.

3. Clahsen, Sonnenstuhl, and Blevins (2003) reported evidence for the combinatorial status of *–ung*. In a priming paradigm, they observed that access to a stem (e.g. *gründen*, "to found") was facilitated when preceded by a derived form suffixed with *–ung* (e.g. *Gründung*, "foundation").

4. With regard to the latency differences of the N400 elicited by incorrect *–heit* and *–keit* forms, Janssen and colleagues assume that these might be attributable to the different sizes of the prosodic domains that must be checked in the two cases (depending on the stress pattern of the base form). See Janssen et al. (2005) for details.

6

Syntax and morphology at the word level: Summary and critical evaluation

As already mentioned at the beginning of this section, the main theoretical and empirical debates regarding the neurocognition of syntax and morphology at the word level have revolved around the distinction between "rule-based" and "network-based" approaches. Whereas both of these model types come in several different flavors, the basic controversy between them pertains to the question of whether linguistic regularities are generated by rule-based knowledge or not. Crucially, this debate should not be taken to suggest that proponents of connectionist models deny the existence of regular structures in language. When proposing their original past tense model, Rumelhart and McClelland (1986) exemplified this point with an analogy originally due to Bates (1979): "The regular structure of the honeycomb arises from the interaction of forces that wax balls exert on each other when compressed. The honeycomb can be described by a rule, but the mechanism which produces it does not contain any statement of this rule" (Rumelhart and McClelland 1986: 217). The theoretical disagreement, then, concerns the question of whether linguistic rules are explicitly represented or not.

Given that the two opposing sides agree on the fact that language exhibits regularities and that some patterns are "more regular" than others, how can these perspectives be distinguished empirically? Recall from Chapter 4 that behavioral findings regarding this issue are often equivocal (i.e. claimed to be compatible with both types of models). Many researchers therefore placed their hopes in neurocognitive observations. The first of these were obtained from patient studies and either presented themselves in the form of deficit-lesion correlations or as double dissociations between ostensibly different functions. Initial findings from this domain suggested that patients with damage to anterior perisylvian regions (including the IFG, anterior portions of the temporal lobe and the basal ganglia), who are more likely to show Broca's aphasia/agrammatism, have a higher likelihood of a regular morphology deficit. By contrast, patients with lesions in inferior or posterior temporal/parietal regions, who are more likely to suffer from Wernicke's aphasia or conditions like anomia or semantic dementia, have a higher likelihood of an impairment with irregular morphology. It therefore only appears natural that the increasing availability of neuroscientific methods inspired researchers to attempt to generalize these broad correlations by examining neural responses in healthy individuals. Thus, attempts were made to associate regular vs. irregular morphological processes with particular neural regions on the one hand, and with qualitatively distinct ERP responses on the other. In keeping with the distinctions drawn from the patient literature, these focused particularly on the notion that left inferior frontal regions/the basal ganglia might be specifically involved in the processing of regular morphology or morphological decomposition more generally, whereas the processing of irregular morphology was expected to engage a distinct set of brain regions (most likely in temporal or parietal cortex). In the ERP domain, the finding of LAN effects in response to syntactic violations (e.g. Kutas and Hillyard 1983) led to the expectation that violations of morphological rules should also yield an electrophysiological response of this type, while lexical/associative processes were predicted to engender N400 effects (Kutas and Hillyard 1980).

Yet even after these data were available, the debate did not end. Firstly, findings that advocates of dual-route models interpreted as evidence for such models were also claimed to be compatible with connectionist approaches (Joanisse and Seidenberg 1999; Seidenberg and Arnoldussen 2003; Seidenberg and Hoeffner 1998). Secondly, from an outside perspective, many aspects of the discussion appear to be reducible to matters of definition. Consider, for example, the contrast between Ullman's declarative/procedural model on the one hand and Joanisse and Seidenberg's connectionist model on the other. Whereas Ullman (2001, 2004) associates inferior frontal and temporal regions with the processing of procedural and declarative knowledge, respectively, Joanisse and Seidenberg (2005) ascribe phonological and semantic functions to the very same regions. Of course, the different groups involved in the debate would almost certainly deny that differing functional neuroanatomical interpretations of this type simply amount to "a rose by any other name", but such labels do raise the question of what is actually behind them. For example, Pinker and Ullman (2002a) argue that the localist semantic representations in Joanisse and Seidenberg's model (one unit per lexeme) in fact amount to a "lexicon". While it is beyond the scope of the present volume to pass judgment on theoretical interpretations of this type, this line of argumentation strikes us as a particularly clear example of how circular the debates in this field have become.

Perhaps even graver from an empirical perspective is the fact that the data themselves are anything but consistent. Similar neuroanatomical regions have been implicated in very different aspects of morphological processing – including what essentially amounts to inverse findings for similar contrasts in different studies. In the ERP domain, the original conception that combinatorial processing aspects (however these are to be modeled theoretically) are reflected in LAN effects also cannot be upheld in view of the overall data pattern. As shown in the studies by Bartke et al. (2005), Janssen et al. (2005), and Koester et al. (2007), and as will be discussed in much greater detail in the following chapters, combinatorial regularities can clearly also be reflected in modulations of the N400.

In the face of these types of empirical problems, one of the leading groups within this domain recently argued as follows: "In a commentary (Münte et al., 1999), two of us have argued that brain imaging should not only be used to test predictions derived from psycholinguistic models but that patterns of activations might be used to derive brain-inspired hypotheses about processing differences between regular and irregular words, for example" (de Diego Balaguer et al. 2006: 884, referring to Münte, Rodriguez-Fornells, and Kutas 1999a).[1] Indeed, the existing state of the art on the neurocognition of morphological processing strongly argues against the perspective that neuroscientific methods can simply be applied "slavishly" in order to verify or falsify the predictions of psycholinguistic or cognitive models of language. Rather, given the fact that this field is still very young and we still have much to learn about the neurocognitive bases of language processing, we agree that a data-driven re-evaluation of theoretical predictions would often be beneficial to the advancement of the field. For example, in view of the evidence that combinatorial structure may modulate N400 effects, a characterization of the LAN as *the* electrophysiological correlate of rule-governed linguistic processes becomes highly questionable. It is therefore problematic to use this component as a diagnostic tool for combinatorial structure or linguistic rule application. Nevertheless, LAN effects are clearly qualitatively different from N400 effects and this dissociation must have some kind of functional significance. In order to ascertain what this significance might be, it sometimes appears important to let the available sets of experimental evidence (not individual data points!) "speak for themselves" and, thereby, generate new perspectives and predictions.

Of course, this does not mean that theoretical considerations should be ignored completely. On the one hand, such considerations play an essential role in the development of experimental designs by informing the manipulations that serve to generate particular neural activations/ ERP patterns. On the other hand, approaches which simply use language as a medium for the examination of more general aspects of higher cognition (e.g. regarding the structure of working memory, theory of mind) often underestimate the inherent complexity of linguistic stimuli. This problem becomes especially clear when data from languages other than English are considered: for example, while many neuroimaging studies of inflectional morphology cite Laine et al.'s (1999) examination of Finnish, the theoretical consequences of this experiment's finding of a similar activation for morphological case marking as others have reported for verb inflection is rarely – if ever – discussed. Most generally, however, both sides of the problem (i.e. the uncritical application of neuroscientific methods to predefined theoretical issues and the underestimation of the inherent complexities of language) will continue to concern us in subsequent sections of this volume.

Note

1. For a similar line of argumentation, see Marslen-Wilson (2007).

Part II
Syntax and Morphology in Sentence Processing

Overview

Perhaps not surprisingly, Part II is the longest of the four parts of this monograph. In the following six chapters, we discuss the core aspects of syntactic and morphological processing at the sentence level, focusing on a range of languages and a variety of experimental techniques. It is important to note that, throughout this section, we have attempted to remain quite closely within the bounds of the core domains of syntax and morphology. Extensions to this perspective, for example with respect to the interaction between syntax and prosody or information structure, will be discussed in Part III of this volume.

We begin by introducing some major questions and considerations relevant to sentence-level processing (Chapter 7), before going on to present a neurocognitive perspective on different aspects of sentence processing in a functionally-oriented manner. Chapter 8 focuses on neurocognitive correlates of constituent structure processing, i.e. on basic operations of phrase structure building and their status within the overall language processing architecture. Chapter 9 then discusses the processing of what we refer to as "relational structure". This term encompasses all of the relations that are established between the elements within the constituent structure. Subsections of the chapter focus on verb–argument relations such as agreement, valency, and subcategorization (Chapter 9.1), and aspects of verb-independent argument processing (Chapters 9.2/9.3). The latter two sections place particular emphasis on the question of which representations are assigned prior to the availability of the verb (e.g. grammatical functions, thematic relations, word order). Unambiguously (case-)marked and (case-)ambiguous structures are discussed separately in this regard (in sections 9.2 and 9.3, respectively). Throughout the entire chapter, we attempt to establish correspondences between findings from different languages and from different neurocognitive data sources (e.g. ERPs and fMRI).

As will quickly become apparent, the overall organization of Part II of this book departs from the traditional approach in psycholinguistics and neurolinguistics, in which complex structures and modifiers (e.g. relative clauses) have long played a major role. Thus, the discussion in Chapters 8 and 9 focuses exclusively on the processing of simple sentences and obligatory sentence constituents. Chapter 10 then turns to the processing of complex structures (i.e. relative clauses and long-distance dependencies), while Chapter 11 focuses on the processing of modifying information (e.g. the argument-over-adjunct preference, modifier attachment preferences, etc.).

In Chapter 12, we turn our attention to an ERP component that appears to defy interpretation in terms of the functionally-oriented domains discussed in the preceding chapters: the P600 or late positivity. As will become clear in this final, component-oriented chapter, the P600 is subject to a multitude of influences from a variety of domains (both language-internal and language-external) and should possibly be viewed as a whole family of components rather than a single type of effect.

Finally, before launching into the discussion of "syntax and morphology in sentence processing", we would like to end this overview with an important caveat. Even though the field of "sentence processing" traditionally encompasses both comprehension and production, the following chapters focus almost exclusively on aspects of comprehension. The reasons for this apparent selectivity are very simple: beyond the word level, processes of language production have only been examined in an exceedingly small number of neurocognitive experiments. Furthermore, the majority of these studies employed what Indefrey (2007) described as "narrative production paradigms", i.e. they contrasted free production with baseline conditions not involving language production. Studies of this type are therefore not suited to isolating syntactic and morphological aspects of the production process. From an even smaller number of more controlled production experiments, Indefrey (2007) concludes that BA 44 (and perhaps adjacent areas, BA 45 and BA 6) are crucially involved in syntactic encoding. As it currently appears impossible to draw any further conclusions with respect to the neurocognitive correlates of syntactic and morphological aspects of sentence production, we have no other choice but to focus on comprehension in the following chapters.

7

Mapping form onto meaning: The requirements for a sentence processor

This chapter aims to provide an introduction to the main issues in sentence processing. In particular, it is concerned with the question of which "ingredients" are required in a sentence processor and, by extension, with the possible relationship between the characteristics of the processing architecture and properties of the grammar. Furthermore, the specific characteristics of neurocognitive investigations of sentence comprehension and their consequences for psycholinguistic modeling will be emphasized.

7.1 The goal: From form to meaning

Most essentially, the language comprehension architecture must be able to map the form of a perceived utterance onto its corresponding meaning. Possible input forms are an acoustic speech stream, written text or gestures (i.e. sign language) depending on the modality with which the perceiver is confronted. The requirements of the form-to-meaning mapping thus constrain the architecture of the comprehension system. To fulfill the demands of effective real time communication, the mapping must be accomplished very rapidly and it must take place in an incremental fashion, i.e. by attempting to maximize the degree of meaning assigned at each possible point within the input (Marslen-Wilson 1973; Crocker 1994; Stabler 1994). This means that decisions must be made even in the absence of complete and certain information, since the comprehension system cannot wait until the end of a sentence in order to begin interpreting it. To accomplish incremental interpretation in this sense, the sentence processor must be equipped to perform the operations described in (7.1). Each of these will be discussed in more detail below.

(7.1)   Properties of the processing system required by incremental comprehension
The processing system must:

a. Impose a structure on the input as quickly as possible (*structure building*)

b. Assign to this structure the "maximal" (i.e. most detailed) meaning allowed by the degree of information available (*linking*)

c. Use the structure/meaning assigned so far to generate predictions about the incoming input (*prediction*)

d. In the case of an ambiguity in the input, decide on an interpretation (*ambiguity processing*)

e. Efficiently resolve processing conflicts if at all possible (*conflict resolution*)

f. Store information that has not been fully interpreted (*storage*)

Structure building must clearly be constrained by the grammar assumed for the language being processed. Thus, the grammar constrains the types of structures that can be constructed from the input (cf. the difference in constituent order between *the green frog* in English and the corresponding *la grenouille verte* "the frog green" in French). Furthermore, it provides the processing system with knowledge regarding the terminal elements (input items) in these structures and how to recognize them. For example, word category plays an important role in the definition of terminal elements, but how different categories can be recognized differs from language to language (e.g. on the basis of distributional or morphological criteria).

Linking defines the way in which a structure is associated with an interpretation. This is again subject to constraints imposed by the grammar. For example, whether a specific structural position can be assumed to link to a specific meaning depends both on the language being processed and on the representational assumptions of the grammar. As a simple example, consider the difference between English and German. English has a designated subject position and, in an active sentence (e.g. *Jim often visits his aunt's farm in summer*) the subject (*Jim*) always corresponds to the highest-ranking thematic role.[1] The linking between the subject position and the interpretation assigned to

the argument encountered in that position is therefore highly constrained. In German, by contrast, it has been argued that there is no
similar position for a subject: not only does the language allow non-
nominative initial base orders, it also permits VP topicalizations including the subject (Haider 1993).[2] Moreover, in a transitive construction, the
subject need not bear the highest-ranking thematic role, e.g. in structures
with dative object-experiencer verbs (e.g. Wunderlich 1997; Primus 1999;
Fanselow 2000) and in passivized ditransitives (see Note 2). Thus, the
mapping between a structural position and a particular interpretation is
much less constrained in German (and other languages showing similar
properties) than in languages of the English type.

Prediction is a very pervasive property throughout the processing
architecture. It thus applies at a number of different levels of processing. On the one hand, predictions are generated by the structural
properties of a language. This means, for example, that on account of
the internal structure of sentential constituents (e.g. noun phrases, verb
phrases, etc., all of which consist of a head that projects the phrase and
additional elements), the occurrence of a non-head within a constituent
whose head has not yet been processed will give rise to the prediction of a
head. On the other hand, predictions can also be assumed at the non-
structural (relational) level. For example, in languages that do not allow
subjects to be dropped, the occurrence of an object that is unambiguously
marked as such will engender the prediction of a subject (e.g. Gibson
1998). While the two levels of prediction may coincide under certain
circumstances (cf. the discussion of English and its close association
between structural positions, grammatical functions, and argument interpretation above), they are logically independent, since not all languages
provide for such close correlations (e.g. German).

Most generally, as a consequence of the predictive component of the
processing architecture, identical elements may be processed in different ways depending on the position in which they are encountered and
the predictions associated with this position. Consider, for example, a
split-ergative language such as Hindi/Urdu.[3] This language's aspect-
based split and verb-final basic word order induces an ambiguity with
respect to the role of a non-case-marked (nominative/absolutive) argument when it is encountered before the verb (e.g. *kitaab*, "book"): it
could either be the sole argument of an intransitive relation (7.2), the
higher-ranking argument of a transitive relation in a non-perfective
construction (7.3), or the lower-ranking argument of a transitive relation in a perfective construction (7.4).

(7.2) किताब   गिर   गयी।
       kitaab   gir   gay-ii
       book[F]   fall   go-PFV.F
       "The book dropped."

(7.3) किताब   शिक्षक को   आश्चर्यचकित करती   है।
       kitaab   sikshak-ko   ashcaryacakit kar-tii   hai
       book[F]   teacher[M]-ACC   surprise   do-IPFV.F   AUX
       "The book surprises the teacher."

(7.4) शिक्षक ने   किताब   पढ़ी   है।
       sikshak-ne   kitaab   padh-ii   hai
       teacher[M]-ERG   book[F]   read-PFV.F   AUX
       "The teacher read a book."

Now consider what happens when the processing system encounters an
unmarked argument during real time comprehension. If this argument is
the first to be encountered in the sentence currently being processed, it
will interpreted as the subject of an intransitive verb in order to avoid the
assumption of unnecessary dependencies (Demiral, Schlesewsky, and
Bornkessel-Schlesewsky 2008; Bornkessel-Schlesewsky and Schlesewsky
in press). By contrast, when this type of argument follows an ergative-
marked NP, the situation is different. At least in those dialects of Hindi/
Urdu in which the ergative can only occur in transitive constructions
(Mohanan 1994), the occurrence of an ergative predicts that there will be
an absolutive at some upcoming point in the input string. Thus, when
the unmarked (absolutive) argument (e.g. *book* in 7.4) is subsequently
processed, it is interpreted as the lower-ranking argument of a transitive
relation as a result of this prediction. The processing of input elements
with identical morphological marking therefore differs crucially depending on the environment in which they are encountered and on the
predictive properties of that environment.

   Ambiguity processing has long been considered one of the most
fascinating properties of the comprehension system. As ambiguities
abound in natural language – and particularly in the incomplete
input on which incremental comprehension is typically based – the
ability to handle ambiguities efficiently, i.e. without a significant delay
in processing, constitutes a central feature of the processing architecture. Consider, for example, the degree of ambiguity displayed by an
initial non-case-marked argument in Hindi/Urdu, which permits an
intransitive reading (7.2), a transitive subject reading (7.3) and a

transitive object reading.[4] The latter possibility can come about when the object of a sentence such as (7.4) is scrambled to a position in which it precedes the subject (7.5) or in a sentence with a dropped subject (7.6).

(7.5) किताब   शिक्षक ने   पढी   है।
       kitaab   sikshak-ne   padh-ii   hai
       book[F]   teacher[M]-ERG   read-PFV.F AUX
       "The teacher read a book."

(7.6) किताब   पढी   है।
       kitaab   padh-ii   hai
       book[F]   read-PFV.F   AUX
       "(Someone) read a book."

It is undisputed that, in dealing with ambiguities such as these, the processing system displays certain preferences regarding the structure/interpretation assumed, i.e. it neither delays structuring or interpretation until disambiguating information is encountered, nor does it pursue all possible alternatives in an equal (unweighted) manner. By contrast, the precise mechanism employed for ambiguity processing has been subject to a substantial amount of debate (see section 7.2).

Conflict resolution is a requirement that goes hand in hand with the existence of ambiguity. When the heuristics employed for ambiguity processing fail in the sense that they lead the system to prefer the wrong alternative, a conflict arises at the point where disambiguation towards the dispreferred reading occurs. The situation thus arising is that of the classical "garden path", as in the famous example *The horse raced past the barn fell* (Bever 1970). The need to switch from one reading to another engenders additional processing cost. Garden path effects vary substantially in strength, ranging from very mild (not consciously perceived, but measurable) to strong (leading to a failure to understand the sentence, requiring conscious reprocessing). The example sentences in (7.7), which are taken from Sturt and Crocker (1996), illustrate differing degrees of garden path strength.

(7.7) An illustration of different garden path strengths (Sturt and Crocker 1996)

    a. John knows the truth hurts.
    b. While Philip was washing the dishes crashed onto the floor.
    c. The boat floated down the river sank.

Many different approaches to conflict resolution in language comprehension have been proposed, ranging from the assumption that all differences in processing difficulty derive from the restructuring of the input (e.g. Sturt and Crocker 1996) to the notion that restructuring per se is cost free, and that it is rather the classification of the problem that causes these differing costs (Fodor and Inoue 1994). Finally, it has been argued that the point of departure for conflict resolution cannot be a completely new parse. Rather, the processing system appears to have the capacity to selectively revise the erroneous processing choices (Inoue and Fodor 1995).

Storage, namely the need to temporarily maintain intermediate products of the computation until they can be fully interpreted, is undisputedly required in order for sentence comprehension to be successful. Many approaches thus make reference to storage components that may be more or less explicit in their formulation (e.g. Gibson 1998; McElree et al. 2003; Lewis, Vasishth, and Van Dyke 2006). The precise mechanisms underlying the storage component of the human language comprehension system, namely the precise architecture of the store, how information is entered into it, and how this information is later retrieved, are far from being fully understood. However, the field is beginning to converge on the perspective that "working memory" in language comprehension should be viewed as an activated portion of long-term memory (supplemented by a very limited focus of attention), rather than as a separable buffer (e.g. McElree et al. 2003; Van Dyke and McElree 2006; Martin and McElree 2008; Lewis 1996; Lewis and Vasishth 2005; Lewis et al. 2006).

Having sketched out the underlying properties that the processing architecture must fulfill, we will now turn to a discussion of how these characteristics have shaped the major questions in psycholinguistic research.

7.2 Sentence comprehension: the major questions

As discussed above, one of the main characteristics of the processing architecture is that it must be equipped to handle the processing of ambiguity. Indeed, many of the other requirements for a sentence processor that were described in section 7.1 are intimately tied to the question of how ambiguity is dealt with (either forming the basis for the need to resolve ambiguities, e.g. structure building and linking, or resulting from it, e.g. conflict resolution). We will therefore introduce the major questions that have been posed in sentence comprehension research with reference to a sentence fragment containing an ambiguity. Consider example (7.8).

(7.8) Nach   dem   Wettkampf   erfuhren   alle,
       after   the   competition   heard   all
       dass [die Kufen]   [des Schlittens]...
       that [the runners] [NOM/ACC] [the sledge] [GEN]...
       "After the competition, everyone heard that the runners of the sledge..."

The following discussion will be concerned with the analysis of the complex NP *die Kufen des Schlittens* ("the runners of the sledge"). This argument is ambiguous between nominative and accusative case marking and, thereby, between a subject and an object reading. In the subsequent sections, we will examine the issues that this ambiguity raises for processing from several perspectives.

7.2.1 *Serial vs. parallel processing*

One major debate in the sentence processing literature has focused on whether, in the case of a local ambiguity as in (7.8), the processing system recognizes the fact that the input is compatible with several analyses, or whether it processes the ambiguity in a similar manner to the corresponding preferred unambiguous structure (in this case, an unambiguously case-marked subject). Perhaps even more importantly, if the ambiguity is recognized, does this lead to more than one analysis being pursued throughout the subsequent parse? If this is the case, the system is described as a *parallel* processor. The parallel models that have been proposed all assume that the multiple readings that are pursued are ranked with respect to one another according to how preferred they are. As mentioned in section 7.1, global parallelism (i.e. parallelism without a ranking) has not been seriously pursued as an option in the sentence processing literature, since a model of this type could not explain why certain readings are preferred over others. Existing ranked parallel models differ as to how the weighting between the alternative readings is computed and with respect to the question of whether readings with a very low ranking are "pruned" (i.e. no longer pursued as alternatives) or not. Non-parallel (serial) models all have in common that only a single reading is pursued beyond the ambiguous regions. They differ, however, regarding their stance on the

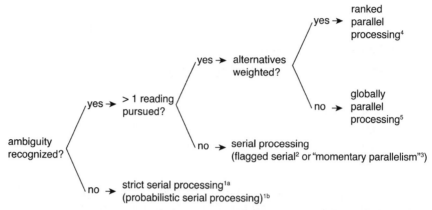

Figure 7.1 A schematic illustration of the different possibilities for ambiguity resolution. References: 1a (Frazier and Fodor 1978; Frazier 1987a); 1b (Traxler et al. 1998); 2 (Inoue and Fodor 1995); 3 (Altmann and Steedman 1988); 4 (Kurtzmann 1985; Gorrell 1987; Gibson 1991); 5 (not assumed within psycholinguistics). An alternative class of models (not depicted in the figure) assumes that the analysis is underspecified or delayed until sufficient information is encountered (Berwick and Weinberg 1984; Pritchett 1988).

visibility of the ambiguity: the ambiguity must be recognized, for example, in a "flagged serial" system, in which the point of ambiguity is marked in order to facilitate reprocessing in the case of a conflict. Strictly serial models, by contrast, assume that the ambiguity is not recognized at all. Figure 7.1 presents a summary of the different possibilities for ambiguity resolution together with references to proponents of each of these models.

Depending on which of the model types in Figure 7.1 is assumed, the NP *die Kufen* in (7.8) will therefore either be exclusively associated with a subject interpretation (for a discussion of the subject-first preference, see section 7.3) or the reading in which this NP is the subject will be pursued in parallel to an analysis assuming an object reading, but nonetheless weighted higher.

7.2.2 Modular vs. interactive processing

Irrespective of whether a serial or a parallel model of ambiguity processing is assumed, it is generally undisputed that there is a preference for one reading over the other in the case of most ambiguities. But how is such a preference determined? Which types of information are relevant for determining incremental interpretation? As an illustration, consider once again the example in (7.8) and recall from section 7.1

that position is not an unequivocal indicator of grammatical function in German. Despite the absence of an unambiguous structural cue, there is a clear preference for a subject reading, as this reading is associated with a potentially much simpler structure than an object reading: the assumption of an object entails that a subject must also be present in the structure, but not vice versa. However, in addition to the structurally-based subject preference, a second information type is potentially relevant to the resolution of the ambiguity: the critical NP is inanimate. Since subjects are usually also higher-ranking arguments from a thematic perspective (Agents, Causers, Experiencers etc.), an inanimate argument is less compatible with this typical range of inter-pretations and might therefore serve to contradict the subject preference.

There are therefore two main possibilities regarding the way in which the preference in (7.8) is determined. The first is that the preference is entirely based on structural properties, while animacy does not play a role. This is assumed by a class of models that has been labeled as "modular", "autonomous", or "syntax-first". Alternatively, both relevant information types may interact to yield the overall preference, an assumption that is made by "interactive" or "con-straint-satisfaction" models. The two classes of models are compared and contrasted in more detail in Box 7.1. In the case of a serial ambiguity-resolution architecture, an interaction between structure and animacy would either result in a reversal of the preference (such that only the object reading is pursued) or in an increase of the proportion of cases in which the object reading is chosen. This latter assumption is made by (non-deterministic) probabilistic serial (or "race-based") models, which assume that the preferred reading may differ from trial to trial even though only a single reading is ever pursued at one time (Traxler, Pickering, and Clifton 1998; van Gom-pel, Pickering, and Traxler 2001; van Gompel et al. 2005). The pro-portion of cases in which one or the other reading is chosen depends on how strong the preference for one reading over the other is, i.e. when the preference is very strong, the alternative reading will virtu-ally never be pursued. In a parallel model, by contrast, the interaction between the two factors would serve to modulate the relative distance between the two readings (in terms of their weights), with the result-ing overall ranking depending on the relative strength of the two information types.[5]

While the difference between modular and interactive models is well defined from a theoretical perspective, the two types of architectures are

Box 7.1 Modular vs. interactive models of sentence processing

Since the earliest days of psycholinguistic investigation, researchers have debated whether the sentence processing architecture is structured in a modular or an interactive fashion. In the most extreme views of modularity, syntactic processing is thought to proceed independently of other (linguistic or non-linguistic) information types such as semantics (Forster and Ryder 1971; Forster 1979). At the complete opposite end of the spectrum, it has also been proposed that all information types interact fully during all stages of sentence comprehension (Marslen-Wilson and Tyler 1980). Notably, as numerous empirical studies have demonstrated effects of non-syntactic information types (such as discourse context or pragmatic plausibility) on sentence processing, the crucial question underlying the debate on modularity vs. interactivity is not *whether* these information sources influence processing (which appears indisputable) but *when* this influence occurs. In this regard, the last decades of psycholinguistic theorizing in the domain of sentence comprehension have been dominated by two main approaches.

The first of these, which is often referred to as the "garden path model" (GPM), was developed by Lyn Frazier and her colleagues (e.g. Frazier 1978; Frazier and Fodor 1978; Frazier and Rayner 1982; Frazier 1987a; Frazier and Clifton 1996). The GPM is a two-stage approach to sentence processing. It assumes an initial stage of analysis that only draws upon syntactic category information and a small set of structural preference principles. In a subsequent second processing stage, the processing system then checks whether these initial processing choices are compatible with other information sources such as animacy, plausibility, discourse context, and frequency of occurrence. Thus, different information types interact with one another rapidly, but only after an initial (modular) stage of syntactic processing.

The second type of approach that has been proposed is fully interactive in nature. From this perspective, it is assumed that all available information types are jointly taken into account from the very first stages of processing (e.g. MacDonald et al. 1994; Trueswell and Tanenhaus 1994). Thus, the *generation* of syntactic structure is jointly determined by all available information sources and their relative weighting. A further important characteristic of interactive (or "constraint-based", "constraint satisfaction") models of this type is that they are typically *lexicalist* in nature. This means that syntactic structures are not generated via an abstract set of rules. Rather, they are constructed via the combination (unification) of partial structures that are lexically stored and associated with individual lexical items (for a detailed description of one such proposal, see Vosse and Kempen 2000). For an illustration of such lexically-stored syntactic structures, see Plate 6.

The differing predictions of two-stage vs. interactive models are best illustrated with respect to an example. Consider the sentences in (i), from an eye-tracking study by Ferreira and Clifton (1986).

(i)   Example stimuli from Ferreira and Clifton (1986)
       a. The witness examined by the lawyer turned out to be unreliable.
       b. The evidence examined by the lawyer turned out to be unreliable.

Like the classic garden-path sentence *The horse raced past the barn fell* (Bever 1970), the sentences in (i) involve a main-clause/relative-clause (MC/RC) ambiguity: the verb *examined* could either be the finite verb of the main clause (as in *The witness examined the evidence*) or the verb of a reduced relative clause (as in examples (ia/b)). The main clause reading is clearly preferred, thus leading to increased processing difficulty when the sentence is disambiguated towards a relative clause analysis (e.g. Rayner, Carlson, and Frazier 1983). From the perspective of the modular–interactive debate, the crucial question is whether an initial misanalysis still occurs even when the animacy status of the first noun phrase is incompatible with an analysis of this NP as the subject of the following verb. As two-stage models assume that the initial (modular) processing stage only takes word category into account, they would predict a garden path effect in both (ia) and (ib). However, (ib) may well still be easier to process than (ia) because the animacy information can help the processing system to recover from the initial misanalysis. By contrast, interactive models predict that animacy should directly modulate structure building in the ambiguous region, making it more likely that a reduced relative reading will be initially adopted in (ib) as opposed to (ia).

Whether the empirical findings on sentences such as (i) support one or the other theoretical perspective or whether they are, in fact, inconclusive, remains a matter of debate. In accordance with the predictions of modular models, Ferreira and Clifton (1986) originally observed that the reanalysis effect (i.e. the reading time increase at the disambiguating by-phrase) did not differ between sentences with animate (ia) and inanimate (ib) first NPs. This result led to much discussion within the sentence processing literature, with subsequent studies either reporting contradictory findings (i.e. a reduced garden-path effect for initial inanimate NPs: Trueswell, Tanenhaus, and Garnsey 1994) or converging evidence (Clifton et al. 2003). However, as noted by Clifton et al. (2003), a comparison of the effects in the disambiguating region of sentences such as (ia/b) cannot dissociate between modular

> and interactive models, as an attenuation of processing costs for sentences
> with inanimate first NPs could be due to a difference either in structure
> building or in computing the correct interpretation during reanalysis. Thus,
> this example not only serves to illustrate the different predictions of two-
> stage models and interactive models but also shows how difficult these may
> be to dissociate empirically.

very difficult to distinguish empirically (see also Box 7.1). Thus, in the
case of a sentence such as (7.8), the difference between the competing
predictions can only be examined when disambiguating information
becomes available at some later point in the sentence. However, any
differences measured in the disambiguating region need not necessarily
be due to mechanisms of initial choice, but could also result from
differences in reanalysis (conflict resolution). For example, animacy
may not impact upon the initial analysis of the first NP as subject, but it
may render the reanalysis of the argument towards the dispreferred
object reading easier (see Mitchell 1994). This issue will be discussed
further in section 7.3.

7.2.3 Frequency-based explanations

A very well-known phenomenon in the domain of word processing is
that the recognition/interpretation of a word directly correlates with its
frequency of occurrence (see Jurafsky 2003, for a review). This observation has led to the question of whether similar mechanisms might
also apply during processing at the sentence level (e.g. MacDonald,
Pearlmutter, and Seidenberg 1994; Trueswell and Tanenhaus 1994;
Mitchell et al. 1995; Jurafsky 1996; Vosse and Kempen 2000; Crocker
and Keller 2006; Hale 2006; Levy 2008). Applying this to example (7.8),
we can therefore ask whether the preference for a particular interpretation of the complex NP (*die Kufen des Schlittens*, "the runners of the
sledge") is modulated or even determined by the likelihood that an
inanimate NP in this position is the subject of the clause. Depending
on the type of model assumed, different frequencies can potentially
interact to determine the overall preference: (a) How often is an NP in
this position the subject?; (b) How often are inanimate NPs subjects?;
(c) How often is an inanimate NP in this position the subject?; (d)
What is the transitional probability between two or three adjacent

words (bigram or trigram frequency), i.e. the probability of the determiner *die* following *dass* instantiating a subject reading? Frequency-based approaches thus potentially provide a rather elegant way of deriving differences in the strength of a preference, depending on the relative frequency weightings of the factors involved.

In spite of this inherent appeal of frequency-based (probabilistic) approaches, however, they also raise a number of questions. Firstly, even if a phenomenon can be explained via frequency of occurrence, the underlying cause of the frequency distribution still remains to be explained. Secondly, given the many different possible grain sizes of frequency-based measures (e.g. possibilities (a)–(d) in the preceding paragraph, among many others), on what basis should precise frequency-based predictions be derived? Thirdly, for certain cases in which frequency influences have been demonstrated, subsequent research has suggested that these may not tell the whole story as to how processing preferences are derived. For example, Trueswell, Tanenhaus, and Kello (1993) reported empirical evidence in favor of a frequency-based modulation of so-called "NP-S" ambiguities, in which a noun phrase could either be the direct object of the main clause verb or the subject of a sentential complement (e.g. *The student forgot the solution.* vs. *The student forgot the solution was incorrect.*). They argued that the analysis of the ambiguous NP (*the solution*) is determined by how frequently the main clause verb occurs with a direct object vs. a sentential complement. However, using the same type of ambiguity, Pickering, Traxler, and Crocker (2000) demonstrated effects of direct object plausibility in the ambiguous region even for verbs with a frequency bias towards an intransitive reading. They therefore suggest that, rather than being determined entirely by frequency, initial processing choices are also influenced by "informativity", which includes how testable the assumption of a particular reading is.

In summary, the role of frequency in sentence-level processing mechanisms remains controversial. Future research must therefore seek to determine whether these types of models can indeed account for the full range of processing phenomena that cannot be derived with reference to lexical properties and that therefore call for the assumption of abstract representations (Jurafsky 2003). This difficulty is mirrored in the finding that simple frequency counts within existing corpora often do not reveal any straightforward correspondence to processing properties with respect to such lexically independent phenomena (Kempen and Harbusch 2005). This stands in contrast to the very clear correlations that have been found between corpus frequencies and processing findings at the lexical level (up to and including lexical effects at the sentence level, e.g. on the basis of subcategorization information). Thus, while it appears relatively implausible to assume that frequency plays no role whatsoever in the processing of morpho-syntactic information at the sentence level, the precise role of this type of information and how far-reaching its consequences may be is currently difficult to evaluate.

7.2.4 *Processing obligatory vs. non-obligatory information*

Many studies on sentence comprehension have examined the process-ing of non-obligatory constituents (modifiers such as PPs or relative clauses) and have used the results thus obtained to draw conclusions with respect to the properties of the processing architecture. However, the high degree of variability manifest across a range of phenomena in these studies stands in stark contrast to the very robust preferences observed in the processing of core constituents (i.e. obligatory argu-ments). This observation led Frazier and Clifton (1996) to propose that modifiers ("secondary relations" in their terminology) are processed in a fundamentally different way to obligatory information ("primary relations"). Notably, their *Construal* hypothesis states that only primary relations are subject to initial structure-based processing preferences (see the description of the garden path model in Box 7.1), while sec-ondary relations are only "associated" with a particular structural domain such that their final interpretation can be subject to a much wider range of influences (e.g. plausibility, frequency, etc.). This pro-posal not only helped to explain a wide range of otherwise puzzling results, it also appears plausible in view of a fundamental conceptual difference between the two constituent types. While obligatory infor-mation can be predicted and induce predictions, this is not the case for modifiers. Consider the following example:

(7.9)   Whom did the boy see on Sunday?

In (7.9), the argument *the boy* is predicted on the basis of two informa-tion sources: the wh-pronoun *whom* is unambiguously marked as an object and therefore leads to the prediction of a subject; a similar prediction at the structural level is generated at the position of *did*. Similarly, a wh-phrase such as *to whom* would engender a prediction for a subject and a direct object. By contrast, the temporal PP *on Sunday* can never be predicted by any information source. (Modifiers may, however, serve to guide structural predictions in demarcating certain portions of the clause, e.g. the left edge of VP).

A second important phenomenon with respect to the processing of obligatory vs. modifying information is the "argument-over-adjunct" preference. Thus, a constituent (e.g. a PP) that is ambiguous between an argument and an adjunct reading is preferably interpreted as an argument (e.g. Abney 1989; Clifton, Speer, and Abney 1991; Boland and Boehm-Jernigan 1998; Schütze and Gibson 1999). An example for this preference (from Boland and Boehm-Jernigan 1998) is given in (7.10).

(7.10)   John gave a letter *to his son* to a friend a month ago.

When the PP *to his son* is first encountered in a sentence such as (7.10), it is preferentially analyzed as the recipient of *give*, i.e. as an argument of the verb. When the second PP (*to a friend*) is subsequently encountered, this original analysis must be revised towards an adjunct interpretation (*a letter to his son*). In the spirit of *Construal*, the argument-over-adjunct preference might be attributed to the processing system's endeavor to maximize incremental interpretation. If interpretation is delayed for modifying elements in comparison to obligatory constituents (as the former are only structurally associated), a preference for arguments straightforwardly follows.

Because of the differences that have been postulated between the processing of obligatory and non-obligatory constituents, we will discuss the processing of modifiers separately from the processing of core constituents (see Chapter 11).

7.3 The neurocognitive perspective

The increasing availability and use of neuroscientific methods for the examination of language processing allows many of the major questions for psycholinguistic theory to be examined in a new light. In particular, neurocognitive methods can provide additional fine-grained information that can be used to flesh out details of the processing architecture. While behavioral measures such as acceptability (grammaticality) judgments or reaction times provide a unidimensional perspective on processing difficulty, neural responses are inherently multidimensional. As described in detail in Chapter 2, this applies to both electrophysiological activity (as measured, for example, by ERPs) and to characterizations of functional neuroanatomy (as provided, for example, by fMRI). In both cases, inherent aspects of stimulus-related processing can – at least in principle – be separated from output characteristics (e.g. task-related processing requirements). Therefore, modulations that appear unidimensional in the output can be dissociated further using these types of methods, particularly if a single critical manipulation is examined in different experimental environments. By this, we do not mean to suggest that neurocognitive measures per se provide a more informative window on the grammar underlying the processing system. However, they do allow for a more fine-grained characterization of the language architecture by helping to disentangle which aspects of the output signal stem from domain general systems (e.g. for evaluative judgments, cognitive control, etc.) and which should be attributed to inherent properties of the linguistic manipulation itself.

In spite of these advantages of neurocognitive measures, these techniques are not a panacea, i.e. they remain subject to a number of limitations associated with empirical validations of psycholinguistic models. A case in point is the debate on modularity vs. interactivity in initial processing choices. While neurocognitive methods are highly sensitive and provide multidimensional measures, they nonetheless cannot overcome the problem that any effect measured at a point of disambiguation is no longer informative with respect to the mechanisms of initial choice, as (a) the preference could have been modulated by a post-initial mechanism by that point, or (b) modulations of the observable effect could be attributable to difference in conflict resolution (see section 7.2.2).

However, neurocognitive experiments – particularly using ERPs – have been used to approach this problem from a somewhat different perspective, by using so-called "violation paradigms". A violation paradigm involves a comparison between an ungrammatical sentence, which induces a violation with respect to one particular linguistic property, and a minimally differing control sentence. The logic behind this kind of design is that the violation should lead to processing problems within that part of the comprehension architecture that is responsible for the processing of the information type that induces the violation.[6] For example, a phrase structure violation should engender some kind of response from the system responsible for phrase structure processing because this is where a problem arises. This type of approach appeared very fruitful in light of early ERP investigations, which revealed distinct electrophysiological processing signatures for violations within different linguistic domains (Kutas and Hillyard 1980;

Kutas and Hillyard 1983). From the perspective of psycholinguistic modeling, violation paradigms may help to overcome the "reanalysis problem" described above, because they provide a means of examining the mechanisms of immediate incremental processing. Thus, the response to violations induced by different information types may be contrasted at the position of the same critical input element. This allows for an examination of their relative timing and independence or mutual interdependence.

Notes

1. At a first glance, object-experiencer verbs such as *frighten* may appear to constitute a counterexample to this claim. However, it is generally assumed in the literature that these verbs are associated with a causative reading, thereby maintaining the "canonical" mapping between thematic roles and grammatical functions, i.e. the subject remains the higher-ranking argument (e.g. Grimshaw 1990; Pesetsky 1994).

2. The two constructions are illustrated in (i) and (ii), respectively

   (i) Unmarked dative-nominative order in passivized ditransitives
       ... dass dem Jungen der Roller   gestohlen wurde.
       ... that [the boy]$_{DAT}$ [the scooter]$_{NOM}$ stolen   was.
       "... that the boy had (his) scooter stolen."
   (ii) VP-topicalization including a subject (nominative)
       Ein Fehler   unterlaufen ist noch keinem Linguisten.
       [an error]$_{NOM}$ occurred-to is PRT no   linguist
       "Never has an error occurred (to a linguist)."

3. In an ergative language, the "subject" of an intransitive sentence and the "object" of a transitive sentence are coded by the same morphological case, while the transitive subject is assigned a distinct case, the "ergative". The case which marks the transitive object and intransitive subject is often referred to as "absolutive". In the vast majority of languages showing this coding pattern, it is the absolutive argument that agrees with the verb (see example 7.4). Split-ergativity refers to a situation in which a nominative-accusative system (as in German, Japanese, Turkish, etc.) and an ergative-absolutive system coexist within a single language (see Dixon 1994, for a comprehensive introduction to ergativity and split-ergativity).

4. Note that "subject" and "object" are used in an intuitive sense here to refer to the higher- and lower-ranking arguments in a transitive relation, respectively. A detailed discussion of the problems associated with a cross-linguistic definition of grammatical relations is beyond the scope of this

volume. Readers interested in this topic are referred to Keenan (1976), Comrie (1989), Farrell (2005), and Bickel (in press).

5. Note that the aim of this discussion is to illustrate that the dimensions of serial vs. parallel processing and modular vs. interactive processing are, in principle, orthogonal to one another. In practice, however, a strong correlation is assumed between the two such that modular models are typically serial, whereas interactive models are typically parallel.

6. The use of violation paradigms is not entirely uncontroversial. It is sometimes argued that reactions to the processing of a violation may constitute little more than an "error response" and that they are therefore not suited to revealing details of the normal processing architecture. However, this perspective cannot easily explain why different types of violations robustly correlate with different types of neurocognitive responses.

8

Constituent Structure

Psycholinguistic investigation at the sentence level essentially began with the question of how the processing system structures individual input items (words) into larger constituents. One of the initial motivations for this research focus was the need to explain why words in a sentence are processed more quickly and recalled more easily than words in a list containing the same number of items (Johnson 1970; Miller and Isard 1964). It was assumed that, by providing a means to quickly structure input elements into larger chunks, constituent structuring reduced the number of elements needing to be maintained in working memory, thus facilitating processing (Frazier and Fodor 1978). In addition, the structures built in this way are clearly not arbitrary in their internal makeup, but rather follow known regularities of constituent structuring.

While the need for constituent (phrase) structure is undisputed in both theoretical linguistics and psycholinguistics,[1] its precise role in real time comprehension is somewhat more controversial. A number of positions on this issue have been advocated, the two extremes of which can be described as follows: (a) constituent structuring is the prerequisite for all further processing steps, both syntactic and interpretive in nature, and (b) constituent structure is not afforded any special role but rather interacts with all other available information types (e.g. animacy, frequency, thematic roles) to determine sentence structure and interpretation. The former perspective is typically associated with two-stage models such as the garden path model, while the later is assumed by interactive (or constraint-based) models (see Box 7.1).

The debate on the status of constituent structure in sentence comprehension is thus intimately tied to the question of whether different information types are associated with distinct time course profiles. While syntax-first models would assume a temporal precedence for constituent structure over other information types, strongly interactive models should assume that such a temporal ordering either never occurs or that there are at least certain instances in which other information types show an equally early response.[2] Note that the crucial issue here is not whether an interaction occurs at all – for example in the surface response to a critical stimulus – but how this interaction comes about. As an illustration, consider the example in Box 7.1, which also served to show that the competing predictions of two-stage and interactive models are virtually impossible to tease apart by examining disambiguating regions, since any effect observed there might also reflect the relative ease or difficulty of reanalysis.

In view of the difficulties arising with respect to ambiguous structures, a promising alternative way of examining the status of constituent structure during processing lies in tracking the time course profiles of the different critical information types in unambiguous structures. In studies adopting this approach, the critical manipulation has typically been induced through the use of violation paradigms (see section 7.3). This was first accomplished behaviorally in a series of SAT experiments conducted by McElree and Griffith (1995). (See Chapter 2.4.2 for an introduction to the SAT method.) These authors contrasted the processing of phrase structure (word category) information (8.1a) in comparison to thematic information (8.1b). The grammatical control condition is given in (8.1d).

(8.1)   Example stimuli from McElree & Griffith (1995)

    a. *Some people hastily books. (phrase structure violation)
    b. *Some people amuse books. (thematic violation)
    c. *Some people agree books. (subcategorization violation)
    d. Some people love books. (grammatical control)

McElree and Griffith observed faster SAT dynamics by approximately 100 ms for sentences such as (8.1a) in comparison to (8.1b). This finding indicates that, at least within the domain of obligatory constituents, phrase structure is associated with a faster processing time course than interpretive structure such as thematic information.[3] Note, however, that McElree and Giffith (1995) found that subcategorization information (8.1c) was processed just as quickly as phrase structure information (8.1a). They therefore argue that their data are compatible with a modified two-stage model in which lexical access provides the first stage of processing with both category and subcategorization information (on the importance of subcategorization information, see also Clifton, Frazier, and Connine 1984).

The SAT results provide converging evidence for an overall picture that grew out of a number of ERP findings in the 1990s. The first study to examine the processing of constituent structure in comparison to other information types by means of ERPs was reported by Neville et al. (1991). Among several further conditions, these authors contrasted the processing of phrase structure violations (8.2a) with that of semantic violations (8.2c) using visual presentation. Note that, here and in the following, the critical words in ERP studies are underlined.

(8.2) Example stimuli from Neville et al. (1991)

    a. *The man admired Don's of sketch the landscape. (phrase structure violation)

    b. The man admired a sketch of the landscape. (control for a)

    c. *The man admired Don's headache of the landscape. (semantic violation)

    d. The man admired Don's sketch of the landscape. (control for c)

Neville et al. found an early anterior negative response (N125) followed by a late positivity to the phrase structure violation in (8.2a), while the semantic violation in (8.2c) elicited a classical N400 effect. This observation of a substantial latency difference (approximately 250 ms) between the critical effects indicates that the two information types are indeed associated with different time course profiles. This finding was replicated for German using the auditory modality (Friederici, Pfeifer, and Hahne 1993).

(8.3) Example stimuli from Friederici et al. (1993)

    a. phrase structure violation
       *Der   Freund wurde im   besucht.
       the   friend was in-the   visited

    b. semantic violation
       *Die   Wolke   wurde   begraben.
       the   cloud   was   buried

    c. grammatical   control
       Der   Finder   wurde   belohnt.
       the   finder   was   rewarded

Despite the different language and modality employed in comparison to the Neville et al. study, structures such as (8.3a) elicited an early left anterior negativity (termed "ELAN" by the authors; followed by a late positivity), while sentences of the form in (8.3b) engendered an N400 effect. The ELAN effect for sentences such as (8.3a) is shown in Figure 8.1.

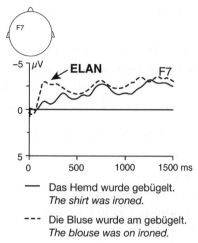

Figure 8.1 Illustration of a typical early left anterior negativity (ELAN) effect.
Source: Adapted from Friederici 2002.

Beyond showing differences in the time course of processing for constituent structure and semantic (selectional restriction) information, ERP studies have revealed a hierarchical dependency of the latter information upon the former. This was accomplished by combining both of the critical violation types within a single word (Hahne 1998; Hahne and Friederici 2002).

(8.4)   Combined phrase structure and semantic violation (Hahne and Friederici 2002)
        *Das   Gewitter   wurde   im   gebügelt.
        the   thunderstorm   was   in-the   ironed

Strikingly, the combined violation in (8.4) engendered precisely the same response as only a phrase structure violation (cf. 8.3a), namely an ELAN (+ late positivity), but not an N400. This finding shows that, when the critical information is contained within a single word, phrase structure information can "block" the processing of semantic information. Hahne and Friederici's result thus indicates that the processing of semantic information is not simply delayed in time in comparison to constituent structure information. Rather, phrase structure relations appear to constitute a necessary precondition for the processing of semantic (selectional restriction) information.

Studies of this type have sometimes been criticized because the temporal availability of the two critical information types typically also differs within the auditory presentation of a word. In the Hahne and

Friederici study, for example, there was a high correlation between the phrase structure violation and the *ge-* prefix on the critical participle, while the semantic information was never available prior to the stem of the word (e.g. *bügelt* in 8.4). From an interactive perspective, one might therefore argue that an apparent hierarchical dependency could also be induced in the opposite direction if the temporal availability of the critical information types within a word was reversed. However, this is not the case, as shown by an auditory ERP study from van den Brink and Hagoort (2004), who examined sentences such as (8.5).

(8.5) *Het   vrouwtje   veegde   de   vloer   met   een   oude
       the   woman   wiped   the   floor   with   an   old
       <u>kliederde</u>   gemaakt   van   twijgen.
       messed   made   of   twigs

The critical word *kliederde* combines a word category violation encoded within the suffix (*-de* indicating a verb rather than the required noun) with a semantic violation that is recognizable from the stem. Crucially, the category violation became apparent approximately 300 ms after the semantic violation (at what the authors termed the "category violation point", CVP). Van den Brink and Hagoort observed an N400 in response to the (semantically) incongruent fragment with an onset clearly before the CVP. This effect was followed by an anterior negativity and a late positivity, which can both be analyzed as reflections of the category mismatch induced by the suffix. This finding therefore shows that, even when the semantic information is available earlier than the category information and has already served to reject a plausible interpretation of the sentence, the N400 thus resulting *cannot* block the ELAN that arises as a response to the phrase structure violation.

   In contrast to this interpretation, van den Brink and Hagoort argue that their observation of an N400 preceding an ELAN disconfirms the assumptions of "syntax-first" models, since these should expect the processing system to delay its response until word category information has been processed. However, this line of explanation overlooks the fact that the stem of the critical word in examples such as (8.5) is fully compatible with the expected word category, namely: noun (especially in view of the highly predictive sentence context, in which a determiner and an adjective preceded the critical word). Thus, there is no reason for the processing system to assume that there is a word category problem, since there is no evidence to this effect.

Regarding the question of how the ERP responses to combined phrase structure and semantic violations are conditioned by the relative temporal availability of the different information types, it appears most informative to contrast the study by van den Brink and Hagoort (2004) with an experiment by Friederici et al. (2004). These investigators also aimed to examine combined violations in words in which the semantic information becomes available earlier than the word category information. In contrast to van den Brink and Hagoort, however, Friederici and colleagues used stimuli in which the suffix conveying the critical category information formed part of the same syllable as the stem (conveying the critical semantic information). Example stimuli from this study are given in (8.6) (note that the stem of the participle *verpflanzt* "replanted" is also compatible with a noun reading: *Verpflanzung*, "replanting").

(8.6)   Example stimuli from Friederici et al. (2004)

    a. control
       Der Strauch wurde <u>verpflanzt</u> von einem Gärtner...
       the bush   was   replanted   by   a   gardener...

    b. semantic violation
       *Das Buch wurde <u>verpflanzt</u> von einem Verleger...
       the book was   replanted by a   publisher...

    c. phrase structure violation
       *Der Strauch wurde trotz   <u>verpflanzt</u> von einem Gärtner...
       the bush   was   despite replanted   by a   gardener...

    d. double violation
       *Das Buch wurde trotz   <u>verpflanzt</u> von einem Verleger...
       the book was   despite replanted   by a   publisher...

Even though the semantic information was available earlier than the word category information, Friederici et al. (2004) observed the same ERP pattern for the double violation as for the phrase structure violation (i.e. an (E)LAN – late positivity pattern with no N400).[4] This finding thus stands in striking contrast to that reported by van den Brink and Hagoort (2004).

Taken together, the experiments by van den Brink and Hagoort (2004) and Friederici et al. (2004) appear to speak in favor of a hierarchically organized processing architecture in which phrase structure processing hierarchically dominates the processing of "semantic" information. Thus, while ELAN effects block N400s, an N400 does not block an ELAN even if the N400 appears at an earlier point in time. In addition, a comparison of the two studies suggests that there is a certain "integration window" during which a word category violation may affect the processing of semantic information even if it is encountered later on in the auditory input (cf. Poeppel 2003, for a discussion of temporal integration windows in speech perception). In Friederici et al.'s study, the word category violation occurred within this window, thereby blocking the N400. In van den Brink and Hagoort's experiment, by contrast, the word category violation occurred too late for such a blocking effect to take place. This overall data pattern suggests that the processing stages may be organized in a cascaded, rather than a strictly serial fashion, i.e. the second stage can be initiated on the basis of a partial (rather than a full) input from the first stage. Thus, for a short period of time, the processes from both stages overlap. If a word category problem occurs within this integration window and stage 1 processing therefore fails, semantic processing may still be aborted. By contrast, once stage 2 processing reaches a particular threshold ("point of no return"), semantic processing proceeds and the N400 can no longer be blocked. While we can only speculate on the exact size of this integration window at present, the within vs. across syllable boundary distinction between the two studies at issue here could constitute a valuable starting point for future research in this regard.

In summary, existing ERP findings provide strong converging support for the assumption that constituent structure information *hierarchically dominates* other information types such as semantics/plausibility. This hierarchical structure is typically mirrored by temporal precedence, but this is not a necessary prerequisite. This example therefore also serves to show that dependencies between ERP components appear to be more informative with respect to the characteristics of the processing architecture than absolute latency values, as these can vary depending on the precise properties of the input.

The conclusions from the ERP data are corroborated by neuroimaging findings. Examining similar structures to those in (8.3) in the auditory modality, Friederici et al. (2003) found that phrase structure violations engendered increased activation in the anterior portion of the left superior temporal gyrus (STG), in the left deep frontal operculum, and the left basal ganglia, while semantic violations gave rise to bilateral activation increases in the middle portion of the STG and in the anterior insula. In addition, both violation types showed an activation in the posterior left STG. Friederici et al.'s findings therefore revealed neuroanatomical regions within which constituent structure and semantic information are processed separately from one another, and a further region common to both information types. This pattern appears highly compatible with the observations from the temporal perspective that constituent structure can be dissociated from other information types, while it must interact with them at some point during processing to enable a complete form-to-meaning mapping.

Notes

1. The precise representation of constituent structure of course depends upon the grammatical theory assumed. However, a number of basic character-istics are shared by the vast majority of theories, for example the notion that constituents consist of a projecting head together with additional (dependent) constituents (arguments).

2. Temporal precedence of constituent structure over other information types could be modeled in a constraint-based approach by assuming that con-stituent structure is associated with an inherently higher activation level than other information sources. However, independently of the possible sources of this higher activation, an interactive model assuming a domin-ance of constituent structure under all circumstances would be empirically indistinguishable from a modular model assuming a primacy of word category-based constituent structuring.

3. Additional evidence in support of this assumption was provided by McEl-ree and Griffith (1998) by means of an experiment examining the process-ing of the same information types in cleft constructions (see Chapter 10, for a more detailed discussion).

4. In this experiment, the ELAN was temporally delayed, thus showing up in a time window more typically associated with left anterior negativity (LAN) effects (see Chapter 9). However, this slightly longer latency relative to the critical stimulus onset was likely due to the fact that the critical word category information became available at a later point within the auditory signal. This finding thus serves to highlight a very important consideration that should be kept in mind in the interpretation of ERP data: component/ effect latencies are relative rather than absolute. This means that the latency of an effect may change depending on the presentation conditions (e.g. auditory vs. visual presentation) and differences in the availability of particular information types that result from changes in these conditions.

9

Relational Structure

Beyond constituent structure, the next level in the form-to-meaning mapping comprises the relations between different constituents in a sentence. Consider, for example, the dependency between a verb and its arguments: the lexical entry of the verb specifies how many arguments it requires (or is potentially compatible with), of which type these arguments are (e.g. whether they are NPs, PPs, etc.), which cases they bear in languages with morphological case marking, and so on. In addition, many languages require the verb to agree with one or more of its arguments with respect to features such as number, person, or gender. All of these properties are "relational" in the sense that the dependencies in question do not hold between an element and its position in the constituent structure but rather between different elements within that structure. For example, while it is an inherent characteristic of phrase structure that constituents must have a head, the existence of something akin to a "subject position" is not. Grammatical theories differ with respect to how they express relational properties of this type: Chomskyan approaches construe them as corresponding to particular phrase structure configurations (e.g. in assuming that an accusative object can be defined as a complement of the verb), while other theories either attribute them to an independent level of representation (e.g. Lexical–Functional Grammar, LFG; Bresnan 2001) or to aspects of the linking between form and meaning (e.g. Role and Reference Grammar, RRG; Van Valin 2005). Likewise, psycholinguistic theories disagree as to whether relational structure is processed simultaneously with phrase structure information or in a post-initial processing phase (see the discussion of interactive vs. modular processing models in Box 7.1). Thus, models of sentences processing differ along two orthogonal dimensions, namely: (a) whether relational structure can be derived from phrase structure representations or whether it is afforded an independent status, and (b) whether the two information types are processed simultaneously or not.

Interestingly, there is evidence to suggest that the combinatorial properties of relational structure are not determined entirely by those of constituent structure. Thus, a number of recent findings on processes of "enriched composition" suggest that some aspects of sentence-level interpretation must go beyond the combination of elements in the phrase structure. Consider the following sentences, which were examined in an MEG study by Pylkkänen and McElree (2007).

(9.1)   Example stimuli from Pylkkänen and McElree (2007)

    a. Enriched composition (complement coercion)
       The journalist began the <u>article</u> after his coffee break.

    b. Control
       The journalist wrote the <u>article</u> after his coffee break.

    c. Anomalous
       The journalist astonished the <u>article</u> after his coffee break.

Sentences requiring enriched composition are thought to involve additional inferential processes for the computation of an implied meaning (see, for example, Pustejovsky 1995; Jackendoff 1997). This is the case, for example, in sentences such as (9.1a): the verb *begin* requires an event complement, as would typically be expressed by a verb phrase (e.g. *began to write the book*). When, as in (9.1a), *began* is followed by a (non-eventive) object NP such as *the book* instead, this NP must be "coerced" from an entity to an event representation. As argued by Pylkkänen and McElree (2006), coercion does not appear to constitute a syntactic process. In addition, it engenders activation in different brain regions to other aspects of sentence processing (namely in the so-called "anterior midline field", i.e. a frontomedian area approximately at the border between BA 8 and 9, see Plate 2C). Thus, sentences such as (9.1a) involve processes of relational (semantic) composition that cannot be derived entirely from a sentence's constituent structure.

Throughout the remainder of this chapter, we will therefore assume that relational structure is logically independent of constituent structure (though the two may, of course, overlap under certain circumstances). Following the classical assumption that the majority of relational dependencies can be derived from the verb, we will begin with some observations within this area (section 9.1). In particular, we will discuss whether all types of verb-related information are processed in a similar manner (as defined by temporal and spatial signatures) and whether they interact or show a similar hierarchical behavior to that found in the area of early constituent structuring. Moving away from the verb-based perspective and turning to morphological case as a second fundamental way of defining relational dependencies at the sentence level, the following sections examine how pre-verbal dependencies are processed in verb-final languages and how the different position of the predicate in SVO vs. SOV languages can be used as a predictor for basic properties of the comprehension architecture. These questions are first discussed on the basis of word order phenomena (section 9.2). Subsequently, insights on the processing of arguments without explicit verbal information form a basis for the discussion of grammatical function assignments in ambiguous environments from the perspective of different psycholinguistic approaches (section 9.3).

9.1 Relational aspects of verb and verb–argument processing

As described above, dependencies induced by the verb can be either formal or interpretive in nature. However, as we will illustrate with reference to case marking, the boundary between these two domains is not always clear-cut from an empirical perspective. Interpretive aspects have mainly been used to examine the interaction between lexical/ semantic information and constituent structure (e.g. the combination of animacy and verb-based information in *The evidence examined…* vs. *The witness examined*; see the discussion in Box 7.1 above). Formal dependencies, by contrast, were long viewed as "givens" in psycholinguistic research in the sense that they were typically employed to examine other aspects of processing (e.g. to disambiguate relative clause attachments or grammatical function assignments) rather than being subject to investigation in their own right. This tendency is most evident with respect to agreement.

9.1.1 *Agreement*

One of the most prominent discussions of agreement in the psycholinguistic literature concerns the erroneous assignment of plural verb-agreement under particular circumstances. This occurs, for example, following a complex subject NP such as *the key to the cabinets* (singular–plural) and has been observed both in production (e.g. Bock and Cutting 1982; Bock and Miller 1991; Bock and Eberhart 1993; Vigliocco and Nicol 1998) and comprehension (Nicol, Forster, and Veres 1997; Pearlmutter, Garnsey, and Bock 1999). The reversed assignment of singular agreement following a plural–singular NP, by contrast, does not occur. This asymmetry is typically attributed to the difference in markedness between plural and singular. Studies of this type have been used to contrast linear precedence with hierarchical structure as structure building properties during language processing (for discussion, see Pearlmutter 2000).

While the discussion of feature-based interference arose mainly with reference to findings from language production, the major field of "application" for agreement in the domain of comprehension has lain in the disambiguation of ambiguous structures. For example, agreement has been used to disambiguate the attachment of a relative clause in contexts where more than one potential attachment site is available (Cuetos and Mitchell 1988; Gilboy et al. 1995; Frazier and Clifton 1996). An example is shown in (9.2) (from Frazier and Clifton 1996; Chapter 4.4).

(9.2)   Agreement as a disambiguating feature (from Frazier and Clifton 1996)

Max met the only one of Sam's employees . . .
a.   . . . who have teeth who drives a pickup truck
b.   . . . who has teeth who drives a pickup truck

All of these studies, therefore, examined how agreement relations are used during processing rather than how they are established.

With the increasing availability of neurocognitive methods, questions regarding the processing of agreement per se began to be posed more directly. Specifically, researchers were concerned with the question of whether agreement as a relational syntactic feature could be dissociated from semantic information on the one hand and constituent structure on the other. Thereby, they aimed to shed light on possible distinctive neurocognitive signatures of agreement as opposed to other information types. This was typically accomplished by contrasting sentences containing an agreement error with minimally differing grammatical controls. As described with respect to the processing of constituent structure above, violation paradigms of this type are based on the assumption that a conflict encountered within a particular domain will engender increased processing costs within that domain. Thus, if agreement is processed differently to semantic information, for example, this should be reflected in a differential neurocognitive response to an agreement as opposed to a semantic violation. That this is indeed the case was first shown by Kutas and Hillyard (1983), who contrasted errors in subject–verb agreement as in (9.3) with semantic violations.

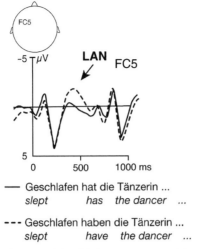

Figure 9.1 Illustration of a typical focal left anterior negativity (LAN) effect.
Source: Adapted from Burkhardt et al. 2007.

(9.3)   Example agreement violation from Kutas and Hillyard (1983)
        *Some shells <u>is</u> even soft.

While semantic violations engendered an N400 effect (see Chapter 2 and the discussion in Chapter 8), Kutas and Hillyard (1983) found that the increased processing costs associated with the agreement mismatch in (9.3) gave rise to a left anterior negativity (LAN), i.e. to an effect within approximately the same time range as the N400 but with a different topographical distribution. From a neuroanatomical perspective, subject–verb agreement violations as in (9.3) have been shown to engender increased activation in the pars opercularis (BA 44) of the left inferior frontal gyrus (Newman et al. 2003). The correlation between subject–verb agreement violations and LAN effects was shown to be very consistent, as attested by a number of subsequent studies in different languages (see 9.4). A typical LAN effect is illustrated in Figure 9.1.

(9.4)   Examples of subject–verb agreement conflicts producing a LAN
        (typically + late positivity)
        a. English (Coulson, King, and Kutas 1998b; see also Osterhout
           and Mobley 1995)
           *Every Monday he <u>mow</u> the lawn.

b. Italian (de Vincenzi et al. 2003)
   *Il cameriere anziano <u>servono</u>   con espressione distratta.
   [the waiter old][SG]   serve-3PL with look   vacant

c. Dutch (Hagoort and Brown 2000)
   *Het verwende kind   <u>gooien</u>   het speelgoed
   [the spoilt child][SG]   throw-3PL   the toys
   op de grond.
   on the floor

d. German (Roehm et al. 2005; see also Burkhardt, Fanselow, and
   Schlesewsky 2007; Münte, Matzke, and Johannes 1997)
   *Den Auftrag   bearbeiten   <u>er</u>   dennoch
   [the order][ACC.SG]   execute-3PL   he[SG]   nonetheless
   nicht.
   not

Further findings indicate that the appearnce of a LAN is not restricted
to the processing of subject–verb agreement, but that it rather appears
to constitute a more general response to increased demands in the
processing of agreement relations. This was shown by several studies
examining violations in verb–auxiliary agreement (9.5) and in gender
agreement during sentence processing (9.6).

(9.5) Verb–auxiliary agreement violations engendering a LAN (+ late
       positivity)

a. Auxiliary error in German (Rösler et al. 1993)
   *Der   Dichter   hat
   the   poet   has
   <u>gegangen</u>. (instead of *ist gegangen*, "was gone")
   gone

b. Participle form error in German (Friederici et al. 1993)
   *Das   Parkett   wurde
   The   parquet   was-being
   <u>bohnere</u>. (instead of *wurde gebohnert*, "was being polished")
   polish

c. Participle form error in Dutch (Gunter, Stowe, and Mulder
   1997)
   *De vuile matten   wurden door de hulp
   the dirty doormats were   by   the housekeeper
   <u>kloppen</u>. (instead of *gekloppt*)
   beat

(9.6)   Gender agreement conflict engendering a LAN + late positiv-
        ity (Gunter et al 2000; see also Barber and Carreiras 2005)
        *Sie   bereist   den   Land   auf   einem
        she   travels   the[M]   country[N]   on   a
        kräftigen   Kamel.
        strong   camel

Moreover, similarly to the study by Hahne and Friederici (2002) (see
Chapter 8), Gunter et al. (1997; see 9.7a) and Gunter et al. (2000; see 9.7b)
used a combined violation paradigm in order to examine the interdependence of agreement processing and semantic (selectional restriction)
processing, i.e. of formal and interpretive relational properties.

(9.7)   a.   Combined semantic + participle form violation in Dutch
             (Gunter et al. 1997)
             *De   vuile   matten   wurden   door   de   hulp
             the   dirty   doormats   were   by   the   housekeeper
             koken.
             cook

        b.   Gender agreement violation + low cloze word in German
             (Gunter et al. 2000)
             *Sie   befährt   den   Land   mit   einem
             she   drives.across the[M]   country[N]   with an
             alten   Wartburg.
             old   Wartburg (car)

Strikingly, both studies revealed an additive processing pattern for the
double violation, i.e. a pattern showing both an N400 and a LAN
within the same time range, followed by a late positivity. This shows
that, in contrast to conflicts arising during the processing of constituent structure, which lead to a blocking of the N400 (see Chapter 8), the
processing of relational syntactic information (agreement) co-occurs
with the establishment of interpretive relations. This observation is
consistent with initial evidence that a LAN can also be blocked by an
ELAN (Rossi et al. 2005). Taken together, these distinctions between
the ELAN and the LAN – which clearly go beyond mere issues of
timing – suggest that the two components indeed index functionally
separate processes (for a different view, see Lau et al. 2006).

  Despite the co-occurrence of LAN and N400 in a second phase of
processing, the additive nature of the component pattern observed by
Gunter et al. (1997; 2000) indicates that the two information types are

processed in parallel but do not interact with one another during the LAN/N400 time range (i.e. between approximately 300 and 500 ms). By contrast, there is evidence that such an interaction does indeed occur during later processing stages, as shown by an interaction of agreement and semantic information in the subsequent late positivity (Gunter et al. 1997; Gunter et al. 2000). For a more detailed discussion of the late positive effects that co-occur with left anterior negativities, see Chapter 12.

A further issue warranting discussion with respect to the electro-physiological correlates of agreement processing is that violations of subject–verb agreement/verb form do not always engender LAN effects. Thus, a range of studies employing comparable manipulations to those in (9.4/9.5) have only revealed late positivities – but no LANs – in response to agreement or verb form violations (e.g. Hagoort, Brown, and Groothusen 1993; Osterhout and Nicol 1999; Nevins et al. 2007). This variability appears to suggest that LAN effects may only reflect a certain subset of agreement mismatches, i.e. mismatches that come about under particular conditions. In this regard, Nevins et al. (Nevins et al. 2007: 89) speculate that the presence of a LAN may depend on "individual variables, or on the details of the morphological forms being tested, or on the linear relation between the agreement controller and the verb". The possible influence of these and other factors in modulating the brain's response to agreement violations thus clearly requires further investigation.

Finally, it should be noted that a number of studies using the so-called "mismatch negativity" (MMN) paradigm have been used to argue for a substantially earlier timing of relational syntactic processing and specifically of agreement information. The MMN is a negativity with a fronto-central distribution and a typical latency between approximately 100 and 200 ms post critical stimulus onset. It occurs in response to (typically) auditory stimuli which deviate from an expected "standard" stimulus, e.g. a rarely occurring high tone presented in a series of low tones (for a review, see Paavilainen et al. 2001). In the domain of phonological processing, the MMN has been used to argue for particular feature representations according to the logic that, in order for a mismatch to be elicited between a standard and a deviant differing with respect to only a single abstract feature, that feature must be neurally represented (e.g. Eulitz and Lahiri 2004). A similar experimental approach has also been applied to syntactic processing. For example, Pulvermüller and Shtyrov (2003) examined

the processing of grammatical and ungrammatical pronoun–verb sequences (*we come* vs. **we comes*), both of which were presented as
standard and deviant stimuli. The two verb forms were also compared
without a pronoun to ensure that possible differences could indeed be
attributed to the grammaticality contrast. Grammaticality and context
interacted in the MMN response around 150 ms, i.e. at a substantially
earlier point in time than typical LAN responses to agreement violations. Since the MMN is elicited without participants' conscious attention, Pulvermüller and Shtyrov concluded that it constitutes an
automatic response to grammatical processing (see also Pulvermüller
et al. 2008).

Recent findings from German further suggest that agreement violations and word category violations engender MMN effects in approximately the same time range (Hasting, Kotz, and Friederici, 2007).
Hasting and colleagues conclude that their data do not confirm the
"timing of syntactic ERP effects" as evidenced in other studies and
that this timing is "greatly influenced by methodological factors such
as the precision of time-locking (i.e. word onset vs. violation point) or
the linguistic complexity of the presented stimulus material (i.e. longer
sentences vs. two-word utterances)" (Hasting et al. 2007: 398).

While we agree that it is problematic to base timing assumptions in
language processing on the absolute latency of ERP effects (cf. Bornkessel and Schlesewsky 2006a), we also believe that it may be worth
considering an alternative explanation of the existing syntactic MMN
findings. In all of the studies using this paradigm of which we are
aware, there was a feature overlap within the critical stimuli (e.g. *he
[3.SG] come-s[3.SG]*) which was not present in the ungrammatical case.
Hence, independently of the precise manipulation, these very early effects
could be modeled as resulting from some type of spreading activation of
feature content (which is likely enhanced by the repetition of a standard
stimulus). In essence, this explanation is in line with the syntactic
priming-based interpretations of the syntactic MMN that have been
advanced in the literature (e.g. Pulvermüller and Shtyrov 2003; Hasting
et al. 2007). However, it also calls into question whether results of this
type could be viewed as evidence for the timing of syntactic composition.

9.1.2 *Verb–argument relations*

Beyond the formal properties encoded by agreement relations, there are
a number of dependencies between verbs and their arguments that may

be considered somewhat more interpretive in nature. These concern the number of arguments, their type (e.g. with respect to categories such as NP, PP, etc. or other features such as animacy) and their form (e.g. case marking). One of the earliest neurocognitive studies to examine the effects of verb–argument relations during online comprehension was conducted by Osterhout, Holcomb, and Swinney (1994) using sentences such as (9.8).

(9.8) Example stimuli from Osterhout et al. (1994)
    a. only S-complement
       The doctor hoped the patient <u>was</u> lying
    b. NP- or S-complement
       The doctor believed the patient <u>was</u> lying.
    c. only NP-complement
       *The doctor forced the patient <u>was</u> lying.

The verbs in sentences (9.8a–c) differ with respect to their subcategorization properties: *hoped* (9.8a) is incompatible with an NP argument and requires a sentential complement; *forced* (9.8c) does not permit a finite complement clause, rather requiring an NP argument followed by an infinitival (e.g. *to lie*); *believe* (9.8b) is compatible with both an NP and a finite clause complement. At the position of *was*, Osterhout et al. (1994) observed a biphasic N400-late positivity pattern in response to (9.8c), while (9.8b) only engendered a late positivity. This finding suggests that the late positivity may reflect revisions of incorrect structural commitments as well as occurring in response to violations (see Chapter 12 for further discussion). In addition, the observation of an N400 in response to a conflict with respect to argument type provides a first indication that verb-based relations may indeed differ qualitatively depending on whether they are formal or lexical-interpretive in nature.

Corroborating findings for this assumption stem from a study comparing the processing of valency (number of arguments) and object case in German (Friederici and Frisch 2000).

(9.9) Example sentences from Friederici and Frisch (2000)
    Anna weiss, ...
    Anna knows ...
    a. Valency violation
       * ... dass der Kommissar   den Banker
       ... that [the inspector][NOM]   [the banker][ACC]
       <u>abreiste</u>   und wegging.
       departed   and left

b. Object case violation
   * ... dass der Kommissar   den Banker
   ... that [the inspector][NOM]   [the banker][ACC]
   <u>beistand</u>   und wegging.
   stood.by(DAT)   and left

c. Grammatical control
   ... dass der Kommissar   den Banker
   ... that [the inspector][NOM]   [the banker][ACC]
   <u>*abhörte*</u>   und   wegging.
   wiretapped   and   left

For the valency violation condition, Friederici and Frisch found an N400 followed by a late positivity (in comparison to the control condition). This observation thus supports the interpretation advanced on the basis of Osterhout et al.'s (1994) findings that the processing of lexical information concerning verb–argument relations can be dissociated from that of agreement. Recent results from Mandarin Chinese suggest that these processing mechanisms not only apply to verb-specific restrictions on the number of arguments but also extend to verb type restrictions in particular sentence constructions (Ye, Zhan, and Zhou 2007). Furthermore, the N400 effect for valency violations can be blocked by a phrase structure violation just like a plausibility-induced N400 (Frisch, Hahne, and Friederici 2004), thus suggesting that phrase structure processing also takes priority over the processing of verb–argument relations of this type. Interestingly, for the processing of a wrong object case, Friederici and Frisch (2000) observed a LAN-late positivity pattern. On the basis of the results discussed so far, the finding of a LAN in these types of structures might be taken to suggest that the relation established between an argument and a verb via case reflects formal properties similar to those encoded by agreement. Before we investigate this hypothesis further in the context of an in-depth discussion of case information, we will turn to a further interpretive aspect of verb–argument processing.

In addition to specifying the number of required arguments and their category (and case), it has often been assumed that a verb's lexical entry also encodes further restrictions with respect to possible arguments. While theories differ with respect to the types of properties that may be thought to be lexically encoded, probably the most uncontroversial feature in this regard is animacy. Thus, if a particular argument slot is only compatible with an animate argument, for example, this typically reflects an inherent property of the verb's meaning (e.g. the verb *love* requires an animate (human) higher-ranking argument, because the ability to experience psychological states comprises an inherent property of what it means to love something or someone). This type of verb-inherent restriction was contrasted with world knowledge-based interpretive anomalies in a study by Kuperberg et al. (2007).

(9.10)   Example stimuli from Kuperberg et al. (2007)
   a. Animacy violation
      For breakfast the eggs would <u>eat</u> toast and jam.
   b. World knowledge violation
      For breakfast the boys would <u>bury</u> toast and jam.
   c. Combined animacy/world knowledge violation
      For breakfast the eggs would <u>bury</u> toast and jam.
   d. Control
      For breakfast the boys would <u>eat</u> toast and jam.

For both conditions involving an animacy violation, Kuperberg and colleagues observed a late positivity and no N400, while the world knowledge violation in (9.10b) engendered the expected N400 effect. This finding is interesting in several respects. First of all, it suggests that animacy restrictions concerning the higher-ranking argument can be dissociated from interpretive restrictions based simply on world knowledge. In addition, the overall data pattern appears to suggest that an animacy violation can "block" the appearance of an N400 even without the concomitant appearance of a different ERP component within the same or an earlier time range. If this were not the case, the combined violation (9.10c) should have shown a biphasic N400-late positivity pattern rather than only a late positive effect. However, while these data indicate that the processing system distinguishes animacy from other interpretive information types, the precise interpretation of the positivity observed in (9.10a/c) poses an interesting challenge to neurocognitive models of sentence comprehension. In fact, the study by Kuperberg et al. (2007) is only one of a larger range of experiments to have found "semantic positivities". These will be discussed in more detail in Chapter 12.

   To summarize, the neurocognitive findings on the processing of verb–argument relations suggest that valency and subcategorization information (i.e. information concerning the number and type of arguments) is distinguished from verb–argument agreement relations during incremental processing. Whereas increased processing effort arising from the former is typically reflected in N400-late positivity patterns, conflicts induced within the latter domain mainly engender component patterns consisting of a LAN and a late positivity. However, in contrast to ELAN and N400 effects, LANs and N400s within the verb–argument domain can co-occur, thus suggesting that these components reflect the same hierarchical stage of processing.

9.2 From case to word order – establishing relations between arguments in verb-final constructions

Without wishing to deny the important role of verb-based relations in sentence processing, it should be kept in mind that these only constitute one side of the coin. Thus, while an overwhelming number of the insights on sentence comprehension have been obtained from studies conducted in English (an SVO language, in which the verb thus typically becomes available before both arguments have been processed), the most frequent basic word order among the languages of the world is SOV (Dryer 2005). The cross-linguistic proliferation of verb-final structures therefore raises the question of whether – in accordance with the endeavor to maximize incremental comprehension – relations between the arguments might be established even before the verb is encountered and, if so, how this can be accomplished.

9.2.1 Incremental processing in verb-final structures: First observations and considerations

Several early psycholinguistic approaches assumed that parsing is driven by lexical heads, thus implying that the building of structure and the establishment of dependencies must be delayed until the verb is encountered (Abney 1989; Pritchett 1992; Pritchett 1988). Remnants of such assumptions can still be found in modern lexicalist approaches (MacDonald et al. 1994; Trueswell and Tanenhaus 1994; Vosse and Kempen 2000). However, the validity of assuming that parsing is indeed "head-driven" began to be questioned from the late 1980s onward, primarily on the basis of findings from Dutch, German and Japanese (Frazier 1987b; Bader and Lasser 1994; Kamide and Mitchell 1999). It is therefore now standardly assumed that pre-verbal structure building and interpretation indeed take place in verb-final constructions. The following example from Japanese illustrates that, under these circumstances, the properties of both the structure and the interpretation assigned cannot be solely a function of category information.

(9.11) 数時間前   演技者を   カメラマンが
       suujikanmae   engisya-o   kameraman-ga
       a few hours ago actor-ACC   photographer-NOM
       呼び止めました
       yobitomemasita
       ran-after-stopped
       "A few hours ago, the photographer ran after the actor and stopped him/her."

Example (9.11) is a sentence with a "scrambled" word order, i.e. the object precedes the subject. Scrambling changes the interpretation of the sentence in the sense that the first argument is no longer the Actor. Because of its word order, sentence (9.11) is further associated with a distinct discourse function from that of a subject-before-object sentence. In addition, in grammatical theories modeling argument interpretation with reference to structural positions, object-initial orders of this type are typically represented as involving a syntactic movement operation. Crucially, all of these properties cannot be derived solely on the basis of word category (NP). In addition, they are also not simply a function of the first NP and its morphological features (case marking), since Japanese allows subject-drop as in (9.12).

(9.12) 数時間前   演技者を   呼び止めました
       suujikanmae   engisya-o   yobitomemasita
       a few hours ago actor-ACC   ran after-stopped
       "A few hours ago, (someone) ran after the actor and stopped him/her."

Thus, while the morphological properties of the first NP are informative with respect to that NP's potential thematic interpretation (i.e. *o*-marking implies that an argument is the lower-ranking argument in a two-argument relation), they cannot unambiguously signal whether the NP has been scrambled or not. This can only be decided when the second NP is reached, when a specification of the relational properties of both NPs to one another can be undertaken.

    The examples from Japanese provide a first illustration of a universal tendency for verb-final languages to be associated with a richer case morphology than languages in which the verb appears in an earlier position in the clause (Greenberg's universal of grammar number 41; Greenberg 1966). From a processing perspective, such a correlation appears plausible because morphological marking directly constrains the range of interpretations that the arguments may be assigned even in absence of the verb. At the very least, this information may serve to specify an argument's grammatical function. At the opposite extreme, it may provide a very precise indication of its degree of causality in the event being described. This latter property is illustrated in (9.13) with reference to the East-Caucasian language Avar (examples cited from Blake 1994).

(9.13) Morphological marking of thematic roles in Avar

    a. ínssu-cca   j-as   j-écc-ula   (Agent)
       father-ERG F-child F-praise-PRS
       "Father praises the girl."

    b. ínssu-je   j-as   j-óλ'-ula   (Experiencer)
       father-DAT F-child F-love-PRS
       "Father loves the girl."

    c. ínssu-da   j-as   j-íx-ula   (Perceiver)
       father-LOC F-child F-see-PRS
       "Father sees the girl."

Whereas the examples in (9.13) show how an interpretation can be derived from the case marking of one of the two arguments (namely the higher-ranking argument), the following sentences from German indicate how this type of information can be encoded by the relation between two arguments (examples adapted from Primus 1999).

(9.14) Ich hörte,...
     I heard...

    a. ...dass dem Graphiker   (*absichtlich)
      ...that [the graphic.designer][DAT] (*deliberately)
      der Rahmen   zerbrach.
      [the frame] [NOM] broke.
      '~...that the frame (*deliberately) broke on the graphic designer.'

    b. ...dass der Graphiker   (absichtlich)
      ...that [the graphic.designer][NOM] (deliberately)
      den Rahmen   zerbrach.
      [the frame] [ACC] broke.
      '~...that the graphic designer (deliberately) broke the frame.'

In both sentences in (9.14), the relation between the two arguments is such that the graphic designer is responsible for the breaking of the frame. The two structures differ, however, with respect to how they construe the fine-grained thematic relations within this breaking-event: the dative-nominative case pattern in (9.14a) indicates that the degree of volitionality is reduced (i.e. the frame must have been broken inadvertently), while the relation of causality is maintained just as in the example with nominative-accusative case (9.14b). Examples such as these therefore illustrate that case marking can provide rather fine-grained interpretive information that is not dependent on the specific lexical properties of a verb and that might therefore provide for an early partial interpretation of the relations between the arguments even before the verb is encountered. How specific the relations thus constructed actually are has been examined in a number of empirical studies.

The first empirical evidence for incremental structuring in verb-final sentences was provided by behavioral studies examining a variety of different sentence types in several languages (see 9.15).

(9.15) Early studies providing evidence for pre-verbal structure assignment

a. Dutch (Frazier 1987b)
   Karl hielp   de mijnwerkers   die
   Karl helped [the mineworkers$_i$][PL] who$_i$
   de boswachter   vond
   [the forester][SG]   found[SG]
   "Karl helped the mineworkers who the forester found."
   (preferred: "Karl helped the mineworkers who found[PL] the forester.")

b. German (Bader and Lasser 1994)
   ...dass [sie   nach   dem   Ergebnis
   ...that [she/them[NOM/ACC]   for   the   result
   zu   fragen] tatsächlich   erlaubt   worden ist.
   to   ask]   indeed   permitted   been is
   "...that it was indeed permitted to ask her/them for the result."
   (preferred:...dass sie [nach dem Ergebnis zu fragen] tatsächlich erlaubt hat/haben., "...that she/they indeed permitted (someone) to ask for the result.")

c. Japanese (Kamide and Mitchell 1999)

Kyooju-ga	gakusee-ni	toshokansisho-ga	kasita
professor-NOM	student-DAT	librarian-NOM	lent
mezurasii	komonjo-o	yabutta.	
unusual ancient	manuscript-ACC	tore	

"The professor tore the unusual ancient manuscript which the librarian had lent the student."

(preferred: *Kyooju-ga gakusee-ni toshokansisho-ga yabutta mezurasii komonjo-o miseta*; "The professor showed the student the unusual ancient manuscript which the librarian had torn.")

All of these studies employed a reanalysis logic, i.e. they reasoned that, if incremental structuring were to take place before the verb in the constructions under examination, a disambiguation towards a dispreferred structural option at the position of the verb would lead to increased processing costs. This was indeed the case: each of the sentence types shown in (9.15) engendered increased processing costs at or immediately following the critical disambiguating verb positions (underlined) in comparison to preferred control structures (Frazier 1987b, and Bader and Lasser 1994, used speeded acceptability judgment tasks, whereas Kamide and Mitchell 1999 conducted a self-paced reading study). In (9.15a), the higher processing costs reflect the disambiguation towards object-before-subject order in the relative clause by the final auxiliary. This finding provided the first demonstration of the so-called "subject-first" preference, i.e. the tendency of the processing system to incrementally analyze an ambiguous initial argument as the subject of the clause (see section 9.3 for detailed discussion). Example (9.15b), by contrast, is centered around an ambiguity that is twofold: the pronoun *sie* is ambiguous between nominative and accusative case and, as a consequence, introduces an ambiguity with respect to whether this pronoun is to be understood as part of the embedded infinitival clause or not. Under a nominative reading of the pronoun, the only possible analysis would be one in which the pronoun is not part of the subordinate clause (resulting in a reading such as "... that she indeed permitted (someone) to ask for the result."). This interpretation, however, is incompatible with the disambiguation towards passive voice in (9.15b). Thus, the increased processing costs for this structure in comparison to its minimally differing active counterpart again result from a reanalysis of the preferred subject analysis of the pronoun to an object analysis and the restructuring of the subordinate clause resulting from this reanalysis. A similar ambiguity between a main clause and a subordinate (in this case relative) clause reading – but without a concomitant ambiguity of case marking – was induced in Japanese sentences such as (9.15c). Here, the dative argument *gakusee-ni* ("student-DAT") must be reanalyzed as a part of the relative clause when the clause-final verb is encountered, because this verb does not take a dative argument. (Note that, prior to this position, the dative NP could either be an argument of the main clause or of the subordinate clause because dative arguments of ditransitive verbs are optional in Japanese. Thus, even though the relative clause verb *kasita*, "lent", is ditransitive, this does not disambiguate between the two possible readings for the dative.) At the position of the disambiguating clause-final verb, Kamide and Mitchell observed increased reading times in comparison to control conditions in which the dative argument was either required as a main clause argument or which allowed both a relative and a main clause reading of this constituent. Taken together, all of these findings therefore attest to the pre-verbal assignment of (at least) constituent structure and grammatical functions in verb-final constructions.

Furthermore, pre-verbal structuring is not only measurable in ambiguous contexts but can also be observed at the position of an unambiguously marked initial accusative object. This was shown by several studies employing reading time measures (self-paced and eye-tracking).

(9.16)   Studies showing increased pre-verbal processing costs in case-marked structures

a. German, clause-initial declarative (Hemforth, Konieczny, and Strube 1993)

Den guten Schauspieler	bewundert	die	kluge
[the good actor][ACC]	admires	the	smart

Frau.
woman
"The smart woman admires the good actor."

b. German, clause-initial wh, animate (Fanselow, Kliegl, and Schlesewsky 1999a)

Welchen Mann	denkst	Du	kennt	der
[which man][ACC]	think	you	knows	the

Professor   seit   Jahren?
professor   since   years
"Which man do you think the professor has known for
years?"

c. German, clause-initial wh, inanimate (Fanselow et al. 1999a)
Welchen Diamanten   denkst   Du   findet   der
[which diamond][ACC]   think   you   finds   the
Professor   bei   der   Ausgrabung?
professor   at   the   excavation
"Which diamond do you think the professor will find
during the excavation?"

d. Finnish (Hyönä and Hujanen 1997)
Lopulta   politiikan   tuhoaa   jatkuvasti
finally   politics-GEN   destroys   continuously
kasvava   nukkuvien   puolue.
growing   body of   non-voters
"Finally, the politics are destroyed by the continuously
growing body of non-voters."

All of the studies cited in (9.16) observed increased reading times (as
measured via eye-tracking in the Finnish study and via self-paced
reading elsewhere) for the unambiguously marked clause-initial objects
in comparison to subjects in the same position. Whereas, from the
perspective of a strictly head-driven approach, one might argue that the
processing disadvantages for the structures in (9.15) reflect increased
integration costs at the position of the verb rather than reanalysis, the
findings for the unambiguous sentences in (9.16) are very difficult to
reconcile with a head-driven account. First attempts to model these
disadvantages for object-initial orders via differences in the frequency
of occurrence of object- vs. subject-initial sentences revealed that the
correspondence between the two domains is not trivial. Firstly, a strong
processing disadvantage for initial objects is observed even in sentence
constructions in which the frequency ratio of subject-initial:object-
initial sentences is approximately 1:1, e.g. in wh-questions in German
(Fanselow et al. 1999a). Secondly, native speakers have been shown to
have very fine-grained intuitions about the relative acceptability of
structures which do not occur in large-scale corpora (Crocker and
Keller 2006; Kempen and Harbusch 2005). Hence, while the basic
observation of a subject-first preference is generally in accordance
with corpus frequencies, it has not yet been demonstrated how entirely

frequency-based approaches might derive the very fine-grained distinctions that can be observed with respect to word order processing. This observation therefore suggests that the processing costs observed cannot be fully reduced to frequency-based mismatches, but that they rather appear to reflect properties of incremental, pre-verbal sentence analysis (but see Levy 2008, for a recent probabilistic approach).

9.2.2 Beyond grammatical functions: Pre-verbal thematic interpretation

The empirical findings described in section 9.2.1 can clearly be interpreted as evidence for the assignment of grammatical functions prior to the verb (for a more fine-grained neurocognitive investigation, see section 9.3). However, as grammatical functions and thematic relations typically covaried in these studies (i.e. the subject was also the argument bearing the higher-ranking thematic role), these two levels of analysis are difficult to tease apart. The first study to examine whether the assignment of grammatical functions is in fact driven by thematic considerations during online comprehension was reported by Scheepers, Hemforth, and Konieczny (2000).

(9.17)   Example sentence from Scheepers et al. (2000)
Vielleicht   ängstigte   die stille Schülerin
perhaps   frightened   [the quiet pupil][NOM/ACC]
der strenge Lehrer   ein   wenig,   so wurde vermutet
[the strict teacher][NOM]   a   little   so was   suspected
"People suspected that the strict teacher perhaps frightened the quiet pupil a little."

Scheepers and colleagues varied the type of verb preceding the arguments such that it was either a "subject-experiencer" verb (i.e. a verb assigning the Experiencer role to the subject such as *fürchten*, "to fear") or an "object-experiencer" verb (i.e. a verb assigning the Experiencer role to the object such as *ängstigen*, "to frighten" in 9.17). Assuming that the Experiencer argument always outranks its co-argument (Theme or Stimulus) on the thematic hierarchy and that an ambiguous argument is preferentially associated with the higher-ranking thematic role, the processing of a case-ambiguous argument following an object-experiencer verb should lead to a preference for an object-initial structure. However, the authors observed a general disadvantage for the object-initial reading in terms of first-pass reading times at the disambiguating position (NP2). By contrast, the regression path durations for the sentence-final adverbial phrase revealed an interaction between word order and verb class, thereby indicating that – sentence-finally – object-initial orders were easier to process in the context of an accusative object-experiencer verb. Scheepers et al. thus concluded that the preference for subject-initial structures is not derivable from thematic properties.

As already noted by Scheepers and colleagues, a potential caveat with respect to this interpretation concerns the type of verbs examined in their experiment. Similarly to object-experiencer verbs in English (Grimshaw 1990; Pesetsky 1994), accusative object-experiencer verbs in German have been described as causative in many theoretical analyses (e.g. Wunderlich 1997; Primus 1999; Fanselow 2000). As a consequence, the nominative argument is potentially a Causer rather than a Theme/Stimulus, thereby outranking the Experiencer on the thematic hierarchy. It thus appears plausible that, on account of the availability of the causative reading, these types of verbs cannot override the subject-first preference. Nonetheless, as a result of the ambiguity between the two readings, the object-initial structure is rendered more acceptable and thereby easier to integrate sentence-finally.

This problem can be overcome by using dative object-experiencer verbs, which are undisputedly associated with a "true" object-experiencer reading in which the object outranks the subject in terms of thematic properties.[1] Using a similar design to Scheepers et al. (2000) in an ERP study, Schlesewsky and Bornkessel (2006; see also Bornkessel 2002; and Schlesewsky and Bornkessel 2004) examined the processing of case-ambiguous arguments following dative object-experiencer verbs (9.18).

(9.18)   Example sentence from Schlesewsky and Bornkessel (2006)
         Vielleicht   gefällt   Richard
         perhaps   is.pleasing.to   Richard[NOM/ACC/DAT]
         der Regisseur...
         [the director] [NOM]...
         "Perhaps the director is pleasing/appealing to Richard..."

Even though behavioral studies attest to the fact that, in sentences with dative object-experiencer verbs, object-initial orders are more acceptable than their counterparts with active verbs (Schlesewsky and Bornkessel 2003; Bornkessel et al. 2004b; Haupt et al. 2008), sentences of the type in (9.18) show a subject preference. This was reflected in increased processing costs (in the form of an N400) at the position of the second NP when this NP was marked for nominative as opposed to dative. (For further discussion of the "reanalysis N400" see section 9.3). This finding thereby supports the interpretation advanced by Scheepers et al. (2000) that the preference for subject-initiality in ambiguous structures is independent of thematic properties.

Perhaps somewhat surprisingly in view of these considerations, evidence for an immediate assignment of thematic relations has been observed in studies examining the processing of unambiguously case-marked structures. By manipulating the thematic properties of the clause-final verb such that they either confirmed the preferred mapping of a nominative argument onto the higher-ranking thematic role (active verbs; 9.19a) or disconfirmed it (object-experiencer verbs; 9.19b), Bornkessel, Schlesewsky, and Friederici (2002a; 2003b) were able to elicit a "thematic reanalysis effect" in a visual ERP study (see Leuckefeld 2005, for a replication in the auditory modality).

(9.19)   Example stimuli from Bornkessel et al. (2003b)
          Maria glaubt...
          Maria believes...

     a.   ... dass der Priester   dem Gärtner
          ... that [the priest][NOM]   [the gardener][DAT]
          folgt   und...
          follows   and...
          "... that the priest follows the gardener."

     b.   ... dass der Priester   dem Gärtner
          ... that [the priest][NOM]   [the gardener] [NOM]
          gefällt   und...
          is-pleasing/appealing-to   and...
          "... that gardener finds the priest appealing."

At the position of the clause-final verb, Bornkessel et al. observed an early parietal positivity (between approximately 300 and 600 ms) for object-experiencer as opposed to active verbs. This effect shows that the arguments must have been ranked thematically even before the verb was encountered (note that the difference between verb types cannot be attributed to lexical properties, see Bornkessel et al. 2002a; Schlesewsky and Bornkessel 2006). Since the early positivity occurred independently of argument order (nominative-dative vs. dative-nominative), thematic interpretation appears to hinge solely upon morphological case marking and not upon an argument's position in the sentence. Bornkessel et al. (2003b) argue that the thematic assignments undertaken prior to the verb do not involve individual thematic roles (such as Agent or Patient), but rather generalized roles such as Actor/Undergoer (Proto-Agent/Proto-Patient) or simply an interpretive hierarchy between arguments (see Box 9.1 for a discussion of the status of thematic information in sentence comprehension). Furthermore, as the above-mentioned independence of position-based preferences for the assignment of grammatical functions (the subject preference) would lead one to expect, case-ambiguous versions of sentences like (9.19) do not show a difference between active and object-experiencer verbs (Bornkessel et al. 2002a).[2]

A mirror image of these temporal aspects of relational argument interpretation (i.e. assignment of thematic relations in unambiguously case-marked but not in case-ambiguous structures, thematic reanalysis with object-experiencer verbs) can be found in the neuroanatomical domain. On the basis of an fMRI study using an analogous manipulation to that shown in (9.19), Bornkessel et al. (2005) concluded that increased effort in the processing of interpretive argument–argument relations correlates with activation in the posterior portion of the left superior temporal sulcus (pSTS). In an overall network of frontal, temporal, and parietal regions correlating with argument processing, the left pSTS was the only region that proved sensitive to all of the relevant factors outlined above. It is therefore the only region that has hitherto been identified as a possible neural substrate for the establishment of hierarchical thematic relations between arguments (for converging evidence, see Grewe et al. 2007).[3]

While morphological case clearly plays a very important role in preverbal argument interpretation, it is not the only information type involved. As in the discussion of verb-based relations in section 9.1, evidence in this regard again converges on one of the usual suspects, namely animacy. Example (9.20) provides a representative illustration of the interaction between case and animacy in verb-final structures (Frisch and Schlesewsky 2001; Roehm et al. 2004).

(9.20)   Example sentence from Frisch and Schlesewsky (2001)
         Peter fragt sich, . . .
         Peter asks himself . . .
         . . . welchen Lehrer   der Zweig   streifte.
         . . . [which teacher][ACC]   [the twig][NOM]   brushed
         ". . . which teacher the twig brushed against."

Box 9.1 On the status of thematic information in sentence comprehension

Thematic roles have long played a major role in all domains of linguistic explanation, including theory of grammar, language typology, and psycholinguistics/neurolinguistics. This strong degree of interest is grounded mainly in the need for suitable interface representations that can mediate between syntax and semantics. As thematic roles serve to characterize core relational meaning with a certain degree of abstraction, they have been implicated in the linking between the relevant semantic aspects of an underlying meaning and the abstract requirements of the corresponding surface form. However, despite the obvious appeal of such interface representations and the high degree of interest afforded to them during the last decades of linguistic research, there is still no fully satisfactory model of how the syntax-to-semantics linking is accomplished. One reason for this appears to lie in the problems regarding the definition and scope of thematic roles that have continually reappeared since the very beginnings of research in this domain (Gruber 1965; Fillmore 1968; Jackendoff 1972). For example, researchers made vastly differing assumptions with regard to how many roles should be assumed, how these should be characterized both in semantic and in syntactic terms, how the different roles can be dissociated from one another, and which syntactic phenomena should be derivable from them.

Essentially, the literature suggests two possible ways of overcoming these difficulties. On the one hand, it has been proposed that the hierarchical relations between thematic roles are more important with regard to the form-to-meaning mapping than the content of individual roles (Jackendoff 1972; Bierwisch 1988; Bresnan and Kanerva 1989; Grimshaw 1990; Wunderlich 1997). While the further degree of abstraction provided by a hierarchy-based approach resulted in a major advance in the characterization of linking properties, the formulation of hierarchies in terms of individual role labels is inherently subject to similar problems as the individual roles themselves. Thus, a number of conflicting hierarchies have been proposed, all of which can account for certain syntactic phenomena, but at the same time fail to provide a comprehensive solution to the challenges of argument linking (for discussion, see Levin and Rappaport Hovav 2005; Primus 2006).

A second type of approach to the problems described above lies in the assumption of "generalized semantic roles" (GSRs), which have been referred to as macroroles (Foley and Van Valin 1984), proto-roles (Dowty 1991), and hyperroles (Kibrik 1997). GSRs differ from individual semantic roles in that they abstract over the content of several individual roles and therefore allow for a highly reduced role inventory (typically including only two generalized roles). By focusing on a small number of role oppositions, GSRs appear well suited to modeling argument linking. However, this obvious advantage comes at the cost of a reduced degree of semantic resolution such that fine-grained differences between, say, volitional Agents and inadvertent Causers must be expressed at a different level of representation.

This "grain problem" with regard to the nature of thematic roles also carries over to the psycholinguistic domain. Thus, one major question to be addressed by psycholinguistic models of language comprehension concerns the nature of the thematic representations used during language comprehension. A second and equally important issue relates to the time course of thematic processing: if thematic information is viewed as psychologically real, does it serve to determine the syntactic analysis or can it simply constrain it?

With regard to the question of how thematic information is represented, most psycholinguistic approaches have drawn upon the theoretical assumptions of Government and Binding Theory (Chomsky 1981). From this perspective, the lexical entry of a verb is assumed to contain a thematic grid which specifies the number and type of thematic roles assigned by the verb (e.g. *hit* <Agent, Patient>). In constraint-based approaches, it is typically assumed that this information is immediately available as soon as the verb is processed and that it may serve to drive processing preferences independently of syntactic information (e.g. Carlson and Tanenhaus 1988). This view thus postulates that thematic information can influence initial structure-building. Advocates of two-stage approaches, by contrast, have proposed that thematic information comes in *after* an initial (syntactic) stage of processing and is then used to check the syntactic (phrase structure) assignments. Perhaps the most well-known approach of this kind was put forward in the form of Rayner et al.'s (1983) "thematic processor". Rayner and colleagues assumed that this processor, which was thought to operate independently of the syntactic analysis of the sentence and to not influence initial syntactic processing choices, "[e]xamines the alternative thematic structures of a word (to compare the relative plausibility of each) and selects the semantically and pragmatically most plausible one" (Rayner et al. 1983: 371).

An alternative view of thematic information during sentence processing has been put forward by Ken McRae and his colleagues (e.g. McRae, Ferretti, and

Amyote 1997; McRae, Spivey-Knowlton, and Tanenhaus 1998; Ferretti, McRae, and Hatherell 2001). Within the overall scope of an interactive processing architecture, these investigators have assumed that thematic information is even more fine-grained than typical theoretical approaches to individual thematic roles (like Agent, Theme, Experiencer) would propose. In their approach, the lexical entry of a verb not only contains a specification of the thematic roles assigned by that verb but also of typical fillers for those roles (e.g. *detective* is a highly typical filler for the Agent role of *arrest*, but a low typicality filler for the Patient role of this verb; the reverse is true for *crook*). As in other constraint-based approaches, McRae and colleagues assume that thematic information – in the sense of these world knowledge-based role specifications – is immediately accessed when the verb is processed and that it may thus influence syntactic structure building.

In our own approach to sentence processing, we have advocated an approach that is diametrically opposed to that of MacRae and colleagues. From this perspective, the thematic relations constructed during sentence comprehension are based entirely on generalized semantic roles (Bornkessel 2002; Bornkessel et al. 2003b; Schlesewsky and Bornkessel 2004; Bornkessel and Schlesewsky 2006a; Bornkessel-Schlesewsky and Schlesewsky 2009). We have argued that the assumption of generalized roles, which serve to emphasize the hierarchical dependency between the arguments rather than specific semantic aspects of their interpretation, may help to account for the incremental interpretation of arguments in verb-final sentences. See Chapter 15.4 for a more detailed discussion of these theoretical claims.

In summary, when considering the status of thematic information in sentence comprehension, at least two separate dimensions must be considered, namely the grain size of the thematic representations and the time-course of their application. Both issues have been subject to substantial debate in the psycholinguistic literature. Finally, if it is indeed the case that thematic information can be assigned pre-verbally in verb-final structures (see section 9.2.2), the way in which this information is extracted online must also be considered.

At the position of the inanimate nominative-marked NP in the subordinate clause in (9.20), an N400 was observable in comparison to an animate nominative in the same position. Crucially, this effect cannot simply be due to the inherent animacy difference between the nouns, as there was no analogous effect in the comparison between the accusative-marked second NPs in two subject-initial structures in the same experiment. Furthermore, the N400 in these structures also does not appear to reflect the costs of processing an inanimate nominative argument per se (e.g. due to the relative infrequency of inanimate subjects): an experiment using the identical stimuli to Frisch and Schlesewsky (2001) revealed no comparable effect for inanimate vs. animate subjects in the clause-initial position (Ott 2004). Thus, only the processing of an inanimate nominative *following* an (animate) accusative gives rise to an increased N400. This effect can be explained as follows: when the initial accusative is encountered, it is interpreted as a lower-ranking thematic argument (Undergoer) on the basis of its case marking (see above). In a language such as German, this entails that a higher-ranking (nominative-marked) argument must be encountered at some later point in the clause. Since the prediction of an "ideal" higher-ranking argument (Actor or Proto-Agent, see Box 9.1) entails not only nominative case marking but also the interpretive properties associated with such an argument – including the fact that this type of argument should ideally be animate rather than inanimate – only an animate nominative in second position can fully satisfy this prediction. The divergence from the predicted prototype engenders increased processing effort at the relational interpretive level and is thus reflected in an N400.

Findings of this type are not restricted to German but have also been observed in English sentences such as (9.21), thus attesting to a more general association between animacy, relational argument processing, and the N400.

(9.21) Example sentences from Weckerly and Kutas (1999)

    a. The <u>novelist</u> that the <u>movie</u> inspired praised the director for staying true to the complicated ending.

    b. The <u>movie</u> that the <u>novelist</u> praised inspired the director to stay true to the complicated ending.

In addition to a number of further effects, Weckerly and Kutas observed an N400 for inanimate vs. animate first nouns as well as a further N400 at the position of the relative clause subject in (9.21a) vs. (9.21b) (*movie* vs. *novelist*). The N400 effect for the first noun might be taken as an indication of the conflict between the position-based tendency to interpret the first argument as thematically highest-ranking in English (see Note 2) and the inanimacy of this argument. By contrast, the second N400 effect closely mirrors the findings from German (9.20) in that the processing of an inanimate subject following an animate object requires increased processing effort.[4] Very similar results were obtained by Mak, Vonk, and Schriefers (2006), who used eye-tracking to examine the influence of animacy in the processing of relative clauses in Dutch (see Chapter 10).

Taken together, these findings of non-lexical animacy effects prior to the verb in verb-final constructions provide strong converging support for pre-verbal argument interpretation (i.e. for the pre-verbal assignment of (generalized) thematic roles). They further suggest that incremental argument interpretation (a) involves a predictive component, and that, at least in a language like German, it is (b) inherently relational in nature (i.e. increased processing costs due to animacy mismatches are only observable when more than one argument has already been processed). Strikingly, as shown by recent findings from Mandarin Chinese, the applicability of this type of processing mechanism is neither confined to verb-final languages nor to languages with morphological case marking. Thus, in an auditory ERP experiment examining Chinese sentences such as (9.22), Philipp et al. (2008) observed an N400 at the position of an inanimate Actor argument following an initial Undergoer argument.

(9.22) a. 王子　　　被　挑战者　　　刺死　了
        wáng zǐ　bèi　tiǎo zhàn zhě　cì sǐ　le
        Prince　bèi　contender　　stab　PFV
        "The prince was stabbed by the contender."

    b. 王子　　　被　绳子　　勒死　　　了
        wáng zǐ　bèi　shéng zi　lēi sǐ　le
        Prince　bèi　cord　　strangle　PFV
        "The prince was strangled by the cord."

The examples in (9.22) illustrate the so-called bèi-construction in Mandarin Chinese, which is often described as a passive-like construction.[5] Crucially for present purposes, the coverb *bèi* unambiguously identifies the first argument as an Undergoer, thus leading to an analogous comprehension situation to that in the German examples in (9.20). Just as in German, the processing of an Actor argument that is lower on the animacy hierarchy than the preceding Undergoer argument gave rise to an N400 effect in Mandarin Chinese (Philipp et al. 2008). Note that, using further experimental conditions, Philipp and colleagues also contrasted animate and inanimate initial NPs (which were lexically identical to the critical second NPs) and found no difference in terms of ERPs. This observation therefore again shows that the effect in question does not result from simple animacy differences at the single argument level but that it must rather be analyzed as a correlate of relational argument processing.

To summarize the last two sections, there is a great deal of evidence to suggest that, even before the verb is encountered, assignments and predictions are made with respect to both the interpretation of individual arguments and the hierarchical interpretive relation between arguments.

9.2.3 *Argument–argument relations vs. verb–argument relations: A comparison*

Having introduced some fundamental characteristics of the processing of argument–argument relations, a natural next question concerns how these relations might be integrated into the overall picture introduced earlier. In this regard, the possible relation between argument–argument and verb–argument dependencies is of particular interest. We have already outlined above that – even in terms of the very fine-grained temporal dissociations permitted by ERPs – these two domains appear to be processed within a similar time range. This initial observation fits well with the distinction between constituent structure and relational structure that was derived in Chapter 8 and section 9.1, since argument–argument relations are also clearly attributable to the post-constituent-structure domain. Yet how should the interaction between verb–argument and argument–argument relations be envisioned? Do the two interact during processing (e.g. in the sense that one information type hierarchically dominates the other) or are they kept separate?

These questions were addressed in a study by Roehm et al. (2005), which combined an agreement violation with a violation belonging to the domain of argument–argument relations (9.23) (for an example of a single agreement violation in this study, see example 9.4g).

(9.23)   Example stimuli from Roehm et al. (2005)

    a. Combined agreement and double case violation
        *Den Auftrag   bearbeiten   ihn
        [the order][ACC.SG]   process-3.PL   he[ACC.SG]

> dennoch   nicht.
> nevertheless   not

b. Grammatical control

> Den Auftrag   bearbeiten   sie
> [the order][ACC.SG]   process-3.PL   they[NOM.PL]
> dennoch   nicht.
> nevertheless   not

"Nevertheless, they did not process the order."

The logic of the study is based on the well-established assumptions of case-based processing predictions (see example 9.20 above). When the initial accusative argument and the verb have been processed, at least two predictions are open: a prediction for a nominative argument and a prediction for an argument that agrees with the verb (and should therefore bear plural number marking in the context of the present example). In the grammatical control condition (9.23b), the pronoun immediately right-adjacent to the verb fulfilled both of these predictions. In the critical condition (9.23a), both predictions were violated by the pronoun encountered in this position. While the agreement violation per se should be expected to engender a LAN-P600 pattern (see section 9.1.1), the predictions for the case violation were based on a number of previous studies in German, all of which had observed an N400-P600 pattern for sentences with two identically case-marked arguments. This pattern occurred at the position of the second NP in both NP–V–NP and NP–NP–V structures and can thus be interpreted as reflecting the processing of (verb-independent) argument–argument relations (Frisch 2000; Frisch and Schlesewsky 2001; Frisch and Schlesewsky 2005). As expected, structures such as (9.23a) engendered all three critical components, a LAN, an N400, and a P600, thus attesting to the fact that verb–argument and argument–argument relations are processed within the same time range but separately from one another (i.e. neither of the two effects "blocks" the other).

One of the interesting conclusions that can be drawn from these observations and that has not yet been discussed concerns the relation between the role of case in the argument–argument as opposed to the argument–verb domain. While processing conflicts with respect to the former engender an N400 (see the discussion of the Roehm et al. study above), conflicts in the latter are associated with a LAN (see section 9.1.2, example 9.9). This distinction indexes the different functions played by morphological case in each domain: while its role is clearly interpretive in nature in the argument–argument domain, it appears more formal (almost akin to that of agreement) in the verb–argument domain. Thus, violations of subcategorized object case involve the processing of an unlicensed case marker. In double case violations, by contrast, the case of the argument inducing the violation is always licensed by the verb (or the clause in the case of nominative), while the conflict obtains with respect to the interpretive hierarchization of both arguments (i.e. with respect to the question of "who is acting on whom"). In a language such as English, by contrast, in which case morphology has lost its interpretive capacity, a LAN is observable even for structures very similar to double case violations in German (e.g. *The plane took we to paradise and back.*; Coulson et al. 1998b).

The multidimensional nature of case as reflected in its roles as both an interpretive and a formal feature will be explored further in the next section, in which we examine the relationship between case and argument position.

9.2.4 *Case marking and word order permutations*

Approaches to word order permutations in psycholinguistics have traditionally focused mainly on wh-questions and relative clauses. This can plausibly be attributed to two reasons. On the one hand, English does not permit object-initial orders in many other constructions. On the other, the distinction between competence and performance (Chomsky and Miller 1963), which provided a major impulse for early psycholinguistic research, originally also focused on the processing limitations observable in complex constructions. In this section, we depart from this traditional perspective in that we will examine the processing of argument order in simple sentences (for a discussion of complex constructions, see Chapter 10). Furthermore, to avoid potential confounds due to reanalysis processes, we will focus on the processing of unambiguous sentences, in which the case (grammatical function) of the first argument is immediately clear when that argument is processed. From this perspective, four types of relevant structures can be distinguished.

(9.24)   Structure types of interest in the examination of word order permutations
   a. permutation to the clause-initial position (declarative)
   b. permutation to the clause-initial position (wh)
   c. permutation to a clause-medial position (declarative)
   d. permutation to a clause-medial position (wh)

We distinguish between permutations to clause-medial and clause-initial positions because this distinction has been shown to have a fundamental influence on the neurocognitive processing correlates of object-initial orders in German (see below). In other languages, the distinction is more difficult to make and/or there is little or no empirical evidence on how it might relate to processing. Finally, not all languages allow a distinction between the two types of wh-clauses in (9.24) on account of requirements on the positioning of the wh-phrase. However, such a difference is potentially relevant to the processing of Japanese, which will be discussed below.

Word order permutations have played a significant role in psycholinguistic and neurolinguistic theory in at least three respects. Firstly, they are clearly of interest from a linguistic perspective, since they can potentially be used to address questions related to the dislocation of elements and their reconstruction (e.g. with respect to the debate on the psychological reality of traces; for discussion, see Fodor 1995). Secondly, these constructions have been of great interest to researchers interested in the interaction between language and cognitive processing at a more general level. Thus, it is widely assumed that the dislocation of an element leads to increased working memory costs, since this element must be maintained in memory until it can be integrated into its base position/associated with its subcategorizer. Finally, word order phenomena are significant from a neurocognitive perspective because they are associated with one of the most reliably observed neuroanatomical correlates of sentence-level language comprehension.

9.2.4.1 Neuroanatomical correlates of word order permutations   From a neuroanatomical perspective, word order processing has come to be closely tied to Broca's region (see Plate 2B). Recall from Chapter 2 that the classical neurological perspective on this region – namely that it is primarily responsible for language production – has been questioned on the basis of both patient and neuroimaging data. In fact, the patient findings that first called this long-standing correlation into question came from the word order domain. Consider the following examples.

(9.25)   a. This is the boy who chased the girl.
          b. This is the boy who the girl chased.
          c. This is the mouse that the cat chased.

As firstly shown by Caramazza and Zurif (1976), patients with Broca's aphasia have no problems in understanding subject cleft sentences such as (9.25a), but show chance-level performance for object clefts such as (9.25b). When the relation between the arguments is semantically biased (as in 9.25c), by contrast, they again perform well. This pattern of results was interpreted as evidence for a specific grammatical deficit, since these ("agrammatic") patients apparently cannot reconstruct an object-initial word order when there is no semantic cue to help them do so. The subsequent discussion of findings of this type has been strongly associated with the name of Yosef Grodzinsky and his "trace deletion hypothesis", which assumes that agrammatic patients are specifically impaired with respect to the reconstruction of a dislocated element to its base (i.e. trace) position (see Grodzinsky 2000 and the references cited therein). For an alternative position, which maintains that grammatical knowledge is preserved in these patients and that their comprehension impairment rather results from a deficit in mapping syntactic relations onto thematic roles, see Linebarger, Schwartz, and Saffran (1983) and Mauner, Fromkin, and Cornell (1993).

In the domain of unimpaired language comprehension, a reliable association between Broca's region and word order processing has been established via neuroimaging. The first fMRI study to observe such a correlation in unambiguously marked, simple sentence structures of the type to be focused upon in this section was reported by Röder et al. (2002). Note, however, that this study must also be viewed as part of a longer neuroimaging tradition examining word order and Broca's region in complex constructions in English. These findings will be discussed in Chapter 10.

(9.26)   Example stimuli from Röder et al. (2002)

    a. Complex

       Jetzt   wird   dem Forscher   den Mond
       now   will   [the scientist][DAT]   [the moon][ACC]
       der Astronaut   beschreiben.
       [the astronaut][NOM]   describe
       "Now the astronaut will describe the moon to the scientist."

    b. Simple

       Jetzt   wird   der Astronaut   dem Forscher
       now   will   [the astronaut][NOM]   [the scientist][DAT]
       den Mond   beschreiben.
       [the moon][ACC]   describe
       "Now the astronaut will describe the moon to the scientist."

   c. Pseudoword complex (PW = pseudoword)
Jetzt   wird   dem Schorfer   den Rond
now   will   [the PW][DAT]   [the PW][ACC]
der Trosanaut   bebreuschen.
[the PW][NOM]   PW

   d. Pseudoword simple
Jetzt   wird   der Trosanaut   dem Schorfer
now   will   [the PW][NOM]   [the PW][DAT]
den Rond   bebreuschen.
[the PW][ACC]   PW

For the comparison between structures with an object-before-subject order (in which both the direct and the indirect object preceded the subject, e.g. 9.26a) and subject-initial structures (either with the unmarked[6] word order shown in 9.26b or with the direct object preceding the indirect object), Röder et al. observed increased activation within the pars opercularis (BA 44) and pars triangularis (BA 45) of the left inferior frontal gyrus (IFG), i.e. within two subregions of Broca's area (see Plate 2A).[7] As will become clear below, the pars opercularis in particular appears to be highly sensitive to word order processing. In addition, the Röder et al. study examined the processing of pseudoword sentences (e.g. 9.26c/d), in which the words were devoid of lexical meaning but retained morphosyntactically relevant information (e.g. case marking). The word vs. pseudoword manipulation interacted with the word order manipulation within the inferior frontal area described above, i.e. the effect of word order in this region was larger for sentences with real words. On the basis of this observation, Röder and colleagues concluded that this region "might specifically contribute to the use of syntactic structure to compute the meaning of a sentence" (Röder et al. 2002: 1011).

While the word order manipulation employed by Röder et al. (2002) only differentiated between "difficult" (DAT-ACC-NOM/ACC-DAT-NOM) and "easy" (NOM-DAT-ACC/NOM-ACC-DAT) sentences, subsequent research revealed that the pars opercularis of the left IFG (BA 44) is in fact sensitive to parametric variations of word order. This was shown for German using similar structures to those in the Röder et al. experiment (Friederici et al. 2006b).

(9.27)   Example of a medium-complexity sentence from Friederici et al. (2006b)

Heute   hat   dem Jungen   der Opa
today   has   [the boy][DAT]   [the grandfather][NOM]

den Lutscher   geschenkt.
[the lollipop][ACC]   given
"Today the grandfather gave the lollipop to the boy."

In Friederici and colleagues' fMRI study, the activation of the pars opercularis directly correlated with the number of deviations from the unmarked word order. Hence, the studies discussed so far indicate that the pars opercularis (BA 44) is highly sensitive to syntactic complexity. This pattern of results is potentially compatible with a number of more specific interpretations, i.e. the increased activation might result from (a) an increased number of permutations (Grodzinsky 2000; Grodzinsky and Friederici 2006), (b) a decrease in acceptability, (c) an increase in working memory load (e.g. Stowe et al. 1998; Caplan et al. 2000; Kaan and Swaab 2002; Müller, Kleinhans, and Courchesne 2003; Fiebach et al. 2005), or (d) a decrease in frequency of occurrence. These possible options were examined more closely in several further studies.

A study indicating that the activation pattern of the left pars opercularis (BA 44) cannot be straightforwardly reduced to any of these factors was reported by Grewe et al. (2005).

(9.28) Example sentences from Grewe et al. (2005)

    a.   Permuted non-pronominal object
        Dann   hat   dem Gärtner   der Lehrer
        then   has   [the gardener][DAT]   [the teacher][NOM]
        den Spaten   gegeben.
        [the spade][ACC]   given
        "Then the teacher gave the spade to the gardener."

    b.   Permuted pronominal object
        Dann   hat   ihm   der Lehrer
        then   has   him[DAT]   [the teacher][NOM]
        den Spaten   gegeben.
        [the spade][ACC]   given
        "Then the teacher gave him the spade."

    c.   Combined condition
        Dann   hat   ihm   den Spaten
        then   has   him[DAT]   [the spade][ACC]
        der Lehrer   gegeben.
        given   [the teacher][NOM]
        "Then the teacher gave him the spade."

The logic of the manipulation employed by Grewe and colleagues was as follows. Sentences with a pronominal object at the left edge of the German *middlefield*[8] are unmarked on account of an independent principle requiring pronouns to precede non-pronominal arguments in the middlefield (i.e. pronouns are fronted to the so-called "Wackernagel" position, e.g. Bierwisch 1963; Lenerz 1977). Thus, while sentences such as (9.28b) – like minimally differing sentences with a non-pronominal initial object (9.28a) – involve the dislocation of an object to the left of the subject (thereby requiring increased working memory resources) and are less frequent than their subject-initial counterparts, they are just as acceptable as comparable subject-initial sentences. By contrast, structures such as (9.28a) engender a pronounced acceptability drop in the absence of a suitable context. The difference between (9.28b) and (9.28a) can therefore be characterized as a contrast between a "licensed" and an "unlicensed" dislocation. Condition (9.28c) combines both types of dislocation and, crucially for the purposes of the study, is associated with an even greater acceptability drop than (9.28a). The activation patterns predicted by the competing explanations described above are summarized in (9.29).

(9.29)   Predictions for the stimuli used by Grewe et al. (2005) in different approaches

    a. Number of permutations: $c > a = b$
    b. Working memory: $c > a \geq b$ (and $b >$ control)
    c. Frequency: $c > a > b$ (and $b >$ control)
    d. Acceptability: $c > a > b$ (and $b =$ control)
    e. Licensing of permutations: $c = a > b$ (and $b =$ control)

The results of Grewe et al.'s (2005) study are shown in Plate 3. Object-initial sentences without pronouns (9.28a) gave rise to a significant increase in pars opercularis activation in comparison to the subject-initial control condition (see Plate 3B). By contrast, no such activation increase was observed for the condition with an initial pronominal object (9.28b; see Plate 3A). Finally, the activation engendered by the combined condition (9.28c) did not differ from that for the non-pronominal object-initial condition (9.28a). These results are compatible only with the "licensing-based" account outlined in (9.29e) and thus formed the basis for a new account of pars opercularis function in the processing of word order permutations, the "linearization hypothesis". This account assumes that pars opercularis activation reflects the interaction of a range of principles governing linear order in language. Further converging support for the linearization hypothesis was observed in a series of studies showing an influence of the linearization of thematic role information (Bornkessel et al. 2005), animacy (Grewe et al. 2006), and definiteness/specificity (Bornkessel-Schlesewsky, Schlesewsky, and von Cramon submitted) on pars opercularis activation.

Interestingly, an fMRI study on the processing of unambiguous object-initial orders in declarative main clauses in German (i.e. permutations of type 9.24a rather than 9.24c) revealed increased activation with a maximum in the pars triangularis of the left IFG (BA 45) rather than in the pars opercularis (Bahlmann et al. 2007). An example of an object-initial sentence from this study is given in (9.30). (Note that Bahlmann and colleagues also examined locally ambiguous sentences requiring a reanalysis towards an object-initial order, see Note 15.)

(9.30)   Example stimulus from Bahlmann et al. (2007)

> Den   begabten   Sänger   entdeckte   während
> [the   gifted   singer][ACC]   discovered   during
> der   Weihnachtsfeier   der   talentierte   Gitarrist.
> the   christmas.party   [the   talented   guitar.player] [ACC]
> "The talented guitar player discovered the gifted singer during the Christmas party."

The discrepancy between Bahlmann et al.'s (2007) finding of activation in BA 45 and previous observations of BA 44 activation for word order permutations in German could be due to several factors.[9] On the one hand, the differences might be related to some aspect of the distinction between main and subordinate clauses or to differences in the sentence-initial as opposed to non-initial positioning of objects. On the other hand, they could be due to the different properties of the German middlefield (as examined in previous studies; see also Note 8) and prefield (the clause-initial position, as examined by Bahlmann and colleagues). In contrast to the middlefield, the prefield can host only a single constituent and it need not be occupied by a subject in order for the sentence to be unmarked (i.e. it could also be filled by an adverb or a prepositional phrase in an unmarked sentence). Theoretical accounts of German syntax thus typically assume that the prefield is a derived position (Drach 1939). This means that all arguments in the prefield – even subjects – must have undergone movement and thus cannot be interpreted in this position (for an alternative view, see Travis 1984). However, pending further investigation, the data currently available cannot distinguish between an account based on these rather fine-grained aspects of German syntax and other alternative explanations.

Interestingly, there is some initial cross-linguistic evidence to suggest that the shift between word order-related activation maxima in BA 45 and BA 44 may indeed be somehow related to the positioning of the object within the overall clause. In an auditory fMRI study on argument order permutations in Hebrew, Ben-Shachar, Palti, and Grodzinsky (2004) observed increased activation in the left IFG for object-initial main clauses such as (9.31).

(9.31)   Example sentences from Ben-Shachar et al. (2004)

    a. Topicalization (OSV order)
       'et ha-sefer ha-'adom   John   natan
       [ACC the-book the –red]   John   gave
       la-professor   me-oxford
       [to-the-professor   from-Oxford]
       "John gave the red book to the professor from Oxford."

    b. Control (SVO order)
       John   natan   'et ha-sefer ha-'adom
       John   gave   [ACC the-book the –red]
       la-professor   me-oxford
       [to-the-professor   from-Oxford]
       "John gave the red book to the professor from Oxford."

For sentences with a fronted object such as (9.31a), Ben-Shachar and colleagues observed increased activation within the left pars triangularis (BA 45) and pars opercularis (BA 44) in comparison to subject-initial sentences such as (9.31b). As in the study by Bahlmann et al. (2007), the activation maximum was located in BA 45. Increased activation for object- vs. subject-initial sentences with a maximum in BA 45 has also been reported for Japanese (Kinno et al. 2008). These findings from languages which lack the prefield–middlefield distinction and in which object scrambling or topicalization thus typically targets the clause-initial position are thus very similar to those for German main clauses.

Interestingly, Ben-Shachar et al. did not observe an activation increase within the left IFG for a second type of word order permutation, in which an indirect (dative) object was positioned in front of a direct (accusative) object (a phenomenon which, in analogy to English, the authors describe as "dative shift"). Here, the more marked word order engendered increased activation in the right anterior insula and right ventral precentral sulcus, thus leading the authors to conclude that different movement types may be associated with differing neural correlates. In other words, only A-bar movement (see Haegeman 1994, for a introduction) is supposed to engender increased activation in the left IFG. While the finding of different activations for the different types of word order permutations in Hebrew is certainly very interesting, an explanation of these distinctions in terms of different kinds of movement operations appears somewhat problematic. On the one hand, scrambling in German – which, as described above, reliably yields activation increases within the pars opercularis – is often described in terms of A-movement (e.g. Haider and Rosengren 2003). On the other hand, superficially similar word order variations to Ben-Shachar et al.'s "dative shift" examples have been shown to lead to increased activation of the left pars opercularis in Japanese (Koizumi 2005). Taken together, the studies on Japanese and German therefore suggest that all deviations from the unmarked argument order (nominative-dative-accusative in these two languages) can be correlated with a modulation of activation within the pars opercularis. A possible explanation for why Hebrew deviates from this pattern might be that dative arguments are realized as prepositional phrases in this language and that they are thereby subject to different linearization parameters to dative arguments in German and Japanese. Most notably, datives in Hebrew follow accusatives in the unmarked order, which therefore does not correspond to the thematic hierarchy (i.e. recipients follow patients despite the fact that they are higher-ranking from a thematic perspective). As deviations from the linear argument order which corresponds to the thematic hierarchy have been shown to engender increased pars opercularis activation (Bornkessel et al. 2005) and this thematic influence appears to be equally strong to deviations from the default order of grammatical functions in a particular language (see Grewe et al. 2006), the linearization hypothesis would predict approximately equal pars opercularis activation for unmarked (NOM ACC DAT) and "dative shifted" (NOM DAT ACC) orders in Hebrew.

A second potential confounding factor in Ben Shachar et al.'s (2004) contrast between sentences involving dative shift and control sentences stems from the animacy of the arguments. In this experiment, indirect (dative) objects were always animate, whereas direct (accusative) objects were always inanimate. As demonstrated by Grewe et al. (2006) for German, the relative order of animate and inanimate arguments can modulate activation within the pars opercularis. Consider the sentences in (9.32).

(9.32)   Example stimuli from Grewe et al. (2006)

       a. Dann   wurde   dem   Arzt   der Mantel
           then   was   [the   doctor][DAT]   [the coat][NOM]
           gestohlen.
           stolen
           "Then the coat was stolen from the doctor."

       b. Dann   wurde   der Mantel   dem Arzt
           then   was   [the coat][NOM]   [the doctor][DAT]
           gestohlen.
           stolen
           "Then the coat was stolen from the doctor."

Strikingly, Grewe and colleagues observed *increased activation* for *subject-initial* sentences such as (9.32b) in comparison to their object-initial counterparts (9.32a) within the pars opercularis, i.e. increased activation for sentences with an inanimate-before-animate order. As comparable conditions with two animate arguments did not yield an activation difference within this region, the activation increase for (9.32b) can be unambiguously attributed to the influence of animacy.

In summary, and independently of the precise nature of the explanation given, it seems undisputed that neural activity within the left pars opercularis (BA 44) correlates with word order variations. Under certain circumstances, which remain to be specified precisely but may correlate with the sentence-initial position, this activation appears to spread into the pars triangularis (BA 45). (See Plate 4 for an overview of the relevant findings.) Furthermore, the word order-related principles engendering activation differences within the pars opercularis are by no means entirely syntactic in nature, but rather stem from a variety of domains known to influence linear order in language.

9.2.4.2 Argument order variations from a temporal perspective   In addition to yielding very robust neuroanatomical findings, argument order variations can also be associated with rather fine-grained temporal

processing patterns. The earliest study to examine the processing of unambiguously marked object-initial structures in simple sentences was conducted by Rösler et al. (1998), who examined the processing of clause-medial argument order variations in German ("scrambling") in sentences similar to those used in the fMRI study by Röder et al. (2002) (see 9.26). Rösler and colleagues observed a negativity between approximately 300 and 450 ms in response to the determiner signaling an initial scrambled object in comparison to a nominative (subject) determiner in the same position. The authors classified this component as a LAN and argued that it reflects working memory-related processes (since a dislocated object must be maintained in working memory until it can be integrated into its base position). A number of subsequent findings confirmed this observation of a negativity in response to scrambled structures, while also showing that the topographical distribution of this effect often differs from that of a classical LAN. Rather, the negativity is central, but with a focus to the left (Bornkessel, Schlesewsky, and Friederici 2002b; Bornkessel, Schlesewsky, and Friederici 2003a; Schlesewsky, Bornkessel, and Frisch 2003). On account of this distribution, which is difficult to associate unambiguously with either an N400 or a LAN, Bornkessel et al. (2002b; 2003a) and Schlesewsky et al. (2003) coined the (topographically neutral) term "scrambling negativity" on the basis of the component's functional interpretation.

The "scrambling negativity" shows striking similarities to the neuroanatomical correlates for the processing of scrambled sentences in that it is (a) cross-linguistically stable, and (b) subject to similarly fine-grained distinctions as those demonstrated for the pars opercularis. With respect to the first point, the scrambling negativity was observed in Japanese under circumstances in which a pro-drop reading in rendered unlikely (Wolff et al. 2008).

(9.33)   Example sentences from Wolff et al. (2008). Note that ERPs were timelocked to the case marker of the first NP.

    a. 二週間前   判事を   大臣が
        nisyuukanmae   hanzi-o   daizin-ga
        two weeks ago   judge-ACC   minister-NOM
        招きました
        manekimasita
        invited
    "Two weeks ago, the minister invited the judge."

b. 二週間前　　　判事が　　　大臣を
   nisyuukanmae   hanzi-<u>ga</u>   daizin-o
   two weeks ago judge-NOM   minister-ACC
   招きました
   manekimasita
   invited
   "Two weeks ago, the judge invited the minister."

Wolff and colleagues contrasted the processing of scrambled sentences such as (9.33a) with the processing of their subject-initial counterparts (as in 9.33b) in an auditory ERP study which employed an additional prosodic manipulation. Thus, the sentences in (9.33) either included a prosodic boundary after the first NP or did not. Without a prosodic boundary, one would expect the pro-drop reading to be highly available and the initial object to thus be compatible with a (non-scrambled) OV reading. With a prosodic boundary, by contrast, the pro-drop structure is rendered highly unlikely, since an object in the base position cannot be separated from the verb by a prosodic boundary (see also Hirotani 2005 for empirical evidence that a prosodic boundary after an initial object may serve to signal a scrambled structure). The results of Wolff et al.'s ERP experiment revealed a scrambling negativity for an initial object followed by a prosodic boundary, while an initial object in the absence of such a boundary did not differ from a subject in the same position.[10] This indicates that the scrambling negativity reflects the specific processing costs associated with a scrambled structure, which can be avoided when a scrambling analysis is not necessarily required. A similar finding (i.e. no scrambling negativity at the position of an unambiguously marked initial object) was reported for Turkish, which, like Japanese, allows subjects to be dropped (Demiral et al. 2008). These cross-linguistic findings thus suggest that, rather than constituting a simple mismatch response to the processing of an initial object, the scrambling negativity occurs whenever the initial argument unambiguously signals than an unmarked word order cannot be upheld.

Converging support for such an interpretation stems from a further study on German, in which Bornkessel et al. (2002b) observed a scrambling negativity in response to scrambled accusatives but not scrambled datives in German, despite the fact that both types of objects are associated with approximately the same (in-)frequency of occurrence in comparison to a nominative argument in the same position.

This finding appears to result from the possibility of interpreting a dative following a complementizer as the sole argument of a passivized transitive verb (e.g. ... *dass dem Mönch geholfen wurde.*, "... that [the monk][DAT] helped was."). Similarly to the option of pro-drop in Japanese, an initial dative object in German therefore need not be interpreted as introducing a scrambled structure.

The second point of similarity between the scrambling negativity and the pars opercularis activation for word order variations lies in the specificity of the electrophysiological response, which was already partially apparent in the dative–accusative distinction discussed above. A further study attesting to this specificity (Schlesewsky et al. 2003) employed identical stimuli to those in Grewe et al. (2005) (see examples 9.28a/b) and observed a scrambling negativity in response to initial non-pronominal objects, but not to pronominal objects. Thus, similar to the conclusions of the fMRI study, these data indicate that the scrambling negativity reflects the processing of a marked word order rather than that of an object argument in an unexpected position or in a position in which it occurs infrequently (object pronouns are significantly less frequent than subject pronouns at the left edge of the middlefield; see Schlesewsky et al. 2003).

Finally, and perhaps most strikingly, the occurrence of the scrambling negativity is specific to the processing of this particular word order variation in German, namely to word order permutations in the middlefield (see Haider and Rosengren 2003 for a theoretical characterization of scrambling). This means that this component has been observed neither in response to topicalized objects (Frisch et al. 2002; Matzke et al. 2002) nor to initial objects in wh-questions (Fiebach, Schlesewsky, and Friederici 2002). Rather, these types of word order permutations to the clause-initial (prefield) position are reflected in sustained left anterior negativities (sLANs; Fiebach et al. 2002; Matzke et al. 2002; Felser, Clahsen, and Münte 2003), which have typically been interpreted in terms of increased working memory demands (see Chapter 10.2 and Figure 10.1). A plausible explanation for this difference between clause-medial (scrambling) and clause-initial object-initial orders (topicalization, wh-questions) in German is that it may result from the distinction between the different topological fields within the German clause (*middlefield* vs. *prefield*). As discussed in relation to example (9.30) above, these two positions are associated with differing syntactic properties (e.g. in terms of A- vs. non-A-movement in generative approaches or of core vs. non-core regions

in Role and Reference Grammar; Diedrichsen 2008). This distinction –
however it is best characterized in theoretical terms – thus appears to
map directly onto the observable neurophysiological phenomena.

Further cross-linguistic support for the association between the
scrambling negativity and word order permutations in the middlefield
– at least for languages in which such a topological field can be
distinguished – stems from an ERP study on Swedish (Roll, Horne,
and Lindgren 2007). Roll and colleagues examined the neurophysiological correlates of "object shift" in sentences such as (9.34).

(9.34) Example stimuli from Roll et al. (2007)

  a. Object-shifted pronoun
     Ni   köpte   den   <u>inte</u>   men   ni   målade   ändå.
     you bought it   not   but   you   painted anyway
     "You didn't buy it, but you painted anyway."

  b. Object-shifted definite NP
     *Ni   köpte   färgen   <u>inte</u>   men   ni   målade   ändå.
     you   bought paint-DEF   not   but   you   painted anyway
     "You didn't buy the paint, but you painted anyway."

  c. Object-shifted indefinite NP
     *Ni   köpte   färg   <u>inte</u>   men   ni   målade   ändå.
     you   bought paint not   but   you   painted anyway
     "You didn't buy paint, but you painted anyway."

In the examples in (9.34), the object NPs are positioned to the left of
the negation (which is typically considered a marker for the left edge of
the VP; i.e. negation marks a position to the left of the base position of
the verb, as can be seen when the "verb second" slot is filled by another
constituent like an auxiliary). Hence, when an object precedes the
negation, it has been "shifted" to the left from its base position
(which is to the right of the base position of the verb). In Swedish,
this option ("object shift", Holmberg 1986) is only open to pronouns
(in Icelandic, by contrast, it can also apply to non-pronominal objects). At the position of the negation, where the object shifted structure becomes apparent, Roll and colleagues observed a posterior
negativity between 200 and 400 ms for sentences with indefinite NPs
(9.34c) as opposed to sentences with pronouns (9.34a) and (marginally) sentences with definite NPs (9.34b). Furthermore, both the indefinite and the definite condition (both of which are ungrammatical)
elicited a late positivity. Functionally, the negativity effect appears

highly comparable to the scrambling negativity (for other studies reporting a posterior distribution for this effect, see Bornkessel et al. 2003a; Bornkessel and Schlesewsky 2006b). As also noted by Roll et al. (2007), its slightly earlier latency might be attributable to the properties of the critical word (i.e. the fact that it was a function word rather than an NP as in other studies). These findings from Swedish therefore confirm the role of the scrambling negativity as a cross-linguistic correlate of word order permutations in the middlefield (which, in the Swedish examples in 9.34, begins after the finite verb in second position). Perhaps even more strikingly, they suggest that this effect can be modulated by properties that are not directly syntactic in nature, namely by object definiteness. Thus, in spite of the fact that object shift is not licensed for non-pronominal NPs in Swedish (as also reflected in the late positivity for both non-pronominal conditions), only the indefinite condition engendered a scrambling negativity in comparison to the pronominal condition and, marginally, in comparison to the definite condition. This finding suggests that the scrambling negativity can be modulated by changing argument "prominence" along several dimensions, not all of which are syntactic in nature. It therefore again emphasizes the close correspondence between the scrambling negativity and activation in the pars opercularis of the left IFG, which is also highly sensitive to non-syntactic word order-related factors such as animacy and definiteness (see section 9.2.4.1).

9.2.5 Summary

The discussion in this section revealed that the neural correlates of argument processing are relatively rich – even independently of the verb. Clearly, existing findings suggest that morphological case marking plays an exceptionally important role in determining pre-verbal argument comprehension, both with respect to incremental thematic interpretation and with regard to the processing of argument order permutations. However, it should also be apparent that case marking is not the only information source involved in shaping these comprehension processes. Rather, several further factors need to be taken into account:

(a) An argument's position in the clause. As shown for the processing of word order permutations, several regions within a clause need to be distinguished, i.e. an object preceding the subject is processed differently depending on where in the clause it is encountered.

Importantly, it is not a trivial matter to establish correspondences between these different clausal regions of interest across languages.

(b) A range of non-syntactic factors like animacy and definiteness. These modulate the processing of word order permutations on the one hand and influence incremental argument interpretation on the other.

(c) The predictability of a marked word order at the position of the first argument. A scrambling negativity, i.e. a local correlate of the processing of word order permutations, is only observable when a marked word order is already apparent at this position. Whether this is the case is modulated not only by the factors already mentioned in (b) but also by language-specific properties such as the availability of subject-drop and prosodic properties of scrambled structures.

The comprehension processes modulated by these factors have been associated with a range of electrophysiological and neuroanatomical correlates. In the electrophysiological domain, pre-verbal processes of (thematic) argument interpretation typically yield N400 effects, whereas the processing of word order permutations in core regions of the clause engenders "scrambling negativities". In terms of functional neuroanatomy, the aspects of argument processing considered in this section correlate primarily with activation in a left hemispheric fronto-temporal network, comprising the inferior frontal gyrus (primarily the pars opercularis, BA 44) and the posterior superior temporal sulcus (pSTS). Whereas the pars opercularis appears to be closely involved in the processing of argument order, pSTS activation is more closely tied to the interpretation of argument relations.

9.3 From word order to grammatical functions

The previous section demonstrated that unambiguous morphological case marking serves to drive the incremental comprehension process, particularly in verb-final structures. However, this type of information is not always available – indeed, the proposed universal that verb-final languages typically have a case system (see section 9.2.1) is not without exceptions, e.g. Abkhaz (Hewitt 1979) and Lakhota (Van Valin 1977). This section will therefore be concerned with the question of which processing choices are made in the absence of unambiguous marking on the arguments themselves and which neurophysiological and neuroanatomical correlates of such assignments can be observed.

As a first illustration of the possible degrees of ambiguity that the human language processing system must be equipped to deal with, consider example (9.35) from Riau Indonesian (Gil 2001).

(9.35) Ayam   makan
        chicken eat
        "The chicken is eating."/"The chicken is making somebody eat."/"Somebody is eating where the chicken is."

According to Gil (2001), this sentence has at least three possible meanings. Thus *ayam* "chicken" may be interpreted either as the subject (Actor) of a simple intransitive relation, as the Actor of a causative construction, or even as a locative adverbial. When the processing system encounters *ayam*, it is therefore faced with a relatively high number of possible interpretive choices. Even though no psycholinguistic experiments have been conducted on Riau Indonesian, speaker intuitions provide a relatively straightforward answer to the question of which of these readings is preferred: at least in the absence of a constraining context, sentence (9.35) would be interpreted as "The chicken is eating" (David Gil, personal communication). This simple example provides an impressive illustration of a cross-linguistically observable tendency to analyze an ambiguous first argument as the subject of the sentence (see also section 9.2.1). Investigations of this so-called "subject-first preference" have a long tradition in the psycholinguistic literature.

9.3.1 *The subject-first preference: Initial observations and theoretical approaches*

The most prominent approach to the question of whether an initial ambiguous argument is preferentially analyzed as a subject or an object is couched within the theoretical assumption of "filler-gap" relations. Inspired by developments in generative grammar (Chomsky 1965; Chomsky 1981), early psycholinguistic theorizing assumed that, even though language comprehension is mostly surface structure-driven, underlying (movement- or transformation-based) dependencies may be assumed whenever the input string cannot be straightforwardly derived via phrase structure rules, i.e. directly mapped to base positions in a syntactic structure (Fodor, Bever, and Garrett 1974; Fodor 1980). An initial wh-phrase such as *which boy*, for example, unambiguously indicates such a dependency. It is therefore treated as a "filler", which must be assigned to a "gap" (trace) position at some later point in the sentence in order to be interpreted successfully (see Fodor 1995 for a discussion of the status of empty categories in sentence comprehension). As noted by Fodor (1978), this processing configuration gives rise to two logical possibilities: the processing system may assign the filler to the first possible gap site even in the absence of unambiguous information to support such an integration (*gap-as-first-resort*), or it may wait until there is enough information to support the establishment of a filler-gap dependency (*gap-as-last-resort*). The demonstration of a robust and widespread subject-first preference in subsequent research has been taken as evidence for a first-resort strategy.

As an example, consider the following Dutch sentences, which stem from one of the most well-known psycholinguistic studies on the subject-first preference (Frazier and Flores d'Arcais 1989).

(9.36)   Example stimuli from Frazier and Flores d'Arcais (1989); *e* indicates the correct gap position in each sentence

    a. Welke   arbeiders   hebben   *e* de voorman
       [Which   workers][PL]   have[PL]   [the foreman][SG]
       geprezen?
       praised
       "Which workers praised the foreman?"

    b. Welke   arbeiders   heeft   de voorman
       [Which   workers][PL]   have[SG]   [the foreman][SG]
       e geprezen?
        praised
       "Which workers did the foreman praise?"

The sentences in (9.36) differ with respect to the gap position to which the filler must be assigned: whereas the gap in the subject-initial example (9.36a) is in the first possible gap position, the gap in the object-initial example (9.36b) corresponds to the second possible gap position. A gap-as-first-resort strategy would therefore predict a preference for (9.36a), which was indeed what Frazier and Flores d'Arcais observed in a speeded acceptability judgment experiment. They interpreted these results as evidence for an *Active Filler Strategy* (AFS; Frazier 1987b), which states that an identified filler should be assigned to a gap site as soon as possible, i.e. "rank the option of a gap above the option of a lexical noun phrase within the domain of an identified filler" (Frazier and Flores d'Arcais 1989: 332). In contrast to a purely bottom-up gap-as-first-resort strategy, the AFS postulates that the filler is "active" in the sense that analysis is not delayed until the first potential gap position is reached.

Further behavioral evidence in favor of the subject-first preference stems from a number of experiments on German. As object-initial readings are, in principle, more accessible in this language than in Dutch, these results provide converging support for the generality of the preference to analyze an initial ambiguous argument as the subject of the clause. In addition, these studies showed that the subject-first preference is observable in a wide range of sentence structures (declarative main clauses: Hemforth et al. 1993; relative clauses: Schriefers, Friederici, and Kühn 1995; embedded clauses: Bader and Meng 1999; wh-questions: Schlesewsky et al. 2000), and that it is neither modulated by the animacy of the ambiguous argument (Schlesewsky et al. 2000) nor by the presence of a context supporting the object-first reading (Meng, Bader, and Bayer 1999). Finally, the existence of a subject-first preference even in the German middlefield attests to the fact that this preference is not restricted to situations in which a filler can be unambiguously identified, because the unmarked word order in the middlefield is assumed to be base-generated. Thus, the preference for subject-initial clause-medial word orders in German requires an explanation in terms of filler-independent mechanisms.

A detailed explanation of this type was first proposed by de Vincenzi (1991) on the basis of data from Italian. In this non-case-marking SVO language, an interesting situation arises because of the availability of subject-drop in combination with possible post-verbal subjects. De Vincenzi capitalized upon these characteristics of Italian to investigate whether, in absence of an overt NP before the verb, a preference for a post-verbal subject interpretation would arise. To this end, she contrasted sentences such as the following in a self-paced reading experiment.

(9.37) Example stimuli from de Vincenzi (1991; Experiment 1)

  a. Ieri   pomeriggio ha richiamato il   venditore
     yesterday afternoon   has called-back the seller
     per chiedere uno sconto...
     to ask-for a   discount
     "Yesterday afternoon, (someone) called back the seller to ask for a discount..."

b. Ieri   pomeriggio ha   richiamato il   venditore
yesterday   afternoon   has called-back the   seller
per offrire uno sconto...
to   offer   a   discount
"Yesterday afternoon, the seller called back to offer a discount..."

In the critical region (*per chiedere uno sconto* vs. *per offrire uno sconto*), de Vincenzi observed significantly longer reading times for sentences such as (9.37b), in which the post-verbal NP turns out to be the subject of the sentence. She interpreted this finding as evidence for a processing strategy which she termed the *Minimal Chain Principle* (MCP): "Avoid postulating unnecessary chain members at S-structure, but do not delay postulating required chain members" (de Vincenzi 1991: 30). The MCP predicts that, in sentences such as (9.37) the empty category in the pre-verbal base position of the subject is preferentially analyzed as a *pro* (i.e. a lexically unexpressed NP) rather than as a trace of a post-verbal subject.[11] Thus, a singleton chain (containing only a *pro*) is preferred over a chain with more than one member. In this way, the MCP also derives the subject preference in the German middlefield: here, a base-generated subject-initial structure is preferred over a scrambled structure, in which the object is moved from its base position to a position preceding the subject (hence creating a multi-membered chain).

In addition to the preference strategies discussed so far, all of which depend on the basic assumption of filler-gap dependencies in combination with particular structural configurations, several further explanations for the subject-preference have been proposed. A purely structure-based alternative, termed *Simplicity*, was formulated by Gorrell (1995). In essence, the simplicity principle states that there should be no vacuous structure building. Together with the assumption that subject-initial structures are simpler than object-initial structures (e.g. Travis 1984; Zwart 1997), this derives the subject-first preference. However, as it seems doubtful whether a structural analysis along these lines can be upheld under all circumstances (for discussion, see Schwartz and Vikner 1996; Gärtner and Steinbach 2003a; Gärtner and Steinbach 2003b), the assumption of phrase structure simplicity as a general explanation for the subject-first preference appears problematic.

An approach that is more closely motivated by general psychological concepts such as working memory and capacity limitations was proposed by Gibson (1998; 2000). Within his *Syntactic Prediction Locality*

Theory (SPLT)/*Dependency Locality Theory* (DLT), Gibson assumes that object-before-subject orders are more costly to process (at least in languages such as English, German, and Dutch) because the processing of an object introduces an additional dependency by calling for a subject in a later position in the clause. An initial subject, by contrast, does not give rise to such a dependency because of the possibility of an intransitive reading. As dependencies are thought to lead to additional memory costs, a subject analysis is pursued for initial ambiguous arguments because this analysis is less taxing with respect to working memory load.

Finally, explanations for the subject-first preference have also been proposed within lexicalist constraint-based processing models (e.g. MacDonald et al. 1994; Vosse and Kempen 2000). As described in Box 7.1, this class of approaches assumes that partial syntactic structures are stored in the lexicon and connected to the lexical entries of individual words and that the composition of larger structures during sentence comprehension depends upon the interaction of a variety of factors (e.g. argument structure, frequency, discourse context). The most detailed account of the subject-first preference in a model of this kind was provided by Vosse and Kempen (2000). They assume that, in a language of the English type, the preference for a subject-initial (SVO) analysis over an object-initial (OSV) analysis results from the increased competition for the subject function that arises between the two preverbal NPs in the latter case.[12] However, a competition-based mechanism of this type cannot account for the subject-first preference in verb-final structures (SOV vs. OSV), in which both arguments precede the verb independently of whether the subject precedes the object or vice versa (e.g. example 9.15a). Thus, an additional mechanism is required to derive the subject-first preference under such circumstances. The most obvious candidate in this regard appears to be frequency of occurrence (e.g. Jurafsky 1996; Tabor, Juliano, and Tanenhaus 1997), i.e. a subject-initial analysis may be preferred because it is more frequent than its object-initial counterpart. However, frequency-based accounts are challenged by the observation that not all word order preferences are mirrored by differences in corpus frequency (Kempen and Harbusch 2005; Crocker and Keller 2006). Thus, while frequency of occurrence clearly appears to be able to account for relatively coarse-grained differences in processing preference (i.e. the most frequent structure is also the most acceptable and the easiest to process in the vast majority of cases), it is currently not clear how many of the more fine-grained distinctions can be derived in such an approach (see also section 7.2.3).

9.3.2 *A neurocognitive perspective on subject–object ambiguities*

The behavioral findings on the subject-preference have been corroborated and extended by neurocognitive findings, particularly from experiments using ERPs. The first study of this kind was reported by Mecklinger et al. (1995), using German relative clauses such as (9.38).

(9.38)   Example stimuli from Mecklinger et al. (1995), non-biased versions

    a. Subject relative clause
        Das   ist   die Professorin,   die
        this   is   [the professor][SG]   who[SG]
        die Studentinnen   gesucht   <u>hat</u>.
        [the students][PL]   sought   has[3.SG]
        "This is the professor who was looking for the students."

    b. Object relative clause
        Das   sind   die Studentinnen,   die
        these   are   [the students][PL]   who[PL]
        die Professorin   gesucht   <u>hat</u>.
        [the professor][SG]   sought   has[3.SG]
        "These are the students who the professor was looking for."

At the position of the critical final auxiliary, Mecklinger and colleagues observed an early parietal positivity for a disambiguation towards an object reading of the relative pronoun and, therefore, towards an object-before-subject order (9.38b). They named this component the "P345" because the effect reached its maximal amplitude at this time point. In addition, the experiment contained sentences that were biased semantically towards either a subject or an object reading of the relative pronoun:

(9.39)   Example stimuli from Mecklinger et al. (1995), semantically biased versions

    a. Subject relative clause
        Das ist die Professorin,   die   die Studentinnen
        this is [the professor][SG]   who[SG]   [the students][PL]
        geprüft   <u>hat</u>.
        examined   has[3.SG]
        "This is the professor who examined the students."

    b. Object relative clause

Das	sind	die	Studentinnen,	die
these	are	[the	students][PL]	who[PL]

die	Professorin	geprüft	<u>hat</u>.
examined	has[3.SG]	[the	professor][SG]

    "These are the students who the professor examined."

As it is much more plausible for a professor to examine students than the other way around, the processing of the participle *geprüft* in the sentences in (9.39) introduces a semantic bias with respect to the thematic roles and, thereby, the grammatical functions of the two arguments already encountered. If this information is actively used to evaluate the processing choices made up to this point and to initiate a reanalysis if necessary (i.e. in case of a mismatch between the subject-first preference and the plausibility information), the positivity observed at the position of the final auxiliary should be modulated by the semantic bias. This was not the case: even though the biased object relative clauses engendered an N400 effect at the position of the biasing participle, there was no modulation of the P345 at the auxiliary as a function of semantic bias. Mecklinger and colleagues interpreted this result as suggesting that contradicting semantic information is not used to initiate a syntactic reanalysis.

    Subsequent studies revealed that the P345 as a correlate of subject-object reanalysis appears to be confined to grammatical function ambiguities in relative clauses. For complement clauses (i.e. ambiguities in the German middlefield), by contrast, Friederici and Mecklinger (1996) and Friederici et al. (2001) observed a late positivity (P600). Similar electrophysiological correlates were reported for the disambiguation towards object-initial readings – either via subject–verb agreement or case marking of the second argument – in wh-clauses (German: beim Graben et al. 2000; Italian: Penolazzi et al. 2005) and German declarative main clauses (Frisch et al. 2002; Matzke et al. 2002). In addition, Knoeferle et al. (2008) showed that a P600 can also be elicited when disambiguation towards an object-initial order in German declarative main clauses is effected via a visual scene context. To this end, they presented scenes as in Figure 2.7B concurrently with (auditorily presented) NP–V–NP structures containing a case-ambiguous first NP. For an initial sentence fragment such as *Die Prinzessin wäscht...* ("[the princess][NOM/ACC] washes..."), the first NP is disambiguated towards an Agent/subject reading by the scene in

2.7BI and towards a Patient/object reading in 2.7BII. At the position of the verb in 2.7BII (i.e. at the scene-based point of disambiguation towards an object-initial order), Knoeferle and colleagues observed a P600 even though no disambiguating information had yet been encountered in the sentence itself.

In this way, subject–object reanalyses were long thought to cluster with other structure-related reanalysis processes in engendering positive ERP effects.[13] However, counterevidence to this generalization began to emerge when the domain of examination was extended to subject–object ambiguities involving dative case. Thus, Bornkessel et al. (2004b) reported a late positivity as a correlate of a reanalysis towards an accusative-initial complement clause structure (9.40a), but an N400 for reanalyses towards dative-initial orders in otherwise identical sentences (9.40b).

(9.40)   Example stimuli from Bornkessel et al. (2004b)

    Alle wussten, . . .

    everyone knew . . .

    (a) . . . dass   Friedrich   Gönnerinnen   lieben, . . .
        . . . that   Friedrich[SG]   patrons [PL]   love(ACC) [PL]
        ". . . that patrons love Friedrich."

    (b) . . . dass   Friedrich   Gönnerinnen   zuwinken, . . .
        . . . that   Friedrich[SG]   patrons [PL]   wave.to(DAT) [PL]
        ". . . that patrons wave to Friedrich."

At a first glance, the observation of an N400 for reanalyses in dative constructions such as (9.40b) might appear to lend itself to an explanation in terms of the exceptional status of the dative case in transitive constructions in German (described, for example, as a "lexical case", Chomsky 1981; or "exceptional case", Fanselow 2000) or via the need to interpret one of the arguments as non-macrorole-bearing (Van Valin 2005). However, an account along these lines is not straightforward because the subject-initial condition which served as a control for (9.40b) also involved a disambiguation towards dative object case at the position of the critical verb. In addition, subsequent studies provided strong converging evidence against an "exception"-based analysis by showing that the N400 still emerges even when the requirement for dative case is unambiguously clear even before the point of word order disambiguation (Schlesewsky and Bornkessel 2006). These findings therefore indicate that an adequate explanation of the component distinctions must go beyond an account based simply on a "lexical" or "exceptional" status of the dative case (as proposed, for example, in Bader and Bayer 2006). Furthermore, they suggest that reanalysis processes are not associated with only a single neurocognitive correlate, but rather that the complexity of the overall neurophysiological pattern mirrors the multiplicity of environments in which these reanalyses occur (for further discussion, see Schlesewsky and Bornkessel 2006).[14]

Having examined the neurophysiological correlates of subject–object ambiguity processing, let us now turn to the functional neuroanatomy of grammatical function reanalyses. In contrast to the ERP findings, which show marked differences between word order variations in unambiguously case-marked structures (see section 9.2.4.2) and sentences involving a local ambiguity, such a distinction has not manifested itself as straightforwardly in neuroimaging findings. Thus, Bornkessel et al. (2005) found that structures requiring a reanalysis towards an object-initial order in the German middlefield (see 9.40b) engendered increased activation within the pars opercularis of the left inferior frontal gyrus and thereby behaved identically to their unambiguously case-marked object-initial counterparts. However, because of the temporal insensitivity of the BOLD signal (see section 2.2.1.2), it is virtually impossible to disentangle neuroanatomical correlates of the reanalysis processes themselves from more general processes related to the overall integration and evaluation of the structures in question. Additional support for the idea that more general processes of this type are crucially involved in engendering the observable fMRI activation stems from the observation that some of the fine-grained differences observable in ERP studies on reanalysis are not mirrored in the fMRI findings. For example, while being associated with qualitatively distinct ERP components, reanalyses in dative and accusative structures such as (9.40) correlate with very similar neural activation patterns in the pars opercularis and a larger frontal-parietal-basal ganglia network (Bornkessel-Schlesewsky et al. submitted).[15] This indistinguishability between (at least some types of) word order permutations in ambiguous and unambiguous structures – as demonstrated in languages allowing for such a contrast to be undertaken – raises the question of whether word order related activation differences in languages such as English (e.g. Just et al. 1996; Stromswold et al. 1996), which always involve a local ambiguity, should be viewed as correlates of word order complexity or reanalysis towards a dispreferred order. We shall return to this point in our discussion of the neuroanatomical correlates of relative clause processing in Chapter 10.1.3.

Finally, it is interesting to note that the pars opercularis of the left IFG has proven sensitive to syntactic ambiguity per se, i.e. this cortical region shows increased activation in response to case-ambiguous as opposed to unambiguous sentences (Fiebach, Vos, and Friederici 2004; Bornkessel et al. 2005). This finding provides for an interesting parallel to the observation that initial case-ambiguous NPs in German declarative main clauses are associated with a similar ERP response (in comparison to unambiguous NPs in the same position) to that observed for a disambiguation towards an object-initial order at a later point in the same sentences (P600; Frisch et al. 2002).

9.3.3 *The subject-first preference: A "universal" processing strategy?*

The wealth of psycholinguistic findings on the subject-first preference indicates that this ambiguity resolution strategy is very robust and, moreover, that it applies in a variety of languages. One might therefore suspect that a subject analysis of an ambiguous initial argument might be universally preferred. As example (9.35) showed, an ambiguity resolution strategy of this kind certainly appears very useful even in languages with very different characteristics to typical European languages. Indeed, a number of behavioral results have been used to argue for a processing advantage for subjects over objects in several non-European languages (e.g. Japanese: Ishizuka 2005; Korean: Kwon, Polinsky, and Kluender 2006). However, these experiments examined relative clauses, they are not straightforwardly comparable to the data described in the preceding sections, and will therefore be discussed further in Chapter 10 on the processing of complex constructions.

On the other hand, a small set of initial neurocognitive findings directly supports the cross-linguistic applicability of the subject-preference. Demiral, Schlesewsky, and Bornkessel-Schlesewsky (2008), for example, report an ERP study which investigated whether this preference can also be observed in Turkish, an SOV language permitting subject-drop. The interest in examining a language of this type lies in the fact that, in contrast to all of the languages examined previously (see sections 9.3.1–9.3.2), it permits an unmarked object reading of an ambiguous initial argument. This is illustrated in example (9.41).

(9.41)   Subject–object ambiguities in Turkish (from Demiral et al. 2008)

    a. Dün   pilot   gördüm.
       yesterday   pilot   see-1sg.past
       "Yesterday I saw (a) pilot."

    b. Dün   pilot   uyudu.
       yesterday   pilot   sleep-3sg.past
       "Yesterday (the) pilot slept."

The first NP in example (9.41a), *pilot*, is the object of a sentence with a dropped subject; its objecthood is clearly indicated by the first person singular agreement marking on the verb. Nevertheless, the sentence is unmarked in the sense of Note 6. Subject-drop is licensed here even without contextual support because the first person subject – and its referent – is fully recoverable from the agreement marking borne by the verb. However, when the NP *pilot* is first encountered, it is ambiguous between an object and a subject reading, as illustrated by example (9.41b). To examine whether Turkish shows a subject-preference for an initial argument, Demiral and colleagues therefore contrasted ERPs at the position of the disambiguating verb in sentences such as (9.41a) with those at the analogous position in comparable sentences in which the initial NP was unambiguously marked as an object.[16] This comparison revealed an early positivity for the disambiguation towards an object reading in comparison to the unambiguous control condition, thus indicating that speakers initially pursued a subject analysis of the first NP. Furthermore, this initial preference was not modulated by semantic factors, as the same ERP effect was observable in a second ambiguous sentence condition with an initial inanimate argument. The latter point is especially interesting because only initial ambiguous animate arguments show a bias towards a subject reading in terms of structural frequency in Turkish (Demiral 2007).

   The findings on Turkish are supported by ERP evidence from Japanese (Wolff, Schlesewsky, and Bornkessel-Schlesewsky 2007). Like Turkish, Japanese is an SOV language with a preponderance for subject-drop. However, a subject–object ambiguity is somewhat more difficult to implement because, unlike in Turkish, both nominative and accusative case are overtly marked and there is no differential object marking. Wolff and colleagues therefore examined sentences in which the first argument bore the topic-marker – *wa*, which is compatible with both a subject and an object reading (the sentences were otherwise identical to those shown in example 9.33) and observed a broadly distributed negativity at the position of disambiguation towards an object reading. While the functional significance of the component distinction between Japanese (negativity) and Turkish (positivity) is not yet entirely clear, these findings provide clear evidence for a subject-first preference in the two languages.

Notably, while Turkish and Japanese behave very similarly to the other languages examined in that they show a subject-preference for initial ambiguous arguments, an interesting contrast arises with respect to the processing of unambiguously marked initial objects. Recall that, in German, scrambled objects engender a scrambling negativity at the position of the object itself (see section 9.2.4.2). By contrast, such an effect is observable neither in Turkish (Demiral et al. 2008) nor in Japanese (Wolff et al. 2007) under default circumstances (but see Note 10). Yet as discussed in section 9.2.4.2, it can be elicited in Japanese when the prosodic structure of the sentence renders subject-drop unlikely. It therefore appears that the absence of a processing disadvantage for unambiguous initial objects in Turkish and Japanese can be attributed to the availability of subject-drop, i.e. because of this property, an initial object does not unambiguously signal a scrambled structure. Moreover, these findings indicate that the subject-first preference in ambiguous structures and processing costs arising in unambiguous object-initial structures cannot simply be viewed as two sides of the same coin (as proposed, for example, by Gibson 1998; Gibson 2000). Rather, the two phenomena seem to be independent of one another.

A cross-linguistically motivated explanation of the subject-first preference, which can also account for the difference between ambiguous and unambiguous structures, was proposed by Bornkessel and Schlesewsky (2006a). This account is based on the assumption of a general least-effort principle called *Minimality*.

(9.41)   Minimality (Bornkessel and Schlesewsky 2006a: 790)

In the absence of explicit information to the contrary, the human language comprehension system assigns minimal structures. This entails that only required dependencies/relations are created.

Minimality is thought to apply at all levels of the processing architecture. With respect to the phenomena under consideration, two levels of Minimality are particularly important: relational minimality (prefer a minimal interpretation; i.e. prefer intransitive events over events with more than one participant), and phrase structure minimality (prefer a minimal phrase structure). The subject-first preference directly follows from relational minimality: an initial argument will be analyzed as the sole argument of an intransitive event whenever possible. In a nominative-accusative language, the "subject" analysis follows directly from this assumption. Note that relational minimality is an interpretive principle, i.e. it is neither concerned with the realization of the arguments in the syntactic structure (which will vary, for example, according to whether a language permits argument-drop), nor with the saturation of agreement at the earliest possible point in time (see Burkhardt et al. 2007, for evidence against a dominant role of agreement in deriving the subject-preference). By contrast, increased processing costs at the position of an unambiguously-marked initial object derive from phrase structure minimality in concert with phrase structure representations that do not contain any empty categories. Recall from section 9.2.4.2 that the scrambling negativity only arises under circumstances in which the initial object unambiguously signals a scrambled reading and, thereby, a (non-minimal) two-argument phrase structure. The ERP effect thus reflects the costs arising when a minimal phrase structure cannot be upheld. Therefore, no such effect is observable when a minimal phrase structure is not ruled out by an object in the first position (e.g. because of the possibility of subject-drop in Turkish and Japanese).

In this way, the minimality-based approach derives the cross-linguistic applicability of the subject-preference while also accounting for the language-specific differences with respect to processing difficulties in unambiguous sentences (see Chapter 15.4 for a slightly revised version of this approach). In addition, the assumption that the "subject"-preference does not, in fact, result from any properties related to subjecthood per se but that it is rather an epiphenomenon of a preference for intransitivity appears appealing in view of the problems associated with defining the subject function from a cross-linguistic perspective (cf. Keenan 1976; Comrie 1989). This view therefore also predicts that a similar preference (namely for the argument type that corresponds to the sole argument of an intransitive clause) should be observable in languages in which several dimensions of subjecthood conflict, e.g. ergative languages.

9.3.4 *Beyond subjects and objects: Further grammatical function ambiguities*

Besides ambiguities between a subject and an object reading of a locally ambiguous argument, an ambiguity may also arise between a direct and an indirect object analysis ("object-object ambiguities"). In fact, the psycholinguistic literature on "gap filling" in English (see section 9.3.1) has focused more closely on this type of ambiguity than on subject–object ambiguities. Consider the following examples from an early self-paced reading study (Crain and Fodor 1985).

(9.42)   Example stimuli from Crain and Fodor (1985)

      a. Who could the little child have forced us to sing those French songs for last Christmas?

      b. Could the little child have forced us to sing those French songs for Cheryl last Christmas?

The rationale behind presenting sentences of the type in (9.42a) is that, according to a gap-as-first-resort strategy (such as the AFS), the processing system should postulate a gap position for the wh-filler immediately following the verb *forced*. However, as this position is already occupied by *us*, a processing conflict should arise if a gap is indeed predicted for this position (the so-called *filled-gap effect*). This was exactly what Crain and Fodor observed: reading times were significantly longer for an overt post-verbal NP in sentences such as (9.42a) in comparison to controls such as (9.42b), in which there is no wh-filler. Findings such as these (see also Stowe 1986) were therefore used to argue for online gap filling at the first possible position.[17]

    Two further behavioral methodologies have featured prominently in the literature on gap filling in object–object ambiguities. The first aimed to provide direct evidence for the reactivation of a filler at the gap position by means of the cross-modal lexical priming (CMLP) paradigm. In this method, participants listened to sentences such as (9.43) (from Nicol and Swinney 1989) and, at the same time, performed a lexical decision task to probe words presented at different points during the sentence.

(9.43)   Example sentence from Nicol and Swinney (1989)
      The policeman saw the boy that the crowd at the party accused of the crime.

The logic behind this experimental setup is that, via lexical priming, a probe word that is semantically related to the filler and presented at the gap position should be recognized faster than an unrelated probe word in the same position. Nicol and Swinney found exactly this pattern of results: related probe words were recognized more quickly at the position of the direct object (i.e. directly following *accused*), but not at earlier or later points in the sentence. A similar finding was reported for English direct object wh-questions by Burkhardt, Piñango, and Wong (2003). These investigators additionally contrasted the processing behavior of Broca's aphasics with that of unimpaired comprehenders and observed a delayed priming effect for the aphasic patients (i.e. priming for a probe word related to the wh-filler at 650 ms rather than 100 ms after the critical verb). They therefore argue that Broca's aphasia (agrammatism) is characterized by *delayed* syntactic dependency processing ("slow syntax") rather than by the principled inability to process or represent such dependencies (e.g. Haarmann and Kolk 1991; Piñango 2000). Note, however, that while findings such as these are sometimes cited as evidence for the psychological reality of empty categories, the reactivation of a filler directly after the verb in English could also result from the "direct association" between the argument and its subcategorizer (Pickering and Barry 1991).

The preference for a direct as opposed to an indirect object inter-pretation of an initial wh-phrase in English was also demonstrated using the so-called stop-making-sense technique, in which participants are asked to press a button as soon as a sentence "stops making sense". To apply this methodology to object–object ambiguities, Tanenhaus et al. (1989) presented sentences such as (9.44a), in which the verb *called* introduces an implausibility under the condition that the which-phrase is taken to be the direct object. These sentences were contrasted with plausible controls such as (9.44b).

(9.44)   Example stimuli from Tanenhaus et al. (1989) and Garnsey et al. (1989)

    a. The businessman knew which article the secretary called at home.

    b. The businessman knew which customer the secretary called at home.

Tanenhaus and colleagues found that participants detected an anomaly at the position of *called* in (9.44a), thus suggesting that the wh-phrase is indeed preferentially interpreted as a direct object. (Note that the detection of an anomaly at this position is indeed crucially dependent on a direct object interpretation of the wh-phrase since alternative plausible continuations are also possible, e.g. *The businessman knew which article the secretary called about this morning.*) A very similar finding was obtained in an ERP study using an identical manipulation (Garnsey, Tanenhaus, and Chapman 1989), which revealed an N400 at the position of *called* for sentences such as (9.44a) vs. (9.44b).

A preference for direct objects (accusative case) has also been argued for on the basis of German, despite the fact that this language has a different basic word order to English (indirect objects precede direct objects). In addition, German permits different object cases in two-argument constructions, thus permitting an examination of the case preferentially assigned when a nominative (subject) analysis is already ruled out. Hopf et al. (1998) investigated these questions by means of an ERP experiment employing sentences such as (9.45).

(9.45)   Example stimuli from Hopf et al. (1998)

Dirigenten,   die   ein   schwieriges   Werk
conductors[NOM/ACC/DAT] who   a   difficult   opus
einstudiert   haben, ...
rehearsed   have ...
"Conductors who have rehearsed a difficult opus."
a. ... kann   ein Kritiker   ruhig   umjubeln.
    ... can   [a critic][NOM]   safely   cheer(ACC)

b. ... kann   ein Kritiker   ruhig   applaudieren.
    ... can   [a critic][NOM]   safely   applaud(DAT)
    "A critic can safely cheer/applaud conductors who have rehearsed a difficult opus."

The sentence-initial NP in the examples in (9.45), *Dirigenten*, is ambiguous between nominative, dative, and accusative case. The nominative reading of this argument (which should initially be preferred because of the subject-first preference) is ruled out when the modal verb *kann* is encountered, because the singular number marking prevents the establishment of subject–verb agreement. At the position of the clause-final verb, the NP is then disambiguated towards either an accusative (9.45a) or a dative reading (9.45b). In comparison to a minimally differing unambiguous control (with a dative-marked initial NP), the dative verb in (9.45b) engendered a

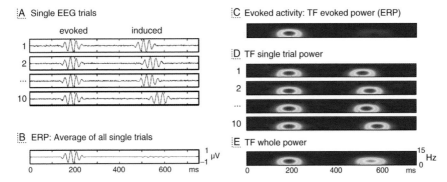

Plate 1. Frequency-based measures of EEG activity and their relation to ERPs. Panel A depicts evoked and induced EEG activity at the single trial level. Both types of neural activity are stimulus-related, but only evoked responses occur with a fixed latency relative to the critical stimulus of interest. Hence, only evoked activity "survives" the averaging procedure and is thereby observable in ERP measures (see Panel B). Panels C–E show the relationship between frequency characteristics of the EEG at the single trial level and common frequency-based measures. Evoked power (Panel C) is obtained by applying a frequency transform to the averaged ERP signal, thereby revealing the frequency ranges underlying the observable ERP components. Like the ERP, evoked power thus only includes evoked activity. Whole power (Panel E), by contrast, is obtained by applying the frequency transformation and the averaging procedure in a different order, namely by averaging over the frequency transforms of each single trial (Panel D). Whole power therefore includes both evoked and induced activity.

Source: Adapted from Herrmann, Munk, and Engel 2004.

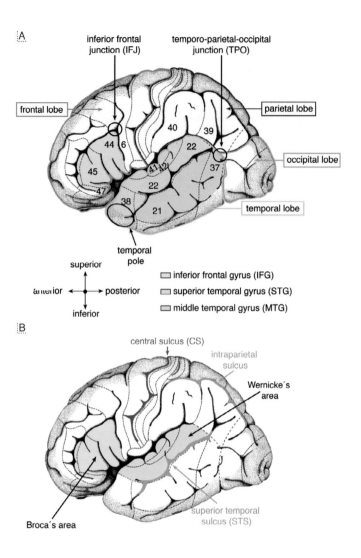

A

inferior frontal junction (IFJ)

temporo-parietal-occipital junction (TPO)

frontal lobe

parietal lobe

occipital lobe

44 6

45

47

41 42

40

39

22

37

38

22

21

temporal lobe

temporal pole

superior

anterior ← → posterior

inferior

☐ inferior frontal gyrus (IFG)

☐ superior temporal gyrus (STG)

☐ middle temporal gyrus (MTG)

B

central sulcus (CS)

intraparietal sulcus

Wernicke's area

Broca's area

superior temporal sulcus (STS)

C

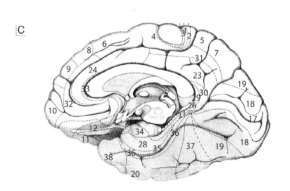

4 3 2

5

8 6

9 24

33

32

10

12

1

38

34

28 35

36

37 19

20

31

23

30

26

5

36

7

19

18

18

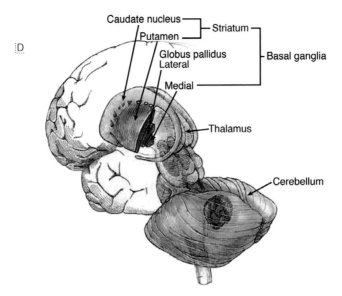

D

Caudate nucleus
Putamen
Striatum
Basal ganglia
Globus pallidus
Lateral
Medial
Thalamus
Cerebellum

Plate 2. This plate provides an introduction to language-related regions in the human brain. Panels A and B depict schematic lateral views of the left hemisphere, whereas Panel C shows a schematic medial view of one of the hemispheres. Panel A shows the major language-related regions of the left hemisphere, with relevant gyri indicated by color-coding. To provide an orientation for the reader unfamiliar with neuroanatomy, the different lobes of the brain are also marked by color-coded borders. Numbers indicate language-relevant Brodmann Areas (BA), which Brodmann (1909) defined on the basis of their cytoarchitectonic characteristics. The coordinate labels superior–inferior indicate the position of a gyrus within a lobe (e.g. superior temporal gyrus) or within a BA (e.g. superior BA 44). The coordinate labels anterior–posterior indicate the position within a gyrus (e.g. anterior superior temporal gyrus). Panel B shows the two classical language areas ("Broca's area" and "Wernicke's area"). Relevant major sulci are also marked. Panel C shows medial brain regions that have been implicated in language processing. The location of subcortical regions involved in language processing (basal ganglia, thalamus) is depicted in Panel D. A further region which has proved sensitive to language processing but is not shown in this plate is the insula, a cortical region located deep to the brain's lateral surface at the junction between the frontal, temporal, and parietal lobes.

Source: Adapted from Bornkessel-Schlesewsky and Friederici 2007.

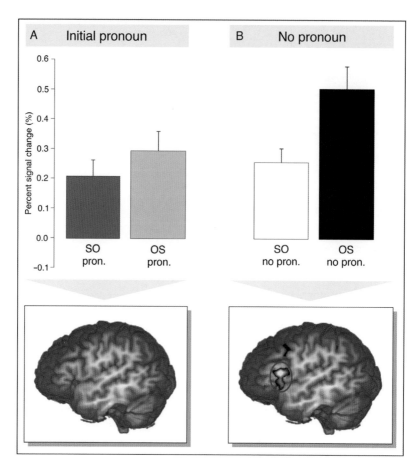

Plate 3. Averaged activation (N=16) for object- vs. subject-initial sentences with pronouns (panel A) and without pronouns (panel B) in the fMRI study by Grewe et al. 2005. The bar graphs show the percent signal change within the pars opercularis of the left IFG (BA 44) for each individual condition, with error bars indicating the standard error of the mean.

Source: Grewe et al. (2005).

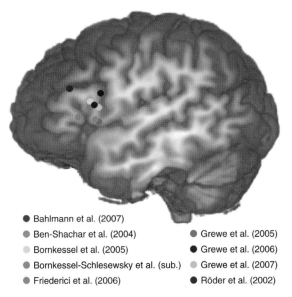

● Bahlmann et al. (2007)
● Ben-Shachar et al. (2004)   ● Grewe et al. (2005)
○ Bornkessel et al. (2005)   ● Grewe et al. (2006)
● Bornkessel-Schlesewsky et al. (sub.)   ○ Grewe et al. (2007)
● Friederici et al. (2006)   ● Röder et al. (2002)

Plate 4. Activation maxima in neuroimaging studies of word order permutations (restricted to studies of simple sentences).

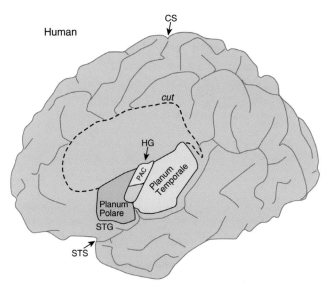

Plate 5. Brain regions implicated in the processing of prosodic information. Note that the Rolandic operculum, which is also mentioned in the text, is situated at the inferior end of the central sulcus, deep to the lateral surface of the brain.

Abbreviations: CS – central sulcus; HG – Heschl's gyrus; PAC – primary auditory cortex; STG – superior temporal gyurs; STS – superior temporal sulcus. *Source*: Adapted from Hall, Hart, and Johnsrude 2003.

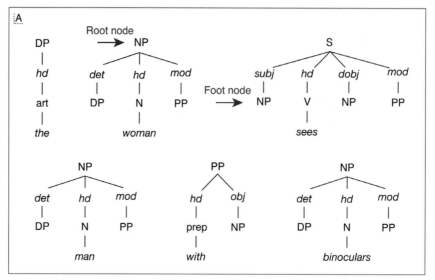

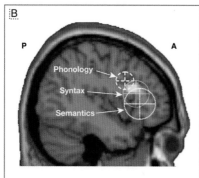 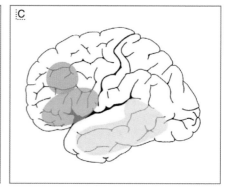

Plate 6. Schematic depiction of the main features of the memory, unification, and control (MUC) framework. Panel A shows sample syntactic frames, which may be unified with one another if the category and features of a root node in one frame match those of a foot node in another (cf. Vosse and Kempen 2000). The assumed "unification gradient" in the left inferior frontal gyrus and the left ventral premotor cortex (see the text for details) is depicted in Panel B. The basic neuroanatomical assumptions of the MUC framework are shown in Panel C: regions implicated in the memory component are shaded in yellow, the neural substrate for unification is shaded in blue, and regions engaging in control are shaded in gray.

Source: Adapted from Hagoort 2005.

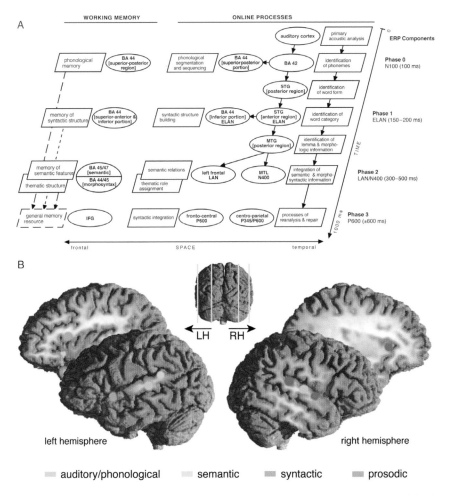

Plate 7. Schematic illustration of the main features of the neurocognitive model of language comprehension. Panel A shows the main architectural assumptions of the model, whereas Panel B depicts its neuroanatomical claims.

Source: Adapted from Friederici 2002; Friederici and Alter 2004.

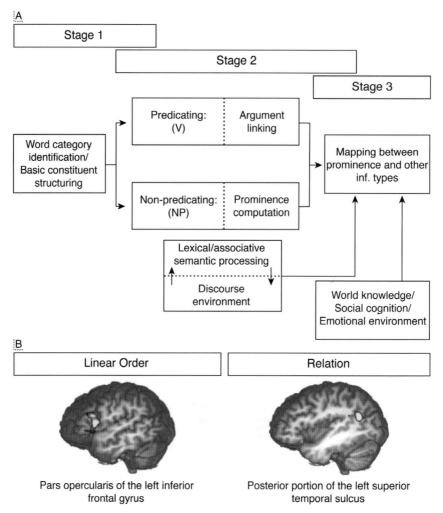

A

Stage 1

Stage 2

Stage 3

Word category
identification/
Basic constituent
structuring

Predicating:
(V)

Argument
linking

Non-predicating:
(NP)

Prominence
computation

Mapping between
prominence and other
inf. types

Lexical/associative
semantic processing

Discourse
environment

World knowledge/
Social cognition/
Emotional environment

B

Linear Order

Relation

Pars opercularis of the left inferior
frontal gyrus

Posterior portion of the left superior
temporal sulcus

Plate 8. The architecture of the extended argument dependency model. The basic
claims of the model architecture are shown in Panel A. Panel B depicts the neuroanatomical correlates of prominence processing with regard to linear order and
argument relations (Actor/Undergoer), respectively.

Source: Adapted from Bornkessel-Schlesewsky and Schlesewsky 2008; Bornkessel-Schlesewsky and Schlesewsky 2009.

centro-parietal negativity between 300 and 900 ms, while there was no difference between the ambiguous and unambiguous accusative conditions. On the basis of this finding, Hopf et al. (1998) argued for an accusative-over-dative preference in German (see also Bader and Bayer 2006).

However, findings by Kulik (2000) call into question the general applicability of an accusative-preference in object–object ambiguities in German. Using sentences such as (9.46), she examined whether the intervening relative clause in Hopf et al.'s critical sentence conditions played a crucial role in engendering the observed data pattern.

(9.46)   Example stimuli from Kulik (2000)

Das   Mädchen   dachte,...
the   girl   thought...

a. ...dass   man   Freundinnen,   denen   man
    ...that   one   friends[ACC/DAT],   who[DAT]   one
    nachfühlt,   zuhören   und   beistehen sollte.
    empathizes.with,   listen.to(DAT)   and   support should
    "...that one should listen to and support friends with whom one empathizes."

b. ...dass man Freundinnen,   die   man
    ...that one   friends[ACC/DAT], who[NOM/ACC] one
    besitzt,   zuhören   und   beistehen   sollte.
    owns,   listen.to(DAT)   and   support   should
    "...that one should listen to and support friends that one has."

In the examples in (9.46), the bare plural NP *Freundinnen* is ambiguous between accusative in dative (the nominative reading is ruled out by the preceding impersonal pronoun *man* which is obligatorily a subject), thus introducing a very similar ambiguity to that examined by Hopf et al. (1998). However, in contrast to Hopf and colleagues, Kulik manipulated the relative clause modifying the critical ambiguous argument such that the relative pronoun either bore dative (9.46a) or accusative case (9.46b). The ERP results showed a negativity very similar to that observed by Hopf et al. for (9.46b) in comparison to an unambiguous control condition, while no such effect was observed for (9.46a). This finding indicates that, in contrast to the subject-first preference, the preference for accusative over dative case is highly dependent on the environment in which the ambiguous object argument is encountered.

This observation is supported by behavioral findings. In an eye-tracking experiment, Scheepers, Hemforth, and Konieczny (1998) only observed an accusative-over-dative preference when the ambiguous NP occurred at the beginning of a German clause (9.47b), but not when it was positioned within the middlefield (9.47a).

(9.47)   Example stimuli from Scheepers et al. (1998)

   a. Die   Gemeinderäte   werden   Pastor Steffens
      [the city.councillors][PL] will[PL] [Pastor Steffens][SG]
      auf der Hauptversammlung wahrscheinlich nicht
      at   the annual.meeting   probably   not
      antreffen / begegnen.
      meet(ACC) / meet(DAT).
      "The city councillors probably won't meet Pastor Steffens at the annual general meeting."

   b. Pastor   Steffens   werden   die Gemeinderäte
      [Pastor Steffens][SG]   will[PL] [the city.councillors][PL]
      wahrscheinlich nicht   antreffen / begegnen.
      probably   not   meet(ACC) / meet(DAT)
      "The city councillors probably won't meet Pastor Steffens."

The critical ambiguity in (9.47) concerns the reading of *Pastor Steffens*. In both (9.47a) and (9.47b), this argument can only be an object because a possible subject reading is ruled out on account of the plural morphology of the finite auxiliary (*werden*). Unambiguously case-marked control sentences were also included in the study. A reading time disadvantage (in terms of regression path durations) for the disambiguation towards a dative reading was only observable for sentences such as (9.47b). As the linear distance between the ambiguous argument and the point of disambiguation was matched across the two-sentence types, these results appear compatible with two possible interpretations: the difference between (9.47a) and (9.47b) may be attributable, (a) to the distinction between the middlefield and prefield in German, or (b) to the fact that (9.47b) involves a reanalysis of the initial subject preference for the ambiguous argument, while (9.47a) does not. The second option appears to provide a more principled explanation, as it is compatible with a revision along markedness hierarchies of case and/or grammatical function (NOM < ACC < DAT;

subject < direct object < indirect object). Whichever explanation finally turns out to be correct, however, the data clearly speak against a general preference for accusative over dative case in German.

Finally, more recent electrophysiological evidence also speaks against an object case preference in the German middlefield. In their study on subject–object ambiguities with accusative and dative case (example 9.40), Bornkessel et al. (2004b) observed an increased N400 effect for accusative as opposed to dative verbs in the clause-final position. This finding suggests that, if anything, accusative verbs yield increased processing load in comparison to dative verbs following two case-ambiguous arguments. However, a possible problem with this conclusion is that the comparison between accusative and dative verbs was implemented as a between-participants factor in the Bornkessel et al. (2004b) study, i.e. each participant read either only sentences with dative verbs or with accusative verbs. This potential caveat was ruled out by a subsequent experiment (Schlesewsky and Bornkessel 2006), in which accusative and dative sentences were contrasted in a within-participants design and verb type disambiguation was separated from word order disambiguation.

(9.48)   Example stimuli from Schlesewsky and Bornkessel (2006)
          . . . dass Richard   Künstlerinnen
          . . . that Richard[NOM/ACC/DAT]   artists[NOM/ACC/DAT]
          gesehen/gedankt   hat, . . .
          seen(ACC)/thanked(DAT)   has
          ". . . that Richard has seen/thanked artists."

In sentences such as (9.48), accusative-assigning participles again elicited an N400 in comparison to dative participles, despite (a) equally probable disambiguations towards accusative and dative case, and (b) no potentially confounding influence of a simultaneous subject–object order disambiguation (which took place at the following auxiliary). Schlesewsky and Bornkessel (2006) interpret the difference between the two verb types in the spirit of a proposal by Gennari and Poeppel (2003), who suggest that lexical/aspectual complexity of verbs engenders increased processing effort in ways that may sometimes appear counterintuitive (e.g. *build* is more costly to process than *love* because it denotes an event rather than a state). A similar approach can be applied to the accusative–dative distinction with German two-argument verbs: as assumed by classical German grammarians (Helbig and Buscha 1996) and more recent functional approaches (Van Valin 2005), dative verbs are lower in transitivity than accusative verbs and there-fore lower in lexical complexity. Furthermore, as the electrophysio-logical difference between the two verb types was more pronounced when the preceding arguments were case-ambiguous, there is no evidence to suggest that this general lexical difference could have overridden a possible accusative-over-dative preference.[18]

In summary, the full range of findings on German indicates that a preference for accusative over dative is only observable as a consequence of a preceding reanalysis, i.e. when the initial subject-preference for the ambiguous argument could not be upheld. The German data pattern is thus very similar to that reported for English, in which the direct object interpretation of an initial wh-phrase is always second to a subject analysis (see Note 17). Note that these results can also be derived via the so-called "NP accessibility hierarchy" (Keenan and Comrie 1977), accord-ing to which the direct object is the second unmarked choice when the subject interpretation of a "filler" must be abandoned. Whether the N400 that has been reliably observed as a correlate of object–object reanalyses should be interpreted in a similar way to the N400 effects for subject–object reanalyses (see section 9.3.2) presently remains an open question.

Notes

1. Note that the interpretive characteristics of dative object-experiencer verbs such as *auffallen* ("to be striking to") correlate with a number of gram-matical properties. For example, verbs of this type can undergo neither passivization nor nominalization. As argued by Jackendoff (1972), these syntactic/morphological operations presuppose an argument hierarchy in which the subject thematically outranks the object, a criterion which verbs such as *auffallen* do not fulfill. The impossibility of passivization/nomin-alization thereby provides independent confirmation of the classification of dative object-experiencer verbs as "true" object-experiencer verbs. By contrast, accusative object-experiencer verbs in German (and object-experiencer verbs in English) can undergo these operations (cf. *The mask frightened the boy.* vs. *The boy was frightened by the mask.*).

2. In languages with a close correlation between linear (structural) position and thematic interpretation, the two dimensions (i.e. grammatical func-tions and thematic relations) may again converge. Initial evidence in this regard stems from studies examining Dutch (i) and English (ii):

   (i) Example stimuli from Lamers (2001)

a. De	oude	vrouw	in	de	straat	verzorgde	hij
the	old	woman	in	the	street	took.care.of	he[NOM]

       vrijwel   elke   dag.
       almost   every   day
       "He took care of the old woman in the street almost every day."

   b. Het oude plantsoen in de   straat <u>verzorgde</u> hij
      the   old   park   in the   street took.care.of he[NOM]
      vrijwel   elke   dag.
      almost   every   day
      "He took care of the old park in the street almost every day."

(ii) Example stimuli from Phillips, Kazanina, and Abada (2005)

   a.... who <u>the man</u>...
   b.... that <u>the man</u>...

Both Lamers (2001) and Phillips et al. (2005) observed early positivities (at the position of *verzorgde* in (ib) vs. (ia) and of *the man* in (iia) vs. (iib)) when the association between the first argument and the highest-ranking thematic role was disconfirmed. In the Dutch examples, this was the case at the position of the verb in (ib), because the verb type employed was not compatible with an inanimate subject (highest-ranking argument). In (iia), by contrast, the NP *the man* disambiguates towards an object relative clause. The appearance of a similar effect as for the reanalysis of case-based thematic assignments in German in these two non-case-marking languages appears to indicate that here thematic relations may be assigned on the basis of an argument's position in the sentence. For further discussion, see Schlesewsky and Bornkessel (2004), and Bornkessel and Schlesewsky (2006a).

3. A further study in the literature argues for a correlation between thematic processing and the pars triangularis of the left inferior frontal gyrus on the basis of a violation paradigm with sentences that contained an additional verb (*The coach watched the poet and told the visitor took in the evening*) (Newman et al. 2003). However, on account of the nature of the violation, the contribution of thematic processing to this frontal activation is not clear. Thus, an additional verb could induce difficulties with respect to agreement, subcategorization, word order and a number of other dimensions.

4. The N400 effect at the position of the relative clause subject in fact only reached significance in participants that were "good comprehenders" (scoring 75% correct or above on the comprehension task employed). These individual differences might be attributable to the fact that, in contrast to the German study described above, Weckerly and Kutas' experiment employed complex structures involving object relative clauses (for further discussion of the particular properties of these structures, see Chapter 10). An interpretation along these lines appears plausible in view of the finding that individual differences in verbal working memory

capacity can influence plausibility-based N400 effects in syntactically complex structures, i.e. that participants with a low verbal working memory capacity do not show an N400 effect for plausibility violations in such sentences (Gunter, Jackson, and Mulder 1995). Furthermore, the group effect in the Weckerly and Kutas study is interesting in that it appears to rule out a simple lexical explanation of the N400 effects in both positions (which always occurred in response to the inanimate vs. the animate noun), but rather suggests that the second N400 at least must be due to higher-level relational processing.

5. Note, however that the *bèi*-construction also differs from "European-style" passive constructions in that it is traditionally associated with an adversative reading, i.e. a reading in which the first NP (the Undergoer) is negatively affected by the event described (e.g. Chappell 1986; Bisang 2006).

6. An "unmarked" word order is typically defined as an order that can be felicitously uttered in the absence of any constraining context (Siwierska 1988). For a critical review of the notion of markedness in general, see Haspelmath (2006).

7. Note that Röder and colleagues additionally observed activation in the middle portion of the left superior temporal gyrus (STG) in response to the word order manipulation. This finding is interesting because none of the studies on word order in German to be discussed in the remainder of this chapter observed a comparable activation. One reason for this difference might be modality-related: the Röder et al. study used auditory presentation, while all of the other experiments presented sentences visually.

8. The *middlefield* ("Mittelfeld") is defined as the region of the German clause delimited to the left by the complementizer (in embedded clauses) or the finite verb (in main clauses) and to the right by an infinitive, participle, or particle.

9. Note, however, that the distinction between the left pars triangularis (BA 45) and pars opercularis (BA 44) seems to involve a shift of the word order-related activation maximum rather than a double dissociation, since Bahlmann et al. (2007) also observed a modulation of activation in BA 44 in a region of interest analysis based on the comparison of all sentence conditions vs. rest. Conversely, at least two previous studies of word order permutations in the German middlefield (Röder et al. 2002; Bornkessel et al. 2005) showed activation maxima in BA 44, but with activation extending into BA 45.

10. The first electrophysiological study on scrambling in Japanese was reported by Ueno and Kluender (2003). However, the results of this experiment are not directly relevant to the discussion of the scrambling negativity, as the authors did not contrast ERPs to an initial scrambled object with those elicited by a subject in the same position. By contrast,

Hagiwara et al. (2007) observed a central negativity (between 300 and 400 ms) in response to an initial accusative as opposed to an initial topic-marked NP (which is preferably interpreted as a subject) in an ERP experiment using visual presentation. This effect, which was followed by a sustained negativity for the accusative-initial sentences (which involved long scrambling) might also be interpreted as a scrambling negativity. A possible explanation for the appearance of this effect in Hagiwara et al.'s study may be that the segmented visual presentation employed could have fostered the insertion of prosodic boundaries between the visual chunks. Thus, with this type of presentation, the likelihood that an initial object will be interpreted as scrambled is increased substantially (as with an explicit auditory cue in the Wolff et al. study); for further discussion, see Wolff et al. (2008).

11. Adopting an analysis proposed by Rizzi (1982), de Vincenzi (1991: 31) in fact assumes that the empty category in question is a *pro* in both cases, but that it forms a chain with the post-verbal subject and transmits case and a thematic role to it in (9.37b).

12. MacDonald and Christiansen (2002) put forward a somewhat similar explanation on the basis of a connectionist model. However, rather than appealing to the increased competition between the two NPs in the OSV structure, they assume that the SVO structure in an English relative clause is more easily amenable to association with simple main clause structures. Thus, even in the absence of a frequency advantage for subject-first relative clauses, the model generalizes from its experience with other structures. Nonetheless, this explanation crucially relies upon the difference between SVO and OSV configurations. Thus, it can essentially be viewed as a variant of the "canonical sentoid strategy" proposed in the 1970s (Bever 1970; Fodor et al. 1974). This strategy stated that "whenever one encounters a surface sequence NP V (NP), assume that these items are, respectively, subject, verb and object of a deep sentoid" (Fodor et al. 1974: 345).

13. The latency differences between the P345 in relative clauses and the late positivity in all other sentence constructions were interpreted as reflecting an "easier" reanalysis in the former construction (Friederici and Mecklinger 1996). Thus, in relative clauses, the position of the relative pronoun itself is not affected by the reanalysis operation. Rather, only a repositioning of the relative pronoun trace is required. An alternative explanation in the spirit of Fodor and Inoue's *Diagnosis Model* (Fodor and Inoue 1994; Fodor and Inoue 1998) was advanced by Friederici (1998), who proposed that the P345 reflects "diagnosis" of a processing conflict rather than structural reanalysis proper.

14. The overall pattern is complicated further by more recent findings of robust N400 effects in accusative structures such as (9.40a) when these are

presented in the auditory modality (Leuckefeld 2005; Haupt et al. 2008). These results indicate that, while reanalyses in dative structures show a higher affinity for N400 effects, there is no one-to-one correspondence between dative reanalyses and the N400 on the one hand and accusative reanalyses and the P600 on the other. Rather, it appears that the status of the N400 as a regular correlate of reanalysis should no longer be neglected. From such a perspective, three possible consequences for the interpretation of reanalysis-related ERP components (and, by extension, ERP components more generally) arise: (a) ERP components are not systematic and therefore cannot be interpreted as evidence for qualitative processing distinctions; (b) the simple mapping between ERP components and macroscopic linguistic domains (e.g. in terms of rule-based vs. lexically stored information) cannot be upheld; or (c) the status of grammatical function reanalyses within the processing architecture needs to be reconsidered. The first option is clearly not desirable and, in addition, appears to be contradicted by the high degree of reliability with which particular components are observed within similar experimental paradigms. Thus, complex component patterns of the type described here rather seem to indicate that the driving factors behind the processing of the manipulation in question have not yet been fully understood. Point number two, by contrast, indeed appears to follow from the full range of existing data. Nonetheless, even if an N400 effect cannot be taken as an unambiguous marker of lexical/semantic processing effort and a direct association between the P600 and syntactic processing is also problematic (see Chapter 12), this does not mean that component distinctions are principally uninformative. Rather, it only suggests that the level of generalization at which component distinctions are described needs to be modified. Finally, if we continue to take the qualitative distinction between components seriously, processing models are confronted with the phenomenon that grammatical function reanalyses reliably elicit a distinct component pattern from other syntactic reanalysis types (e.g. main verb – reduced relative ambiguities, see Chapter 12.1). This might be explained, for example, by assuming that the relative ordering of subject and object in simple sentences does not affect the phrase structure representation of the sentence (see Bornkessel and Schlesewsky 2006a and Chapter 15.4 for a processing model incorporating this assumption; and Fanselow 2001; Van Valin 2005, for theoretical motivations from the perspective of two very different grammatical theories). In this way, a reanalysis towards an object-initial order would not require alterations to the phrase structure (as required by other types of reanalysis) but only a reindexation of the arguments (Haupt et al. 2008).

15. In contrast to these findings on the German middlefield (Bornkessel et al. 2005; Bornkessel-Schlesewsky et al. submitted), Bahlmann et al. (2007)

observed a dissociation between unambiguous and locally ambiguous object-initial sentences involving the German prefield. Whereas unambiguous object-initial sentences yielded increased activation in left BA 45 (see the discussion of example 9.30 in section 9.4.2.1), comparable sentences requiring a reanalysis towards an object-initial order showed an activation increase in the left supramarginal gyrus and the posterior portion of the left middle temporal gyrus. The overall data pattern thus again points towards a distinction between the processing of word order permutations in the prefield and the middlefield in German (see section 9.2.4).

16. This manipulation of object ambiguity is possible because Turkish is a language with "differential object marking" (DOM, cf. Bossong 1985; Aissen 2003). This means that, in Turkish, direct objects are only marked with accusative case when they are specific. The following examples (from Comrie 1989) illustrate the interpretive difference between objects with and without accusative marking:

   (i) Hasan   öküz-ü   aldı
       Hasan   ox-ACC   bought
       "Hasan bought the ox."

   (ii) Hasan   öküz   aldı
       Hasan   ox   bought
       "Hasan bought an ox/oxen."

17. However, the early findings from English also raised the following well-known problem: the first *possible* trace position in sentences such as (9.42a) is, in fact, the subject position following the auxiliary (i.e. the position occupied by *the little child*), so that the first filled-gap effect should be expected at this position. Yet the available data are not fully clear on this matter. Whereas Stowe (1986) found no filled-gap effect for the subject position, Lee (2004) did observe such an effect. More specifically, the filled subject-gap effect in the Lee study appeared to be driven primarily by differences between sentences in which the region between filler and gap was lengthened by the insertion of an adjunct clause (although the interaction between length and gap presence did not reach significance).

18. In general, the situation in German is more complex than in English because the unmarked word order in ditransitive constructions is nominative-dative-accusative. Thus, an advantage for accusative case for the second argument encountered necessarily presupposes that a transitive analysis of the sentence is pursued. (In English, by contrast, the direct object is always right-adjacent to the verb, irrespective of whether an indirect object follows or not.) ERP evidence for a dative-before-accusative preference in German stems from the observation of a scrambling

negativity for an accusative vs. a dative argument following an initial nominative in the middlefield (Rösler et al. 1998). However, as this experiment contained only ditransitive sentences, it cannot be ruled out that the effect was strategically driven. Thus, while it clearly speaks in favor of a dative-before-accusative order in ditransitive sentences, it may not be informative with respect to the general preference arising at the position of the first non-subject argument when the valency of the clause-final verb is not yet known.

10

The processing of complex structures

By way of analogy with Friedrich Nietzsche's 1872 book *Die Geburt der Tragödie aus dem Geiste der Musik* ("The birth of tragedy from the spirit of music"), one might well speak of the birth of psycholinguistics from the spirit of complex sentences. Thus, the interest in examining how sentences are processed had its origins in the classical debate on linguistic competence vs. performance (Miller and Chomsky 1963; Chomsky 1965). From this perspective, it was primarily important to differentiate between linguistic and non-linguistic (e.g. working memory-based) factors in the comprehension of complex sentence constructions (e.g. multiple center embeddings), rather than to model the mechanisms operative in simple sentences.[1] The overwhelming number of studies on the processing of relative clause constructions may be considered a consequence of this original motivation for studying how people process sentences. Yet this historical motivation notwithstanding, psycholinguistic examinations of relative clauses have provided many insights on the architecture and mechanisms of human language comprehension. A related line of investigation that has been pursued concerns the establishment and reconstruction of long-distance dependencies during comprehension. This chapter will therefore focus on these two domains in turn.

10.1 Processing relative clauses

10.1.1 *Basic observations*

One of the earliest observations with respect to the comprehension of relative clauses was that object relatives such as (10.1a) lead to increased processing cost in comparison to subject relatives such as (10.1b).

(10.1)   Example stimuli from Ford (1983)

> a. The managers that the designer praised examined the sketches.
> b. The managers that praised the designer examined the sketches.

The disadvantage for object relatives was originally reported for both English and French, with evidence stemming from a variety of behavioral methods such as comprehension tasks, eye-tracking, phoneme monitoring, and continuous lexical decision (e.g. Wanner and Maratsos 1978; Frauenfelder, Segui, and Mehler 1980; Ford 1983). The second "wave" of studies on relative clause processing was later initiated in the early 1990s, beginning with an experiment by King and Just (1991). In a self-paced reading study manipulating concurrent memory load, they observed that readers with a low verbal working memory capacity (as measured by the "reading span" task, Daneman and Carpenter 1980)[2] read object relative sentences more slowly than subject relatives and also performed worse on a comprehension task than high capacity readers. This finding played a central role in motivating a model of sentence comprehension centered around individual differences (particularly in terms of working memory capacity) and possible differences in processing behavior resulting from them (the "CC Reader" model; Just and Carpenter 1992).

Even though a number of problems have been noted with respect to the working memory task used in this line of work (Waters and Caplan 1996) and the underlying conceptualization of working memory during sentence processing assumed therein also proved controversial (Caplan and Waters 1999), this finding was highly influential with respect to a whole class of psychologically inspired processing models. While all of these approaches were concerned with deriving the higher processing costs of object relatives and other complex constructions (e.g. center embeddings), they differ with respect to the question of which mechanism is held responsible for these costs. Gibson (1998; 2000), for example, proposed an approach based on classical assumptions regarding working memory as a limited-capacity system. In his model, processing costs arise when dependent elements are integrated with one another (e.g. arguments and verbs) and increase when this integration must take place over a longer distance (i.e. when integration is non-local). English object relatives are therefore more difficult to process than subject relatives because of the required non-local integration of the object with the verb that arises from the OSV order. Adopting a rather different conceptualization of working memory (see Jonides et al. 2008), Lewis et al.

(2006) model the differences in reading times between object and subject relative clauses as a function of activation, decay, and retrieval from working memory (see also McElree et al. 2003, for an approach relying upon retrieval and content-addressable memory structures). Finally, Gordon, Hendrick, and Johnson (2001) put forward a similarity-based interference account of the processing difficulty arising in object relatives. This idea builds upon an observation initially made by Bever (1974) that center-embedded object relatives become easier to process when NPs of different types are used (cf. *The reporter everyone I met trusts said the president won't resign* vs. *The reporter the politician the commentator met trusts said the president won't resign*; cited from Gordon et al. 2001: 1412). According to Gordon and colleagues, English object relative clauses are more susceptible to interference between similar NPs because both arguments occur pre-verbally and must therefore be stored and subsequently accessed. The retrieval of the correct order information is impaired by the similarity of the two NPs.

As is apparent from the preceding discussion, theoretical assumptions about the contrast between subject and object relative clauses have been driven primarily by the word order distinctions between these two clause types in languages such as English or French. However, further studies have attempted to extend the range of available data to languages with different types of relative clause structures: verb-final, post-nominal relative clauses (Dutch: e.g. Frazier 1987b; German: e.g. Schriefers et al. 1995); verb-final, pre-nominal relative clauses (Japanese and Korean: e.g. Miyamoto and Nakamura 2003; Ishizuka 2005; Kwon et al. 2006); and verb-medial, post-nominal relative clauses (Chinese: Hsiao and Gibson 2003; Lin and Bever 2006). For Dutch, German, Japanese, and Korean, a clear processing advantage for subject relative clauses has emerged, whereas matters are more controversial for Chinese: Hsiao and Gibson (2003) reported an advantage for object relatives, while Lin and Bever (2006) argued for the opposite preference. Similarly to the results on the subject-first preference discussed in section 9.3, the lower processing complexity of subject relatives shows a striking cross-linguistic stability in spite of the vastly differing structural configurations in the individual languages examined.

In addition to structural and more general cognitive factors, several further parameters influencing the subject vs. object relative distinction have been identified. The most prominent of these concerns the animacy of the two arguments. Traxler, Morris, and Seely (2002) found that the disadvantage for English object relative clauses (as measured via eye-tracking) is virtually eliminated when the relative clause subject is animate and the head noun is inanimate (e.g. *The movie that the director watched received a prize at the film festival*). Note that this facilitation was not due simply to the presence of an animacy distinction between the two critical arguments but crucially required a constellation in which an animate argument (relative clause subject) acted upon an inanimate argument (head noun and relative clause object). Furthermore, this relational animacy effect cannot be accounted for in terms of verb class differences (Traxler et al. 2005). Very similar results from Dutch attest to the stability of the animacy influence (Mak, Vonk, and Schriefers 2002; Mak et al. 2006).

Finally, the examination of relative clauses is rendered even more complex by the fact that influences from outside the relative clause must also be considered. In particular, the coreference relation between the head noun and the relative pronoun leads to a mutual influence of these two elements upon one another. The earliest observation of this type was made by Sheldon (1974) in a study examining the acquisition of relative clauses. She found that sentences containing relative clauses are easier to understand when the head noun and the relative pronoun share the same grammatical function (the *parallel function hypothesis*). Thus, object relative clauses are much less difficult to process when they modify a head noun that is also an object. In a somewhat similar spirit, the *perspective-taking* account proposed that sentences are easy to process when they allow for the same perspective to be maintained (MacWhinney 1977; MacWhinney and Pléh 1998). This account is based on the assumption that listeners adopt a particular perspective depending on the grammatical function of the first argument encountered and may subsequently need to shift this perspective, for example when encountering a relative clause. Thus, an object relative clause modifying a subject will require a perspective shift at the beginning of the relative clause and again at its end if it is center-embedded (because the perspective of the matrix clause must be readopted). The concept of feature sharing between the head noun and the relative pronoun is also of primary importance within a more linguistically-driven account centered around the notion of *case matching* (Schlesewsky 1997; Fanselow et al. 1999b; Stevenson and Smolensky 2006). Here, it is assumed that less processing effort is required when the case features of the head noun and the relative pronoun match. Evidence for processing strategies based on case matching have been observed in

German (Schlesewsky 1997). In this language, such a strategy can be viewed as a relict of grammatical principles in earlier stages of the language (i.e. case matching occurred overtly in Old High and Middle High German, in the sense that the case of a head noun could "overwrite" the required case of a relative pronoun or vice versa when the two independently required cases did not match).

10.1.2 Neurophysiological evidence

The earliest electrophysiological studies on relative clause processing were published in the mid-1990s. Whereas experiments conducted in German were primarily interested in examining the subject-first preference in case-ambiguous relative clauses (Mecklinger et al. 1995, see the discussion in section 9.3.2), King and Kutas (1995) aimed to investigate ERP correlates of the overall complexity difference between subject and object relative clauses in English. To this end, they computed multi-word ERPs spanning the length of the relative clause and the remainder of the matrix clause. They found a sustained left anterior negativity (sLAN) for object as opposed to subject relative clauses throughout this entire region of analysis (for a replication in the auditory modality, see Müller, King, and Kutas 1997) and interpreted this effect as a correlate of the increased demands on working memory engendered by the object relatives (see Figure 10.1, for an illustration of a typical sLAN effect). However, one potential concern with respect to this result is that any comparison of subject and object relative clauses in English necessitates a contrast between ERPs to different word categories. This factor cannot be neglected as trivial, as the ERP method is very sensitive to word category distinctions (cf. Federmeier et al. 2000; for an application to the difference between NP-V-NP and NP-NP-V word orders, see Schlesewsky, Bornkessel, and Meyer 2002). Nonetheless, a similar sLAN effect was also observed in German embedded wh-clauses, which are structurally similar to relative clauses and allow for the comparison of two verb-final constructions (Fiebach et al. 2002; see section 10.2 for further discussion). The electrophysiological findings thereby appear to support the basic assumption that object relative clauses are more complex than subject relative clauses.

The influences of animacy found in eye-tracking and self-paced reading studies (see above) are also mirrored in the electrophysiological domain. As discussed in section 9.2.2, Weckerly and Kutas

(1999) contrasted object relative clauses with an animate or inanimate head noun and a relative clause subject of inverse animacy (see example 9.21). In this study, the behavioral disadvantage for object relatives with an animate head noun and an inanimate relative clause subject was reflected in the occurrence of an N400 at the position of the relative clause subject and of an anterior negativity at the position of the matrix verb following the relative clause. Interestingly, these effects were most pronounced for "good comprehenders" (see Note 4 to Chapter 9), an observation that may be related to Traxler et al.'s (2005) finding that participants with a high verbal working memory capacity showed a stronger influence of animacy on the processing of object relative clauses.

Working memory influences have also been found with respect to the processing of German relative clauses. Employing a similar design to Mecklinger et al. (1995), i.e. using locally ambiguous relative clauses with disambiguation effected by a clause-final auxiliary (see example 9.38), Vos et al. (2001) additionally varied concurrent memory load and contrasted high and low span participants. For the high span group, disambiguation towards an object relative clause engendered a similar early positivity to that found by Mecklinger and colleagues for fast comprehenders. The low span readers, by contrast, showed a late frontal positivity in the same comparison, which moreover varied in latency depending on the number of items concurrently memorized. Vos et al. interpreted the early positivity as reflecting a relatively fast and automatic diagnosis of the processing conflict (see also Friederici 1998), while they viewed the late positivity as a correlate of "regular", controlled processes of reanalysis.

A puzzle raised by the ERP findings on locally ambiguous relative clauses in German concerns the interpretation of the early positivity. Recall from section 9.3.2 that this effect is engendered exclusively by subject–object reanalyses in relative clauses, while reanalyses in declarative main clauses (Frisch et al. 2002; Matzke et al. 2002; Knoeferle et al. 2008), wh-questions (beim Graben et al. 2000), and complement clauses (e.g. Friederici and Mecklinger 1996; Bornkessel et al. 2004b; Schlesewsky and Bornkessel 2006; Haupt et al. 2008) correlate with late positivities and N400s. The exceptional status of relative clauses is further supported by the finding of a late positivity for unambiguous accusative relative pronouns in relative clauses modifying a nominative head noun in sentences such as (10.2b) (from Friederici et al. 1998).

(10.2) Example stimuli from Friederici et al. (1998)

> a. Das ist der Direktor,   der...
>   this is   [the director] [NOM] who[NOM]...
>
> b. Das ist der Direktor,   den...
>   this is   [the director] [NOM] who[ACC]...

By contrast, this effect does not occur at the position of an accusative wh-pronoun in embedded German wh-questions (Fiebach et al. 2002). As these are deemed similar to relative clauses in all structural respects, but do not share the close association to a clause-external antecedent, the overall data pattern provides strong converging support for the idea that the processing of a relative pronoun (and, thereby, of the relative clause as a whole) cannot be viewed as independent of the properties of the head noun. The electrophysiological findings thus directly support the assumptions of accounts on the processing of relative clauses which stress the importance of the relation between head noun and relative pronoun (Sheldon 1974; MacWhinney 1977; Schlesewsky 1997).

   Bornkessel and Schlesewsky (2006a) proposed that these insights can also contribute to the interpretation of the early positivity for grammatical function reanalysis in relative clauses. As discussed in section 9.2.2, a very similar ERP effect has been observed for the reanalysis of hierarchical thematic relations in German verb-final clauses, albeit only in the presence of unambiguously case-marked arguments (Bornkessel et al. 2002a; Bornkessel et al. 2003b; Leuckefeld 2005). A parsimonious account of the effect in relative clauses would therefore assume that this result can also be explained in terms of thematic reanalysis. Yet how can this be possible given that other findings have shown that this type of reanalysis does not occur in ambiguously case-marked sentences? This apparent paradox can be reconciled by appealing to the notion of case-based feature-sharing between head noun and relative pronoun: the relative pronoun receives an interpretation in terms of a generalized thematic role by way of its association with the nominative-marked head noun. When this interpretation is disconfirmed by the clause-final auxiliary, an early positivity results. This account straightforwardly derives the striking difference between the electrophysiological correlates for the processing of relative clauses in comparison to all other clause types, both with respect to the early positivity for word order disambiguation and regarding the late positivity at the position of a non-matching relative pronoun.

10.1.3 *Neuroanatomical evidence*

Relative clause structures have also played a predominant role in the literature on the functional neuroanatomy of sentence processing. In particular, many early studies on this topic used the contrast between subject and object relative clauses to isolate brain activity correlating with increases in linguistic (syntactic) complexity (Just et al. 1996 using fMRI; Stromswold et al. 1996 using PET). While Just et al. (1996) contrasted sentences very similar to those in example (10.1) with conjoined clauses as an additional control (*The reporter attacked the senator and admitted the error*), Stromswold et al. examined sentences such as (10.3).

(10.3)   Example stimuli from Stromswold et al. (1996)

        a. The juice that the child spilled stained the rug.

        b. The child spilled the juice that stained the rug.

In addition to several other regions of activation (e.g. superior temporal cortex, "Wernicke's area"), Just et al. (1996) and Stromswold et al. (1996) observed that activation in "Broca's region" in the left inferior frontal gyrus (IFG) correlated with increasing sentence complexity. Subsequent research showed that the pars opercularis of the left IFG in particular (BA 44) – and sometimes adjacent BA 45 – is sensitive to this type of linguistic manipulation. Complexity-related activation in this region is independent of the modality (visual or auditory) of presentation (Caplan, Alpert, and Waters 1999; Constable et al. 2004). Furthermore, it is modulated by the critical factors that were shown to influence the processing of object relative clauses in behavioral and ERP studies. Examining sentences with an animacy contrast between head noun and relative clause subject, Chen et al. (2006) observed increased pars opercularis activation only for object relatives with an animate head noun and an inanimate relative clause subject (e.g. *The golfer that the lightning struck survived the incident*). However, as the control condition in this study consisted of subject relative clauses attached to an object head noun (e.g. *The lightning struck the golfer that survived the incident*), the absence of a relative activation increase in the object relative condition with an animate relative clause subject might also be due to the function or perspective mismatch between head noun and relative pronoun in the control sentences. Nonetheless, this finding is consistent with the observation that processing costs are alleviated in object relative clauses with an inanimate head noun and an animate relative clause subject (cf. Weckerly and Kutas 1999; Traxler et al. 2002; Traxler et al. 2005; Mak et al. 2002; Mak et al. 2006).

Converging support for the idea that increases in pars opercularis activation for object relative clauses may be modulated by the relation between the relative pronoun and the head noun adjacent to it stems from a study employing sentences such as (10.4) (Caplan et al. 2001).

(10.4)   Example stimuli from Caplan et al. (2001)

    a. The reporter covering the big story carefully who the photographer admired appreciated the award.

    b. The reporter covering the big story carefully who admired the photographer appreciated the award.

When the head noun and relative pronoun were not adjacent (as in 10.4), no increased inferior frontal activation was observable for object relative (10.4a) as opposed to subject relative clauses (10.4b) (Caplan et al. 2001). As results from case marking languages have indicated that case-matching effects during language comprehension crucially require adjacency between the head noun and the relative pronoun (Schlesewsky 1997), this finding suggests that the commonly observed processing disadvantage for object relative clauses in English does not appear to depend solely on relative clause-internal complexity differences.

Whereas neuroimaging data from English have shown a reliable correlation between increased processing cost in relative clauses and the pars opercularis of the left IFG, findings from other languages indicate that this region cannot be considered a universal locus for relative clause processing. On the one hand, data from Hebrew seem to support the observation of increased activation for object relative clauses in this cortical region (Ben-Shachar et al. 2003).

(10.5)   Example stimuli from Ben-Shachar et al. (2003)

    a. azarti   la-yalda še   Mary   ra'ata ba-park
       I-helped   the-girl   who   Mary   saw   in-the-park

    b. amarti   le-Mary   še   ha-yalda   raca   ba-park
       I-told   Mary   that   the-girl   ran   in-the-park

As shown in example (10.5), Ben-Shachar et al. contrasted object relatives with complement clauses with the aim of comparing a sentence condition with a transformation (10.5a) with a sentence condition without a transformation (10.5b). In this way, the increased activation observed for object relatives in this study cannot be straightforwardly compared to the findings from English discussed above. Nonetheless, the data from Hebrew do not contradict the association between linguistic complexity – as measured via object relative clauses – and the pars opercularis.

Matters become more complex, however, when data from German are considered. Fiebach, Vos, and Friederici (2004) compared subject and object relative clauses with early and late word order disambiguation.

(10.6)   Example stimuli from Fiebach et al. (2004)

      a. Das   sind die Einwohner, die
          these are   the residents   who[NOM/ACC]
          der Polizist   angehört   hat, weil
          [the policeman][NOM] interviewed has because
          in den Garten eingebrochen wurde.
          in the   garden broken-into   was
          "These are the residents who the policeman interviewed because the garden was broken into."

      b. Das ist die Sportlerin, die
          this is   the athlete   who[NOM/ACC.SG]
          die Trainerinnen   gesucht haben,   weil
          [the trainers][NOM/ACC.PL] sought have[PL] because
          der Diskus fehlte.
          the discus was-missing
          "This is the athlete who the trainers were looking for because the discus was missing."

The example sentences in (10.6) illustrate the early (10.6a) and late (10.6b) disambiguation conditions for the object relative clauses used by Fiebach et al. (2004). These were compared to minimally differing subject relative clauses (including an accusative-marked NP within the relative clause in the early disambiguation condition and an auxiliary agreeing in number with the relative pronoun in the late disambiguation condition). Fiebach and colleagues found *no* main effect of relative clause structure in the pars opercularis, but rather an effect of the position of disambiguation (i.e. increased activation in the superior portion of BA44 for late disambiguation).[3] The latter observation is consistent with the finding that the pars opercularis is sensitive to the costs of syntactic ambiguity (see section 9.3.2). By contrast, the absence of increased activation for object relative clauses, which is corroborated by findings for embedded wh-questions (see section 10.2

below), suggests that there may be important cross-linguistic differences with respect to the processing of these structures even between
closely related languages such as English and German.

Cross-linguistic differences with respect to the comprehension of
relative clauses and related structures have also been reported in the
literature on language impairments in aphasia. Here, too, the original
observation was that English-speaking agrammatic aphasics (Broca's
aphasics) have difficulty in understanding object relative clauses such
as (10.7a) (from Caramazza and Zurif 1976).

(10.7) Example stimuli from Caramazza and Zurif (1976)

    a. The girl whom the boy is pushing is tall.
    b. The apple that the boy is eating is red.

Caramazza and Zurif found that, while Broca's aphasics can understand sentences with non-reversible relations such as (10.7b), their
comprehension of potentially reversible relations is impaired in object
relative clauses (10.7a), object clefts (*It is the girl who the boy is pushing*)
and passives (*The girl was pushed by the boy*).[4] While it has been known
for some time that the pattern for passives is subject to cross-linguistic
variation (with speakers of German and Dutch showing much better
performance: e.g. Friederici and Graetz 1987; Kolk and van Grunsven
1985), more recent results suggest that this variation also extends to
relative clause constructions. A case in point is Mandarin Chinese.

(10.8) Example stimuli from Su (2000, as cited in Grodzinsky 2006)

    a. Zhui   gou de   mao   hen   da.
       chased   dog RC-marker cat   very big
       "The cat that chased the dog is very big."

    b. Mao zhui   de   gou hen   xiao.
       cat   chased   RC-marker dog very small
       "The dog that the cat chased is very small."

Recall from section 10.1.1 that there is a debate in the comprehension
literature on Mandarin Chinese as to whether subject or object relative
clauses are easier to process. The data from Broca's aphasics appear to
support the preference for object relatives (Hsiao and Gibson 2003) in
that they show the inverse pattern to that found in English: subject
relative clauses such as (10.8a) give rise to chance-level performance,
while object relatives such as (10.8b) are above chance (Law 2000; Su
2000, as cited in Grodzinsky 2006). However, this contrast may also be

influenced by the fact that object relative clauses in fact respond to canonical Chinese word order (SVO), whereas subject relatives instantiate a VOS order.

10.1.4 *Processing relative clauses: Summary*

As the preceding sections have shown, the comprehension of relative clause constructions is a highly complex domain. While the contrast between subject and object relative clauses has provided psycholinguists and neurolinguists with a reliable source of complexity differences during the comprehension process, a comprehensive model of how these structures are processed is currently still lacking. This must be attributed at least in part to the many influencing factors that interact to produce the measurable processing patterns, both in terms of behavioral responses and neurocognitive activity.

(10.9)   Summary of the factors currently known to influence relative clause processing

    a. cross-linguistic variation as a result of different sentence structures (differences with respect to relative clause-internal word order and to the relative positioning of head noun and relative clause)

    b. relational animacy effects between head noun/relative pronoun and the NP within the relative clause

    c. influences of the relation between head noun and relative pronoun with respect to function/case

    d. individual differences such as verbal working memory capacity, speed of processing, and/or comprehension accuracy

Most approaches to the processing of relative clauses have focused on only a subset of these factors. However, this clearly cannot provide a unified explanation of the full range of available findings. Rather, the level of complexity associated with relative clause constructions currently appears to defy satisfactory modeling.

10.2 Processing long-distance dependencies

In many instances, experimental findings on relative clauses have been treated as a means of investigating "unbounded" dependencies. This is based on the standard assumption in generative grammar that the dependency between the relative pronoun (or the phonologically null relative clause operator) and its base position within the relative clause is of a similar nature to that allowing for long-distance dependencies (wh-movement; see Haegeman 1994 for an introduction). However, dependencies of this type have also been examined in non-relative-clause settings, in which case they can be investigated without the additional influences known to arise in relative clause constructions. In addition, long-distance dependencies have been used to raise questions about the relationship between the parser and the grammar, for example with respect to whether island constraints are immediately used to constrain possible processing choices or not.[5]

Early results on the processing of unbounded dependencies gave rise to a debate about whether the processing system initially overgenerates structures without taking island constraints into account. While Freedman and Forster (1985) argued in favor of such a position, Crain and Fodor (1987) questioned their conclusions. Clifton and Frazier (1989) also proposed that island constraints behave like lexical information in the sense that they do not initially prevent gaps from being posited, but are then rapidly used to filter out ungrammatical structural variants. Further research, however, has resolved the issue in favor of an immediate application of island constraints. Traxler and Pickering (1996), for example, used eye-tracking to examine short passages such as the following.

(10.10)   Example stimuli from Traxler and Pickering (1996)
            WAITING FOR A PUBLISHING CONTRACT
            The big city was a fascinating subject for the new book.
    a. We like the book that the author wrote unceasingly and with great dedication about while waiting for a contract.
    b. We like the city that the author wrote unceasingly and with great dedication about while waiting for a contract.
    c. We like the book that the author who wrote unceasingly and with great dedication saw while waiting for a contract.
    d. We like the city that the author who wrote unceasingly and with great dedication saw while waiting for a contract.

The sentence conditions in (10.10) manipulate the plausibility of a direct object filler association (books can be written: 10.10a/c; but cities cannot: 10.10b/d) and the island status of the critical region (no island: 10.10a/b; complex noun phrase island: 10.10c/d) in a 2x2 design. Traxler and Pickering found an effect of filler plausibility only in the non-island sentences, as shown by first fixations in the region *wrote unceasingly* and by later measures in this and the following regions. On the basis of these results, they argued for an immediate use of island constraints during online processing.

Similar conclusions were drawn by McElree and Griffith (1998), who contrasted the time course of island constraint application with that of (verb-based) lexical information concerning thematic roles and sub-categorization. The critical sentences from their experiment are illustrated in (10.11).

(10.11)   Example stimuli from McElree and Griffith (1998)

a. Island violation
   *It was the essay that the writer scolded the editor who admired.
b. Subcategorization violation
   *It was the essay that the writer knew the editor had gloated.
c. Thematic role violation
   *It was the essay that the writer knew the editor had amazed.

McElree and Griffith observed that the detection of island violations was exceptionally fast: the SAT intercept (see Figure 2.6) for sentences such as (10.11a) was approximately 360 ms shorter than that for sub-categorization violations (10.11b) and approximately 420 ms shorter than that for thematic role violations (10.11c). Similarly to Traxler and Pickering, they therefore argued that gaps are not posited within islands and that this structural constraint on processing is operative at an earlier point in time than constraints deriving from lexical information.

The earliest study on the neurophysiological correlates of movement constraints was reported by Neville et al. (1991), who examined sentences such as (10.12).

(10.12)   Example stimuli from Neville et al. (1991)

a. *What was a sketch of <u>admired</u> by the man?
b. Was a sketch of the landscape <u>admired</u> by the man?

In (10.12a), the verb *admired* induces an island violation, because the absence of a noun following the preposition *of* forces an association of the wh-word with a gap position within the subject NP. In comparison to the same verb in the grammatical control condition (10.12b), Neville and colleagues observed an increased early positivity (P200) and a late positive effect.

Subsequent ERP studies were concerned with the processing of various types of island violations (or, more generally, "subjacency violations", Kluender and Kutas 1993a; Kluender and Kutas 1993b; McKinnon and Osterhout 1996), as illustrated in example (10.13).

(10.13)   Example stimuli from McKinnon and Osterhout (1996), Experiment 1

    a. *I wonder which of his staff members the candidate was annoyed <u>when</u> his son was questioned by.

    b. I wonder whether the candidate was annoyed <u>when</u> his son was questioned by his staff member.

Example (10.13a) is rendered ungrammatical at the position of *when*, because this wh-word excludes the possibility of a grammatical gap site within the remainder of the sentence and no potential gap has as yet been encountered for the filler *which of his staff members*. McKinnon and Osterhout contrasted the ERP response to *when* in the violation condition (10.13a) to that in the grammatical control to (10.13b) and, similarly to Neville et al. (1991), observed both an early (150–300 ms) and a late (500–800 ms) positivity. Kluender and Kutas (1993a; 1993b), by contrast, reported left anterior negativities, which they associated with the holding of a filler in memory.

In another experimental manipulation, McKinnon and Osterhout (1996) examined sentences such as (10.14).

(10.14)   Example stimuli from McKinnon and Osterhout (1996), Experiment 2

    a. *The man seems <u>that</u> it is likely to win.

    b. It seems <u>that</u> it is likely that the man will win.

The use of *seems* in the matrix clause of example (10.14a) ensures that the noun phrase *the man* must be analyzed as the subject of the subordinate clause. However, this is not grammatical in English when the subordinate clause is introduced by a complementizer (cf. the grammatical *The man seems likely to win.*). At the position of *that* in (10.14a), McKinnon and Osterhout observed a broadly distributed positivity between 300 and 800 ms post word onset in comparison to (the first) *that* in (10.14b).[6]

In summary, the ERP findings support the idea that constraints on dislocations are rapidly used by the processing system during online comprehension. Moreover, the application of these constraints is *predictive* in the sense that their effect can be measured even before possible gap positions are reached. The late positivity observed in response to the processing of these violations is very similar to the ERP effects engendered by ill-formed structures in general (see also section 9.1.2 and Chapter 12). It can therefore be interpreted as a neurophysiological correlate of a well-formedness check and/or repair processes.

The electrophysiological correlates of long-distance dependency processing have also been investigated using grammatical sentences. In a study aiming to test the predictions of Gibson's Syntactic Prediction Locality Theory (SPLT; see Chapter 9.3.1), Kaan et al. (2000) examined sentences such as (10.15).

(10.15)   Example stimuli from Kaan et al. (2000)

    a. Emily wondered who the performer in the concert had *imitated* for the audience's amusement.

    b. Emily wondered which pop star the performer in the concert had *imitated* for the audience's amusement.

    c. Emily wondered whether the performer in the concert had *imitated* a pop star for the audience's amusement.

Both (10.15a) and (10.15b) introduce a "filler-gap" configuration as discussed above, whereas (10.15c) does not. Following Gibson's approach, (10.15a/b) should therefore lead to increased integration costs at the position of the subcategorizing verb (*imitated*). Indeed, the comparison of *imitated* in the three conditions revealed a late positivity for the *who-* and *which-* as opposed to the *whether-*sentences. Kaan and colleagues interpreted this finding as evidence that syntactic integration processes are initiated at the position of the verb subcategorizing for a wh-object and that the resulting integration complexity is reflected in a late positive ERP component. An association between the degree of integration cost and the size of the ERP effect is supported by the finding that the late positivity was somewhat more pronounced for the *which-*condition in comparison to the *who-*condition. Kaan and colleagues assumed that additional discourse-related processes are required in the former (as it involves selecting one referent out of the group of pop stars in the discourse), thereby leading to a more complex integration. The finding of a late positivity for dependency integration at a subcategorizing verb was replicated by Phillips, Kazanina, and Abada (2005). These authors also observed a sustained anterior negativity (sLAN) spanning the length of the dependency between the wh-phrase and the subcategorizer (as originally reported by Kluender and Kutas 1993a; Kluender and Kutas 1993b; and King and Kutas 1995).

Both of these ERP correlates of dependency processing (sLAN and late positivity) have also been observed in indirect wh-questions in German such as (10.16) (from Fiebach et al. 2002).

(10.16)   Example stimuli from Fiebach et al. (2002)
          Thomas fragt sich, . . .
          Thomas asks himself, . . .

a.   . . . wer   am   Dienstag   nachmittag   nach   dem
     . . . who[NOM]   on   Tuesday   afternoon   after   the
     Unfall   den   Doktor   verständigt   hat.
     accident   [the   doctor][ACC]   called   has.
     " . . . who called the doctor on Tuesday afternoon after the
     accident."

b.   . . . wen   am   Dienstag   nachmittag   nach   dem
     . . . who[ACC]   on   Tuesday   afternoon   after   the
     Unfall   der   Doktor   verständigt   hat.
     accident   [the   doctor][NOM]   called   has.
     " . . . who the doctor called on Tuesday afternoon after the
     accident."

Because of the verb-final order of subordinate clauses in German, the base positions for the subject wh-pronoun (10.16a) and the object wh-pronoun (10.16b) both precede the verb. However, while the gap for the subject pronoun *wer* can be postulated immediately upon the processing of this element, the gap for the object pronoun *wen* can only be posited once the subject is encountered. In the latter case, the filler therefore needs to be maintained throughout the intervening prepositional phrases. As a correlate of this maintenance, Fiebach et al. (2002) observed an sLAN for object vs. subject questions from approximately 1,000 ms post onset of the wh-pronoun to the position of the second NP (see Figure 10.1). This effect was more pronounced for low span readers than for high span readers, thus supporting a working memory-based interpretation.[7] In addition, the data revealed a positivity between 400 and 700 ms for (10.16b) vs. (10.16a) at the position of the second argument, which Fiebach and colleagues interpreted as an integration effect similar to that found by Kaan et al. (2000).[8] (For

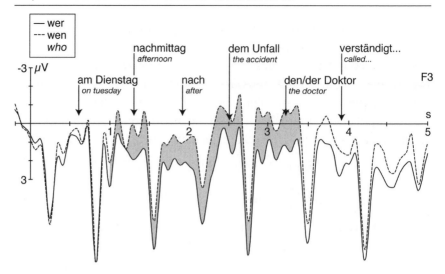

Figure 10.1 Illustration of a typical sustained left anterior negativity (sLAN) effect. The dashed line shows the ERP response to object wh-questions (introduced by the accusative wh-pronoun *wen*), whereas the solid line shows the ERP response to subject wh-questions (introduced by the nominative wh-pronoun *wer*).

Source: Adapted from Fiebach et al. 2002.

similar findings in long-distance scrambling constructions in Japanese, see Hagiwara et al. 2007.) This result was analyzed as suggesting that, in German, an object filler can be integrated into its base position before the verb is reached (see Fanselow et al. 1999a for converging support from self-paced reading; and Muckel 2002 for evidence from cross-modal priming). Note, however, that this finding cannot be seen as unequivocal evidence for the psychological reality of traces (despite the fact that a direct association between the filler and the subcategorizing verb can be ruled out), as the effect can also be accounted for in terms of other mechanisms (e.g. pre-verbal argument interpretation or hierarchization between the arguments, see section 9.2).

In a follow-up study, Fiebach et al. (2005) examined sentences similar to those in (10.16) using fMRI. These were contrasted with sentences with a short distance between wh-pronoun and the following subject or object NP, i.e. sentences in which the two prepositional phrases were positioned after *der/den Doktor*. Fiebach and colleagues observed increased activation in the left IFG at the border between BA 44 and BA 45 for long vs. short object wh-questions. They therefore concluded that word order-related activation in this region is primarily conditioned by the additional working memory demands which arise from the required maintenance of the filler (i.e. to a mechanism functionally equivalent to that reflected in the sLAN in ERP studies of long-distance dependencies). (For a somewhat similar conclusion based on relative clauses in English, though with a localization to BA 47, see Cooke et al. 2001). However, as pointed out by Bornkessel et al. (2005), one problem with the interpretation of the Fiebach et al. (2005) results lies in the fact that the long object question condition (10.16b) involves the non-canonical positioning of two prepositional phrases to the left of the subject. Since word order permutations in the German middlefield engender increased activation in the pars opercularis (BA 44) of the left IFG (see Chapter 9.4.2.1), it cannot be ruled out that it was this aspect of the stimuli that was responsible for the increased inferior frontal activation for sentences like (10.16b) rather than increased working memory demands.

Returning to the electrophysiological domain, it is interesting to note that an integration effect in the form of a late positivity – like that observed by Fiebach et al. (2002), Phillips et al. (2005), and Hagiwara et al. (2007) – has also been observed in raising constructions such as (10.17b) in comparison to minimally differing subject control sentences such as (10.17a) (from Featherston et al. 2000).

(10.17)   Example stimuli from Featherston et al. (2000)

      a. Subject control construction
         Der Sheriff   hoffte [...]   <u>den</u> Täter   endlich
         the sheriff   hoped [...]   the offender   at last
         verurteilen   zu   können.
         sentence   to   can
         "The sheriff hoped to be able to sentence the offender at last."

      b. Raising construction
         Der Sheriff schien [...]   <u>den</u>   Täter   endlich
         the sheriff   seemed [...]   the   offender   at last
         verurteilen zu   können
         sentence   to   can
         "The sheriff seemed to be able to sentence the offender at last."

Featherston and colleagues account for the positivity at the NP within the subordinate clause in terms of processing differences between NP-traces (10.17b) as opposed to PRO (10.17a). However, in analogy to the Fiebach et al. (2002) findings, this result could also be interpreted in terms of the integration of a filler (*der Sheriff*) into a gap site (which becomes identifiable at the position of *den Täter*). An integration of this type is only required in the raising construction, because – following standard generative assumptions – only this sentence type establishes a filler-gap dependency (i.e. involves movement of a subordinate clause subject to the matrix clause). This alternative analysis could also be formulated in non-movement terms: in (10.17a), *Sheriff* is assigned an interpretation (thematic role) by *hoffte*, whereas in (10.17b), it receives no interpretation until the subordinate clause verb is processed.

To summarize, the processing of long-distance dependencies correlates with two main electrophysiological effects: an sLAN, which is typically interpreted as a reflection of increased demands on working memory during the maintenance of an open dependency;[9] and a late positivity, which is observable at the point at which the dependency created by the dislocated element (filler) is resolved. A comparison of the results in the literature suggests that the point of integration/ interpretation giving rise to the positivity differs depending on the structural properties of the language under investigation.

Notes

1. Some early studies also examined simple sentences, or, more precisely, contrasted pairs of sentences differing with respect to only a single hypothesized grammatical operation/transformation (Miller 1962; Mehler 1963; Clifton, Kurcz, and Jenkins 1965).
2. In the reading span task, participants are asked to read sets of sentences aloud and to memorize the last word of each sentence. The size of the sets continually increases from two to six and a participant's reading span is defined as the set size for which he/she can reliably recall the sentence-final words. A number of refinements to this original version of the task have been proposed in subsequent research (see Waters and Caplan 1996, for an overview).
3. The only activation difference within the pars opercularis that was related to relative clause type was observed for object vs. subject relative clauses with late disambiguation for the low span group. However, it presently remains somewhat unclear how this result – and capacity-related differences in pars opercularis activation more generally – should be interpreted. Thus, other studies have suggested that speed of processing rather than working memory capacity is the crucial determining factor for whether IFG activation is observed or not (Waters et al. 2003).

4. Note that the interpretation of findings of this type is rendered more difficult by a variety of factors: (a) there is a high degree of inter-individual variability (for discussion, see Drai and Grodzinsky 2006 and the commentaries on this article in the same volume); (b) comprehension is seldom impaired to 100%; (c) performance improves when patients are given more time (e.g. Burkhardt, Piñango, and Wong 2003; Piñango 2006); (d) neuropsychological classification and neuroanatomical classification in terms of lesion location don't always correspond (see, for example, Dronkers et al. 2004; Thompson-Schill, Bedny, and Goldberg 2005).

5. The term "island constraints" (Ross 1967) refers to a class of restrictions on unbounded dependencies. For an introduction to phenomena of this type and their status in language comprehension, see Phillips and Wagers (2007). An example from their chapter which illustrates the so-called "complex noun phrase constraint" (CNPC) is given in (i). The ill-formedness of this sentence shows that a wh-word (*what*) in a matrix clause cannot be construed as the direct object of an embedded relative clause (i.e. as part of a complex noun phrase).

(i) *What did the agency fire the official that recommended _?

Island constraints are often modeled as constraints on syntactic transformations or movement operations (e.g. Chomsky 1973). However, they have also been derived via movement-independent mechanisms in other grammatical approaches (e.g. Generalized Phrase Structure Grammar: Gazdar et al. 1985; Head-driven Phrase Structure Grammar: Pollard and Sag 1994; Role and Reference Grammar: Van Valin 2005).

6. Interestingly, the impossibility of extracting subjects out of a subordinate clause introduced by a complementizer ("*that*-trace effect") is not cross-linguistically applicable. For example, while it has sometimes been claimed that German is also subject to this constraint (e.g. Grewendorf 1988; Featherston 2005), it is now commonly acknowledged that *that*-trace violations are permitted in at least certain German dialects (e.g. Bayer 1984). In addition, and perhaps even more interestingly from a psycholinguistic perspective, it has been shown that speakers of German dialects that are subject to the *that*-trace effect can be trained to accept, interpret, and produce "*that*-trace violations" when they are confronted with them on a regular basis (Fanselow, Kliegl, and Schlesewsky 2005).

7. Subsequent studies suggest that the relationship between inter-individual differences, ERP components, and the maintenance of long-distance dependencies is, in fact, somewhat more complex. Thus, Bornkessel, Fiebach, and Friederici (2004c) reported qualitatively different sustained ERP effects for high vs. low span readers in case-ambiguous wh-constructions in German. In a further study examining similar ambiguities in the German middlefield, Bornkessel et al. (2004a) observed that

reading span did not provide an adequate means of participant classification and that individual alpha frequency (IAF), a neurophysiologically-based classificational criterion, proved more sensitive to inter-individual differences.

8. This relative polarity difference between the ERPs to NP2 in object- and subject-initial German wh-clauses was replicated in Bornkessel et al. (2004c). In this study, however, the morphology of the ERP waveforms clearly suggested that the observable effect should be considered a negativity for the subject-initial condition rather than a positivity for the object-initial condition. Further evidence for this interpretation stems from a recent study on Japanese (Wolff et al. 2008). According to Bornkessel-Schlesewsky and Schlesewsky (in press), the negativity can be analyzed as a correlate of revision from an intransitive reading of a sentence towards a transitive reading. As described in the discussion of the *Minimality* principle in section 9.3.3, an initial argument is analyzed as the sole argument of an intransitive relation whenever possible (e.g. when it is case-ambiguous or marked for nominative). Thus, when the second NP of a nominative-initial sentence is encountered, this assumption must be revised and a transitive reading assumed. In an accusative-initial sentence, by contrast, no such revision is necessary because the accusative case marking makes clear from the very beginning that the relation in question is transitive.

9. This interpretation of the sLAN is compatible with the finding of similar electrophysiological effects for the maintenance of dependencies in other domains (e.g. in the area of temporal relations; Münte et al. 1998). Münte et al. (1998) observed an sLAN for sentences such as (ii) in comparison to sentences similar to (i), i.e. for sentences in which the order of the clauses does not correspond to the temporal order of events. Here, the event expressed in the "before clause" needs to be maintained until the second event is processed in order to allow for a reconstruction of the correct temporal order.

(i) After the scientist submitted the paper, the journal changed its policy.
(ii) Before the scientist submitted the paper, the journal changed its policy.

11

The processing of modifiers

If any domain within sentence processing can be said to be even more complex than the processing of relative clauses, it is the processing of non-obligatory information. In spite of the wealth of findings on the comprehension of modifiers (e.g. attachment of prepositional phrases and relative clauses) to be found in the literature, there is no general agreement about the status of this information within the comprehension architecture. Whereas some researchers treat the results of experiments on modifiers as suited to revealing core properties of the sentence processing system (e.g. Tanenhaus et al. 1995), others have argued that the comprehension of modifying information is subject to fundamentally different principles to that of obligatory information (Frazier and Clifton 1996). What does appear certain is that the processing of modifiers is subject to a wide variety of influencing factors (including, for example, frequency of occurrence, plausibility, discourse context, and prosody) and that preferences in modifier processing seem to differ across languages (e.g. Mitchell and Brysbaert 1998). Furthermore, there is evidence to suggest that online and offline methods yield different preference patterns within this domain (e.g. Kamide and Mitchell 1997; Augurzky 2006). In this way, a comprehensive discussion of the processing of modifying information could fill a monograph of its own.

In complete contrast to the many behavioral results available on this topic, only very few neurocognitive experiments have examined modifier processing. However, despite the scarcity of the available results, most of the primary issues have at least been touched upon using ERPs. In the following, we will therefore begin by discussing what happens when the processing system can choose between an obligatory (core) constituent analysis and a modifier reading (periphery), before introducing the neurocognitive picture on attachment phenomena.

11.1 Preferences for core over periphery

As already discussed in section 7.2.4, many experiments have provided evidence for an "argument-over-adjunct" preference, i.e. a preference for an argument interpretation of a constituent that is ambiguous between an argument or an adjunct analysis (e.g. Abney 1989; Clifton et al. 1991; Boland and Boehm-Jernigan 1998; Schütze and Gibson 1999). The only ERP study to have examined this question to date yielded converging evidence for this perspective. Capitalizing upon the verb-finality of German, Juranek (2005) examined the default processing preference (argument or adjunct) for the analysis of a prepositional phrase in sentences such as (11.1).

(11.1)   Example stimuli from Juranek (2005)

    a. Argument PP
        Gestern   wollte   der   Berater   die   Graphik   auf
        Yesterday   wanted   the   consultant   the   diagram   on
        der   Leinwand   <u>abbilden.</u>
        the   screen   to-project
        "Yesterday, the consultant wanted to project the diagram onto the screen."

    b. Adjunct PP
        Gestern   wollte   der   Berater   die   Graphik   auf
        Yesterday   wanted   the   consultant   the   diagram   on
        der   Leinwand   <u>überprüfen.</u>
        the   screen   to-check
        "Yesterday, the consultant wanted to check the diagram on the screen."

When the clause-final verb disambiguated the PP towards an adjunct reading (11.1b), an N400 effect was observed in comparison to the argument condition (11.1a). As a control comparison of the two verb types (PP-argument vs. PP-adjunct verbs) in a position where they preceded their arguments (i.e. topicalized to the sentence-initial position) did not yield any significant differences, a purely lexical source of the effect in (11.1) can be ruled out. Rather, this finding suggests that a prepositional phrase is preferentially analyzed as an obligatory sentence constituent when there is no evidence to the contrary.[1]

Further findings indicate that this processing phenomenon seems to be part of a more general tendency to prefer core constituents over modifying information. A case in point is Osterhout and

Holcomb's (1992; 1993) classic ERP comparison of the sentences in (11.2).

(11.2)   Example stimuli from Osterhout and Holcomb (1992; 1993)

    a. The broker persuaded to sell the stock...
    b. The broker hoped to sell the stock...

Example (11.2a) illustrates the well-known "main clause–reduced relative clause" (MC–RC) ambiguity, i.e. *persuaded* could either be the finite verb in a main clause (e.g. *The broker persuaded the investor...*) or the past participle in a reduced relative clause as in the actual example. Whereas, in the main clause reading, *persuaded* is clearly a core constituent, it is part of the periphery in the reduced relative reading. Similarly to the processing preferences described for argument–adjunct ambiguities above, it is uncontroversial that, in the default case, the MC–RC ambiguity is resolved towards the core constituent (i.e. main verb) analysis (see also Box 7.1). In Osterhout and Holcomb's ERP findings, this preference was reflected in a late parietal positivity at the position of *to* in (11.2a) in comparison to (11.2b). At this position, the main clause reading is ruled out following *persuaded* because this verb requires a direct object. *Hoped*, by contrast, subcategorizes for a sentential complement and therefore requires the preferred main clause reading to be upheld even when *to* is encountered. The increased processing costs observable in the form of the late positivity at the position of *to* in (11.2a) therefore reflect the required revision from an obligatory core constituent analysis to a modifier reading.[2]

The qualitatively different ERP components observed for a revision towards an adjunct reading in (11.1) and (11.2) indicate that there is no single neurophysiological correlate of "core to periphery reanalysis", but rather that the effects observed differ depending on the precise processing choices that need to be revised. On the one hand, the MC–RC ambiguity also comprises a phrase structure ambiguity; indeed, the classic explanation of the preference for the main clause reading is that it allows the processing system to opt for a simpler structure. The late positivity may therefore be viewed as a correlate of phrase structure-affecting reanalysis processes. On the other hand, no phrase structure reanalysis is required in (11.1). Here, only assumptions about the transitivity of the event being described need to be revised (from a ditransitive to a transitive reading). The finding of an N400 effect for a phrase structure-independent reanalysis of transitivity properties is consistent with similar findings from other structures (see Note 8 to Chapter 10).

While the existing ERP findings clearly appear to support a preference for core constituents over adjuncts, they are not suited to shedding light on a debate which has existed in the behavioral literature for several decades. This debate concerns the question of which information types can influence the preference in ambiguities such as those described in the preceding paragraphs (see section 7.2.2 and Chapter 8). The MC–RC ambiguity in particular has been examined extensively in this regard, but, as discussed in Box 7.1, no consensus has been reached (see, for example, Crain and Steedman 1985; Ferreira and Clifton 1986; MacDonald et al. 1994; Trueswell et al. 1994; McRae et al. 1997; Clifton et al. 2003). The main point of disagreement concerns whether the initial preference is determined exclusively by structural information or whether it can also be modulated by other information types such as animacy, plausibility, frequency of occurrence, and discourse context. Whereas neurocognitive findings have not contributed to these issues with respect to the MC–RC ambiguity, van Berkum, Brown, and Hagoort (1999) used ERPs to examine the effects of referential context in the resolution of a further ambiguity concerning the core–periphery distinction: the complement vs. relative clause ambiguity. Their critical (Dutch) contexts and sentences are illustrated in (11.3).

(11.3)   Example stimuli from van Berkum et al. (1999)

One-Referent context

De aardige reus werd onderweg vergezeld door een elfje en een kabouter. Het elfje had zich vastgeklampt aan zijn bovenarm, de kabouter had zich genesteld in een comfortabele broekzak.

On the road, the gentle giant was accompanied by an elf and a goblin. The elf had clung [itself] to his upper arm, the goblin had ensconced itself in a comfortable trouser pocket.

Two-Referent context

De aardige reus werd onderweg vergezeld door twee elfjes. Het ene elfje had zich vastgeklampt aan zijn bovenarm, het andere had zich genesteld in een comfortabele broekzak.

On the road, the gentle giant was accompanied by two elfs. One of the elfs had clung [itself] to his upper arm, the other had ensconced itself in a comfortable trouser pocket.

    a. Complement target

De	reus	waarschuwde	het	elfje	dat	ze	niet
the	giant	warned	the	elf	that	she	not

moest	vallen.
must	fall

"The giant warned the elf that she shouldn't fall off."

    b. Relative target

De	reus	waarschuwde	het	elfje	dat	zich	had
the	giant	warned	the	elf	that	itself	had

vastgeklampt	niet	te	vallen.
clung		not	to	fall

"The giant warned the elf that had clung on not to fall off."

The critical ambiguity in the target sentences concerns the analysis of the word *dat*, which could either be a complementizer introducing a complement clause or a relative pronoun. Findings from English indicate that, in the absence of a context, the complementizer reading is preferred, but that the garden path effect is substantially attenuated when the critical sentence is preceded by a context introducing two referents (Altmann, Garnham, and Dennis 1992). Therefore, van Berkum and colleagues examined target sentences disambiguated towards a complement or a relative clause analysis in contexts introducing either one or two referents. The critical disambiguating position in the target sentences was the pronoun *ze* in the complement and the reflexive *zich* in the relative clause. The pronoun can only refer to the antecendent *het elfje* in a complement clause, whereas coreference with the reflexive is only possible in a relative clause construction. At the point of disambiguation, van Berkum et al. observed a late positivity (500–700 ms) for the two-referent as opposed to the one-referent context in the complement condition, but the inverse effect (i.e. a late positivity for the one-referent context) for the relative clause condition. The reversal of the effect clearly shows that referential context affects the processing of the relative–complement ambiguity. However, this result cannot distinguish between the assumption of an immediate contextual determination of the preference and a non-initial modulation of this preference (see sections 7.2.2 and 7.3 and Box 7.1 for detailed discussion). The simplest interpretation of the late positivity therefore appears to be that it reflects a mismatch between the target sentence and the context in which it is encountered rather than reanalysis per se. An account along these lines is supported by the finding of a similar late positive effect for unambiguous complement clauses in an inappropriate (two-referent) context.

11.2 Attachment ambiguities

Within the domain of modifying information per se, the most extensively studied processing phenomenon concerns the attachment of relative clauses, as exemplified in (11.4).

(11.4)   Relative clause attachment ambiguity (from Cuetos and Mitchell 1988)

Andrew had dinner yesterday with the niece of the teacher who belonged to the Communist party.

In example (11.4), the relative clause *who belonged to the Communist party* could either modify (be attached to) *the niece* or *the teacher*. In contrast to ambiguities concerning the attachment of PPs, which often also involve an argument–adjunct ambiguity, relative clause attachment ambiguities are entirely ambiguities of modification. As such, they are subject to influences from a wide variety of different factors, as discussed at the beginning of this chapter (see also Frazier and Clifton 1996). The literature on this topic comprises a vast amount of experimental studies in a variety of languages (see Augurzky 2006, for an overview), but only a handful of experiments on relative clause attachment have been conducted in the neurocognitive domain. The first of these was reported by Kaan and Swaab (2003), who examined sentences such as (11.5).

(11.5)   Example stimuli from Kaan and Swaab (2003)
   a. I cut the cake beside the pizzas that <u>were</u> brought by Jill.
   b. I cut the cakes beside the pizza that <u>were</u> brought by Jill.

In example (11.5), the agreement information of the auxiliary *were* disambiguates towards either a low (11.5a) or a high attachment (11.5b) of the relative clause. As low attachment is preferred in English, increased processing costs are to be expected in (11.5b). Indeed, Kaan and Swaab observed a late positivity at the position of *were* in this condition.

A similar effect, albeit reflecting a preference for high attachment, was reported by Carreiras, Salillas, and Barber (2004) for relative clause processing in Spanish (see 11.6).

(11.6)   Example stimuli from Carreiras et al. (2004)

    a. Juan   felicitó   a   la   cocinera del
       John   congratulated to   the   cook[F] of-the
       alcalde   que   fue <u>premiada</u>
       mayor[M] who   was   awarded.a.prize[F]
       y   laureada en las   fiestas.
       and   honored at   the   party.
       "John congratulated the cook of the mayor who was awarded a prize and honored at the party." (~ The cook was awarded a prize.)

    b. Juan   felicitó   al   cocinero   de la
       John   congratulated to   the cook[M] of-the
       alcaldesa que   fue <u>premiada</u>
       mayor[F] who   was   awarded.a.prize[F]
       y   laureada en las   fiestas.
       and   honored at   the   party.
       "John congratulated the cook of the mayor who was awarded a prize and honored at the party." (~ The mayor was awarded a prize.)

Similarly to the sentences used by Kaan and Swaab, the relative clauses in (11.6) are disambiguated towards a high or a low attachment reading via agreement information. Here, however, the crucial feature is gender rather than number. In accordance with the high attachment preference that has been reported for Spanish (Cuetos and Mitchell 1988), Carreiras and colleagues found a late positivity at the disambiguating position for (11.6b) in comparison to (11.6a). The late positive effects observed in both English and Spanish may be interpreted as reflecting the reanalysis towards the dispreferred structure/recomputation of the dispreferred attachment site. Alternatively they can be construed as correlates of a process which serves to map peripheral information onto properties of the core ("generalized mapping"; Bornkessel and Schlesewsky 2006a). Interestingly, neither Kaan and Swaab nor Carreiras and colleagues observed LAN effects as are often elicited by agreement mismatches (see section 9.1.1). This could be taken as a first indication that agreement processes applying between core constituents and modifiers may differ from those within the core proper.

The neurocognitive findings on relative clause attachment discussed so far appear to suggest that the ERP results neatly mirror previous behavioral results: disconfirmation of an attachment preference is reflected in a late positivity and the preferences observed in the individual languages are as behavioral results would lead one to expect (low attachment for English, high attachment for Spanish). However, as with all reanalysis-based findings, these data are not informative with respect to the *initial* preference arising in the processing of the ambiguous region, namely at the point of the relative pronoun. In order to examine the processing preference at this point, unambiguous attachments need to be examined, as this allows for ERPs to be measured at the position of the relative pronoun. An experiment of this type was conducted by Augurzky (2006), who examined German sentences such as the following.

(11.7) Example stimuli from Augurzky (2006)

    a. Das ist der   Schüler   der Lehrerin,
       this is [the student][NOM.M] [the teacher][GEN.F]
       dessen...
       who[GEN.M]...
       "This is the student of the teacher whose..." (relative clause modifies student)

    b. Das ist der   Schüler   der Lehrerin,
       this is [the student][NOM.M] [the teacher][GEN.F]
       deren...
       who[GEN.F]...
       "This is the student of the teacher whose..." (relative clause modifies teacher)

The sentences in example (11.7) immediately force a high attachment (11.7a) or a low attachment (11.7b) of the relative clause because of the gender features of the relative pronoun. Despite the fact that German has been described as a high attachment language from a behavioral perspective (e.g. Hemforth, Konieczny, and Scheepers 2000), Augurzky found increased processing costs for the high attachment at the position of the relative pronoun. These were observable in the form of a central negativity between 400 and 650 ms post onset of the relative pronoun. A similar finding was observed for sentences in which the genitive NP was replaced by a prepositional phrase (e.g. *von der Lehrerin*, "of the teacher"), for which sentence-final behavioral results clearly show a low attachment preference. These observations suggest that there is a general initial preference for low attachment, which may, under certain circumstances, be modulated towards a high attachment preference as processing proceeds. The finding of a negativity for an attachment that does not conform to the initial preference differs qualitatively from the positivities observed for revisions towards a dispreferred reading at a later point in the relative clause (Augurzky 2006 also reports positivities for a late disambiguation). Note that the finding of initial "mismatch" responses being modulated by further information over the time course of processing is by no means unprecedented; see for example Bornkessel et al. (2004b) and Demiral et al. (2008). For a theoretical discussion of this phenomenon, see Mitchell (1994).

11.3 Summary

Even though the neurocognitive literature on the processing of modifying information is not nearly as rich as the behavioral literature on this topic, a number of clear tendencies with respect to the comprehension of non-obligatory information can already be recognized. Firstly, the available neurophysiological findings clearly support the preference for core constituents over non-obligatory (peripheral) information. This preference is not only apparent in the argument-over-adjunct advantage but also in the default analysis observable for the main clause–reduced relative clause ambiguity and the complement–relative clause ambiguity. In addition to providing a confirmation of these well-known preferences, the ERP data can also help to shed further light on the processes involved when initially preferred analyses need to be revised. Thus, while recomputations affecting the phrase structure representation typically engender late positivities, phrase structure-independent revisions (e.g. of verb transitivity) elicit (non-lexical) N400 effects. Finally, the findings on pure modifier processing (relative clause attachment) indicate that initial preferences may differ crucially from those observed at a later point in the sentence in the sense that further information types continually serve to modulate the analysis currently under consideration. In this regard, modifying information appears substantially more volatile to preference-shifting than obligatory constituents.

Notes

1. Konieczny et al. (1997) argue for a principle of "Parameterized head attachment", according to which the interpretation preference for PPs (and other constituents) is influenced by head (verb) position. They assume that, when a verb precedes an ambiguous PP, the interpretation

preference is determined by the properties of the verb (i.e. whether the PP is compatible with a thematic role assigned by the verb or not). In verb-final sentences, by contrast, a preference for NP-attachment of a PP in an NP-PP sequence is predicted, because the PP attaches to the closest head already encountered. However, in their experiments, Konieczny et al. did not contrast PP-argument with PP-adjunct verbs, but rather varied the likelihood of a VP-attachment (instrument) reading for the PP. Their findings therefore do not speak to the question of whether an argument or an adjunct reading of an ambiguous constituent is preferred. In addition, the finding of a general argument-over-adjunct preference in sentences such as (11.1) is incompatible with the claim that an adjunct (NP-attachment) reading should be preferred in verb-final sentences if this attachment is not ruled out by considerations of plausibility.

2. The main clause–relative clause ambiguity has also been examined using fMRI (Noppeney and Price 2004). However, the aim of this study was neither to examine the core–periphery distinction nor to shed light on the neural substrates supporting reanalysis processes. Rather, Noppeney and Price investigated neural effects of syntactic priming, i.e. whether the neural activation engendered by a particular structure is attenuated when similar sentence types precede the critical sentence item. Thus, no direct contrast between dispreferred and preferred resolutions of the ambiguity are reported. However, it is interesting to note that the primary effect of syntactic priming was observed in the left temporal pole (i.e. the anterior tip of the left temporal lobe; see Plate 2A). As Noppeney and Price examined preferred and dispreferred sentences involving a phrase structure ambiguity, this result is in line with the association that has been drawn between the anterior portion of the left superior temporal gyrus and constituent structure processing (see Chapter 8).

12

On the functional interpretation of late positive ERP effects in language processing

In this chapter, we depart from our functionally-oriented discussion in order to focus on a particular language-related ERP effect (or perhaps even class of ERP effects), namely the late positivity. Late positivities are often observed in response to (morpho)syntactic violations, either as monophasic components or following an (E)LAN. As will have become clear throughout the preceding chapters, however, late positivities are by no means restricted to this type of sentential environment. Rather, they have been observed in response to a wide range of language-related manipulations, thereby warranting a component-oriented chapter of their own.

Because of their typical peak latency at approximately 600 ms post stimulus onset, language-related late positivities are most commonly labeled "P600" (a term coined by Osterhout and Holcomb 1992). However, they have also been referred to as the "syntactic positive shift" (SPS; Hagoort et al. 1993), as "late positivities" (Bornkessel and Schlesewsky 2006a), or, primarily in the context of word-level manipulations, as the "late positive complex" (LPC; e.g. Van Petten et al. 1991). Here, we refer to this type of effect, a typical instance of which is illustrated in Figure 12.1, using both "P600" and "late positivity".

The remainder of this chapter is organized as follows. We begin by discussing the "classic" syntactic perspective on the P600 (section 12.1), before showing that this effect is also sensitive to non-syntactic information (section 12.2). Section 12.3 takes this perspective one step further by presenting recent findings on "semantic P600s". Finally, we conclude

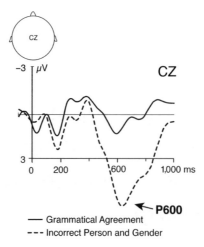

Figure 12.1 Illustration of a typical late positivity (P600) effect, as elicited by subject–verb agreement violations in Hindi.

Source: Adapted from Nevins et al. 2007.

the chapter by considering the relationship between language-related late positivities and ERP effects related to more general aspects of cognitive processing (section 12.4).

12.1 The late positivity as a correlate of syntactic processing?

Language-related late positivities were first observed in response to the dispreferred resolution of syntactic ambiguities (Osterhout and Holcomb 1992; Osterhout and Holcomb 1993) and to grammatical violations (Hagoort et al. 1993). These findings, which were already described in more detail in the preceding chapters (see, for example, Chapter 9.1 and Chapter 11), originally led to the conclusion that the P600 should be viewed as a correlate of syntactic processing.

Subsequent research revealed that P600 effects are not only elicited by (morpho)syntactic violations and garden path sentences but that they also occur in grammatical (and unambiguous) but complex structures (see Chapter 10.2). Hence, Kaan et al. (2000) proposed that the P600 is a more general marker of "syntactic integration". A more fine-grained functional distinction between different types of late positivities was proposed by Friederici, Hahne, and Saddy (2002) on the basis of an ERP study with German stimuli such as (12.1).

(12.1)   Example stimuli from Friederici et al. (2002)

    a. Complex structure

       Dem Vater   <u>getragen</u> hat   er

       [the father][DAT] carried   have[3.SG] he[NOM.SG]

       den Mantel.

       [the coat][ACC]

          "He carried the coat for the father."

    b. Ungrammatical structure

       *Dem Vater   trugen   <u>er</u>   den Mantel.

       [the father][DAT] carry-3.PL he[NOM.SG] [the coat][ACC]

       "He carried the coat for the father."

    c. Control

       Dem Vater   <u>trug</u>   <u>er</u>   den Mantel.

       [the father][DAT] carry-3.SG he[NOM.SG] [the coat][ACC]

       "He carried the coat for the father."

Friederici and colleagues contrasted the ERP response to complex German sentences involving a VP-topicalization (12.1a) (vs. simple control sentences (12.1c)) with that engendered by an ungrammaticality (a subject–verb agreement violation; 12.1b). Both 12.1a and 12.1b elicited a P600 (following a broadly distributed negativity in the case of 12.1b), but the two effects differed in their topographical distribution: centro-parietal for the ungrammatical structures vs. fronto-central for the complex structures. From this finding, Friederici et al. (2002) concluded that repair-related and complexity-related P600s are generated by different neural substrates. A similar conclusion – namely that the P600 is not a unitary component – was reached by Kaan and Swaab (2003), who compared reanalysis- and repair-related positivity effects (using sentences such as 11.5 and an additional ungrammatical condition). Like Friederici and colleagues, they assumed that repair-related P600s show a parietal scalp distribution. In addition, they proposed that reanalysis-related positivity effects pattern with complexity-related effects in showing an anterior scalp distribution.

    Finally, to complete the collection of syntactically-related late positivity effects, Frisch et al. (2002) observed a (broadly-distributed) P600 in response to syntactic ambiguity. In declarative main clauses in German, case-ambiguous initial arguments (which thereby rendered the input ambiguous between a subject- and an object-initial structure) engendered a P600 in comparison to unambiguously case-marked

(subject and object) NPs in the same position. When the locally ambiguous sentences were subsequently disambiguated towards a (dispreferred) object-initial reading, a second P600 was observable. Frisch and
colleagues therefore argued that the P600 reflects both the recognition
of an ambiguity and its resolution.

To summarize, late positivities have been observed in response to a
wide range of syntax-related manipulations, including reanalysis, repair, integration in complex structures and ambiguity. On the basis of
these observations alone, one would thus be justified in assuming that
P600 effects can serve as a diagnostic tool for aspects of syntactic
processing. As we shall see in the following sections, however, matters
are not quite that simple.

12.2 The late positivity as a correlate of the syntax–semantics interaction?

Beyond the syntax-related modulations of late positivities that were
discussed in the preceding section, several studies have revealed an
influence of both syntactic and semantic factors on these effects. Recall
from Chapter 9.1.1 that Gunter et al. (1997; 2000) observed additive
patterns of a LAN and an N400 for combined syntactic and semantic
manipulations, but an interaction between the two factors in the late
positivity time window. These observations have been interpreted as
evidence for an early autonomy of syntactic and semantic processes,
followed by a later period of interaction (Friederici 2002; see also
Chapter 15.3). With respect to the functional interpretation of the
P600, they suggest that this component is not exclusively sensitive to
syntactic aspects of sentence processing.

This non-syntactic perspective on late positivities is further corroborated by the finding of such effects in non-syntactic manipulations.
For example, Roehm et al. (2007a) observed a biphasic N400-late
positivity pattern for the processing of sentences such as *The opposite
of black is nice*, in which the prediction for an antonym is not fulfilled.
Here, there is no syntactic processing problem whatsoever. Rather, the
late positive effect might be interpreted as a correlate of a global
evaluation of the sentence's well-formedness (Bornkessel and Schlesewsky 2006a; see also Chapter 15.4). The finding of a late positivity for
semantic (antonym) violations further appears related to results from
the priming literature, which have revealed modulations of the
so-called late positive complex (LPC) in response to repetition and

semantic priming (see Camblin, Gordon, and Swaab 2007, for a recent summary of the relevant results).

In summary, there is good evidence to suggest that late positive effects during language processing are not exclusively syntactic in nature.

12.3 The late positivity as a correlate of semantic processing?

As already mentioned briefly in Chapter 9.1.2, the recent literature has seen a debate on seemingly "semantic" P600 effects. Thus, even more gravely for classical interpretations of the P600 than the observation of an interaction between syntax and semantics within this component, a number of studies have revealed that, under certain circumstances, P600 effects appear to reflect entirely semantic processes. Semantic P600s have been observed, for example, in response to sentences involving an implausible thematic role assignment to an argument that would be a highly plausible filler for a different thematic role of the same verb (e.g. Kolk et al. 2003; Kuperberg et al. 2003; Hoeks, Stowe, and Doedens 2004; Kim and Osterhout 2005). Consider the following examples.

(12.2)   Example stimuli from Kim and Osterhout (2005)

   a. The hearty meal was <u>devouring</u>... (P600)
   b. The dusty tabletops were <u>devouring</u>... (N400)

For sentences such as (12.2a), which Kim and Osterhout termed (semantic) "attraction violations", they observed a P600 effect in comparison to both active and passive control sentences. By contrast, "non-attraction violations" such as (12.2b) yielded an N400 effect. On the basis of these results, Kim and Osterhout argue that a strong semantic attraction between a predicate and an argument may lead the processing system to analyse a syntactically well-formed sentence as syntactically ill-formed. They therefore adopt a conservative (i.e. syntactic) interpretation of the "semantic" P600, which they analyze as resulting from a syntactic mismatch between the present participle form encountered by the processing system and the semantically-based expectation for a past participle (cf. *The hearty meal was devoured*...).Kim and Osterhout therefore argue that, if the evidence is compelling enough, semantic analysis can override syntactic analysis even in unambiguous structures. From this line of argumentation, it should be readily apparent why semantic P600 effects have sparked controversial discussions in the literature on sentence processing.

In a series of papers, Kolk and colleagues have also argued for a crucial role of semantic attraction in engendering semantic P600 effects (Kolk et al. 2003; van Herten, Kolk, and Chwilla 2005; van Herten, Chwilla, and Kolk 2006). These investigators envision an influence of semantic information in the form of a plausibility heuristic, which computes the most plausible relation between the words in a sentence and may thereby generate representations that conflict with the syntax. In contrast to Kim and Osterhout (2005), however, they interpret the P600 as a domain-general correlate of "conflict monitoring" rather than as a correlate of a syntactic mismatch. This proposal was based on a range of empirical findings. For example, van Herten et al. (2005) showed that semantic P600 effects are not restricted to sentential environments in which there is a mismatch between an expected (morphosyntactic) form and the form actually encountered. To this end, they presented Dutch sentences such as (12.3).

(12.3)   Example stimuli from van Herten et al. (2005)

    a. Semantic reversal anomaly (different number)
        De vos   die op de stropers
        [the fox][SG] that at [the poachers][PL]
        joeg   sloop   door   het bos.
        hunted[SG] stalked through the woods.
        "The fox that hunted the poachers stalked through the woods."

    b. Semantic reversal anomaly (same number)
        De vos   die op de stroper
        [the fox][SG] that at [the poacher][SG]
        joeg   sloop   door   het bos.
        hunted[SG] stalked through the woods.
        "The fox that hunted the poacher stalked through the woods."

Both of the sentences in (12.3) are implausible because the syntactic structure calls for a "reversed" interpretation of what would otherwise be a plausible event (i.e. poachers normally hunt foxes and not the other way around). From the perspective of an account assuming that a semantic/plausibility-based computation of the relation between the arguments and the verb overrides the syntactic analysis, this should lead to a syntactic mismatch in (12.3a), in which the two arguments differ in number and a plural verb agreeing with the more plausible Agent (*poachers*) should be expected on the basis of the plausibility heuristic. In (12.3b), by contrast, no such mismatch should arise because both arguments are singular and should therefore call for the same verb form. However, as van Herten et al. (2005) observed P600 effects in both cases, these findings speak against a syntactic mismatch account of the semantic P600. On the basis of these and further findings, van Herten, Kolk, and colleagues argue that semantic P600 effects reflect the conflict that arises when the output of the plausibility heuristic contradicts the syntactic analysis. This may already be the case when a globally implausible sentence contains a plausible frag-ment (van Herten et al. 2006). Furthermore, as conflict-related P600 effects have also been observed in other domains, for example in response to orthographical errors (Vissers, Chwilla, and Kolk 2006) or sentence-picture mismatches (Vissers et al. 2008), the semantic P600 is viewed as one instance of a more general electrophysiological correlate of "conflict monitoring" during language processing.

Finally, it has also been suggested that semantic P600 effects are crucially related to aspects of thematic processing. Recall from the discussion of example (9.10) in Chapter 9.1.2 that Kuperberg et al. (2007) observed a P600 – and no N400 – for sentences such as *For breakfast the eggs would bury...*, i.e. for animacy violations in the absence of a close semantic relation between the critical argument and the verb. This finding suggests that "semantic attraction" is not a necessary prerequisite for the observation of semantic P600 effects (but see Bornkessel-Schlesewsky and Schlesewsky 2008 for an alternative interpretation of this result). Kuperberg and colleagues attribute the occurrence of a P600 rather than an N400 effect under these circum-stances to aspects of thematic processing, since the animacy violation in their critical sentences can be considered a thematic violation. More precisely, they suggest that "once participants had detected the the-matic role violation, they did not engage in further attempts to se-mantically/pragmatically integrate the meaning of the verb into its preceding context" (Kuperberg et al. 2003: 128).[1] A related proposal was put forward by Hoeks et al. (2004) on the basis of an experiment with verb-final sentences in Dutch. These authors proposed that in sentences such as *The javelin has the athletes thrown* (literal English translation of the Dutch original), the required assignment of an Agent role to an inanimate argument leads to an underspecification of the message-level representation being constructed by the processing system. From this perspective, the absence of an N400 at the clause-final verb (*thrown*) is due to this underspecification, while the P600 observed at this position is viewed as a correlate of increased thematic processing effort.

Taking all of these results together, the findings on semantic P600 effects not only strengthen the perspective that language-related late positivities are not exclusively syntactic in nature. Rather, they also provide further support for the idea that these components involve multiple interacting information types. However, though they may show that the P600 is not a syntactic component, they nonetheless cannot be taken as evidence against (at least certain classes of) syntax-first models of language processing (see Bornkessel-Schlesewsky and Schlesewsky 2008 for an extended discussion).

12.4 The late positivity as a domain-general component?

As shown by the discussion in the preceding sections, language-related late positivities are influenced by a wide range of different information types. It thus appears clear that these effects cannot be taken as correlates of a single language-internal domain. Beyond the question of language-internal domain specificity, however, it has also been debated whether the P600 should be considered a language-specific component or not.

In fact, this type of discussion is not confined to the P600: within the domain of ERPs and language, both the N400 and the P600 have been subjected to a series of discussions regarding the correct grain of their interpretation. Yet since "the propensity to assimilate newly discovered components with more familiar ERP effects has characterized cognitive electrophysiology from the very beginning" (Coulson, King, and Kutas 1998a: 663), these debates can be viewed as part of a longer tradition within the psychophysiological community. For example, as described by Coulson et al. (1998a), an early discussion revolved around whether the P300 – a complex of positive components engendered by improbable, task-relevant and informative stimuli – might in fact be a reflection of a pre-stimulus "contingent negative variation" (CNV), a negative shift in the ERP that is elicited by the anticipation of upcoming events (for discussion, see for example Donchin et al. 1975). Similarly, following the discovery of the N400, it was debated whether this component should be viewed as a (latency-shifted) instance of the N200, an ERP response that is related to the evaluation of stimulus similarity or dissimilarity (e.g. Polich 1985). A further discussion revolved around the question of whether certain modulations of the N400 actually result from underlying differences in the P300 (e.g. Holcomb 1988; Rugg 1990). In the context of the present volume and its focus on the processing of syntax and morphology, however, it is the rather controversial relation between the P600 and the P300 that appears most relevant.

The P300 is one of the earliest cognitive ERP components to have been discovered (Sutton et al. 1965) and it is certainly also one of the best-studied. P300 effects are observed, for example, in response to oddball paradigms, in which a set of frequently occurring stimuli (e.g. tones of a particular pitch or particular shapes) are interspersed with rare "deviants" (e.g. a different tone or different shape). The ERP response to the deviant involves a large positive shift with a peak latency of approximately 300 ms: the P300. It has been demonstrated that this component is larger for task-relevant, informative, salient, and improbable stimuli (Polich 2004). Functionally, it has been related to such cognitive processes as decision-making, stimulus categorization, and context-updating (see, for example, Donchin and Coles 1988; Nieuwenhuis, Aston-Jones, and Cohen 2005). In addition, it is now generally acknowledged that the P300 is not a monolithic component but that it can rather be subdivided into at least two separable subcomponents: the P3a and the P3b. The P3a has an anterior scalp distribution and is typically associated with the processing of novel stimuli, while the P3b is characterized by a posterior distribution and is engendered by target items (Polich 2004). Finally, under certain circumstances, the latency of target-related P300 effects may be "shifted backwards" to a time range which overlaps with that of the P600 (e.g. Bentin et al. 1999). In particular, P300 latencies appear to increase with the required "depth" of processing.

In view of these characteristics of the P300, the notion that the P600 might also be a member of the "P300 family" does not appear overly surprising. As P600 effects were first observed in response to grammatical violations and garden path sentences, they correlated with the processing of improbable, salient, and mostly task-relevant stimulus dimensions. Does this therefore mean that the P600 can simply be viewed as an instance of a P3b that is elicited via linguistic input and shifted in its latency due to the complexity of the processes involved? The first systematic examination of this question was undertaken by Osterhout et al. (1996). In a series of three experiments, these authors compared ERP responses to agreement violations (12.4b), physical deviations (uppercase words, 12.4c), and doubly anomalous words (12.4d).

(12.4)   Example stimuli from Osterhout et al. (1996)
     a. The doctors <u>believe</u> the patient will recover.
     b. *The doctors <u>believes</u> the patient will recover.
     c. The doctors <u>BELIEVE</u> the patient will recover.
     d. *The doctors <u>BELIEVES</u> the patient will recover.

The overall pattern of results in Osterhout and colleagues' study was as follows. Both types of anomalies engendered late positive ERP effects (between approximately 500 and 800 ms). The physical anomaly additionally showed an earlier positivity between 200 and 500 ms. In spite of the fact that both anomaly types engendered late positivities, these differed in a number of respects. Firstly, they were associated with slightly differing topographical distributions. Secondly, only the positivity elicited by the physical anomaly was influenced by the experimental task (acceptability judgment vs. passive reading) and by the probability of an anomalous stimulus occurring. Finally, when the two anomaly types were presented together (12.4d), an additive component pattern was observed (i.e. the late positive response to the doubly anomalous condition approximated a linear summation of the ERP responses to the two single anomalies). Osterhout et al. (Osterhout et al. 1996: 522) interpret these findings as "a preliminary indication that the ERP response to one type of syntactic anomaly is (at least to an interesting degree) both neurally and cognitively distinct from the response to one type of unexpected, task-relevant anomaly that does not involve the grammar".

    This conclusion was subsequently questioned by two groups (Gunter et al. 1997; Coulson et al. 1998b). Both presented ERP studies on the processing of morphosyntactic violations (see Chapter 9.1 for a more detailed discussion) and, like Osterhout et al. (1996), manipulated the probability of anomalous vs. non-anomalous sentence stimuli. The critical violation types are repeated in (12.5/12.6) for convenience. In contrast to Osterhout and colleagues' findings, both Gunter et al. (1997) and Coulson et al. (1998b) observed that stimulus

probability modulated the late positive response to grammatical violations. Coulson and colleagues further showed that the late positivities
engendered by ungrammatical and improbable sentences were statistically indistinguishable in terms of their scalp distribution and that
the effect of probability was larger for ungrammatical stimuli (i.e. there
was no additive component pattern). Finally, the amplitude of the
late positivity was increased by the saliency of the grammatical violation. On the basis of these correlations between the "P300 like" manipulations undertaken and the modulations of the ERPs observed,
both groups concluded that the P600 may be related to the P300
family.

(12.5)   Example violation stimuli from Coulson et al. (1998b)

    a. *The plane took <u>we</u> to paradise and back.
    b. *Every Monday he <u>mow</u> the lawn.

(12.6)   Example violation stimuli from Gunter et al. (1997)

    a. *De vuile matten   werden door de hulp
       the dirty doormats were   by   the housekeeper
       <u>kloppen</u>.
       beat

    b. De   vuile   matten   werden door de   hulp
       the   dirty   doormats were   by   the   housekeeper
       <u>gekookt</u>.
       cooked

    c. *De   vuile   matten   werden door de   hulp
       the   dirty   doormats were   by   the   housekeeper
       <u>koken</u>.
       cook

These different findings and interpretations gave rise to a more general
debate as to whether the P600 should be considered a member of the
P300 family or not (Coulson et al. 1998a; Osterhout and Hagoort 1999).
At approximately the same time, several further findings seemed to
support the similarity between the two components via the observation of (a) a sensitivity of the P600 to task manipulations (Gunter and
Friederici 1999), (b) a probability-induced modulation of P600 effects
in garden-path sentences (Steinhauer et al. 1997), and (c) the observation of very similar late positive effects in linguistic and non-linguistic
manipulations (Patel et al. 1998).

By contrast, converging support for the presumed non-identity of the P600 and the P300 stems from an auditory ERP study with aphasic patients (Frisch et al. 2003). In this experiment, patients with and without basal ganglia lesions were presented with German sentences such as (12.7).

(12.7)   Example stimuli from Frisch et al. (2003)

   a. Im   Garten wurde oft   gearbeitet.
      in.the garden was   often   worked
      ~"Work was often done in the garden."

   b. *Im   Garten wurde oft   streichen.
      in.the garden was   often   paint

As shown in a previous study (Friederici et al. 1993), verb form violations such as (12.7b) elicit a P600 in unimpaired native speakers of German. While Frisch et al. (2003) replicated this effect for patients with lesions excluding the basal ganglia, patients with basal ganglia lesions showed no such effect. By contrast, both patient groups showed a "regular" P300 in an auditory oddball paradigm. From this result, Frisch and colleagues concluded that the P600 and the P300 should be viewed as different components. However, as a P300 response presupposes correct processing of the stimulus properties relevant for the categorization task at hand, it also appears possible that the patients in this study could not generate the correct input to the processes reflected in the P300 in the more complex linguistic task. Nonetheless, the dissociation observed in this study provides an interesting point of departure for further investigations in this regard.

12.5 Summary

From the discussion in this chapter, it will be apparent that a clear and unequivocal functional interpretation of the P600 is still outstanding. In this respect, the P600 thus confronts us with similar difficulties as other language-related ERP components (e.g. the N400, see Chapter 9). However, the emerging picture on late positive effects during language processing suggests: (a) that the P600 is probably not a unitary component, and (b) that ERP responses within the late positivity time range are subject to influences from a wide range of (language-internal and language-external) domains. Possibly, more fine-grained future dissociations between different members of the "P600 family" could also help to resolve the conflicting findings in the "domain-specificity vs. domain-generality" debate, as it appears conceivable that the overlap between the P600 and the P300 could be restricted to particular instances of language-related late positivities.

Note

1. The thematically-based perspective on semantic P600 effects was extended by Kuperberg (2007), who proposed that there is no single necessary or sufficient trigger for this component. Rather she assumes that semantic P600 effects result from an interaction between syntactic processing, thematic processing, semantic memory-based processing, discourse context, and experimental task.

Part III
Processing Syntax and Morphology at the Interfaces

Overview

One of the most fundamental questions within the study of language architecture concerns the nature of the interfaces between different subdomains of the grammar. Thus, both in theory of grammar (e.g. Chomsky 1995; Prince and Smolensky 1997; Jackendoff 2002; Van Valin 2005) and in psycholinguistics (see Box 7.1), it has been debated whether the relationship between distinct grammatical components is interactive or modular in nature. From the perspective of theoretical linguistics, a precise characterization of the interfaces between different grammatical subdomains (e.g. syntax, semantics, phonology) forms a crucial part of understanding how language is organized as a whole (e.g. Müller 1999; Jackendoff 2002; Van Valin 2005). Furthermore, interface considerations are also essential for the modeling of language from the perspective of the speaker and/or hearer, since they can help to specify which pieces of information are taken into account at which point in time during the processing of a linguistic input – an essential aspect of linguistic performance.

The following two chapters seek to provide an overview of the current state of the art of neurocognitive research on the interfaces between syntactic and morphological processing and other information types. While influences of semantic information (in the form of selectional restrictions, thematic roles, animacy, definiteness, etc.) already formed an integral part of the discussion in Part II of this volume, Part III is concerned with the role of prosodic information (Chapter 13) and information structure (Chapter 14) within the language processing architecture. Chapter 13 begins by discussing the neurophysiological and functional neuroanatomical correlates of prosodic phrasing (13.1) before going on to show that this information plays an important role in the establishment of constituent structure and perhaps even in further aspects of sentence-internal processing (13.2).

In Chapter 14, we then turn to the question of how sentence processing is constrained by influences of discourse context by examining the interaction between syntactic and morphological processing, prosodic information, and information structure. To shed light on these issues, we first provide a brief introduction to neurocognitive processing correlates of given vs. new information and the establishment of coreference (14.1). Section 14.2 then focuses on the interaction between contextual requirements and intra-sentential realizations of information structure (as expressed via prosody, syntactic structure, or morphological marking). Finally, we discuss whether contextually determined influences of information structure can alleviate processing difficulties in less preferred structures. Whereas investigations in the domain of word order variations (section 14.3) show mixed results in this regard, such influences may have a larger impact in other areas (section 14.4). Finally, section 14.5 summarizes the discussion of information structural influences on sentence processing.

13

The influence of prosody

Since the earliest days of psycholinguistics, researchers have concerned themselves with the basic units of speech perception. One of the central questions in this domain is how the overall speech stream can be broken down and structured into smaller categories. One of the earliest studies to examine this issue at the sentence level was reported by Fodor and Bever (1965). Using an experimental technique first developed by Ladefoged and Broadbent (1960), they asked participants to report the location of clicks heard during speech and found a significantly higher number of correct responses when clicks were positioned at major syntactic boundaries as well as a tendency for clicks to be "attracted" towards the nearest boundary. These results were taken as evidence for the psychological reality of syntactic constituents independently of the physical presence of pauses in the acoustic signal. Subsequent research was then dedicated to revealing the precise nature of the relationship between syntactic and prosodic structure (e.g. Cooper and Paccia-Cooper 1980). The main theoretical interests in this regard are centered around two complementary perspectives, namely those of the speaker and the hearer. Which prosodic features does the speaker employ and to which end? For example, it may be the case that prosody is used specifically for the avoidance of ambiguity. Alternatively, prosodic realizations of a given sentence may be entirely determined by grammatical regularities without recourse to possible communicative ease or difficulty. Conversely, the hearer faces the problem of having to decode the information provided by the speaker as efficiently as possible. Which role does prosody play in this regard? Which features are taken into account and how are they used? Independently of the precise theoretical stance adopted with respect to these questions, there is a general consensus that prosody plays an important role during language processing (for comprehensive overviews of the behavioral literature in this domain, see Cutler, Dahan, and van Donselaar 1997; Frazier, Carlson, and Clifton 2006). Indeed, it has even been proposed that the establishment of a default prosodic contour crucially constrains processes of language comprehension during reading (e.g. Slowiaczek and Clifton 1980; Fodor 1998).

Behavioral investigations of prosodic information can essentially be subdivided into two major lines of research, namely into the examination of prosodic phrasing on the one hand, and that of prosodic prominence on the other. Within the neurocognitive domain, however, experimental examinations of prosodic processing in isolated sentences have only been undertaken in the first of these domains. By contrast, neurocognitive investigations of prosodic prominence have hitherto been conducted almost exclusively in combination with contextual manipulations. In view of this divergence, the remainder of this chapter will be dedicated to the discussion of prosodic phrasing. Relevant aspects of prosodic prominence will then be addressed as part of Chapter 14 on Information Structure.

13.1 The neurocognitive correlates of prosodic phrasing

In the behavioral literature on sentence comprehension, experiments on prosodic phrasing have primarily concerned themselves with the possible role of prosodic boundaries in the resolution of syntactic ambiguities (for evidence of such an influence, see for example Kjelgaard and Speer 1999). Neurocognitive methods, by contrast, provide us with the opportunity to directly examine the correlates of prosodic phrasing on the sentence level. In the first study to be undertaken in this regard, Steinhauer, Alter, and Friederici (1999) examined sentences such as (13.1).

(13.1)   Example stimuli from Steinhauer et al. (1999); #-marks indicate intonational phrase (IPh) boundaries

    a. Transitive subordinate clause, congruent prosody
       Peter verspricht #   Anna zu entlasten #   und   das Büro
       Peter promises #   Anna to support #   and   the office
       zu putzen.
       to clean
       "Peter promises to support Anna and to clean the office."

    b. Intransitive subordinate clause, congruent prosody
       Peter verspricht Anna #   zu arbeiten #   und das Büro
       Peter promises Anna #   to work #   and the office

zu putzen.
to clean
"Peter promises Anna to work and to clean the office."

   c. Transitive subordinate clause, incongruent prosody

     Peter verspricht Anna #   zu entlasten #   und   das Büro

     Peter promises Anna #   to support #   and   the office

     zu putzen.
     to clean

   d. Intransitive subordinate clause, incongruent prosody

     Peter verspricht #   Anna zu arbeiten #   und   das Büro

     Peter promises #   Anna to work #   and   the office

     zu putzen.
     to clean

At the position of each IPh-boundary in the sentences in (13.1), Steinhauer et al. (1999) observed a parietal positive ERP effect (see Figure 13.1), which they termed "closure positive shift" (CPS) and which they interpreted as a general neural marker of prosodic boundary processing. By means of an

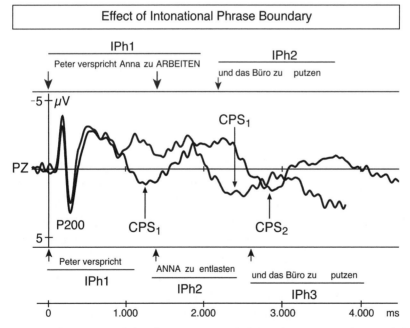

Figure 13.1 Illustration of the closure positive shift (CPS). For a translation of the German sentences, see example (13.1).

Source: Adapted from Steinhauer et al. 1999.

additional prosodic congruency manipulation, they were further able to show that the processing system made use of the position of the prosodic boundaries in order to establish syntactic constituency. Thus, the sentences with an incorrect boundary position (13.1c/d) yielded an N400-late positivity pattern at the position of the first verb in the subordinate clause (*entlasten/arbeiten*). As discussed in Chapter 9.1.2, this corresponds to the standard response to verb valency mismatches (Friederici and Frisch 2000), thereby indicating that the prosodic phrasing led the processing system to treat *Anna* as the argument of a clause to which it did not belong.

Further research attests to the robustness of the CPS as a general neural correlate of prosodic phrasing. This component has been observed in sentences containing pseudowords, in "delexicalized" speech (i.e. speech that has been filtered to remove all lexical information) and even in hummed sentences (Pannekamp et al. 2005). Furthermore, it cannot be considered a simple reflex of a physical pause, as it also occurs when the pause itself is removed from the acoustic signal (Steinhauer et al. 1999; Experiment 3). This point is further underscored by the observation of a comma-induced CPS effect in reading (Steinhauer and Friederici 2001). On the other hand, however, it is also worth noting that the CPS is apparently not uniquely tied to the processing of linguistic prosody as a similar effect has also been reported for the processing of phrase boundaries in music (Knösche et al. 2005).

Following the extensive investigation of the CPS with EEG/MEG, Ischebeck, Friederici, and Alter (2008) attempted to identify the neuro-anatomical bases of this effect using fMRI. To this end, they compared natural and hummed sentences involving either one or two IPh-boundaries. They observed increased activation within the mid STG, the rolandic operculum and Heschl's gyrus for sentences with two IPh-boundaries as opposed to one (see Plate 5). In particular, they suggest that the posterior portion of the rolandic operculum (bilaterally) may be specifically involved in the processing of sentence-level prosodic phrasing, as this region did not show a differential response to natural vs. hummed speech, but increased activation for sentences with an additional IPh-boundary. Furthermore, as the overall activation pattern was slightly more left-lateralized for natural as opposed to hummed sentences, Ischebeck and colleagues argue for a lower degree of hemispheric specialization in the processing of prosodic information as opposed to other linguistic information types. (For a combined ERP/PET investigation of segmented vs. non-segmented speech from a somewhat different perspective, see Strelnikov et al. 2006.)

In view of the critical involvement of the right hemisphere in prosodic processing (see Friederici and Alter 2004 for an overview), it appears of primary interest to ascertain how prosody can interact with other linguistic information types (e.g. syntax), which are associated with a predominantly left-lateralized neural representation. In this respect, Friederici and Alter (2004) hypothesized that the corpus callosum (i.e. the fiber bundles connecting the two hemispheres) may play a crucial mediating role. Empirical evidence for this view stems from a recent ERP study, in which patients with lesions in the corpus callosum (CC) and unimpaired controls were presented with sentences as in (13.1) (Friederici, von Cramon, and Kotz 2007). Whereas the control group and a group of patients with anterior CC lesions showed an N400 effect when there was a mismatch between prosody and syntactic constituency (as in Steinhauer et al. 1999), patients with lesions in the posterior portion of the CC showed no such response. By contrast, a lexical/semantic N400 was observable in all three groups. From these findings, Friederici and colleagues concluded that the posterior third of the CC provides the neuroanatomical basis for the interaction between sentence-level prosodic and syntactic information.

13.2 The role of prosodic phrasing within the neurocognitive processing architecture

Having briefly sketched out the current state of the art concerning the neurocognitive bases of prosodic phrasing, let us now turn to the question of how this information should be situated within the overall language processing architecture. To address this issue, this section will discuss existing studies on the interaction between prosodic phrasing and other information types.

The relationship between word category information and prosodic phrasing in initial structure building was examined by Eckstein and Friederici (2006) using sentences such as (13.2).

(13.2)   Example stimuli from Eckstein and Friederici (2006)
  Maria weiss...
  Maria knows...

  a. ...dass   der   Rentner   im   <u>Alter</u>   kränkelt.
     ...that   the   pensioner in   old.age   sickly.is
     "...that the pensioner is sickly in old age."

b. *...dass   der   Rentner   im   <u>altert</u>   kränkelt.
    ...that   the   pensioner   in   age-3.SG   sickly.is

From a syntactic perspective, the sentences in (13.2) implement a word category violation as described in detail in Chapter 8. In (13.2b), the verb *altert* ("ages") cannot be integrated into the phrase structure because the preposition-determiner complex *im* unequivocally requires that a noun must follow. In addition, Eckstein and Friederici manipulated the prosodic congruence of the critical word such that it was either realized with an appropriate (non-sentence-final) or an inappropriate (sentence-final) prosody. All critical stimuli were created by means of cross-splicing. ERPs timelocked to the suffix of the critical word revealed an early temporal negativity (200–400 ms) for sentences involving syntactic violations. This effect, which the authors interpreted as functionally equivalent to the ELAN, was left-lateralized in the case of a purely syntactic violation, but bilateral for the combined syntactic–prosodic violation. In addition, prosodic violations engendered a broadly distributed negativity between 300 and 500 ms post onset of the critical word and all violation conditions elicited a late positivity (600–1200 ms post word onset and 200–800 ms post suffix onset). On the basis of their results, Eckstein and Friederici argued for an immediate influence of prosodic phrasing on syntactic structure building. They also suggested that right hemispheric contributions to the ELAN component can be attributed to prosodic sources.

The assumption of an early influence of prosodic phrasing on the processing of constituency at a variety of levels receives further converging support from the results of an ERP experiment by Isel, Alter, and Friederici (2005). This study examined the role of prosody in the processing of German sentences with particle verbs, as illustrated in (13.3).

(13.3)   Example stimuli from Isel et al. (2005)

a. Sie   lächelte   den   Arbeiter   am   Vormittag   an
   she   smiled   the   worker   in.the   morning   at
   und...
   and...
   "She smiled at the worker in the morning and..."

b. Sie nannte den Namen <u>am</u>   Vormittag und...
   she said   the   name   in.the morning   and...
   "She said the name in the morning and..."

c. *Sie nannte den Namen <u>an</u> und...
   she   said   the   name   at   and...
   (N.B. only ungrammatical under a particle interpretation
   of *an*, see text)

In their experimental manipulation, Isel et al. (2005) capitalized upon the fact that German has a number of verbs with separable particles (e.g. *anlächeln* "to smile at"). In main clauses, these particles are split off from the finite verb in second position and occur clause-finally (as in 13.3a). In order to examine whether prosodic information helps the processing system to anticipate such particles, Isel et al. examined sentences such as (13.3c), in which a particle co-occurs with a non-particle verb (though, in the absence of prosodic disambiguation, *an* is also compatible with a prepositional reading and, hence, with a grammatical continuation). These sentences were presented to participants in two prosodic realizations: (a) a variant spoken as a particle verb construction, and (b) a cross-spliced variant in which the finite verb (*nannte*, "to call") was replaced with the acoustic realization of the verb from the non-particle construction (13.3b). Notably, a significant N400 was only observed (for 13.3c vs. 13.3b) when prosodic information indicated that a particle would follow. Prosodic information therefore serves to determine whether the verb and the particle are treated as a single constituent or not – and therefore whether sentences such as (13.3c) are treated as well-formed or ill-formed. This suggests that even rather subtle aspects of prosodic phrasing play a crucial role in constraining the processing system's choices regarding matters of morphological and syntactic constituency.

Beyond the level of basic constituent structuring, Wolff et al. (2008) showed that prosodic boundaries can also have a major impact on the processing of word order. Recall from Chapter 9.2.4.2 (examples 9.33) that this study examined the processing of object- and subject-initial sentences in Japanese. An example of an object-initial sentence from this study is repeated here as (13.4), for convenience.

(13.4) 二週間前   判事を   大臣が   招きました
        nisyuukanmae hanzi-o   daizin-ga   manekimasita
        two weeks ago judge-ACC   minister-NOM invited
        "Two weeks ago, the minister invited the judge."

Wolff and colleagues observed a scrambling negativity relative to the case marker of NP1 in sentences such as (13.4) only when the first argument was followed by a prosodic boundary.[1] As such a boundary serves to signal a scrambled structure in Japanese (Hirotani 2005), it renders the initial object incompatible with an analysis of the sentence as an unmarked OV structure with a dropped subject. Hence, prosodic phrasing serves to constrain the mapping between linear order and argument prominence that is reflected in the scrambling negativity (see Chapter 9.2.4.2).

   Finally, in view of the many behavioral investigations of modifier attachment and how processing choices in this domain may be influenced by prosody (see, for example, Fodor 1998; Frazier et al. 2006), it is somewhat surprising that this issue has only been investigated by a single neurocognitive study to date (Augurzky 2006). In an auditory ERP experiment, Augurzky examined sentences such as (13.5) (see Chapter 11 for a discussion of a parallel visual ERP study).

(13.5) Example stimuli from Augurzky (2006)
        a. Das ist der Schüler   der Lehrerin,
           this is   [the student][NOM.M] [the teacher][GEN.F]
           dessen...
           who[GEN.M]...
           "This is the student of the teacher whose..." (relative clause modifies student)

        b. Das ist der Schüler   der Lehrerin,
           this is   [the student][NOM.M] [the teacher][GEN.F]
           deren...
           who[GEN.F]...
           "This is the student of the teacher whose..." (relative clause modifies teacher)

        c. Das ist der Schüler   von
           this is   [the student][NOM.M]   of
           der Lehrerin,   dessen...
           [the teacher][DAT.F]   who[GEN.M]...
           "This is the student of the teacher whose..." (relative clause modifies student)

d. Das   ist   der Schüler   von
  this   is   [the student][NOM.M]   of
  der Lehrerin,   deren...
  [the teacher][DAT.F]   who[GEN.F]...
  "This is the student of the teacher whose..." (relative
  clause modifies teacher)

The sentences in (13.5) were each presented in two alternative prosodic realizations, which favored high attachment (HA) and low attachment (LA) of the relative clause, respectively. In accordance with previous behavioral results from both comprehension (e.g. Clifton, Carlson, and Frazier 2002) and production (Jun 2003), the HA-prosody involved a larger prosodic boundary after NP2 (*der Lehrerin*, "the teacher") as opposed to after NP1, while this relative relation between the two boundaries was reversed in the LA-prosody. Furthermore, Augurzky (2006) assumed (and confirmed via a production study) that the genitive constructions in (13.5a/b) would favor the HA-prosody by default, whereas the prepositional construction in (13.5c/d) would typically be realized with the LA-prosody. The results of the ERP study revealed the following overall pattern of effects at the position of the relative pronoun, which unambiguously signalled an HA or an LA reading. For the genitive conditions (13.5a/b), Augurzky observed an N400-like negativity for HA (13.5a) vs. LA (13.5b) sentences when both were realized with an LA-prosody, but no difference between the two attachment variants with an HA-prosody. The prepositional conditions (13.5c/d), by contrast, showed an N400 for an HA (13.5c) vs. an LA (13.5d) reading with an HA-prosody, but no effect for the conditions with an LA-prosody. Independently of one's preferred theoretical interpretation of this complex data pattern, these findings clearly indicate that prosodic phrasing has a direct impact upon the attachment of the relative clause.

In summary, the existing neurocognitive literature on prosodic phrasing suggests that the placement of prosodic boundaries has a very early impact upon the establishment of syntactic structures and constituency relations. At present, it appears that the CPS is the only direct neurophysiological correlate of prosodic boundary processing. In addition, effects of prosodic information can be observed as modulations of other ERP components that are indicative of particular processes at the sentence level. It is important to note, however, that this modulation is mainly quantitative in nature, i.e. the involvement of prosodic information does not generally lead to a "switch" in the component pattern observed.

Note

1. Note that this study also provided the first demonstration of a CPS in Japanese.

14

Information structure

The question of how the processing of sentence-internal relations is constrained by the discourse context in which these sentences occur has long been a major topic of investigation in the psycholinguistic literature (e.g. Crain and Steedman 1985). Whereas early studies within this domain were mainly concerned with factors such as referentiality and plausibility (see also Chapter 11), recent years have seen an increasing interest in possible influences of information structure. The neurocognitive processing literature presents no exception in this regard: a range of studies have examined the interplay of given and new information within a sentence and how this relates to the processing of prosodic and syntactic information. In addition, a small number of experiments has extended the domain of investigation to more complex information structural factors such as contrast or corrective focus.

In this chapter, we begin by discussing general issues related to the processing of information structure, namely neurocognitive correlates of given vs. new information (section 14.1) and the interaction between information structure and prosodic prominence (section 14.2). We then turn to more specific issues regarding the influence of information structure on sentence-level syntactic processing. These have been examined primarily in the domain of word order, which is the focus of section 14.3. Finally, section 14.4 discusses influences of information structure on other phenomena.

14.1 Neurocognitive correlates of given vs. new information

At the word level, the N400 is certainly the best-known neurophysiological correlate of the distinction between old and new information. Thus, the amplitude of this component is reduced in response to repetition priming (Rugg 1985) and when a word is highly predictable within the sentence or discourse context (see Kutas and Federmeier 2000 and Figure 2.3).

A systematic investigation of the electrophysiological correlates of referential processing was undertaken by Burkhardt (2006). She contrasted the processing of definite noun phrases such as *der Dirigent* ("the conductor") in German sentences such as (14.2) as a function of context (14.1). Within the context provided, the critical NP was either given (14.1a), new (14.1b), or linked to contextually given information via a bridging inference (14.1c).[1]

(14.1)   Example contexts from Burkhardt (2006)

      a. Tobias besuchte einen Dirigenten in Berlin.
        "Tobias visited a conductor in Berlin."

      b. Tobias unterhielt sich mit Nina.
        "Tobias talked to Nina."

      c. Tobias besuchte ein Konzert in Berlin.
        "Tobias visited a concert in Berlin."

(14.2)   Example target sentence from Burkhardt (2006)
      Er erzählte, dass der Dirigent sehr beeindruckend war.
      he said   that the conductor very impressive   was
      "He said that the conductor was very impressive."

As is to be expected, Burkhardt (2006) observed a modulation of the N400 such that given NPs engendered the smallest N400 effect and new NPs elicited the largest N400 effect. The N400 for bridged NPs was intermediary between the two. In addition, both new and bridged NPs engendered a late positivity in comparison to given NPs. Thus, the processing of bridged NPs, which can be linked to a familiar entity within the mental model via an inferential process, is similar to the processing of NPs with an established referent on the one hand (in showing a reduced N400) and similar to the processing of new NPs on the other (in showing a late positivity). Burkhardt therefore argued that the N400 reflects the ease or difficulty of NP interpretation, as determined by the saliency of the information to which it is linked in the discourse. This assumption was supported by a further study (Burkhardt and Roehm 2007), in which the saliency of the antecedent was shown to lead to a modulation of the N400 for inferential dependencies but not for identity relations. By contrast, the late positivity was interpreted as a marker of the establishment of independent reference (i.e. establishment of a new discourse referent).

Box 14.1 Establishing coreference

The establishment of coreference between an anaphoric element (pronoun/reflexive) and its antecedent poses a particular challenge for the language comprehension system. Not only does it call for the establishment of dependencies across what may be quite sizable distances, it also requires the online application of constraints specifying which referents are possible antecedents and which are not. To examine these processes, neurocognitive studies have typically drawn upon violation paradigms.

A number of ERP investigations of coreference establishment have revealed late positivities as correlates of binding violations. As first shown by Osterhout and Mobley (1995) using sentences such as (i), this response is observable under a variety of conditions.

(i) Example stimuli from Osterhout and Mobley (1995)
  a. Reflexive gender mismatch
     The successful woman congratulated herself/*himself on the promotion.
  b. Reflexive number mismatch
     The guests helped themselves/*himself to the food.
  c. Pronoun gender mismatch
     The aunt heard that she/he had won the lottery.

Osterhout and Mobley observed late positivities for all three mismatch conditions in (i). This suggests that the neurophysiological response to problems in the establishment of coreference is similar for different types of anaphoric elements (reflexives/pronouns) and for different types of feature mismatches (gender/number). It further indicates that the language processing system attempts to bind pronouns, which differ from reflexives in that they do not require an antecedent in order for a sentence to be grammatical, to the closest accessible antecedent, independently of whether its features match that of the pronoun or not.

Osterhout and Mobley's (1995) finding of a P600 for reflexives without an accessible antecedent was subsequently replicated by Harris, Wexler, and Holcomb (2000) and, using gender stereotypes, by Osterhout, Bersick, and McLaughlin (1997). Harris and colleagues additionally examined the processing of logophors, i.e. reflexives which occur in non-argument positions and need not be bound by an antecedent within their local syntactic domain (e.g. *themselves* in *[The pilot's mechanics]ᵢ brow-beat Paxton and themselvesᵢ after the race*; see the discussion in Harris et al.). For number-mismatching logophors, Harris et al. (2000) did not observe a P600 but rather a (non-significant) trend towards an N400, thereby suggesting that these types of anaphors are processed differently to regular reflexives and pronouns.

Further ERP findings suggest that feature mismatches in coreference establishment can, under certain circumstances, be modulated by the type of feature involved. In a study contrasting syntactic and biological gender processing in German, Schmitt, Lamers, and Münte (2002) observed a late positivity for syntactic gender disagreement but an N400 for biological gender disagreement. For further findings of N400 effects in this domain and a comparison between German and Dutch, see Lamers et al. (2006). In addition, note that N400 effects have also been observed in response to the formation of dependencies between pronouns and their antecedents in non-violation contexts (Streb, Rösler, and Hennighausen 1999; Streb, Hennighausen, and Rösler 2004; Burkhardt 2005).

Finally, coreference processing has also been examined in several neuroimaging studies. For example, Santi and Grodzinsky (2007a) contrasted the processing of binding dependencies in (English) sentences with reflexives with the processing of (movement) dependencies in wh-questions. They observed a main effect of binding in the right middle frontal gyrus (MFG), left inferior frontal gyrus (BA 45/47)/left orbital gyrus, mid cingulate gyrus, and bilateral medial temporal gyri. (Note that the effect of binding in the right MFG resulted from a decrease rather than an increase in BOLD signal.) This neural network for binding dependencies was quite different to the network that showed activation in response to wh-dependencies, which encompassed the left inferior frontal gyrus (BA 44), the left inferior precentral sulcus and the left posterior superior temporal gyrus. No regions showed an interaction between the two dependency types. (Note that a caveat with respect to these functional-neuroanatomical interpretations is raised by a second study by Santi and Grodzinsky (2007b). Here, the authors also contrasted movement and binding, but used slightly different constructions and employed a parametric design with three levels of increasing dependency distance for each dependency type. While replicating the effect of binding in the right MFG, the results of this second study showed increased movement-related activation in BA 45, but no binding-related left inferior frontal activation. This discrepancy between the two studies indicates that the linguistic manipulations may not have been as comparable as they may appear at first glance.)

A further neuroanatomical dissociation between coreference processing and other aspects of sentence comprehension was observed in an fMRI study on

Dutch (Nieuwland, Petersson, and van Berkum 2007). Nieuwland and colleagues examined sentences with referential ambiguity (e.g. the Dutch equivalent of *Ronald told Frank that he...*) and referential failure (e.g. the Dutch equivalent of *Rose told Emily that he...*) and contrasted these with referentially coherent sentences (with a single gender-matching antecedent) and semantically anomalous sentences. For sentences involving referential ambiguity, the authors observed increased activation in bilateral anterior frontomedian (BA 10) and right superior frontal (BA 8) regions as well as in the left precuneus (BA 7) and bilateral inferior parietal areas. Referential failure led to activations in medial and lateral parietal regions as well as to increased activation of the left middle frontal gyrus. Sentences with unambiguous reference engendered increased activation in the left and right inferior frontal gyri (BA 45/47) in comparison to referentially ambiguous sentences and in the left medial temporal lobe in comparison to sentences with referential failure. Crucially, the networks responsive to increased demands in referential processing did not overlap with those activated in response to semantic anomalies (which comprised bilateral inferior frontal regions; BA 44/45/47). On the basis of these results, the authors argue that the processing of referential ambiguity draws upon similar neural substrates to those involved in decision-making/inferential processes/evaluative judgments. Referential failure, by contrast, is associated with increased activation of areas that may be involved in the reprocessing of episodic memory traces.

In summary, existing neuroimaging findings on coreference processing suggest that these differ in important respects from other aspects of syntactic and semantic processing (for somewhat different conclusions, see Hammer et al. 2007). However, the degree to which coreference-related processes can be explained in terms of domain-general processes such as inferencing and decision-making remains to be explored in future research.

Matters appear to be somewhat different with respect to the processing of proper nouns. This is apparent from the results of an ERP study (Swaab, Camblin, and Gordon 2004), which examined the famous "repeated name penalty" in sentences such as (14.3).

(14.3)   Example stimuli from Swaab et al. (2004)

a. John went to the store so that <u>John/he</u> could buy some candy.

b. John and Mary went to the store so that <u>John/he</u> could buy some candy.

Whereas the continuation with a pronoun did not engender a differential ERP response between (14.3a) and (14.3b), Swaab et al. (2004) observed a larger N400 effect for a proper noun in the context of a single referent (14.3a) as opposed to a coordination (14.3b). Thus, in contrast to Burkhardt and Roehm's findings for definite descriptions, which showed an N400 reduction for the processing of NPs with more prominent/salient antecedents in the discourse, Swaab and colleagues observed the opposite effect for proper nouns. This might be attributable to the fact that, as Swaab and colleagues suggest, the repetition of a proper noun leads to the assumption of "disjoint reference". Thus, in accordance with syntactic (Chomsky 1981) or pragmatic (Reinhart 1983) constraints on the coreference of proper nouns, the second occurrence of *John* in (14.3a) is interpreted as referring to a different referent to that of the first occurrence of *John*. For an overview of further neurocognitive findings in the domain of coreference processing, see Box 14.1.

In summary, the establishment of reference for common nouns correlates with two ERP components: the N400 and the late positivity. Whereas the N400 indexes the accessibility of the referent within the mental model, the late positivity marks the establishment of independent reference.[2]

14.2 The interaction of inter- and intra-sentential information structural requirements

Beyond the processing of old vs. new information at the level of individual sentence constituents, a number of researchers have been concerned with the sentence-internal realization of information structure and how this interacts with contextual requirements. In this regard, ERP research within the auditory domain has seen several investigations of the processing system's response to particular prosodic realizations of information structural requirements. For example, Hruska and Alter (2004) investigated the processing of question–answer pairs in which the prosodic realization of the answer either matched or did not match the information structure imposed by the question. To this end, they presented German sentences such as (14.4).

(14.4) Example stimuli from Hruska and Alter (2004) (capital letters indicate prosodic focus)

    a. VP-focus question
      Was verspricht Peter Anna zu tun?
      "What does Peter promise Anna?"

    a′. VP-focus answer
      Peter verspricht Anna zu ARBEITEN und
      Peter promises   Anna to WORK   and
      das BÜRO   zu putzen.
      the OFFICE to clean
      "Peter promises Anna to WORK and to clean the OFFICE."

    b. Dative-focus question
      Wem verspricht Peter zu arbeiten und das Büro zu putzen?
      "Who does Peter promise to work and to clean the office?"

    b′. Dative-focus answer
      Peter verspricht ANNA zu arbeiten und das Büro
      Peter promises   ANNA to work   and the office
      zu   putzen.
      to   clean
      "Peter promises ANNA to work and to clean the office."

Whereas question (14.4a) sets up an expectation for a VP-focus (which should be realized via a prosodic focus accent on the verb of the first conjunct of the answer; 14.4a′), question (14.4b) calls for a narrow focus on the dative argument in the answer (*Anna* in 14.4b′). When presented as congruent answers to their respective questions, the target sentences in (14.4) engendered a late parietal positivity at the position of the focused constituents (*arbeiten*, "to work", in 14.4a′ and *Anna* in 14.4b′). Note that, as in the study by Steinhauer et al. (1999) (see Chapter 13.1 and Figure 13.1), the two different congruous focus realizations (14.4a′/14.4b′) served as control conditions for one another. On the basis of its latency, topography, and morphology, the authors classified the observed positivity effect as a CPS. In addition, they observed an anterior negativity at each focused position, which they interpreted as reflecting the contextually-induced expectancy for the focused information. Whereas positivity effects were also observable at the same positions when the target sentences were presented in isolation (but with the same prosodic realization), the anterior negativities no longer occurred. Finally, when the target sentences were presented in inappropriate contexts (i.e. 14.4a′ following 14.4b and

14.4b′ following 14.4a), Hruska and Alter observed an N400 for information structurally focused constituents that were missing an appropriate pitch accent (i.e. at *Anna* in 14.4a′ presented in the context of 14.4b), but no such effect for a superfluous pitch accent (i.e. at *Anna* in 14.4b′ presented in the context of 14.4a). For these comparisons, the contextually appropriate counterparts served as control sentences.

These findings were extended in another study on German by Toepel and Alter (2004), who examined the processing of constituents associated with new information pitch accents and contrastive pitch accents in appropriate and inappropriate contexts, respectively. Most generally, both types of inappropriate accents were shown to yield negative ERP deflections. However, while the negativity for a new information accent in a contrastive context appeared independently of the precise experimental task (comprehension task or prosodic judgment), the reversed effect (i.e. the negativity for a contrastive accent in a new information context) only obtained when participants were explicitly required to judge the prosodic appropriateness of the target sentence within the given context. In addition, parietal positivities (again interpreted as CPS effects) were observed at all positions at which new or contrastive information was expected (in comparison to sentences in which no new or contrastive information occurred at this position). These findings thus provide further supporting evidence for the association between positive ERP deflections and the processing of (contextually/prosodically) focused information. Like Hruska and Alter's results, they also suggest that the prosodic underspecification of a particular information structural status leads to higher processing costs than the addition of superfluous prosodic information.

Somewhat different results were obtained in an experiment on the processing of contrastive question–answer pairs in French (Magne et al. 2005). Using a prosodic appropriateness judgment task, Magne and colleagues examined the comprehension of auditorily presented question–answer pairs such as (14.5).

(14.5)   Example stimuli from Magne et al. (2005) (capital letters indicate prosodic focus)

    a. Direct object contrast question
       A-t-il donné une bague ou un bracelet à sa fiancée?
       "Did he give his fiancée a ring or a bracelet?"

    a′. Direct object contrast answer
       Il   a   donné une BAGUE à   sa   fiancée.
       he   have[3.SG] given   a   RING   to his   fiancée
       "He gave a RING to his fiancée."

  b. Indirect object contrast question
     A-t-il donné une bague à sa fiancée ou à sa sœur?
     "Did he give a ring to his fiancée or to his sister?"

  b'. Indirect object contrast answer
     Il a   donné une bague à   sa   FIANCÉE.
     he have[3.SG] given a   ring   to his FIANCÉE.
     "He gave a ring to his FIANCÉE."

By fully crossing the presentation of questions and answers in (14.5), Magne et al. (2005) were able to examine the processing of contrastive information under appropriate and inappropriate prosodic focus conditions in both sentence-medial and sentence-final positions. Sentence-finally, results were comparable to those obtained by Toepel and Alter (2004): inappropriate prosodic focus (i.e. a contrastive pitch accent on a non-contrastive constituent or no such pitch accent on a contrastive constituent) engendered a negative shift (150–1,050 ms) in the ERP record. Clause-medially, by contrast, Magne and colleagues observed a parietal positivity (300–900 ms) for prosodically incongruent constituents. They interpreted this effect as an instance of a surprise-related P300 (see Chapter 12.4 for a more detailed discussion of P300 effects). Indeed, one of the crucial differences between this study and the previous experiments on German was that all dialogues led to an expectation for a contrastive focus. Thus, in combination with the prosodic judgment task, this may have led participants to monitor for the position of the contrastive pitch accent. As the clause-medial position in effect disambiguated the entire prosodic structure of the utterance (i.e. a clause-medial pitch accent implied that there would be no clause-final pitch accent, whereas the absence of a clause-medial pitch accent implied the presence of a clause-final pitch accent) and a mismatch in this position was thus highly task relevant, this may have led to the observation of a P300. By contrast, ERPs for the less task-relevant clause-final position were less likely to be obscured by these strategic considerations and thus patterned more closely with the results by Hruska and Alter (2004) and especially Toepel and Alter (2004). However, it must also be kept in mind that the prosodic realization of the sentence-final constituent was fully predictable from the preceding sentence context. Thus, these conclusions warrant at least some degree of caution.

  The effects of contextually-induced information structural requirements have also been examined in the visual modality. In an ERP study on German, Bornkessel, Schlesewsky, and Friederici (2003a) examined how the processing of an argument is affected by its information structural status (i.e. by whether it occurs in a neutral context, is given by the context, or questioned (focused) by the context). This manipulation was realized by means of question–answer pairs as illustrated in (14.6) and (14.7).

(14.6)   Example context questions for subject-initial sentences from Bornkessel et al. (2003a)

   a. Neutral context
      Klaus fragt sich, was am Sonntag passiert ist.
      "Klaus asks himself what happened on Sunday."

   b. Object-focus context (subject contextually given)
      Klaus fragt sich, wen der Gärtner am Sonntag besucht hat.
      "Klaus asks himself who the gardener visited on Sunday."

   c. Subject-focus context (object contextually given)
      Klaus fragt sich, wer am Sonntag den Lehrer besucht hat.
      "Klaus asks himself who visited the teacher on Sunday."

(14.7)   Example subject-initial target sentence from Bornkessel et al. (2003a)
      Dann   erfuhr   er,   dass   der   Gärtner
      then   heard   he   that   [the   gardener][NOM]
      den Lehrer   besucht   hat.
      [the teacher][ACC]   visited   has
      "Then he heard that the gardener visited the teacher."

Bornkessel and colleagues observed that the processing of focused arguments (i.e. *der Gärtner*, "the gardener" in 14.7 in the context of 14.6c and *den Lehrer*, "the teacher" in 14.7 in the context of 14.6b) engendered a parietal positivity between 280 and 480 ms post NP onset (see Figure 14.1). This effect, which was termed the "focus positivity", also occurred at the position of the verb in both non-neutral contexts.

   The findings by Bornkessel et al. (2003a) therefore indicate that the positive ERP deflections observed in response to focused sentence constituents are engendered by the processing of information structural rather than prosodic focus (similar conclusions were reached for the auditory domain by Johnson et al. 2003). In particular, the focus positivity appears to index the integration of new information into the appropriate slot opened up by the context.

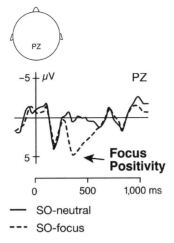

Figure 14.1 Illustration of the focus positivity in the visual modality. The plot shows the ERP response to a nominative-marked NP in a subject-focus (dashed line) as a opposed to a neutral context (solid line).

Source: Adapted from Bornkessel et al. 2003a.

Further observations from the Bornkessel et al. (2003a) study suggest that this integration process is crucially dependent upon the presence of new lexical material rather than on a match between the grammatical function/case marking of the focused information in the context and target sentence. This was shown by means of two "mismatch" conditions, in which the contextually-induced expectations (14.8) were not fully met within the target sentence, which is repeated as (14.9) for convenience.

(14.8) Example mismatch context questions from Bornkessel et al. (2003a)

   a. Klaus fragt sich, wen der Lehrer am Sonntag besucht hat.
       "Klaus asks himself who the teacher visited on Sunday."

   b. Klaus fragt sich, wer am Sonntag den Gärtner besucht hat.
       "Klaus asks himself who visited the gardener on Sunday."

(14.9) Example subject-initial target sentence from Bornkessel et al. (2003a)

   Dann   erfuhr   er,   dass   der Gärtner
   then   heard   he   that   [the gardener][NOM]
   den Lehrer   besucht hat.
   [the teacher][ACC]   visited has
   "Then he heard that the gardener visited the teacher."

In the context of (14.8a), the first argument in (14.9) provides a new referent, but also indicates that the state of affairs must have been different to what was suggested by the context question as this new referent is introduced with nominative rather than accusative case. This situation is reversed when the first argument in (14.9) is encountered in the context of (14.8b). Here, the case marking matches the expected case marking of the new information, but the NP is already given by the context. Both situations therefore require a correction of the contextually-induced expectation. Crucially, however, only the condition which introduced new lexical material (i.e. 14.9 following 14.8a) engendered a focus positivity at the position of the first argument. This result led Bornkessel et al. (2003a) to conclude that it is the introduction of new lexical material that forms the crucial basis for the elicitation of the focus positivity. Subsequent research using hyperonyms (e.g. *carp-fish*) to induce coreference in lexically non-identical noun phrases suggests that the focus positivity is in fact triggered by the introduction of a *new referent* rather than by new lexical material per se (Kulik 2007).

The relation between the sentence-internal realization of information structure and contextual requirements was also the topic of a visual ERP study on English (Cowles et al. 2007). In this experiment, Cowles and colleagues used contexts such as (14.10) to set up an expectation for a contrastive focus. In the following target sentences (14.11), they employed a cleft structure to focus either an appropriate (14.11a) or an inappropriate (14.11b) referent. Thus, in contrast to the auditory German and French studies discussed above, this experiment used a syntactic device to induce the sentence-internal information structure match or mismatch.

(14.10)   Example context from Cowles et al. (2007)
          A priest, a farmer, and a laborer were sitting outside the church.
          Who did the priest pray for, the farmer, or the laborer?

(14.11)   Example target sentences from Cowles et al. (2007)
          a. It was the <u>farmer</u> that the priest prayed for.
          b. It was the <u>priest</u> that prayed for the farmer.

At the position of the clefted noun in the target sentence (*farmer, priest*), Cowles and colleagues observed a centrally distributed negativity (200–800 ms) for incongruent (14.11b) vs. congruent (14.11a) focus. In spite of its long duration, they interpreted this effect as a kind of N400. Furthermore, they observed a positivity between 200 and 800 ms for the clefted noun and the sentence-final word as opposed to all other word positions in the target sentence. In an additional analysis, which used a high-pass filter to control for an overall positive drift throughout the course of the sentence, this positivity was found to be more pronounced for the clefted noun as opposed to the sentence-final word. These findings are therefore in agreement with Bornkessel et al.'s (2003a) results in showing that the processing of focused constituents correlates with a positive ERP effect, which is independent of the contextual appropriateness of the focus assignment. In addition, Cowles and colleagues' results indicate that such a positivity can also be elicited via strong sentence-internal considerations (i.e. via a construction that unambiguously indicates that a particular NP is in focus).

Furthermore, Cowles et al.'s (2007) findings are in line with (the majority of) the results from the auditory domain in revealing a negativity for a mismatch between sentence-internal and contextually given information structure. At a first glance, however, the finding of a negativity for a superfluous sentence-internal focus appears to conflict with Hruska and Alter's (2004) observation that missing but not superfluous prosodic accents engender negativity responses. Cowles and colleagues attribute this apparent discrepancy between the modalities to the fact that cleft constructions unambiguously call for a focus interpretation of the clefted noun, while prosodic information is inherently relational in nature (i.e. prosodic prominence is not absolute but can only be determined by means of a comparison between several constituents). Thus, the processing system might be able to accommodate a superfluous pitch accent more readily than an inappropriate cleft structure.

In summary, the existing ERP findings on inter- vs. intra-sentential information structural requirements suggest that the processing of focused information correlates with an early parietal positivity. This effect either results when a new referent is encountered within a question context, when the syntactic structure of the sentence unambiguously indicates that one particular constituent is in focus, or, as tentatively suggested by Hruska and Alter's (2004) findings, when prosodic prominence is used to the same end. The focus positivity therefore appears to reflect the integration of an expected new referent into the slot opened up within the context. A similar effect has also been observed at the position of the clause-final word (Bornkessel et al. 2003a; Cowles et al. 2007), thereby suggesting that an additional information structural integration may take place at this point (i.e. when the entire proposition has been processed and can be integrated with the context). Both Bornkessel et al. (2003a) and Cowles et al. (2007) suggest that the focus positivity could be viewed as an instance of a P3b (see Chapter 12.4 for further discussion of this component), reflecting the "delivery of crucial information" (Cowles et al. 2007: 239). An interpretation along these lines, which appears compatible with the "context-updating" view of the P300 (see Chapter 12.4), suggests that ERP effects may also be observed in response to the fulfillment of a prediction (i.e. to a "positive" event) rather than only reflecting mismatches of some kind. This perspective is supported by the findings of Bornkessel et al. (2003a), which showed that the early positivity is attenuated – rather than increased – when there is a mismatch between the properties of the first potential focused NP and the discourse context. Finally, in contrast to the positivity reflecting the fulfillment of a contextual expectation, information structural mismatches between context and target sentences are generally reflected in N400-like negativities.

14.3 Information structure and word order

Having discussed the processing of information structure at the sentence level and its interaction with the discourse context, let us now turn to the question of how information structural requirements may influence sentence-internal processing phenomena. The processing of word order is a case in point: as it is often assumed that order permutations in languages with flexible word order are at least partly conditioned by information structure, it appears important to ascertain whether such an influence can also be detected during online language comprehension. This issue has been addressed by several behavioral studies using self-paced reading (Meng et al. 1999) and the visual world paradigm (Kaiser and Trueswell 2004). Kaiser and Trueswell (2004), for example, examined the processing of OVS and SVO word orders in Finnish and observed anticipatory eye movements to new discourse referents (as shown on a visual display; cf. Chapter 2.4.3.1) when participants heard OVS orders, reflecting the fact that the subject was expected to encode new information. From this, they concluded that the processing of a marked word order leads to a rapid use of the associated information structural information.

Within the neurocognitive domain, the first experiment to examine the effects of information structure on word order processing was reported by Bornkessel et al. (2003a). While the subject-initial target sentences employed in this study were already discussed in the last section, the full experimental design also included object-initial constructions. These are illustrated together with their respective contexts in (14.12) and (14.13).

(14.12)   Example context questions for object-initial sentences from Bornkessel et al. (2003a)

    a. Neutral context
       Klaus fragt sich, was am Sonntag passiert ist.
       "Klaus asks himself what happened on Sunday."

    b. Subject-focus context (object contextually given)
       Klaus fragt sich, wer am Sonntag den Gärtner besucht hat.
       "Klaus asks himself who visited the gardener on Sunday."

    c. Object-focus context (subject contextually given)
       Klaus fragt sich, wen der Lehrer am Sonntag besucht hat.
       "Klaus asks himself who the teacher visited on Sunday."

(14.13)   Example object-initial target sentence from Bornkessel et al. (2003a)
       Dann   erfuhr   er,   dass   den Gärtner
       then   heard   he   that   [the gardener][ACC]
       der Lehrer   besucht   hat.
       [the teacher][NOM]   visited   has
       "Then he heard that the gardener visited the teacher."

Recall from Chapter 9.2.4.2 that clause-medial word order permutations ("scrambling") as in (14.13) engender a central negativity between approximately 300 and 450 ms post onset of the initial object (the so-called "scrambling negativity"). Bornkessel et al. (2003a) therefore aimed to examine whether this effect can be modulated when the scrambled word order is embedded in a supporting context. According to the theoretical literature, this should be the case when the scrambled object is given by the context (e.g. Lenerz 1977; Fanselow 2003; Haider and Rosengren 2003), i.e. when (14.13) is presented as an answer to (14.12b). In spite of this contextual support, however, Bornkessel et al.

(2003a) did *not* observe a reduction of the scrambling negativity when the scrambled object was given (in comparison to when it was presented in a neutral context). Thus, while the information structural support for the object-initial order serves to render this order more acceptable, it does not attenuate the local processing costs associated with a scrambled word order. A recent replication of this finding in the auditory modality (Bornkessel-Schlesewsky et al. submitted) further showed that the scrambling negativity still obtains even under conditions of contextual and prosodic support. These observations provides converging evidence for a processing architecture in which contextual/ pragmatic influences are assumed to occur at a post-initial stage of comprehension.

By contrast, Bornkessel et al.'s (2003a) findings showed no indication of a scrambling negativity when the scrambled object was focused, i.e. when (14.13) was presented as an answer to (14.12c). Here, the object-initial order showed a focus positivity (see section 14.2) of the same magnitude as the focus positivity in the corresponding subject-initial order. There was thus no evidence for an additive component pattern comprising both a focus positivity and a scrambling negativity. In contrast to the conclusion drawn above, this result therefore indicates that information structural considerations *can* have an immediate influence on sentence-internal processing considerations under certain circumstances. In addition, this observation might appear to suggest that focus rather than givenness should be considered the "true" information structural licensing condition for scrambling in German. However, several considerations speak against such an interpretation. On the one hand, a focus reading of a scrambled object is less acceptable than a given reading. On the other hand, a strong contextual influence of focus – as induced exclusively by a context question – has also been observed in linguistic domains other than word order, e.g. for closure ambiguities (Altmann et al. 1998). Furthermore, the findings on the focus positivity that were discussed in the last section are indicative of a "special" status for focus integration within the overall processing architecture. Bornkessel and colleagues thus concluded that, rather than indicating a local contextual licensing of scrambling, the absence of a scrambling negativity for focused objects should be attributed to a special processing status of focused constituents per se.[3]

A potential caveat about the findings presented by Bornkessel et al. (2003a) is that the information structural effects of question–answer pairs such as those in (14.12/14.13) may not be strong enough to override the sentence-internal word order considerations leading to the scrambling negativity. This possibility was examined by Bornkessel and Schlesewsky (2006b) in an ERP study using contrastive contexts such as (14.14).

(14.14)   Example of a contrastive context from Bornkessel and Schlesewsky (2006b)

Von den zwanzig Studenten, die im ersten Semester mit dem Chemiestudium begonnen hatten, waren nach vier Jahren nur noch Toralf und Dietmar übrig. Dies kam wohl zum Teil auch daher, dass die beiden schon von Anfang an von zwei Professorinnen für organische Chemie und Umweltchemie protegiert wurden. Allerdings weiss ich nicht genau, wer den Toralf und wer den Dietmar betreute.
Of the twenty students who had begun studying chemistry in the first semester, only Toralf and Dietmar remained after four years. To a certain extent, this was most likely a result of the fact that, from the very beginning, the two were supported by two professors for organic chemistry and environmental chemistry. However, I don't know exactly who supervised Toralf and who supervised Dietmar.

(14.15)   Example target sentence from Bornkessel and Schlesewsky (2006b)

Ich	habe	gehört,	dass	den Toralf	
I	have	heard	that	[the Toralf] [ACC]	
die	Organikerin		sehr	mochte,	während
the	organic.chemist		very	liked,	while
den Dietmar			die	Umweltchemikerin	
[the Dietmar] [ACC]			the	environmental.chemist	
äußerst	begabt	fand.			
extremely	talented	found			

I heard that Toralf was very much liked by the organic chemist, while Dietmar was found to be very talented by the environmental chemist.

The context in (14.14) sets up a contrastive reading of the scrambled object *den Toralf* in the target sentence (14.15) without explicitly questioning this constituent. This manipulation thus tested whether the scrambling negativity can be influenced in a non-question context when the information structural status of the scrambled object is "stronger" than simple givenness. However, this was not the case: Bornkessel and Schlesewsky (2006b) observed a robust scrambling negativity for dialogues such as (14.14/14.15) and for two other types of contrastive dialogues. Strikingly, in all of these cases, the scrambled target sentences were judged to be significantly *more* acceptable than their subject-initial counterparts within the given context. Thus, while the contrastive reading clearly served to license scrambling from a global sentence perspective, it did not alleviate the local processing difficulty that is reflected in the scrambling negativity. The overall data pattern was thus very similar to that previously observed for scrambled objects that were contextually given.

Bornkessel and Schlesewsky (2006b) did, however, observe a modulation of the scrambling negativity in a fourth type of dialogue, namely one involving corrective focus. An example is given in (14.16/14.17).

(14.16) Example of a corrective focus context from Bornkessel and Schlesewsky (2006b)
Von den zwanzig Studenten, die im ersten Semester mit dem Chemiestudium begonnen hatten, waren nach vier Jahren nur noch Toralf und Dietmar übrig. Leider hat aber nur einer von beiden die Diplomprüfung bestanden. Ich vermute, dass es der Toralf war.
Of the twenty students who had begun studying chemistry in the first semester, only Toralf and Dietmar remained after four years. Unfortunately, only one of them passed the final exam. I suspect that it was Toralf.

(14.17) Example target sentence (corrective focus context) from Bornkessel and Schlesewsky (2006b)
Ich   habe   gehört,   dass   <u>den Dietmar</u>
I   have   heard   that   [the Dietmar][ACC]
ein   besonders   wohlwollender   Prüfer   bestehen   ließ.
a   particularly   well.meaning   examiner   pass   let
I heard that it was Dietmar who was passed by a particularly well-meaning examiner.

The dialogue in (14.16/14.17) involves a corrective focus because the target sentence denies and corrects the assertion that *Toralf* passed the exam. Moreover, the need for a correction is already apparent at the position of the first argument, since the context induces a strong expectation that *Toralf* will be the topic of the target sentence. This is contradicted by the positioning of *Dietmar* as the leftmost argument. Under these circumstances, no scrambling negativity was observable for initial objects – in spite of the fact that corrective focus was associated with a general acceptability drop and therefore does not seem to license scrambling from a grammatical perspective. Bornkessel and Schlesewsky (2006b: 38) thus speculate that corrective focus might lead to an extra-grammatical override of sentence-internal word order processing due to its "extreme communicative saliency".

When taken together, existing neurocognitive findings on the effects of information structure in the processing of unambiguously marked word order variations suggest that the effects of a facilitating context typically come into play in a post-initial stage of processing. Thus, contexts which clearly render scrambled orders more acceptable in terms of sentence-final behavioral responses and which are known to favor the production of scrambled sentences do not lead to an attenuation of the scrambling negativity. By contrast, very strong information structural influences such as information focus (as induced by a context question) or corrective focus do seem to be able to influence even the earliest stages of word order processing. This finding suggests that context/information structure *can*, in principle, have an immediate influence on relational syntactic processing. In view of this rather complex overall situation, it is not straightforwardly apparent which conclusions should be drawn for the organization of the language processing architecture. In essence, the existing results appear compatible with two alternative interpretations, namely (a) that information structure can lead to an override of sentence-internal processing considerations only under particular circumstances such as strong contextually-induced predictions, or (b) that the absence of a general early influence of information structure in German should be attributed to language-specific properties (i.e. to the fact that scrambling can never be unambiguously signaled by a particular context in German). The consequences for the status of information structure within the language processing architecture will differ substantially depending on which of these two options turns out to be correct. However, this can only be ascertained on the basis of further systematic cross-linguistic research.

14.4 Information structure in other domains

The relationship between information structure and sentence-internal processing preferences has also been examined in domains other than

word order. In a visual ERP study on the interplay between information structure and implicit prosody in German, Stolterfoht et al. (2007)
examined the processing of contrastive ellipses such as (14.18).

(14.18)   Example sentences from Stolterfoht et al. (2007)

    a. Revision of focus structure
        Am   Dienstag hat   der Direktor
        on   Tuesday   has   [the principal][NOM]
        den Schüler   getadelt,
        [the student][ACC]   reprimanded
        und nicht <u>den Lehrer</u>.
        and not   [the teacher][ACC]
        "On Tuesday, the principal reprimanded the student and
        not the teacher."

    b. Revision of focus structure and implicit prosody
        Am   Dienstag hat   der Direktor
        on   Tuesday   has   [the principal][NOM]
        den Schüler   getadelt,
        [the student][ACC]   reprimanded
        und nicht <u>der Lehrer</u>.
        and not   [the teacher][NOM]
        "On Tuesday, the principal and not the teacher repri-
        manded the student."

    c. Control (object focus)
        Am   Dienstag hat   der Direktor
        on   Tuesday   has   [the principal][NOM]
        nur den Schüler   getadelt,
        only [the student][ACC]   reprimanded
        und nicht <u>den Lehrer</u>.
        and not   [the teacher][ACC]
        "On Tuesday, the principal reprimanded only the student
        and not the teacher."

    d. Control (subject focus)
        Am   Dienstag hat   nur   der Direktor
        on   Tuesday   has   only   [the principal][NOM]
        den Schüler   getadelt,
        [the student][ACC]   reprimanded
        und nicht <u>der Lehrer</u>.
        and not   [the teacher][NOM]
        "On Tuesday, only the principal and not the teacher
        reprimanded the student."

The experimental design in (14.18) is based upon the assumption that a default prosodic contour is assigned during reading and that, in accordance with the default prosody in spoken language, this should normally lead to the assignment of prosodic prominence to the pre-verbal argument (i.e. to the object *den Schüler*, "the student", in 14.18a/b). In addition, without any constraining context, the entire sentence will be interpreted as conveying new information. If these two assumptions are correct, the processing of the contrastive ellipsis in (14.18a) should lead to an information structural revision when *den Lehrer* ("the teacher") in encountered, because this constituent makes clear that only the object of the first conjunct is in focus rather than the entire sentence. Example (14.18b) requires a similar information structural revision, leading to a focusing of the subject of the first conjunct. However, in contrast to (14.18a), (14.18b) also requires a revision of the (implicit) prosodic representation, because the subject focus also requires the assignment of prosodic prominence to this argument. Two additional conditions (14.18c/d) included the focus particle *nur* ("only"), which was assumed to unambiguously specify the correct information structure and the correct placement of prosodic prominence.

In the comparison between (14.18a) and (14.18c), which was assumed to reveal the electrophysiological correlates of an information structural revision, Stolterfoht and colleagues observed a broadly distributed positivity (350–1,300 ms) for (14.18a). By contrast, the comparison between (14.18b) and (14.18d), in which a revision of both the information structure and the prosodic representation was expected, revealed a marginally significant central negativity (450–650 ms) with a focus to the right. This effect reached significance in the comparison between the two conditions without focus particles (14.18b vs. 14.18a). On the basis of these results, Stolterfoht et al. (2007) argued that revisions of information structure correlate with late positive ERP effects, whereas revisions of implicit prosody correlate with a right-central negativity.[4] They further interpreted these results as evidence for the assignment of information structural and prosodic representations during reading.

The effects of information structure on the processing of conjunction constructions were examined from a slightly different perspective by Kerkhofs et al. (2007). These authors investigated the processing of NP-S coordination ambiguities such as (14.20) in contexts such as (14.19).

(14.19) Example contexts from Kerkhofs et al. (2007)

Nog geen dag nadat James "Mad Dog" Johnson werd vrijge-
laten uit de gefangenis was het alweer raak in Painful Gulch.
"Hardly a day since James 'Mad Dog' Johnson's release from
prison, trouble started again in Painful Gulch."

a. Toen Johnson zijn mannen weer opgetrommeld had, was
de grootste boerderij in de buurt het doelwit van hun
actie.
"After Johnson summoned his men, the largest ranch in
the neighborhood was targeted for their raid."

b. Toen ze de boer om hulp hoorden roepen, snelden de
sheriff en de knecht naar de boerderij.
"When they heard the farmer cry for help, the sheriff and
the farm hand rushed to the ranch."

(14.20) Example target sentence from Kerkhofs et al. (2007)

De	sheriff	beschermde	de	boer	en
the	sheriff	protected	the	farmer	and
<u>de knecht</u>		verdedigde	dapper	de	boerderij
the farm.hand		defended	bravely	the	ranch
tegen	Johnson's	bende.			
against	Johnson's	gang.			

"The sheriff protected the farmer and the farm hand bravely
defended the ranch against Johnson's gang."

At the position of the NP following the conjunction *en* ("and"), target
sentences such as (14.20) induce an ambiguity between a coordination at
the level of the noun phrase (as in *The sheriff protected the farmer and the
farm hand.*) and sentence-level coordination (as in example 14.20). It is
well established that NP-coordination is preferred by the processing
system in the default case (e.g. Frazier 1987b), but this preference can
be modulated by means of an appropriate discourse context or by the
inclusion of a disambiguating comma (Hoeks, Vonk, and Schriefers
2002; Hoeks et al. 2006). More precisely, S-coordination is no longer
associated with a processing disadvantage in comparison to NP-coordination even under conditions of local ambiguity when the subject NPs of
both conjuncts have been introduced as a joint topic within the discourse
(e.g. as accomplished by means of the pronoun *ze*, "they", in 14.19b).

Building upon these observations, Kerkhofs et al. (2007) combined a
contextual and a prosodic manipulation within an auditory ERP study:

sentences were presented in either a neutral context (14.19a) or in a context biasing towards S-coordination (14.19b) and with or without a prosodic boundary following NP2 (i.e. the first NP in the conjunction; *de boer*, "the farmer" in 14.20). As is to be expected, the prosodic boundary conditions elicited a CPS relative to the offset of NP2. More interestingly, however, the magnitude of this effect was modulated by the context such that smaller CPS effects were observed when the context also biased towards an S-coordination. By contrast, the CPS was not influenced by the eventual disambiguation, i.e. there were no effects of prosodic/syntactic incongruity vs. congruity.

While Kerkhofs and colleagues interpreted their positivity as a CPS, this classification does not straightforwardly account for the fact that the effect was smaller within a facilitating context. As discussed in Chapter 14.2 above, previous auditory experiments on the relationship between discourse context and prosody have provided no evidence for the attenuation of the CPS within an appropriate context. Thus, an alternative interpretation of Kerkhofs et al.'s (2007) result might be that the late positivity in fact indexes a more general mismatch between the contextually-preferred syntactic analysis of the target sentence and its prosodic realization.

14.5 Summary

To date, the most consistent finding within the neurocognitive literature on the processing of information structure is that focused constituents are afforded a special status within the comprehension process. Thus, a range of ERP studies in both the auditory and visual modalities have revealed rapid effects of focus processing as signaled via a variety of information types (discourse context, syntactic structure, prosody). Focus integration is reflected in a parietal positivity, the timing of which varies depending on the modality of presentation, and which may be an instance of a target-related P3b effect. Mismatches between the contextual and sentence-internal focus requirements, by contrast, typically engender N400-like negativities. These occur more reliably when contextually-required prosodic prominence is missing rather than in response to superfluous prosodic information, thereby again emphasizing the importance of contextually-induced expectations with respect to focused constituents.

While the important role of focus for sentence processing is readily apparent from the data discussed here, it is not yet entirely clear to what degree focus processing interacts with sentence internal processes (i.e. whether and how it impacts upon the construction of constituent structure and relational structure as described in Chapters 8 and 9). For other manipulations of information structure (e.g. givenness, contrast), the evidence presently suggests a global rather than a local influence – at least in the domain of obligatory constituents. In the domain of word order variations, for example, contexts that serve to render an object-initial order highly acceptable sentence-finally none-theless do not attenuate the local processing difficulty engendered by the initial object. However, it remains to be seen whether this state of affairs, which reflects the situation in German, is cross-linguistically valid.

Notes

1. Bridging inferences are required for the interpretation of NPs that do not directly correspond to previously introduced discourse referents, but are inferentially linked to some salient aspect of the current mental model (Clark 1975).

2. For an overview of a range of further studies that show a contextual modulation of N400 effects, see Hagoort and van Berkum (2007). These findings, which attest to the astounding flexibility of the mental lexicon, are orthogonal to questions of syntactic and morphological processing. We thus refrain from discussing them in detail here (but see Chapter 15.2 for some further discussion).

3. This interpretation is supported by the additional finding that the ERP responses to initial objects vs. subjects were only identical when the features of the object fully matched the expectations generated by the context question (see section 14.2 for a discussion of the "mismatch" conditions examined by Bornkessel et al. 2003a). When the scrambled object introduced a new referent but did not match the case marking predicted by the context question, it engendered an attenuated focus positivity, which Bornkessel and colleagues interpreted as the result of a component overlap between a focus positivity and a scrambling negativity. Thus, focus can only override sentence-internal word order constraints when the contextual prediction is entirely fulfilled.

4. A similar claim was made on the basis of an earlier study by Stolterfoht and Bader (2004).

Part IV
Neurocognitive Models of Syntactic and Morphological Processing

Overview

Having provided an overview of empirical findings on the neurocognition of syntactic and morphological processing, the aim of this section is to introduce existing models in this domain. As already became apparent in parts of the discussion in the preceding sections, such models can typically be subdivided according to traditional psycholinguistic distinctions and debates. On the word level, this is reflected in the "rules vs. lexicon" distinction and controversies based on this distinction. On the sentence level, the dominating feature for the classification of models still lies in what may be considered an extension of these word-level questions, namely the debate between modular (two-stage) and interactive models. In essence, the controversies arising in this regard have focused mainly on the relationship between "syntax" and "semantics": How are these two information types represented neurally and how do they interact during online processing? Within the scope of these questions, three neurocognitive models have been proposed: the *declarative/procedural* model (Ullman 2001; Ullman 2004), the *memory, unification, and control (MUC)* framework (Hagoort 2003; Hagoort 2005), and the *neurocognitive model of auditory sentence comprehension* (Friederici 1995; Friederici 1999; Friederici 2002; Friederici and Alter 2004). These models will be discussed in turn in sections 15.1–15.3. In section 15.4, we introduce a model which differs from these approaches in its basic aims and conceptualization, the *extended argument dependency model (eADM)* (Schlesewsky and Bornkessel 2004; Bornkessel and Schlesewsky 2006a; Bornkessel-Schlesewsky and Schlesewsky 2008; Bornkessel-Schlesewsky and Schlesewsky 2009; Bornkessel-Schlesewsky and Schlesewsky in press). The distinguishing feature of the eADM is that it is a model of the syntax–semantics interface at the sentence level, i.e. rather than assuming a clear-cut distinction between syntax and semantics, this model attempts to understand the information types that are "in between" these two categories and that serve to map them onto one another. In addition to introducing these four different models, we will briefly compare and contrast their assumptions and predictions.

In accordance with the primary focus of this volume, we have restricted the discussion in Chapter 15 to models that explicitly address questions related to the processing of syntax and morphology. Of course, somewhat more generally, cognitively or neuroscientifically motivated approaches to the neurocognition of language have also been proposed, e.g. accounts assuming a close relationship between language and action (e.g. Rizzolatti and Arbib 1998; Pulvermüller 2005). These will be discussed briefly in Chapter 16. Furthermore, the interested reader is referred to a recent functional-neuroanatomical model of morphological processing (Marslen-Wilson and Tyler 2007).

Neurocognitive models of language comprehension

15.1 The declarative/procedural model

As briefly described in Chapter 4, the declarative/procedural model (Ullman 2001; Ullman 2004) provides a neurocognitive implementation of a language processing architecture that differentiates between lexical knowledge and rule-based knowledge. Furthermore, rather than positing such a distinction from a purely language-internal point of view, Ullman proposes that it can be situated within the more general cognitive dissociation between declarative and procedural memory (see, for example, Squire and Zola 1996). Declarative memory is responsible for the storage of facts ("semantic memory") and events ("episodic memory"). It allows for the fast learning of associative relationships, is subject to conscious recollection, and can be accessed by other systems. Procedural memory, by contrast, encompasses knowledge of sequences, actions, and skills, both in the sensorimotor and cognitive domains (e.g. learning to ride a bicycle). It has been proposed that this type of knowledge is "informationally encapsulated" (i.e. it cannot be accessed or influenced by other systems); it also cannot be consciously retrieved. On the basis of this distinction, Ullman assumes that rule-based linguistic knowledge (i.e. syntactic and regular morphological knowledge, but also aspects of phonology and compositional semantics) forms part of the procedural system, while lexically stored information (e.g. irregular morphology, lexical semantics) is represented as a declarative information type (see Figure 15.1). As such, processing within the two linguistic subdomains is expected to engage the neural networks associated with the procedural and declarative memory systems, respectively.

In terms of functional neuroanatomy, the declarative memory system is primarily associated with structures in the medial temporal lobe

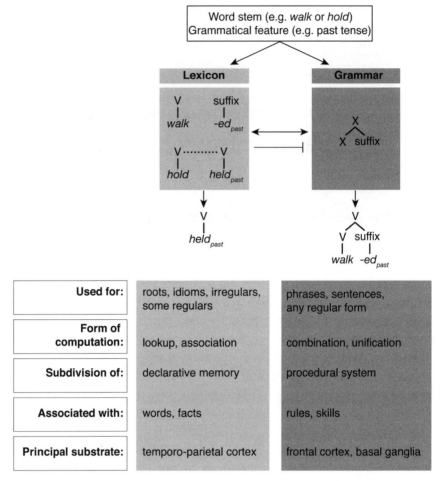

Figure 15.1 Schematic depiction of the main features of the declarative/procedural model.

Source: Adapted from Pinker and Ullman 2002b.

(i.e. hippocampal, parahippocampal, entorhinal and perirhinal cortex). (Ullman notes that midline diencephalic nuclei, in particular the mammillary bodies and portions of the thalamus, are also implicated in declarative memory as they receive input from the hippocampus.) The procedural system is linked to a distinct neural network comprising frontal regions (including the pars opercularis and triangularis of the IFG and premotor cortex) as well as parietal, cerebellar and basal ganglia structures. Within the declarative/procedural model, these different networks are therefore thought to support the processing of rule-based and lexically stored knowledge, respectively. However, rather than positing a complete neural dissociation between the two systems, Ullman assumes a number of points of overlap between them. Firstly, he views superior temporal regions as a possible locus for the interaction between declarative and procedural knowledge, since they appear to play a role in the storage of information types that are relevant for procedural aspects of language (e.g. phonological information and possibly also morphological/syntactic information). Secondly, frontal regions including the inferior frontal gyrus and premotor cortex, which are typically thought to form part of a working memory-related network, have been implicated in the encoding of new memories and in the selection or retrieval of declarative knowledge. According to Ullman, this interaction can be envisioned as follows: "the procedural system is hypothesized to build complex structures, and learn rule-governed patterns over those structures, by selecting lexical items from declarative memory, and maintaining and structuring those items together in working memory" (Ullman 2004: 247). In this regard, Ullman assumes a further subdivision between BA 6/44 on the one hand and BA 45/47 on the other. While the former regions are assumed to engage in phonological processing, the latter are thought to play a similar role with regard to semantics.

In addition to the neuroanatomical assumptions outlined above, Ullman proposes that the declarative and procedural language systems are associated with distinguishable electrophysiological processing correlates. While aspects of declarative memory are thought to be reflected in N400 effects, rule-based/combinatory processing engenders left anterior negativities. Late positivities (P600s), by contrast, are viewed as controlled rather than automatic aspects of procedural memory.

Most generally, the broad neuroanatomical dissociations that form part of the declarative/procedural model are compatible with a range of theoretical assumptions about the functional neuroanatomy of language processing. Indeed, as will become clear throughout the remainder of this chapter, most approaches assume some kind of association between lexically stored representations and parts of the temporal lobe, whereas more "computational" or "compositional" aspects of language are thought to engage frontal regions. There is also some empirical support for the conception of two different memory systems which can both learn structured aspects of the same linguistic input. In this regard, Ullman proposes that "rapid lexical/declarative storage of sequences of lexical forms should provide a database from which grammatical rules can gradually and implicitly be abstracted by the procedural memory system" (Ullman 2004: 247).

In fMRI examinations of artificial grammar learning, Opitz and Friederici (2003; 2004) observed increased hippocampal activation during
early ("similarity-based") stages of learning and increased inferior
frontal/ventral premotor activation during later ("ruled-based") stages
of learning. These findings are very closely in line with the neuroanatomical assumptions of the declarative/procedural model.

However, other claims of the declarative/procedural model are
somewhat more problematic. A case in point concerns the role of the
basal ganglia in language processing. On the one hand, and in support
of the model's assumptions, there is evidence to suggest that these
neuroanatomical structures are involved in the processing of rhythm
and beat (e.g. Grahn and Brett 2007) as well as in aspects of sequencing
(e.g. Schubotz and von Cramon 2001). By contrast, it has also been
observed that basal ganglia dysfunction does not necessarily lead to
selective deficits in the processing of procedural knowledge such as
regular past tense morphology (Longworth et al. 2005). Rather, a
number of findings suggest that the basal ganglia are involved in
controlled aspects of language processing such as the inhibition of
dispreferred representations (for discussion, see Longworth et al.
2005; Friederici 2006). This observation appears problematic for
Ullman's overall conception of the procedural system.

The strengths of the declarative/procedural model clearly lie in its
well-founded assumptions with regard to the neuroanatomical under-
pinnings of the overall language system. Thus, in contrast to other
models, it "provides further specification [of the] anatomical, physiological and biochemical substrates, and the functional roles in language
played by those substrates" (Ullman 2004: 248). From this perspective,
the declarative/procedural model provides a useful framework for the
neuroanatomically-based association between language and more general cognitive functions. However, it seems that these cognitive and
neural motivations sometimes come at the cost of less precise psycholinguistic explanations: since the distinction between declarative and
procedural knowledge is very general, it is thereby somewhat underspecified in language-internal terms. In essence, this problem arises
with regard to all information types that cannot be straightforwardly
categorized as either rule-based or lexically stored (i.e. for most information types that depart from the basic "words and rules" schema).
For example, it is not at all clear how phenomena at the interface
between syntax and semantics such as thematic role representations or
word order (see Chapter 9.2/9.3) could be implemented within the

declarative/procedural model. Furthermore, as the model makes no specific assumptions about the precise nature of the linguistic representations that are drawn upon during language processing, this can lead to difficulties with respect to the classification of a particular phenomenon as declarative or procedural in nature. Consider, for example, the representation of word order. Most generative approaches assume that word order variations are derived via movement operations (i.e. a subclass of linguistic rules), thus rendering word order processing a clearly procedural phenomenon. By contrast, other accounts of word order permutations – framed in terms of a variety of theoretical approaches – do not derive these via syntactic movement but rather describe the markedness of object-initial structures with reference to other factors, e.g. increased complexity of linking from syntax to semantics (Bresnan 2001; Fanselow 2001; Van Valin 2005) or the lower frequency of occurrence of an object-initial construction (Goldberg 2003). For linking-based approaches, it is not clear whether the increased processing costs engendered by word order permutations should be attributed to the procedural or the declarative domain. If construed in terms of constructional frequency, however, they would clearly involve declarative rather than procedural knowledge. Depending on which grammatical theory one favors, the neuroanatomical predictions of the declarative/procedural model would therefore clearly be different.[1] Thus, whereas the underlying neuroanatomical assumptions of the model are well specified and motivated with reference to a range of empirical findings from non-linguistic domains, its predictive capacity is reduced by its underspecification of language-internal processing assumptions.

Most problematic, however, are the model's electrophysiological assumptions. In essence, they correspond to a very classical functional interpretation of language-related ERP components (i.e. LAN effects reflect compositional processing of some description; N400 effects are related to lexical/associative knowledge). However, as shown in detail in Parts I and II of this volume, this strict classification is no longer compatible with the full range of available findings. In particular, there is good evidence to suggest that N400 effects may also reflect combinatorial processes. This is completely unexpected from the perspective of the declarative/procedural model. A second problem arises with respect to late positive (P600) effects. In addition to correlating with syntactic reanalysis (i.e. controlled use of procedural knowledge in terms of Ullman's model), these effects reflect well-formedness mismatches and are engendered by the increased costs of mapping different information types onto one another (see Chapter 12). A clearly "procedural" interpretation of this component (or family of components) is therefore also somewhat too narrow. In the face of these observations, it appears virtually impossible to derive electro-physiological predictions from the declarative/procedural model in its current form.

In summary, while we believe that the declarative/procedural model constitutes an interesting attempt to account for language comprehension mechanisms and their neural bases in terms of more general cognitive (memory) systems, the simple dichotomy between declarative and procedural information assumed in this model does not provide a comprehensive explanation for language processing phenomena in and of itself. The model would therefore benefit from a clearer specification of its underlying linguistic assumptions. Alternatively, the model could be viewed as a general neuroanatomical framework for language, upon which models with more explicit psycholinguistic assumptions could build.

15.2 The memory, unification, and control (MUC) framework

An alternative neurocognitive model of language processing was proposed by Hagoort (2003; 2005). In this approach, the neural language system is thought to encompass three basic components: memory, unification, and control (MUC). The memory component, which is responsible for the storage of linguistic representations and their retrieval, is primarily associated with left temporal cortex. Unification, by contrast, serves to combine the items retrieved from memory into more complex representations. In neuroanatomical terms, this operation is thought to be supported by left inferior frontal regions (BA 44/45/47) and left premotor cortex (BA 6). Finally, the control component aims to account "for the fact that the language system operates in the context of communicative intentions and actions" (Hagoort 2005: 421). It therefore encompasses functions such as action planning and attentional control/inhibition, which are assumed to draw upon regions of the dorsolateral prefrontal cortex (BA 46/9) and the anterior cingulate gyrus.

In a number of respects, these neuroanatomical assumptions (which are summarized in Plate 6C) overlap with those of the declarative/

procedural model: both approaches posit a basic distinction between the storage of representations in temporal cortex and combinatory processing in inferior frontal regions. However, the two models differ in that Hagoort's memory component also encompasses retrieval mechanisms, whereas Ullman attributes these to the procedural system and therefore expects them to be reflected in inferior frontal rather than temporal activation. Finally, Hagoort posits that mechanisms of cognitive control should be viewed as a separate component within the language network, whereas Ullman assumes that they form part of the overall procedural system.

Like the declarative/procedural model, the MUC approach assumes that left inferior frontal cortex supports combinatory operations during language processing. However, in contrast to the very general conception of rule-based processing that forms part of the declarative/procedural model, MUC relies upon the notion of "unification" as proposed within a previous computational model of language comprehension (Vosse and Kempen 2000). In Vosse and Kempen's approach, syntactic structures are stored in the lexicon as pre-compiled representations ("syntactic frames", see Plate 6A). This model is strictly lexicalist in that all syntactic frames are tied to individual lexical representations (e.g. sentence frames are connected to individual verbs). Thus, in stark contrast to the "words and rules" distinction underlying Ullman's model, Vosse and Kempen (2000) and Hagoort (2005) do not assume any lexically independent combinatory rules (except perhaps the unification operation itself). During the comprehension process, syntactic frames are retrieved from the lexicon and combined via unification. Increased processing costs in the unification step arise, for example, when different unification links compete with one another (e.g. in object relative clauses in English, when the two pre-verbal NPs compete for the association with the subject function/node).

In the spirit of this approach, Hagoort (2005) proposes that the storage and retrieval of syntactic frames is supported by the posterior portion of left superior temporal cortex, while template unification ("binding") is accomplished by left inferior frontal areas. The MUC framework also goes beyond Vosse and Kempen's proposal in that it views unification as the basic combinatory operation in all domains of linguistic processing, i.e. in phonology and semantics as well as in syntax. All of these unification operations are assumed to be supported by left inferior frontal regions, with the different information types organized according to a neuroanatomical "unification gradient":

phonological unification is associated with ventral premotor cortex (BA 6) and the pars opercularis of the left IFG (BA 44), syntactic unification draws upon the pars opercularis and pars triangularis (BA 44/45), and semantic unification is supported by the pars triangularis and pars orbitalis (BA 45/47) (see Plate 6B). Note, however, that in contrast to the clear definition of syntactic unification (via Vosse and Kempen's computational model), the processing steps and representations underlying semantic and phonological unification have not as yet been clearly defined.[2]

A further important aspect of MUC's general philosophy is that unification takes place not only within but also across linguistic domains. From this perspective, the left inferior frontal gyrus is thought to play an important role in binding information types from different domains together (i.e. Hagoort assumes that this region serves to solve the "binding problem" for language, cf. Hagoort 2003). A key idea in this regard is that there is no hierarchical dominance of one information type over another. Thus, in the spirit of interactive models of language processing (see Box 7.1), MUC posits that all information types interact with one another right from the outset of the comprehension process. While this is a central assumption of the model, the precise mechanisms of this cross-domain unification have not been specified to date.[3]

The assumption of an immediate interaction between multiple information types (including further factors such as discourse context, language accompanying gestures, speaker information etc.) is motivated by a range of ERP studies and some fMRI evidence. For example, Hagoort et al. (2004) contrasted the processing of lexical/semantic information and world knowledge using sentences such as (15.1). Note that trains in the Netherlands are typically yellow, so that (15.1a) constitutes a violation of world knowledge.

(15.1)   Example stimuli from Hagoort et al. (2004)
    a. World knowledge violation
       The Dutch trains are white and very crowded.
    b. Semantic violation
       The Dutch trains are sour and very crowded.
    c. Control condition
       The Dutch trains are yellow and very crowded.

Both the semantic violation condition and the world knowledge violation condition engendered N400 effects (300–550 ms), which did not differ from one another in scalp topography or onset/peak latency.[4] Furthermore, both violations elicited increased activation in the left inferior frontal gyrus (BA 45/47). Hagoort and colleagues argue that these findings "provide evidence against a nonoverlapping two-step interpretation procedure in which first the meaning of a sentence is determined, and only then is its meaning verified in relation to our knowledge of the world" (Hagoort et al. 2004: 440).

In a further ERP study, Nieuwland and van Berkum (2006) observed a contextual modulation of an argument's animacy status. An example story from their experiment is given in (15.2).

(15.2)   Example story from Nieuwland and van Berkum (2006)
         A woman saw a dancing peanut who had a big smile on his face. The peanut was singing about a girl he had just met. And judging from the song, the peanut was totally crazy about her. The woman thought it was really cute to see the peanut singing and dancing like that. The peanut was salted/in love, and, by the sound of it, this was definitely mutual. He was seeing a little almond.

In the critical sentence (underlined), *salted* engendered an N400 effect (300–600 ms) in comparison to *in love*. Thus, the effect is elicited by the adjective that would normally (i.e. in the absence of a context) provide an appropriate predication for the inanimate NP *peanut* in comparison to an adjective that would typically only be appropriate for animate arguments. (In a control comparison without context, Nieuwland and van Berkum indeed observed the expected N400 increase for *in love* in comparison to *salted*.) This finding was interpreted as evidence that discourse context can override the lexical animacy specification of an argument (i.e. a feature which is often claimed to play an important role in the sentence-internal computation of meaning) and thereby as further converging support that sentence interpretation does not take place in a two-step fashion.

These and other findings (see Hagoort and van Berkum 2007 for an overview) provide an impressive demonstration of the language processing system's flexibility and adaptability as far as the integration of a single word into the overall meaning of an utterance is concerned. As such, they are reminiscent of the results discussed by Kutas and Federmeier (2000) in their overview of N400 findings (see also Figure 2.3). Yet in contrast to Hagoort and van Berkum (2007), Kutas and Federmeier interpret N400 modulations of this type as reflecting semantic memory organization together with a predictive processing strategy. They note that "semantic information accrues gradually and continuously throughout the processing of a sentence, discourse, or even a list of words. This information serves not only to constrain, but in some cases to pre-activate, the perceptual and semantic features of forthcoming items, such that information congruent with the context or the predictions it has engendered is subsequently easier to assimilate and process. This ease of processing, in turn, seems to be manifested electrophysiologically as a reduction in N400 amplitude" (Kutas and Federmeier 2000: 468). In this way, an alternative interpretation of Hagoort, van Berkum, and colleagues' findings is that, rather than providing evidence about semantic composition/unification, they reflect the highly dynamic nature of a neurally represented semantic network.

The consequences of these types of results for semantic composition are also called into question by Pylkkänen and McElree (2006). With regard to Hagoort et al.'s (2004) findings for sentences such as (15.1), they argue that "it is entirely unclear whether compositional processes would draw a distinction between general and culture-specific know-ledge" (Pylkkänen and McElree 2006), since this would, for example, preclude a correct interpretation of figurative sentences. Alternatively, they suggest that pragmatic knowledge might also be used to interpret a sentence such as (15.1b). Given this ambiguity of interpretation, it appears important to examine structures that clearly call for increased effort in semantic composition. Sentences requiring "enriched com-position" are a case in point. An example from this domain, which was discussed in Chapter 9, is repeated in (15.3) for convenience.

(15.3)   Example sentences from Pylkkänen and McElree (2007)

    a. Coercion condition
       The journalist began the <u>article</u> after his coffee break.

    b. Control condition
       The journalist wrote the <u>article</u> after his coffee break.

    c. Anomalous condition
       The journalist astonished the <u>article</u> after his coffee break.

Recall from Chapter 9 that Pylkkänen and McElree (2007) observed a coercion-specific MEG response in the anterior midline field (AMF) between 350 and 450 ms post onset of the object noun. This effect was localized to ventral frontomedian cortex. By contrast, anomalous sentences such as (15.3c) engendered a distinct pattern of results, including increased activity in left and right inferior frontal areas. These results suggest that semantic composition leads to activity in regions distinct from those implicated in Hagoort et al.'s (2004) study. Furthermore, as SAT findings indicate that sentences involving coercion are interpreted more slowly than control sentences (McElree et al. 2006), enriched composition indeed leads to a measurable increase of computational costs. Observations such as these, which speak in favor of increased costs of event-structure composition in the case of a type mismatch, appear to contradict the assumption of a "single step" interpretation which incorporates all available influences. It would thus be very interesting to see how findings such as these might be incorporated into the MUC approach.

Finally, as for the declarative/procedural model, it is presently not clear how the MUC framework might derive processing phenomena that are situated at the interface between syntax and semantics (e.g. word order). For a detailed discussion of this issue, see Bornkessel and Schlesewsky (2006a).

To summarize, the MUC framework constitutes an interesting new approach with potentially far-reaching implications for our under-standing of the neurocognition of language. However, as is apparent from the discussion above, this framework still requires further specification in a number of respects. In this regard, the notion of cross-domain unification and its neural correlates appears particularly intriguing, as this mechanism serves to distinguish MUC from all other existing neurocognitive approaches to language processing. The fur-ther development of the unification concept thus appears suited to providing an important new perspective on the neural language archi-tecture.

15.3 The neurocognitive model of auditory sentence comprehension

An approach which is diametrically opposed to the MUC framework in its basic philosophy is provided by Friederici's (1995; 1999; 2002) neurocognitive model of auditory sentence comprehension. This model posits that online language comprehension takes place in a strictly hierarchical manner, thus providing a neurocognitive imple-mentation of classic two-stage processing assumptions (Frazier and Fodor 1978; Frazier and Rayner 1982). Fine-grained neurophysiological data led to an extension of these architectural assumptions to a three-phase processing model: word category-based phrase structure building is accomplished in phase 1, followed by morphosyntactic and lexical/semantic processing as well as thematic role assignment in phase 2, and, finally, reanalysis, repair, and integration processes in phase 3. Formal and interpretive properties are processed in parallel but independently of one another in the second phase before interacting with one another in phase 3. All of these architectural assumptions are directly reflected in electrophysiological processing correlates. A failure of processing in phase 1 engenders an ELAN, whereas semantic and morphosyntactic processing costs in phase 2 elicit N400 and LAN effects, respectively. Finally, the P600, which is influenced by both syntactic and semantic information, reflects reanalysis/repair/integration processes in phase 3. Crucially, because of the hierarchical organization of the phases, the failure of a processing step in one phase will "block" the application of the subsequent phase (cf. the blocking of an N400 in response to a semantic violation by an ELAN engendered by a phrase structure violation; see Chapter 8). The architectural assumptions of the neurocognitive model are depicted in Plate 7A.

With regard to the functional neuroanatomy of language processing, the neurocognitive model assumes a network of left inferior frontal and left superior temporal regions, with syntactic and semantic processes thought to engage differential subnetworks of the overall language system (see Plate 7B). While syntactic processing draws upon the anterior portion of the STG, the inferior portion of BA 44, and the frontal operculum, the semantic network comprises the mid STG, MTG, and BA 45/47. Both systems interact in the posterior portion of the left STG. Furthermore, Friederici's model goes beyond the other two approaches discussed in the preceding sections in that it also aims to integrate prosody into the neurocognitive architecture. As described briefly in Chapter 13, there is general agreement that prosodic processing draws upon right hemispheric regions to a greater degree than either syntactic or semantic processing. In particular, pitch in isolation is assumed to be processed within the right hemisphere, with the involvement of the left hemisphere increasing for more "linguistic" uses of pitch (Friederici and Alter 2004). The interplay of the two hemispheres in integrating the different information types with one another is assumed to be mediated by the corpus callosum (Friederici and Alter 2004; Friederici et al. 2007).

Even though Friederici's model was the first to make precise theoretical assumptions about the neurocognition of sentence comprehension (Friederici 1995) and the literature has since been supplemented by a wealth of empirical findings, the basic architectural foundations of the model have not been falsified to date (see Part II). In particular, the assumption of successive, hierarchically organized processing phases with distinct neurophysiological and neuroanatomical correlates currently appears to provide the best approximation to the true structure of the human language architecture. Nevertheless, the full range of existing findings suggests that the model would benefit from some further architectural specifications. These concern particularly the relationship between phases 1 and 2 and the representations established in these phases.

For example, Friederici (2004) proposes a neuroanatomical distinction between two aspects of syntactic processing, namely "local transitions" and "long-distance syntactic hierarchies". The former are involved in the local combination of syntactic categories, for example in the combination of a determiner and a noun to form a noun phrase. The latter, by contrast, come into play when structures include "long-distance dependencies involving syntactic movement" (Friederici 2004). In terms of functional neuroanatomy, Friederici proposes that local transitions are supported by the posterior deep frontal operculum, whereas long-distance dependencies engage the lateral surface of the left inferior frontal gyrus (and particularly BA 44). Converging support for this assumption was provided by fMRI findings on artificial grammar learning, which indicate that only the learning of grammars which involve hierarchical dependencies leads to an activation of the left IFG (Friederici et al. 2006a).

This distinction between two types of syntactic information provides an interesting further specification of the neurocognitive model's neuroanatomical bases. However, its integration into the model's representational/processing assumptions currently remains unclear. Whereas the correspondence between the notion of local transitions and the phrase structure building operations in phase 1 appears relatively straightforward, the status of hierarchical syntactic dependencies/movement operations raises a number of questions. In the original formulation of the model, it was proposed that "[a] first syntactic processing phase [. . .] correlates with a first-pass parse defined as the assignment of the initial phrase structure including traces of moved elements" (Friederici 1995: 277). By contrast, the more recent empirical publications showing a dissociation between the processing of local structural transitions and complex structures suggest that Friederici now considers the two as separate phenomena (e.g. Friederici et al. 2006b). This would seem to imply a change of the model's underlying representational assumptions that has not yet been implemented theoretically.

To summarize, the contributions of the neurocognitive model to the field of sentence comprehensions are indisputable. As the first articulated neurocognitive model of sentence comprehension, it has been a driving force behind research in this domain since its original formulation. By providing testable neurophysiological and neuroanatomical predictions, it not only inspired a wealth of experimental studies but also a range of alternative theoretical approaches to the neural bases of language comprehension.

15.4 The extended argument dependency model (eADM)

Finally, we cannot of course complete this chapter without discussing our own neurocognitive model of sentence comprehension, the extended argument dependency model (eADM; Bornkessel 2002; Schlesewsky and Bornkessel 2004; Bornkessel and Schlesewsky 2006a; Bornkessel-Schlesewsky and Schlesewsky 2008; Bornkessel-Schlesewsky and Schlesewsky 2009; Bornkessel-Schlesewsky and Schlesewsky in press). Furthermore, it will hardly be surprising to the reader that the eADM addresses at least some of the concerns that we have noted with respect to competing models above as these, of course, also reflect our own perspective on the field. May the reader therefore forgive us, should the following discussion be a little too enthusiastic and the critique a little too harmless.

The eADM originally grew out of an extension of Friederici's neurocognitive model of sentence comprehension (Bornkessel 2002). Since this first proposal, however, the model has been continually modified and extended such that it now constitutes a full-fledged language processing architecture of its own (Bornkessel and Schlesewsky 2006a). The eADM still shares with the neurocognitive model the assumption that sentence processing takes place in a hierarchically organized manner and can be subdivided into three basic phases. However, as will become clear below, the eADM differs from the neurocognitive model with respect to the functional characterization of the individual processing phases themselves.

The eADM differs from all other existing neurocognitive models of language comprehension in that it explicitly aims to be cross-linguistically adequate. This motivation is based on the observation that the languages of the world differ vastly with respect to how the (surface) structure of a sentence is mapped onto an interpretation (cf. Bornkessel-Schlesewsky and Schlesewsky 2009). To capture this diversity, the eADM assumes a principled separation between phrase structure, which encodes only word category, and relational structure, which encodes the relations between the arguments and the verb as well as between the arguments themselves (for similar assumptions within theoretical linguistic approaches, see, for example, Fanselow 2001; Culicover and Jackendoff 2005; Van Valin 2005). How, then, does argument interpretation take place if not with reference to particular positions in the syntactic structure? To this end, the eADM assumes that arguments are ranked hierarchically and assigned generalized semantic roles (Actor and Undergoer). This ranking/role assignment is derived with reference to a set of cross-linguistically motivated information types (termed "prominence information") and their language-specific weightings as specified in the "interface hypothesis of incremental argument interpretation" (15.4).

(15.4)   *The interface hypothesis of incremental argument interpretation*
        (Bornkessel-Schlesewsky and Schlesewsky 2009)
        Incremental argument interpretation (i.e. role identification and assessment of role prototypicality) is accomplished by the syntax–semantics *interface*, i.e. with reference to a cross-linguistically defined set of prominence scales and their language-specific weighting. The relevant prominence scales are:
        a. morphological case marking (nominative > accusative/ergative > nominative)
        b. argument order (argument 1 > argument 2)
        c. animacy (+animate > −animate)
        d. definiteness/specificity (+definite/specific > −definite/specific)
        e. person (1st /2nd person > 3rd person)

In general, prominence information as in (15.4) serves to map arguments onto an argument hierarchy such that more prominent arguments are preferably interpreted as Actors, whereas less prominent arguments are preferably interpreted as Undergoers. In the languages subjected to psycholinguistic investigation to date, the information types relevant to this mapping can be subdivided into two classes. Primary prominence information serves to fix the Actor-Undergoer hierarchy; for example, in languages like English, the position of an argument in the sentence entirely determines whether that argument will be interpreted as Actor or Undergoer. The modulating prominence scales, by contrast, determine the goodness of fit between the argument and its assigned generalized role. For example, an inanimate Actor is less optimal than an animate Actor, even in languages allowing inanimate Actors.[5] In this way, argument interpretation is determined independently of phrase structure positions and independently of the verb. Crucially, there exists an asymmetric dependency between the two generalized roles such that Undergoers are dependent on Actors but not vice versa (Primus 1999). This dependency relation allows for predictive interpretive processing of arguments to take place even in verb-final structures. Since it also entails that only Actors have defining prototypical features whereas Undergoers are modeled in opposition to the Actor role, it allows for a range of phenomena in online language comprehension to be derived via increased competition for Actor-hood (cf. Bornkessel-Schlesewsky and Schlesewsky 2009; Bornkessel-Schlesewsky and Schlesewsky in press).

The eADM's conception of argument interpretation as determined via prominence information provides a theoretical motivation for the separation between word category and relational information (stages 1 and 2 of processing, respectively; cf. Plate 8). As the computation of a prominence status is only possible for non-predicating elements (i.e. typically noun phrases), word category recognition is a necessary prerequisite for the application of prominence information. Similarly, the notion of prominence-based sentence processing also provides a motivation for the dissociation between a second and a third processing stage. Prominence information only encompasses a restricted set of cross-linguistically motivated features (see 15.4), thereby excluding a range of further information types that play a role in final sentence interpretation (e.g. plausibility, world knowledge, etc.). This principled separation presupposes a processing stage in which prominence information and prominence-external information are mapped onto one another. Within the eADM, this mapping is accomplished within the third stage of processing.

The second processing mechanism within stage 2 of the eADM handles the linking between the argument hierarchy (constructed independently of the verb) and the information specified within verb's lexical entry. This is accomplished via a decomposed semantic structure (logical structure, LS) based on the verb's *Aktionsart*, as illustrated in

(15.5). Note that the LS representations assumed within the eADM are adopted from Role and Reference Grammar (Van Valin 2005).

(15.5)   Example logical structure (LS) for the verb *to hit*
$$\mathbf{do'}(x, \mathbf{hit'}(x,y))$$

The linking between the argument hierarchy and the LS of the verb takes place in such a way that the Actor argument is mapped onto the higher-ranking (leftmost) argument variable within the LS, whereas the Undergoer argument is mapped onto the other argument variable. In languages with subject–verb agreement, the agreement relation serves as the "anchor point" of the linking process in the sense that it serves to align the verb-independent argument hierarchy with the lexical argument hierarchy of the verb. Only if the higher-ranking argument also agrees with the verb (at least in nominative-accusative languages) can linking be initiated.

Whereas the relationship between the three processing stages of the eADM was originally envisioned as strictly serial, more recent developments within the model have led to the proposal of a cascaded processing architecture (Bornkessel-Schlesewsky and Schlesewsky 2008; Bornkessel-Schlesewsky and Schlesewsky 2009). From this perspective (see McClelland 1979), processing in stage n need not be fully complete before processing in stage $n+1$ begins. However, the architecture is strictly feed-forward in the sense that processing in phase $n+1$ can never impact upon processing in *phase n*. The notion of cascaded processing was introduced into the eADM for two basic reasons. Firstly, the assumption of a cascaded relation between the three processing stages provides an elegant account of the different findings on the relationship between the ELAN and the N400 (see Chapter 8): whereas an N400 can never block an ELAN (stage 2 cannot impact upon stage 1), whether an ELAN blocks an N400 crucially depends on the precise processing situation. When there is a strong prediction for a particular word category and no contradictory information early on in the critical stimulus, processing in stage 2 can begin even though stage 1 is not yet complete and an N400 may be engendered. However, if a word category violation is then encountered further down the track, an anterior negativity still ensues due to the continued processing in stage 1. Secondly, and somewhat more speculatively, the idea of a cascaded relation between processing stages 2 and 3 may be able to account for cross-linguistic differences with respect to the influence of prominence-external information types on argument

interpretation (e.g. the strong influence of discourse context in languages like Chinese vs. the delayed application of this information in a
language like German, cf. Bornkessel and Schlesewsky 2006b).

Having described the architectural assumptions of the eADM (see
Plate 8 for an illustration), let us now turn to the neural processing
correlates postulated within this model. With regard to stage 1 of processing, the eADM adopts the assumptions of Friederici's neurocognitive
model: the inability to establish a phrase structure representation on the
basis of word category information is reflected in an ELAN and increased
activation within the left posterior deep frontal operculum/anterior left
STG. Within stage 2 of processing, increased costs of argument prominence computation and argument linking both engender N400 effects and
increased activation within the left posterior STS. By contrast, a
mismatch between argument prominence and linear order leads to an
N400-like effect with a slightly more anterior distribution ("scrambling
negativity") and increased activation in the pars opercularis of the left
IFG. Note also that N400 effects related to plausibility and semantic
association occur in parallel to but independently of the prominence/
linking-related N400 effects in stage 2. These different types of N400 may
be dissociable via their frequency characteristics (Roehm et al. 2007b).
Stage 2 LAN effects (e.g. in response to subject–verb agreement
violations) are viewed as the result of a principled mismatch between
prominence and linking requirements, i.e. they occur when the anchoring between the verb-independent and verb-specific argument hierarchies (see above) fails. From this perspective, agreement mismatches of the
type described in Chapter 9 reflect a more general relational "anchoring
problem" between heads and dependents.

Finally, stage 3 processing encompasses two processing steps, both of
which are reflected in late positive ERP effects. The first of these is a
"generalized mapping" between prominence/linking-information from
stage 2, prominence-independent information such as frequency, world
knowledge, prosody, discourse context, etc. and lexical/semantic associations. In a second step, the well-formedness of the sentence is evaluated
in a task- and environment-dependent manner.

The strengths of the eADM lie in its ability to account for cross-
linguistic similarities and differences in the neurocognition of language
processing and its derivation of phenomena at the syntax–semantics
interface (e.g. word order, case marking, etc.). It is also currently the
only model within this domain which was formulated (almost) exclusively on the basis of findings from the processing of grammatical and

plausible sentence structures. We have recently demonstrated the explanatory capacity of a cross-linguistically motivated architecture of this type (incorporating a hierarchical, word-category-first architecture in which structure does not determine interpretation) by showing how it can derive seemingly puzzling phenomena in well-studied languages like English (e.g. in deriving "semantic P600" effects Bornkessel-Schlesewsky and Schlesewsky 2008). Furthermore, the model architecture incorporates clear assumptions about the representations that are built up during sentence processing and about the way in which they are constructed. Thus, at least with respect to the processing of simple sentences, it overcomes the problem of psycholinguistic "underspecification" that we noted with respect to the models in the preceding sections. Conversely, however, this high degree of language-internal specification also leads to what might be considered the greatest weakness of the model: it is not straightforwardly clear how the processes and representations assumed by the eADM might correspond to more general psychological or neuroscientific concepts. Thus, at present, the neurocognitive assumptions made within the model (i.e. the electrophysiological and neuroanatomical correlates of different processing steps) are purely correlative in the sense that they do not follow from any more general principles about cognitive or neural processing. Future research must therefore seek to specify how the cross-linguistic psycholinguistic generalizations drawn within the framework of the eADM can be situated within a more principally founded neurocognitive setting.

Notes

1. A further potential problem appears to lie in the partially overlapping functions of the cortical regions known to be involved in the processing of word order variations (i.e. especially the pars opercularis of the left IFG; see Chapter 9.2.4.1 and Chapter 10.1.3). While this region clearly forms part of the procedural system, it also engages in the selection/retrieval of declarative information (see above). Presumably, then, the selection of a less frequent alternative could also lead to increased activation in this region as it is subject to increased competition from possible alternative structures (Thompson-Schill et al. 1997). The predictions of the model are therefore no longer clear at this point.

2. For a recent review of empirical findings on semantic unification, see Hagoort and van Berkum (2007). However, this paper also does not

provide a closer specification of the operations thought to underlie this type of unification.

3. Hagoort (2005) refers to Jackendoff's (2002) tripartite model of language architecture in which syntactic, semantic, and phonological representations are all established via independent, parallel combinatory systems and then unified with one another. However, given MUC's assumption of an immediate interaction between the different information types, it appears unlikely that the mechanisms which support cross-domain interaction in Jackendoff's model could also be applied within the MUC framework. In Jackendoff's approach, phonological, semantic, and syntactic structures are unified with one another via a set of post-combinatorial interface levels. Thus, the assumptions of this approach stand in contrast to MUC's proposal of an immediate interaction during structure generation.

4. By contrast, the two violation conditions engendered differing patterns of oscillatory brain activity (see Chapter 2.1.2): whereas semantic violations led to increased induced theta power, world knowledge violations resulted in increased induced power in the gamma band.

5. Note that the question of which features constitute primary and modulating prominence information is presumably not universal. In some languages (e.g. Fore and Awtuw, both of which are spoken in Papua New Guinea), animacy plays a primary role in determining the argument hierarchy. This means that, in the absence of additional morphological marking, the argument that is higher on the animacy hierarchy must be interpreted as the Actor. For detailed discussion, see Bornkessel-Schlesewsky and Schlesewsky (2009).

16

Future directions

The neurocognition of language is a rapidly developing field. Had this book been completed five years earlier, for example, the discussion in the preceding chapters would have been very different. In view of this highly dynamic nature of the field, with relevant new results coming in on almost a daily basis, it is somewhat difficult to draw conclusions about the current state of the art in the domains of syntactic and morphological processing. In this final chapter, we nevertheless attempt to take stock of where the field stands at present and what progress has been made over the last years. On the basis of this discussion, we then present a selection of issues which, in our view, will play an important role in shaping future research in this domain.

Given the wealth of existing findings and the high likelihood that future results will significantly modify our current picture of the neurocognition of language processing, it does not strike us as very fruitful to attempt to provide an overview of the results presented in the preceding chapters here. Rather, we would like to summarize what we have learned from the journey so far and which perspectives this opens up for future developments in the field under discussion.

As a first, tangible indication of the progress that has been made with respect to the neurocognition of syntactic and morphological processing during approximately the last decade, consider Table 16.1. This table summarizes the functional domains in which the relevant language-related ERP components have been observed. It thereby contrasts with Table 2.2, which presented the classical perspective on component interpretations.

Arguably the most striking aspect of Table 16.1 lies in the multiplicity of the component-to-function mappings shown therein: the vast majority of the ERP components listed in the table have been shown to correlate with a variety of functional domains. This applies particularly to the N400 and the P600, i.e. to the two components which were long

Table 16.1: Revised summary of language-related ERP components and their domains of occurrence.

Component			Domains of occurrence										
		Lexical factors	Morpho-syntactic composition factors	Word-level composition	Constituent structure	Sentence-level composition — Gramm. relations	Thematic roles	Linking	Word order	Semantic interpretation	Well-formedness	Complexity	Working memory
NEG	ELAN				✓								
	LAN		✓	✓				✓					
	sLAN								✓				✓
	SCR NEG								✓				
	N400	✓		✓			✓	✓	✓		✓		
POS	P345					✓	✓					✓	
	P600					✓			✓	✓	✓	✓	✓

regarded as relatively specific markers of "lexical/semantic" and "syntactic" processing, respectively. Hence, an important insight of the research conducted during the last years is that language-related ERP components are not as functionally-specific as we once thought.

A possible solution to this "mapping problem" might appear to lie in the choice of a different nomenclature. Consider, for example, the "scrambling negativity", which stands out in Table 16.1 as one of the two components that are associated with only a single functional domain. The reason for this functional specificity is relatively straightforward: in contrast to the other components in the table, the scrambling negativity bears a functional rather than a "physiologically-motivated" label.[1] (Recall from Chapter 9.2.4.2 that the separate labeling of this effect was also motivated by its topographical distribution, which did not straightforwardly correspond to either that of the LAN or to that of the N400.) However, the use of such a functionally-oriented nomenclature is also not without problems. On the one hand, it brings with it the danger of assigning functional interpretations that may be motivated theoretically, but for which there is no empirical evidence. On the other hand, it may obscure neurophysiological similarities between supposedly different effects, thereby preventing us from drawing important inferences about underlying neurocognitive correspondences between domains which we might consider distinct from a theoretical perspective. Of course, the opposite approach to component labeling and interpretation is also not without its problems. As discussed briefly in Chapter 12.4, the high tendency to assimilate new findings to established effects and explanations may gloss over important differences that could be relevant to a correct functional interpretation.

This discussion thus raises the important question of how similarities and differences between components should be defined and under which circumstances two effects should be considered instances of the same component. One way of addressing this issue is to examine correlations between the results of different methods (e.g. ERPs and fMRI). However, given the problem of cross-method comparability (see Chapter 2.3.1), this can only form part of the solution to the problem. Alternatively, a "method-internal" approach has been to include the different manipulations of interest in a single study and to directly compare the components which they engender. This is a good start. But does "statistically indistinguishable" really mean "identical"? Fine-grained data analysis methods, e.g. from the frequency domain (see Chapter 2.1.2), suggest that the answer to this question is probably "no". Using these methods, it has been demonstrated, for example, that different instances of N400 effects which are indistinguishable in terms of their surface characteristics (latency, topography, amplitude) can be differentiated on the basis of their underlying frequency characteristics (frequency band + evoked power/whole power/phase locking index: Roehm et al. 2004; Roehm et al. 2007b). Hence, more fine-grained analysis methods provide an important perspective for future research on component classifications and functional interpretations.

These considerations directly lead us to a further interesting point, namely to the issue of averaging. Group analyses are a critical issue in both the electrophysiological and the neuroanatomical domain. But let's stick with the ERPs for the moment. A variety of studies have reported individual differences between participants, sometimes without having been able to establish a criterion for participant classification (e.g. Osterhout 1997; Roehm et al. 2007a). In other experiments, the expected criteria for the subdivision of participants did not work and had to be replaced by others (Bornkessel et al. 2004a). Thus, there is an obvious need for new data analysis methods which allow for the examination of smaller groups or even single participants. Advances in this regard would clearly also be of interest for patient studies and for other types of studies requiring the investigation of small groups. Initial approaches that might be suited to addressing this issue include single-trial EEG analyses based on independent component analysis (Makeig et al. 2002; Makeig et al. 2004) and EEG analysis methods from non-linear dynamics (beim Graben and Frisch 2004; Frisch and beim Graben 2005).

Given the clear trend towards more fine-grained data analysis methods and combinations of different neuroscientific methods (e.g. Debener et al. 2006), it appears that the complexity of the available data will increase rather than decrease during the next years. This is an exceptionally important issue, because multidimensional data on language processing impose challenging demands on the models in this field. The neurocognitive models of language processing that were discussed in Chapter 15 offer at least some initial proposals on the treatment of multidimensional neurocognitive data. However, it is currently not at all clear how the models in this domain might fit together with models of other data types that have been drawn upon for the examination of language processing (e.g. models of eye movements in reading: Reichle et al. 2003; Engbert et al. 2005), with models based on concepts from cognitive psychology (e.g. Lewis et al. 2006), or computational models based on statistical regularities of the linguistic input (e.g. Hale 2006; Levy 2008). This "correspondence problem" is partly a function of the types of data considered by the different models under consideration, as "non-neurocognitive" models are mostly based on behavioral findings (e.g. judgments, self-paced reading, eye-tracking). In other respects, however, it also reflects the fact that psycholinguistic modeling has traditionally been concerned mainly with a quantification of "processing effort" rather than with qualitative dissociations between different types of processing costs.

Ascertaining the precise relationship between neurocognitive methods and behavioral methods is essential for several reasons. Firstly, only a more precise understanding of these correspondences will allow for a "unification" of psycholinguistic and neurolinguistic research. This is by no means a trivial matter (see, for example, Sereno and Rayner 2003; Bornkessel and Schlesewsky 2006a, for a discussion of the problems involved in establishing correspondences between ERPs and eye-tracking). Nevertheless, on the basis of the research conducted during the last years, we have come a long way in understanding how different experimental methods work and how they are related to one another. This is also an important step with respect to the question of how different data types might serve to inform linguistic theory. For example, systematic cross-method comparisons have revealed that linguistic judgments incorporate a range of different influences, thus questioning whether this data type – at least when considered in isolation – is indeed suited to revealing linguistic competence in an "unadulterated" manner (for discussion, see Bornkessel-Schlesewsky and Schlesewsky 2007). However, independently of the type of data under consideration, psycholinguistic and neurolinguistic methods cannot decide which data types are important for linguistic theory-building. This is rather a matter of choice for the developers of each individual theory: if a theory does not seek to be "psychologically adequate" (in the sense of Dik 1991), it needn't – and shouldn't – concern itself with processing facts.

Furthermore, in spite of the inherent appeal of using neurocognitive data to validate/falsify assumptions from theoretical linguistics, we believe that this is a highly problematic way of proceeding. For example, even if wh-dependencies engender sustained left anterior negativities and, possibly, an integration effect at the hypothesized trace position, this cannot be taken as evidence for the psychological reality of movement/empty categories (see Chapter 9.3 for discussion). Likewise, as discussed in detail throughout Parts I and II of this book, the observation of an N400 in a particular sentence or word condition does not necessarily indicate that the critical information in question is lexically stored. Thus, this type of component cannot be interpreted as evidence for a non-ruled-based representation (e.g. in the sense of a construction at the sentence level). From our perspective, the role of neurocognitive data therefore cannot lie simply in the experimental validation of independently developed theoretical concepts. Rather, as also argued by Münte et al. (1999a) and as discussed in Chapter 6, we believe that the field would benefit from focusing on the development of its own theoretical questions and concepts.

An alternative line of orientation in this regard is offered by domain-general neurocognitive approaches. For example, based on observations in the debate on "mirror neurons", Broca's region can be viewed as part of a larger network for "action understanding" (see Rizzolatti, Fogassi, and Gallese 2002). From this perspective, which assumes that language learning and evolution are crucially grounded in neural mechanisms of imitation (Rizzolatti and Arbib 1998), it has been proposed that language may be modeled via the same type of filler-slot-based associations between arguments and predicates which can be used to represent motor commands (e.g. *grasp(peanut)*). More specifically, Broca's area is viewed as representing "'verb phrases' and constraints on the noun phrases that can fill the slots, but not details of the noun phrases themselves" (Rizzolatti and Arbib 1998: 192). Applying a somewhat similar line of argumentation to the word level, Pulvermüller (2005) assumes that word meaning and action may be interrepresented in distributed cortical networks. These approaches have in common that they assume a crucial role of non-linguistic representations and operations in language processing. However, accounts of this type are currently not specific enough to derive the very fine-grained neurocognitive data patterns that are observable in studies on language. (Consider, for example, the direct correlation between various highly specific influences on word order variations and the activation of Broca's region; see Chapter 9.2.4.1.) This is not to say that neurocognitive correspondences between linguistic and non-linguistic data should be ignored. To the contrary: these are of crucial importance if we are to understand the relationship between language and other domains of higher cognition. Yet, since it is clear that there are currently no domain-general cognitive theories that are detailed enough to fully derive neurocognitive findings on language and to explain the mechanisms of language processing – and especially the rich emerging findings on the processing of grammatical and plausible constructions – it also does not appear satisfactory to assume that these mechanisms can be subsumed under those required in other domains simply because they show activation in the same cortical regions/similar ERP effects.

Hence, one of the major challenges for future approaches to the neurocognition of language lies in the solution of the "grain problem". At present, neurocognitive models of language processing are essentially caught in between (data-independent) linguistic concepts and theories on the one hand and (language-independent) cognitive/neuroscientific concepts and theories on the other. As we have tried to make clear in the preceding sections, neither of these different "sides" is optimally suited to informing neurocognitive models of language. Nonetheless, these influences also cannot be ignored if scientific progress is to be made and true explanations are to be found. It is therefore up to the field to take up the challenge and converge upon its own optimal level of explanation. Finding the ideal balance certainly won't be an easy task. But then again, it is precisely this challenge that makes this line of work so much fun.

Note

1. At a first glance, the ELAN might appear to contradict this generalization because it is also only linked to a single functional domain in Table 16.1 in spite of its physiologically-motivated label. In practice, however, functional considerations have also played an important role with respect to the classification of ELAN effects in different studies. For example, effects occurring in later time ranges have sometimes been interpreted as ELANs, with the latency-shift explained via aspects of stimulus presentations and the point in time at which the critical information became available. Conversely, effects which might have been classified as ELANs on the basis of their latency have been interpreted as instances of other components, with "forward-shifted" latencies again thought to be due to parameters of stimulus presentation.

References

Abney, S. (1989). "A computational model of human parsing". *Journal of Psycholinguistic Research* 18: 129–44.

Aissen, J. (2003). "Differential object marking: Iconicity vs. economy". *Natural Language and Linguistic Theory* 21: 435–83.

Allen, M., Badecker, W., and Osterhout, L. (2003). "Morphological analysis in sentence processing: An ERP study". *Language and Cognitive Processes* 18: 405–30.

Altmann, G.T.M., Garnham, A., and Dennis, Y. (1992). "Avoiding the garden path: Eye movements in context". *Journal of Memory and Language* 31: 685–712.

—— and Steedman, M. (1988). "Interaction with context during human sentence processing". *Cognition* 30: 191–238.

—— van Nice, K.Y., Garnham, A., and Henstra, J.-A. (1998). "Late closure in context". *Journal of Memory and Language* 38: 459–84.

Augurzky, P. (2006). *Attaching relative clauses in German: The role of implicit and explicit prosody in sentence processing.* Leipzig: Max Planck Series in Human Cognitive and Brain Sciences.

Bader, M., and Bayer, J. (2006). *Case and linking in language comprehension.* Dordrecht: Springer.

Bader, M., and Lasser, I. (1994). "German verb-final clauses and sentence processing: evidence for immediate attachment", in C. Clifton, Jr., L. Frazier, and K. Rayner (eds.), *Perspectives on sentence processing.* Hillsdale, NJ: Lawrence Erlbaum Associates,

Bader, M., and Meng, M. (1999). "Subject-object ambiguities in German embedded clauses: An across-the-board comparison". *Journal of Psycholinguistic Research* 28: 121–43.

Bahlmann, J., Rodriguez-Fornells, A., Rotte, M., and Münte, T.F. (2007). "An fMRI study of canonical and noncanonical word order in German". *Human Brain Mapping* 28: 940–9.

Bai, C., Bornkessel-Schlesewsky, I., Wang, L., Hung, Y.-C., Schlesewsky, M., and Burkhardt, P. (2008). "Semantic composition engenders an N400: evidence from Chinese compounds". *Neuroreport* 19: 695–9.

Barber, H., and Carreiras, M. (2009). "Grammatical gender and number agreement in Spanish: An ERP comparison". *Journal of Cognitive Neuroscience* 17: 137–53.

Bard, E.G., Robertson, D., and Sorace, A. (1996). "Magnitude estimation of linguistic acceptability". *Language* 72: 32–68.

Bartke, S., Rösler, F., Streb, J., and Wiese, R. (2005). "An ERP-study of German 'irregular' morphology". *Journal of Neurolinguistics* 18: 29–55.

Basar, E. (1998). *Brain function and oscillations I. Brain oscillations: Principles and approaches.* Berlin: Springer.

Bates, E. (1979). "On the emergence of symbols: Ontogeny and philogeny", in A. Collins (ed.), *Children's language and communication: The Minnesota symposium on child psychology*. Hillsdale, NJ: Erlbaum, 121–57.

Bayer, J. (1984). "COMP in Bavarian syntax". *Linguistic Review* 3: 209–274.

beim Graben, P., and Frisch, S. (2004). "Is it positive or negative? On determining ERP components". *IEEE Transactions on Biomedical Engineering* 51: 1,374–82.

—— Schlesewsky, M., Saddy, J.D., and Kurths, J. (2000). "Symbolic dynamics of event-related brain potentials". *Physical Review E* 62: 5,518–41.

Ben-Shachar, M., Hendler, T., Kahn, I., Ben-Bashat, D., and Grodzinsky, Y. (2003). "The neural reality of syntactic transformations: Evidence from functional magnetic resonance imaging". *Psychological Science* 14: 433–440.

—— Palti, D., and Grodzinsky, Y. (2004). "Neural correlates of syntactic movement: Converging evidence from two fMRI experiments". *Neuroimage* 21: 1,320–36.

Bentin, S., McCarthy, G., and Wood, C.C. (1985). "Event-related potentials, lexical decision, and semantic priming". *Electroencephalography and Clinical Neurophysiology* 60: 343–55.

—— Mouchetant-Rostaing, Y., Giard, M.H., Echallier, J.F., and Pernier, J. (1999). "ERP manifestations of processing printed words at different psycholinguistic levels: Thime course and scalp distribution". *Journal of Cognitive Neuroscience* 11: 235–60.

Beretta, A., Campbell, C., Carr, T.H., Huang, J., Schmitt, L.M., Christianson, K., and Cao, Y. (2003a). "An ER-fMRI investigation of morphological inflection in German reveals that the brain makes a distinction between regular and irregular forms". *Brain and Language* 85: 67–92.

—— Carr, T.H., Huang, J., and Cao, Y. (2003b). "The brain is not single-minded about inflectional morphology: A response to the commentaries". *Language* 85: 531–534.

Berger, H. (1929). "Über das Elrektrenkephalogramm des Menschen" [On the human electroencephalogram]. *Archiv für Psychiatrie und Nervenkrankheiten* 87: 527–70.

—— (1938). *Das Elektrenkephalogramm des Menschen [The human electroencephalogram]*. Halle: Nova Acta Leopoldina.

Berko, J. (1958). "The child's learning of English morphology". *Word* 14: 150–77.

Berndt, R.S., and Haendiges, A. (2000). "Grammatical class in word and sentence production: Evidence from aphasic patients". *Journal of Memory and Language* 43: 249–73.

Bertram, R., Schreuder, R., and Baayen, H. (2000). "The balance of storage and computation in morphological processing: The role of word formation type, affixal homonymy and productivity". *Journal of Experimental Psychology: Learning, Memory and Cognition* 26: 489–511.

Berwick, R.C., and Weinberg, A.S. (1984). *The grammatical basis of linguistic performance*. Cambridge, MA: MIT Press.

Bever, T.G. (1970). "The cognitive basis for linguistic structures", in J.R. Hayes (ed.), *Cognition and the development of language.* New York: Wiley, 279–362.

—— (1974). "The ascent of the specious, or there's a lot we don't know about mirrors", in D. Cohen (ed.), *Explaining linguistic phenomena.* Washington: Hemisphere, 173–200.

Bickel, B. (in press). "Grammatical relations typology", in J.-J. Song (ed.), *The Oxford handbook of typology.* Oxford: Oxford University Press.

Bierwisch, M. (1963). *Grammatik des deutschen Verbs [=A grammar of the verb in German].* Berlin: Akademie-Verlag.

—— (1988). "On the grammar of local prepositions", in M. Bierwisch, W. Motsch, and I. Zimmermann (eds.), *Syntax, Semantik und Lexikon.* Berlin: Akademie Verlag, 1–65.

Bird, H., Lambon-Ralph, M.A., Seidenberg, M.S., McClelland, J.L., and Patterson, K. (2003). "Deficits in phonology and past-tense morphology: What's the connection?". *Journal of Memory and Language* 48: 502–26.

Bisang, W. (2006). "Widening the perspective: Argumenthood and syntax in Chinese, Japanese and Tagalog", in D. Hole, A. Meinunger, and W. Abraham (eds.), *Dative and other cases. Between argument structure and event structure.* Amsterdam/Philadelphia: John Benjamins, 331–81.

—— (2008). "Precategoriality and syntax-based parts of speech: The case of Late Archaic Chinese". *Studies in Language* 32: 568–89.

—— (to appear). "Word classes", in J.J. Song (ed.), *The Oxford handbook of language typology.* Oxford: Oxford University Press.

Blake, B.J. (1994). *Case.* Cambridge: Cambridge University Press.

Bock, K., and Cutting, J.C. (1982). "Regulating mental energy: Performance units in language production". *Journal of Memory and Language* 31: 99–127.

—— and Eberhart, K.M. (1993). "Meaning, sound, and syntax in English number agreement". *Language and Cognitive Processes* 8: 57–99.

Bock, K., and Miller, C.A. (1991). "Broken agreement". *Cognitive Psychology* 23: 45–93.

Boland, J., and Boehm-Jernigan (1998). "Lexical constraints and prepositional phrase attachment". *Journal of Memory and Language* 39: 684–719.

Bornkessel-Schlesewsky, I., Haupt, F.S., Lauszat, A., and Schlesewsky, M. (submitted). "The role of context and prosody in the processing of scrambled structures". *Manuscript submitted for publication.*

—— and Schlesewsky, M. (2007). "The wolf in sheep's clothing: Against a new judgment-driven imperialism". *Theoretical Linguistics* 33: 319–34.

—— and —— (2008). "An alternative perspective on 'semantic P600' effects in language comprehension". *Brain Research Reviews* 59: 55–73.

—— and —— (in press). "Minimality as vacuous distinctness: Evidence from cross-linguistic sentence comprehension". *Lingua.*

—— and —— (2009). "The role of prominence information in the real time comprehension of transitive constructions: A cross-linguistic approach". *Language and Linguistics Compass* 3: 19–58.

—— —— and von Cramon, D.Y. (submitted). "Word order and Broca's region: Evidence for a supra-syntactic perspective". *Manuscript submitted for publication.*

—— and Friederici, A.D. (2007). "Neuroimaging studies of sentence and discourse comprehension", in M.G. Gaskell (ed.), *The Oxford handbook of psycholinguistics.* Oxford: Oxford University Press, 407–24.

Bornkessel, I. (2002). *The Argument Dependency Model: A neurocognitive approach to incremental interpretation.* Leipzig: MPI Series in Cognitive Neuroscience.

—— Fiebach, C.J., Friederici, A.D., and Schlesewsky, M. (2004a). " 'Capacity reconsidered': Interindividual differences in language comprehension and individual alpha frequency". *Experimental Psychology* 51: 279–89.

—— McElree, B., Schlesewsky, M., and Friederici, A.D. (2004b). "Multidimensional contributions to garden path strength: Dissociating phrase structure from case marking". *Journal of Memory and Language* 51: 495–522.

—— Fiebach, C.J., and Friederici, A.D. (2004c). "On the cost of syntactic ambiguity in human language comprehension: an individual differences approach". *Cognitive Brain Research* 21: 11–21.

—— and Schlesewsky, M. (2006a). "The Extended Argument Dependency Model: A neurocognitive approach to sentence comprehension across languages". *Psychological Review* 113: 787–821.

—— and —— (2006b). "The role of contrast in the local licensing of scrambling in German: Evidence from online comprehension". *Journal of Germanic Linguistics* 18: 1–43.

—— —— and Friederici, A.D. (2002a). "Beyond syntax: Language-related positivities reflect the revision of hierarchies". *Neuroreport* 13: 361–4.

—— —— and —— (2002b). "Grammar overrides frequency: Evidence from the online processing of flexible word order". *Cognition* 85: B21–B30.

—— —— and —— (2003a). "Contextual information modulates initial processes of syntactic integration: The role of inter- vs. intra-sentential predictions". *Journal of Experimental Psychology: Learning, Memory and Cognition* 29: 269–98.

—— —— and —— (2003b). "Eliciting thematic reanalysis effects: The role of syntax-independent information during parsing". *Language and Cognitive Processes* 18: 268–98.

—— Zysset, S., Friederici, A.D., von Cramon, D.Y., and Schlesewsky, M. (2005). "Who did what to whom? The neural basis of argument hierarchies during language comprehension". *NeuroImage* 26: 221–33.

Bossong, G. (1985). *Differentielle Objektmarkierung in den neuiranischen Sprachen [= Differential object marking in the New Iranian languages].* Tübingen: Narr.

Bozic, M., Marslen-Wilson, W., Stamatakis, E.A., Davis, M.H., and Tyler, L.K. (2007). "Differentiating morphology, form and meaning: Neural correlates of morphological complexity". *Journal of Cognitive Neuroscience* 19: 1464–75.

Bradley, D. (1980). "Lexical representation of derivational relation", in M. Aronoff, and M.L. Kean (eds.), *Juncture.* Saratoga, CA: Anma Libri, 37–55.

Brázdil, M., Dobšík, M., Mikl, M., Hluštík, P., Daniel, P., Pažourková, M., Krupa, P., and Rektor, I. (2005). "Combined event-related fMRI and intra-cerebral ERP study of an auditory oddball task". *Neuroimage* 26: 285–93.

Bresnan, J. (2001). *Lexical Functional Grammar.* Oxford: Blackwell.

—— and Kanerva, J.M. (1989). "Locative inversion in Chichewa: A case study of factorization in grammar". *Linguistic Inquiry* 20: 1–50.

Brodmann, K. (1909). *Vergleichende Lokalisationslehre der Großhirnrinde.* Leipzig: J.A. Barth.

Brown, R. (1973). *A first language: The early stages.* Cambridge, MA: MIT Press.

Brown, W.S., and Lehmann, D. (1979). "Verb and noun meaning of homo-phone words activate different cortical generators: A topographic study of evoked potential fields". *Experimental Brain Research* 2: S159–68.

Burani, C., and Caramazza, A. (1987). "Representation and processing of derived words". *Language and Cognitive Processes* 2: 217–27.

Burkhardt, P. (2005). *The syntax-discourse interface: Representing and inter-preting dependency.* Amsterdam: John Benjamins.

—— (2006). "Inferential bridging relations reveal distinct neural mechan-isms: Evidence from event-related brain potentials". *Brain and Language* 98: 159–68.

—— Fanselow, G., and Schlesewsky, M. (2007). "Effects of (in)transitivity on structure building and agreement". *Brain Research* 1163: 100–10.

—— Piñango, M.M., and Wong, K. (2003). "The role of the anterior left hemisphere in real time sentence comprehension: Evidence from split-intransitivity". *Brain and Language* 86: 9–22.

—— and Roehm, D. (2007). "Differential effects of saliency: An event-related brain potential study". *Neuroscience Letters* 413: 115–20.

Bybee, J.L. (1988). "Morphology as lexical organization", in M. Hammond, and M. Noonan (eds.), *Theoretical morphology.* San Diego, CA: Academic Press, 119–41.

—— (1995). "Regular morphology and the lexicon". *Language and Cognitive Processes* 10: 425–55.

Camblin, C.C., Gordon, P.C., and Swaab, T.Y. (2007). "The interplay of discourse congruence and lexical association during sentence processing: Evidence from ERPs and eye tracking". *Journal of Memory and Language* 56: 103–28.

Caplan, D. (2001). "Functional neuroimaging studies of syntactic processing". *Journal of Psycholinguistic Research* 30: 297–320.

—— Alpert, N., and Waters, G. (1999). "PET studies of syntactic processing with auditory sentence presentation". *Neuroimage* 9: 343–51.

—— —— —— and Olivieri, A. (2000). "Activation of Broca's area by syntactic processing under conditions of concurrent articulation". *Human Brain Mapping* 9: 65–71.

—— Hildebrandt, N., and Makris, N. (1996). "Location of lesions in stroke patients with deficits in syntactic processing in sentence comprehension". *Brain* 119: 933–49.

—— Vijayan, S., Kuperberg, G.R., West, C., Waters, G., Greve, D., and Dale, A.M. (2001). "Vascular responses to syntactic processing: Event-related fMRI study of relative clauses". *Human Brain Mapping* 15: 26–38.

—— and Waters, G. (1999). "Verbal working memory and sentence comprehension". *Behavioral and Brain Sciences* 22: 77–126.

Cappelletti, M., Fregni, F., Shapiro, K., Pascual-Leone, A., and Caramazza, A. (2008). "Processing nouns and verbs in the left frontal cortex: A transcranial magnetic stimulation study". *Journal of Cognitive Neuroscience* 20: 707–20.

Caramazza, A., and Zurif, E. (1976). "Dissociation of algorithmic and heuristic processes in language comprehension: Evidence from aphasia". *Brain and Language* 3: 572–82.

Carlson, G., and Tanenhaus, M.K. (1988). "Thematic roles and language comprehension", in W. Wilkins (ed.), *Syntax and semantics, Vol. 21: Thematic relations*. New York: Academic Press, 263–88.

Carreiras, M., Salillas, E., and Barber, H. (2004). "Event-related potentials elicited during parsing of relative clauses in Spanish". *Cognitive Brain Research* 20: 98–105.

Chappell, H. (1986). "Formal and colloquial adversity passive in standard Chinese". *Linguistics* 24: 1025–52.

Chen, E., West, W.C., Waters, G., and Caplan, D. (2006). "Determinants of BOLD signal correlates of processing object-extracted relative clauses". *Cortex* 42: 591–604.

—— (1965). *Aspects of the theory of syntax*. Cambridge, MA: MIT Press.

—— (1973). "Conditions on transformations", in S. Anderson, and P. Kiparsky (eds.), *A Festschrift for Morris Halle*. New York: Holt, Rinehart and Winston, 232–86.

—— (1981). *Lectures on government and binding*. Dordrecht: Kluwer.

—— (1995). *The Minimalist Program*. Cambridge, MA: MIT Press.

—— and Halle, M. (1968). *The sound pattern of English*. Cambridge, MA: MIT Press.

—— and Miller, G.A. (1963). "Introduction to the formal analysis of natural languages", in R.D. Luce, R. Bush, and E. Galanter (eds.), *Handbook of mathematical psychology*. New York: Wiley, 269–321.

Clahsen, H. (1999). "Lexical entries and rules of language: A multidisciplinary study of German inflection". *Behavioral and Brain Sciences* 22: 991–1060.

Clahsen, H., Sonnenstuhl, I., and Blevins, J.P. (2003). "Derivational morphology in the German mental lexicon: A dual mechanism account", in
H. Baayen, and R. Schreuder (eds.), *Morphological structure in language
processing*. Berlin: Mouton de Gruyter, 125–55.

Clark, H.H. (1975). "Bridging", in B. Nash-Webber, and R. Schank (eds.),
Theoretical issues in natural language processing. Cambridge, MA: Yale
University Mathematical Society Sciences Board, 188–93.

Clifton, C., Jr., Carlson, K., and Frazier, L. (2002). "Informative prosodic
boundaries". *Language and Speech* 45: 87–114.

—— and Frazier, L. (1989). "Comprehending sentences with long distance
dependencies", in G.N. Carlson, and M.K. Tanenhaus (eds.), *Linguistic
structures in language processing*. Dordrecht: Kluwer, 273–317.

—— —— and Connine, C. (1984). "Lexical expectations in sentence comprehension". *Journal of Verbal Learning and Verbal Behavior* 23: 696–708.

—— Kurcz, I., and Jenkins, J.J. (1965). "Grammatical relations as determinants of sentence similarity". *Journal of Verbal Learning and Verbal Behavior*
4: 112–17.

—— Speer, S., and Abney, S.P. (1991). "Parsing arguments: Phrase structure
and argument structure as determinants of initial parsing decisions". *Journal of Memory and Language* 30: 251–71.

—— Staub, A., and Rayner, K. (2007). "Eye movements in reading words and
sentences", in R.P.G. van Gompel (ed.), *Eye movements: A window on mind
and brain*. Amsterdam: Elsevier, 341–72.

—— Traxler, M.J., Mohamed, M.T., Williams, R.S., Morris, R.K., and Rayner,
K. (2003). "The use of thematic role information in parsing: Syntactic
processing autonomy revisited". *Journal of Memory and Language* 47:
571–88.

Cohen, L.G., Celnik, P., Pascual-Leone, A., Corwell, B., Faiz, L., Dambrosia, J.,
Honda, M., Sadato, N., Gerloff, C., Catalá, M.D., and Hallett, M. (1997).
"Functional relevance of cross-modal plasticity in blind humans". *Nature*
389: 180–3.

Comrie, B. (1989). *Linguistic universals and language typology*. Oxford: Blackwell.

Constable, R.T., Pugh, K.R., Berroya, E., Mencl, W.E., Westerveld, M., Ni, W.,
and Shankweiler, D. (2004). "Sentence complexity and input modality
effects in sentence comprehension: An fMRI study". *Neuroimage* 22: 11–21.

Cooke, A., Zurif, E.B., DeVita, C., Alsop, D., Koenig, P., Detre, J., Gee, J.,
Piñango, M., Balogh, J., and Grossman, M. (2001). "Neural basis for
sentence comprehension: Grammatical and short-term memory components". *Human Brain Mapping* 15: 80–94.

Cooper, W.E., and Paccia-Cooper, J. (1980). *Syntax and speech*. Cambridge,
MA: Harvard University Press.

Corey, V.R. (1999). *The electrophysiological difference between nouns and verbs.* Ph.D. thesis, University of Washington.

Coulson, S., King, J.W., and Kutas, M. (1998a). "ERPs and domain specificity: Beating a straw horse". *Language and Cognitive Processes* 13: 653–72.

—— —— and —— (1998b). "Expect the unexpected: Event-related brain response to morphosyntactic violations". *Language and Cognitive Processes* 13: 21–58.

Cowles, H.W., Kluender, R., Kutas, M., and Polinsky, M. (2007). "Violations of information structure: An electrophysiological study of answers to wh-questions". *Brain and Language* 102: 228–42.

Crain, S., and Fodor, J.D. (1985). "How can grammars help parsers?", in D. Dowty, L. Karttunen, and A. Zwicky (eds.), *Natural language parsing: Psychological, computational, and theoretical perspectives.* Cambridge: Cambridge University Press, 94–129.

—— and —— (1987). "Sentence matching and overgeneration". *Cognition* 26: 171–86.

—— and Steedman, M. (1985). "On not being led up the garden path: The use of context by the psychological parser", in D. Dowty, L. Karttunen, and A. Zwicky (eds.), *Natural language parsing: Psychological, computational, and theoretical perspectives.* Cambridge: Cambridge University Press, 320–57.

Crocker, M.W. (1994). "On the nature of the principle-based sentence processor", in C. Clifton, Jr., L. Frazier, and K. Rayner (eds.), *Perspectives on sentence processing.* Hillsdale: Erlbaum, 245–66.

—— and Keller, F. (2006). "Probabilistic grammars as models of gradience in language processing", in G. Fanselow, C. Féry, R. Vogel, and M. Schlesewsky (eds.), *Gradience in Grammar: Generative Perspectives.* Oxford: Oxford University Press, 227–45.

Croft, W.A. (2001). *Radical construction grammar: Syntactic theory in typological perspective.* Oxford: Oxford University Press.

Cuetos, F., and Mitchell, D.C. (1988). "Cross-linguistic differences in parsing: Restrictions on the use of the late closure strategy in Spanish". *Cognition* 30: 73–105.

Culicover, P.W., and Jackendoff, R. (2005). *Simpler syntax.* Oxford: Oxford University Press.

Cutler, A., Dahan, D., and van Donselaar, W. (1997). "Prosody in the comprehension of spoken language: A literature review". *Language and Speech* 40: 141–201.

Damasio, A.R., and Damasio, H. (1992). "Brain and language". *Scientific American* 267: 89–95.

—— and Tranel, D. (1993). "Nouns and verbs are retrieved with differently distributed neural systems". *Proceedings of the National Academy of Sciences USA* 90: 4957–60.

Daneman, M., and Carpenter, P.A. (1980). "Individual differences in working memory and reading". *Journal of Verbal Learning and Verbal Behavior* 19: 450–66.

Daniele, A., Giustolisi, L., Silveri, M.C., Colosimo, C., and Gainotti, G. (1994). "Evidence for a possible neuroanatomical basis for lexical processing of nouns and verbs". *Neuropsychologia* 32: 1325–41.

de Diego Balaguer, R., Rodriguez-Fornells, A., Rotte, M., Bahlmann, J., Heinze, H.-J., and Münte, T.F. (2006). "Neural circuits subserving the retrieval of stems and grammatical features in regular and irregular verbs". *Human Brain Mapping* 27: 874–88.

de Vincenzi, M. (1991). *Syntactic parsing strategies in Italian.* Dordrecht: Kluwer.

—— Job, R., Di Matteo, R., Angrilli, A., Penolazzi, B., Ciccarelli, L., and Vespignani, F. (2003). "Differences in the perception and time course of syntactic and semantic violations". *Brain and Language* 85: 280–96.

Debener, S., Ullsperger, M., Siegel, M., Fiehler, K., Cramon, D.Y., and Engel, A.K. (2005). "Trial-by-trial coupling of concurrent electroencephalogram and functional magnetic resonance imaging identifies the dynamics of performance monitoring". *Journal of Neuroscience* 25: 11730–7.

Debener, S., Ullsperger, M., Siegel, M., and Engel, A.K. (2006). "Single-trial EEG-fMRI reveals the dynamics of cognitive function". *Trends in Cognitive Sciences* 10: 558–63.

Dehaene, S. (1995). "Electrophysiological evidence for category-specific word processing in the normal human brain". *Neuroreport* 6: 2153–7.

Demiral, Ş.B. (2007). *Incremental argument interpretation in Turkish sentence comprehension.* Leipzig: MPI Series in Human Cognitive and Brain Sciences.

—— Schlesewsky, M., and Bornkessel-Schlesewsky, I. (2008). "On the universality of language comprehension strategies: Evidence from Turkish". *Cognition* 106: 484–500.

Desai, R., Conant, L.L., Waldron, E., and Binder, J.R. (2006). "fMRI of past tense processing: The effects of phonogical complexity and task difficulty". *Journal of Cognitive Neuroscience* 18: 278–97.

Devlin, J.T., Jamison, H.L., Matthews, P.M., and Gonnerman, L.M. (2004). "Morphology and the internal structure of words". *Proceedings of the National Academy of Sciences USA* 101: 14984–8.

—— and Watkins, K.E. (2007). "Stimulating language: insights from TMS". *Brain* 130: 610–22.

Dhond, R.P., Marinkovic, K., Dale, A.M., Witzel, T., and Halgren, E. (2003). "Spatiotemporal maps of past-tense verb inflection". *Neuroimage* 19: 91–100.

Diedrichsen, E. (2008). "Where is the precore slot? Mapping the layered structure of the clause and German sentence topology", in R.D. Van Valin, Jr. (ed.), *Investigations of the syntax-semantics-pragmatics interface.* Amsterdam: John Benjamins, 203–24.

Dik, S. (1991). "Functional grammar", in F. Droste, and J.E. Joseph (eds.), *Linguistic theory and grammatical description*. Amsterdam/Philadelphia: John Benjamins.

Dixon, R.M.W. (1994). *Ergativity*. Cambridge: Cambridge University Press.

Dominguez, A., de Vega, M., and Barber, H. (2004). "Event-related brain potentials elicited by morphological, homographic, and semantic priming". *Journal of Cognitive Neuroscience* 16: 598–608.

Donchin, E., and Coles, M.G.H. (1988). "Is the P300 component a manifestation of context-updating?". *Behavioral and Brain Sciences* 11: 355–72.

—— Ritter, W., and McCallum, W. (1978). "Cognitive psychophysiology: The endogenous components of the ERP", in E. Callaway, P. Tueting, and S. Koslow (eds.), *Event-related brain potentials in man*. New York: Academic Press, 349–411.

—— Tueting, P., Ritter, W., Kutas, M., and Heffley, E. (1975). "On the independence of the CNV and the P300 components of the human averaged evoked potential". *Electroencephalography and Clinical Neurophysiology* 38: 449–61.

Donders, F.C. (1969). "On the speed of mental processes". *Acta Psychologica* 30: 412–31.

Dowty, D. (1991). "Thematic proto-roles and argument selection". *Language* 67: 547–619.

Drach, E. (1939). *Grundgedanken der deutschen Satzlehre*. Frankfurt am Main: Diesterweg.

Drai, D., and Grodzinsky, Y. (2006). "A new empirical angle on the variability debate: Quantitative neurosyntactic analyses of a large data set from Broca's aphasia". *Brain and Language* 96: 117–28.

Dronkers, N.F., Wilkins, D.P., Van Valin, R.D., Jr., Redfern, B.B., and Jaeger, J.J. (2004). "Lesion analysis of the brain areas involved in language comprehension". *Cognition* 92: 145–77.

Dryer, M.S. (2005). "Order of subject, object, and verb", in M. Haspelmath, M.S. Dryer, D. Gil, and B. Comrie (eds.), *The world atlas of language structures*. Oxford: Oxford University Press, 330–4.

Eckstein, K., and Friederici, A.D. (2006). "It's early: Event-related potential evidence for initial interaction of syntax and prosody in speech comprehension". *Journal of Cognitive Neuroscience* 18: 1696–711.

Engbert, R., Longtin, A., and Kliegl, R. (2002). "A dynamical model of saccade generation in reading based on spatially distributed lexical processing". *Vision Research* 42: 621–36.

—— Nuthmann, A., Richter, E.M., and Kliegl, R. (2005). "SWIFT: A dynamic model of saccade generation during reading". *Psychological Review* 112: 777–813.

Ervin, S. (1964). "Imitation and structural change in children's language", in E. Lenneberg (ed.), *New directions in the study of language*. Cambridge, MA: MIT Press.

Eulitz, C., and Lahiri, A. (2004). "Neuoribiological evidence for abstract phonological representations in the mental lexicon during speech recognition". *Journal of Cognitive Neuroscience* 16: 577–83.

Eviatar, Z., Menn, L., and Zaidel, E. (1990). "Concreteness: Nouns, verbs and hemispheres". *Cortex* 26: 611–24.

Fanselow, G. (2000). "Optimal exceptions", in B. Stiebels, and D. Wunderlich (eds.), *Lexicon in Focus.* Berlin: Akademie Verlag, 173–209.

—— (2001). "Features, θ-roles, and free constituent order". *Linguistic Inquiry* 32: 405–37.

—— (2003). "Free constituent order: A minimalist interface account". *Folia Linguistica* 37: 191–231.

—— Kliegl, R., and Schlesewsky, M. (1999). "Processing difficulty and principles of grammar", in S. Kemper, and R. Kliegl (eds.), *Constraints on language: Aging, grammar and memory.* Dordrecht: Kluwer Academic Publishers, 171–202.

—— Kliegl, R., and Schlesewsky, M. (2005). "Syntactic variation in German wh-questions: A rating and training study". *Linguistic Variation Yearbook* 5: 37–63.

—— Schlesewsky, M., Cavar, D., and Kliegl, R. (1999b). "Optimal parsing: Syntactic Parsing preferences and optimality theory". *Rutgers Optimality Archive* 367.

Farrell, P. (2005). *Grammatical relations.* Oxford: Oxford University Press.

Featherston, S. (2007). "Data in generative grammar: The stick and the carrot". *Theoretical Linguistics* 33: 269–318.

—— Gross, M., Münte, T.F., and Clahsen, H. (2000). "Brain potentials in the processing of complex sentences: An ERP study of control and raising constructions". *Journal of Psycholinguistic Research* 29: 141–54.

Federmeier, K.D., and Kutas, M. (1999). "A rose by any other name: Long-term memory structure and sentence processing". *Journal of Memory and Language* 41: 469–95.

—— Segal, J.B., Lombrozo, T., and Kutas, M. (2000). "Brain responses to nouns, verbs and class-ambiguous words in context". *Brain* 123: 2552–66.

Felser, C., Clahsen, H., and Münte, T.F. (2003). "Storage and integration in the processing of filler-gap dependencies: An ERP study of topicalization and wh-movement in German". *Brain and Language* 87: 345–54.

Ferreira, F., and Clifton, C., Jr. (1986). "The independence of syntactic processing". *Journal of Memory and Language* 25: 348–68.

Ferretti, T.R., McRae, K., and Hatherell, A. (2001). "Integrating verbs, situation schemas and thematic role concepts". *Journal of Memory and Language* 44: 516–47.

Fiebach, C.J., Schlesewsky, M., and Friederici, A.D. (2002). "Separating syntactic memory costs and syntactic integration costs during parsing: The processing of German wh-questions". *Journal of Memory and Language* 47: 250–72.

—— —— Lohmann, G., von Cramon, D.Y., and Friederici, A.D. (2005). "Revisiting the role of Broca's area in sentence processing: Syntactic integration versus syntactic working memory". *Human Brain Mapping* 24: 79–91.

—— Vos, S.H., and Friederici, A.D. (2004). "Neural correlates of syntactic ambiguity in sentence comprehension for low and high span readers". *Journal of Cognitive Neuroscience* 16: 1562–75.

Fillmore, C.J. (1968). "The case for case", in E. Bach, and R. Harms (eds.), *Universals in linguistic theory.* New York, 1–88.

Finocchiaro, C., Fierro, B., Brighina, F., Giglia, G., Francolini, M., and Caramazza, A. (2008). "When nominal features are marked on verbs: A transcranial magnetic stimulation study". *Brain and Language* 104: 113–21.

Fitzgerald, P.B., Fountain, S., and Daskalakis, Z.J. (2006). "A comprehensive review of the effects of rTMS on motor cortical excitability and inhibition". *Clinical Neurophysiology* 117: 2584–96.

Fodor, J.A., and Bever, T.G. (1965). "The psychological reality of linguistic segments". *Journal of Verbal Learning and Verbal Behavior* 4: 414–20.

—— —— and Garrett, M.F. (1974). *The psychology of language: an introduction to psycholinguistics and generative grammar.* New York: McGraw-Hill.

Fodor, J.D. (1978). "Parsing strategies and constraints on transformations". *Linguistic Inquiry* 9: 427–73.

—— (1980). "Superstrategy", in W.E. Cooper, and E.C.T. Walker (eds.), *Sentence processing: Studies in psycholinguistics presented to Merrill Garrett.* Hillsdale, NJ: Erlbaum.

—— (1995). "Comprehending sentence structure", in D.N. Osherson (ed.), *An invitation to cognitive science, Vol. 1: Language.* Cambridge, MA: MIT Press.

—— (1998). "Learning to parse". *Journal of Psycholinguistic Research* 27: 285–319.

—— and Inoue, A. (1994). "The diagnosis and cure of garden paths". *Journal of Psycholinguistic Research* 23: 407–34.

—— and —— (1998). "Attach anyway", in J.D. Fodor, and F. Ferreira (eds.), *Reanalysis in sentence processing.* Dordrecht: Kluwer, 101–41.

Foley, W.A., and Van Valin, R.D., Jr. (1984). *Functional syntax and universal grammar.* Cambridge: Cambridge University Press.

Foraker, S. (2007). "Explicit versus implicit prosody: Effects on pronoun interpretation". *20th Annual CUNY Conference on Human Sentence Processing.*

Ford, M. (1983). "A method for obtaining measures of local parsing complexity throughout sentences". *Journal of Verbal Learning and Verbal Behavior* 22: 203–18.

Forster, K., and Ryder, L.S. (1971). "Perceiving the structure and meaning of sentences". *Journal of Verbal Learning and Verbal Behavior* 10: 285–96.

Forster, K.I. (1979). "Levels of processing and the structure of the language processor", in W.E. Cooper, and E.C.T. Walker (eds.), *Sentence processing: Psycholinguistic studies presented to Merrill Garrett.* Hillsdale, NJ: Erlbaum, 27–85.

Frauenfelder, U., Segui, J., and Mehler, J. (1980). "Monitoring around the relative clause". *Journal of Verbal Learning and Verbal Behavior* 19: 328–37.

Frazier, L. (1978). *On comprehending sentences: Syntactic parsing strategies.* Ph.D. thesis, University of Connecticut.

—— (1987a). "Sentence processing: A tutorial review", in M. Coltheart (ed.), *Attention and performance, Vol. 12: The psychology of reading.* Hove: Erlbaum, 559–86.

—— (1987b). "Syntactic processing: Evidence from Dutch". *Natural Language and Linguistic Theory* 5: 519–59.

—— Carlson, K., and Clifton, C., Jr. (2006). "Prosodic phrasing is central to language comprehension". *Trends in Cognitive Sciences* 10: 244–9.

—— and Clifton, C., Jr. (1996). *Construal.* Cambridge, MA: MIT Press.

—— and Flores d'Arcais, G.B. (1989). "Filler-driven parsing: A study of gap filling in Dutch". *Journal of Memory and Language* 28: 331–44.

—— and Fodor, J.D. (1978). "The sausage machine: A new two-stage parsing model". *Cognition* 6: 291–326.

—— and Rayner, K. (1982). "Making and correcting errors during sentence comprehension: Eye movements in the analysis of structurally ambiguous sentences". *Cognitive Psychology* 14: 178–210.

Freedman, S., and Forster, K.I. (1985). "The psychological status of over-generated sentences". *Cognition* 19: 101–31.

Friederici, A.D. (1995). "The time course of syntactic activation during language processing: A model based on neuropsychological and neurophysiological data". *Brain and Language* 50: 259–81.

—— (1998). "Diagnosis and reanalysis: Two processing steps the brain may differentiate", in J.D. Fodor, and F. Ferreira (eds.), *Reanalysis in sentence processing.* Dordrecht: Kluwer, 177–200.

—— (1999). "The neurobiology of language comprehension", in A.D. Friederici (ed.), *Language comprehension: A biological perspective.* Berlin/ Heidelberg/New York: Springer, 263–301.

—— (2002). "Towards a neural basis of auditory sentence processing". *Trends in Cognitive Sciences* 6: 78–84.

—— (2004). "Processing local transitions versus long-distance syntactic hierarchies". *Trends in Cognitive Sciences* 8: 245–7.

—— (2006). "What's in control of language?". *Nature Neuroscience* 9: 991–2.

—— and Alter, K. (2004). "Lateralization of auditory language functions: A dynamic dual pathway model". *Brain and Language* 89: 267–76.

—— Bahlmann, J., Heim, S., Schubotz, R.I., and Anwander, A. (2006a). "The brain differentiates human and non-human grammars: Functional localization and structural connectivity". *Proceedings of the National Academy of Sciences USA* 103: 2458–63.

—— Fiebach, C.J., Schlesewsky, M., Bornkessel, I., and von Cramon, D.Y. (2006b). "Processing linguistic complexity and grammaticality in the left frontal cortex". *Cerebral Cortex* 16: 1709–17.

—— and Frisch, S. (2000). "Verb argument structure processing: the role of verb-specific and argument-specific information". *Journal of Memory and Language* 43: 476–507.

—— and Graetz, P. (1987). "Processing passive sentences in aphasia: Deficits and strategies". *Brain and Language* 30: 93–105.

—— Gunter, T.C., Hahne, A., and Mauth, K. (2004). "The relative timing of syntactic and semantic processes in sentence comprehension". *Neuroreport* 15: 165–9.

—— Hahne, A., and Saddy, D. (2002). "Distinct neurophysiological patterns reflecting aspects of syntactic complexity and syntactic repair". *Journal of Psycholinguistic Research* 31: 45–63.

—— and Mecklinger, A. (1996). "Syntactic parsing as revealed by brain responses: First pass and second pass parsing processes". *Journal of Psycholinguistic Research* 25: 157–76.

—— Mecklinger, A., Spencer, K.M., Steinhauer, K., and Donchin, E. (2001). "Syntactic parsing preferences and their on-line revisions: A spatio-temporal analysis of event-related brain potentials". *Cognitive Brain Research* 11: 305–23.

—— Pfeifer, E., and Hahne, A. (1993). "Event-related brain potentials during natural speech processing: Effects of semantic, morphological, and syntactic violations". *Cognitive Brain Research* 1: 183–92.

—— Rüschemeyer, S.-A., Fiebach, C.J., and Hahne, A. (2003). "The role of left inferior frontal and superior temporal cortex in sentence comprehension: Localizing syntactic and semantic processes". *Cerebral Cortex* 13: 1047–3211.

—— Steinhauer, K., Mecklinger, A., and Meyer, M. (1998). "Working memory constraints on syntactic ambiguity resolution as revealed by electrical brain responses". *Biological Psychology* 47: 193–221.

—— von Cramon, D.Y., and Kotz, S.A. (2007). "Role of the corpus callosum in speech comprehension: Interfacing syntax and prosody". *Neuron* 53: 135–45.

Frisch, S. (2000). *Verb-Argument-Struktur, Kasus und thematische Interpretation beim Sprachverstehen [=Verb-argument structure, case and thematic interpretation during language processing]*. Leipzig: MPI Series in Cognitive Neuroscience.

—— and beim Graben, P. (2005). "Finding needles in haystacks: Symbolic resonance analysis of event-related potentials unveils different processing demands". *Cognitive Brain Research* 24: 476–91.

—— Hahne, A., and Friederici, A.D. (2004). "Word category and verb-argument structure information in the dynamics of parsing". *Cognition* 91: 191–219.

—— Kotz, S.A., von Cramon, D.Y., and Friederici, A.D. (2003). "Why the P600 is not just a P300: the role of the basal ganglia". *Clinical Neurophysiology* 114: 336–40.

Frisch, S., and Schlesewsky, M. (2001). "The N400 indicates problems of thematic hierarchizing". *Neuroreport* 12: 3391–4.

—— and —— (2005). "The resolution of case conflicts from a neurophysiological perspective". *Cognitive Brain Research* 25: 484–98.

—— Schlesewsky, M., Saddy, D., and Alpermann, A. (2002). "The P600 as an indicator of syntactic ambiguity". *Cognition* 85: B83–B92.

Funnell, M.G., Corballis, P.M., and Gazzaniga, M.S. (2001). "Hemispheric processing asymmetries: Implications for memory". *Brain and Cognition* 46: 135–9.

Gardner, H., and Zurif, E. (1975). "Bee but not Be: Oral reading of single words in aphasia and alexia". *Neuropsychologia* 13: 181–90.

Garnsey, S.M., Tanenhaus, M.K., and Chapman, R.M. (1989). "Evoked potentials and the study of sentence comprehension". *Journal of Psycholinguistic Research* 18: 51–60.

Gärtner, H.-M., and Steinbach, M. (2003a). "What do reduced pronominals reveal about the syntax of Dutch and German? Part 1: Clause-internal positions". *Linguistische Berichte* 195: 257–94.

—— and —— (2003b). "What do reduced pronominals reveal about the syntax of Dutch and German? Part 2: Fronting". *Linguistische Berichte* 196: 459–90.

Gaskell, M.G. (2007). "Statistical and connectionist models of speech perception and word recognition", in M.G. Gaskell (ed.), *The Oxford handbook of psycholinguistics*. Oxford: Oxford University Press, 55–70.

Gazdar, G., Klein, E., Pullum, G., and Sag, I. (1985). *Generalized phrase structure grammar*. Cambridge, MA: Harvard University Press.

Gennari, S., and Poeppel, D. (2003). "Processing correlates of lexical semantic complexity". *Cognition* 89: B27–B41.

Gibson, E. (1991). *A computational theory of linguistic processing: Memory limitations and processing breakdown*. Ph.D. thesis, Carnegie Mellon University.

—— (1998). "Linguistic complexity: Locality of syntactic dependencies". *Cognition* 68: 1–76.

—— (2000). "The dependency locality theory: A distance-based theory of linguistic complexity", in Y. Miyashita, A. Marantz, and W. O'Neil (eds.), *Image, language, brain*. Cambridge, MA: MIT Press, 95–126.

Gil, D. (2001). "Creoles, complexity and Riau Indonesian". *Linguistic Typology* 5: 325–71.

Gilboy, E., Sopena, J.-M., Clifton, C., Jr., and Frazier, L. (1995). "Argument structure and association preferences in Spanish and English complex NPs". *Cognition* 54: 131–67.

Gold, B.T., and Rastle, K. (2007). "Neural correlates of morphological decomposition during visual word recognition". *Journal of Cognitive Neuroscience* 19: 1983–93.

Goldberg, A.E. (2003). "Constructions: A new theoretical approach to language". *Trends in Cognitive Sciences* 7: 219–24.

Goodglass, H., and Kaplan, E. (1972). *The assessment of aphasia and related disorders.* Philadelphia: Lea and Febiger.

—— Klein, B., Carey, P., and Jones, K. (1966). "Specific semantic word categories in aphasia". *Cortex* 2: 74–89.

Gordon, P.C., Hendrick, R., and Johnson, M. (2001). "Memory interference during language processing". *Journal of Experimental Psychology: Learning, Memory and Cognition* 27: 1411–23.

Gorrell, P. (1987). *Studies of human sentence processing: Ranked-parallel versus serial models.* Ph.D. thesis, University of Connecticut.

—— (1995). *Syntax and parsing.* Cambridge: Cambridge University Press.

Grahn, J.A., and Brett, M. (2007). "Rhythm and beat perception in motor areas of the brain". *Journal of Cognitive Neuroscience* 19: 893–906.

Greenberg, J.H. (1966). "Some universals of grammar with particular reference to the order of meaningful elements", in J.H. Greenberg (ed.), *Universals of language.* Cambridge, MA: MIT Press, 73–113.

Grewe, T., Bornkessel-Schlesewsky, I., Zysset, S., Wiese, R., von Cramon, D.Y., and Schlesewsky, M. (2007). "The role of the posterior superior temporal sulcus in the processing of unmarked transitivity". *Neuroimage* 35: 343–52.

—— Bornkessel, I., Zysset, S., Wiese, R., von Cramon, D.Y., and Schlesewsky, M. (2005). "The emergence of the unmarked: A new perspective on the language-specific function of Broca's area". *Human Brain Mapping* 26: 178–90.

—— —— —— —— —— and —— (2006). "Linguistic prominence and Broca's area: The influence of animacy as a linearization principle". *Neuroimage* 32: 1395–402.

Grewendorf, G. (1988). *Aspekte der deutschen Syntax. Eine Rektions-Bindungs-Analyse.* Tübingen: Narr.

Grimshaw, J.B. (1990). *Argument structure.* Cambridge, MA: MIT Press.

Grodzinsky, Y. (2000). "The neurology of syntax: Language use without Broca's area". *Behavioral and Brain Sciences* 23: 1–71.

—— (2006). "The language faculty, Broca's region, and the mirror system". *Cortex* 42: 469–71.

—— and Friederici, A.D. (2006). "Neuroimaging of syntax and syntactic processing". *Current Opinion in Neurobiology* 16: 240–6.

Gross, M., Say, T., Kleingers, M., Clahsen, H., and Münte, T.F. (1998). "Human brain potentials to violations in morphologically complex Italian words". *Neuroscience Letters* 241: 83–6.

Gruber, J. (1965). *Studies in lexical relations.* Ph.D. thesis, MIT.

Gunter, T.C., and Friederici, A.D. (1999). "Concerning the automaticity of syntactic processing". *Psychophysiology* 36: 126–37.

Gunter, T.C., Friederici, A.D., and Schriefers, H. (2000). "Syntactic gender and semantic expectancy: ERPs reveal early autonomy and late interaction". *Journal of Cognitive Neuroscience* 12: 556–68.

—— Jackson, J.L., and Mulder, G. (1995). "Language, memory and aging: An electrophysiological exploration of teh N400 during reading of memory demanding sentences". *Psychophysiology* 32: 215–29.

—— Stowe, L.A., and Mulder, G. (1997). "When syntax meets semantics". *Psychophysiology* 34: 660–76.

Haarmann, H.J., and Kolk, H.H.J. (1991). "Syntactic priming in Broca's aphasics: Evidence for slow activation". *Aphasiology.*

Haegeman, L. (1994). *Introduction to Government and Binding Theory.* Oxford: Blackwell.

—— (1995). *The syntax of negation.* Cambridge: Cambridge University Press.

Hagiwara, H., Soshi, T., Ishihara, M., and Imanaka, K. (2007). "A topographical study on the ERP correlates of scrambled word order in Japanese complex sentences". *Journal of Cognitive Neuroscience* 19: 175–93.

—— Sugioka, Y., Ito, T., Kawamura, M., and Shiota, J. (1999). "Neurolinguistic evidence for rule-based nominal suffixation". *Language* 75: 739–63.

Hagoort, P. (2003). "How the brain solves the binding problem for language: A neurocomputational model of syntactic processing". *Neuroimage* 20: S18–S29.

—— (2005). "On Broca, brain, and binding: a new framework". *Trends in Cognitive Sciences* 9: 416–23.

—— and Brown, C. (2000). "ERP effects of listening to speech compared to reading: the P600/SPS to syntactic violations in spoken sentences and rapid serial visual presentation". *Neuropsychologia* 38: 1531–49.

—— Brown, C., and Groothusen, J. (1993). "The syntactic positive shift (SPS) as an ERP measure of syntactic processing". *Language and Cognitive Processes* 8: 439–83.

—— Hald, L., Bastiaansen, M., and Petersson, K.M. (2004). "Integration of word meaning and world knowledge in language comprehension". *Science* 304: 438–41.

—— and van Berkum, J.J.A. (2007). "Beyond the sentence given". *Philosophical Transactions of the Royal Society B* 362: 801–11.

Hahne, A. (1998). *Charakteristika syntaktischer und semantischer Prozesse bei der auditiven Sprachverarbeitung.* Leipzig: MPI Series in Cognitive Neuroscience.

—— and Friederici, A.D. (2002). "Differential task effects on semantic and syntactic processes as revealed by ERPs". *Cognitive Brain Research* 13: 339–56.

Haider, H. (1993). *Deutsche Syntax, generativ.* Tübingen: Narr.

—— and Rosengren, I. (2003). "Scrambling: Nontriggered chain formation in OV languages". *Journal of Germanic Linguistics* 15: 203–67.

Hale, J. (2006). "Uncertainty about the rest of the sentence". *Cognitive Science* 30: 643–72.

Hall, D.A., Hart, H.C., and Johnsrude, I.S. (2003). "Relationships between human auditory cortical structure and function". *Audiology and Neuro-ootology* 8: 1–18.

Hammer, A., Goebel, R., Schwarzbach, J., Münte, T.F., and Jansma, B.M. (2007). "When sex meets syntactic gender on a neural basis during pronoun processing". *Brain Research* 1146: 185–98.

Handy, T.C. (ed.) (2004). *Event-related potentials. A methods handbook.* Cambridge, MA: MIT Press.

Harris, A., Wexler, K., and Holcomb, P. (2000). "An ERP investigation of binding and coreference". *Brain and Language* 75: 313–46.

Haspelmath, M. (2002). *Understanding morphology.* London: Arnold.

—— (2006). "Against markedness (and what to replace it with)". *Journal of Linguistics* 42: 25–70.

Hasting, A.S., Kotz, S.A., and Friederici, A.D. (2007). "Setting the stage for automatic syntax processing: The mismatch negativity as an indictor of syntactic priming". *Journal of Cognitive Neuroscience* 19: 386–400.

Hauk, O., Johnsrude, I.S., and Pulvermüller, F. (2004). "Somatotopic representation of action words in motor and premotor cortex". *Neuron* 41: 301–7.

Haupt, F.S., Schlesewsky, M., Roehm, D., Friederici, A.D., and Bornkessel-Schlesewsky, I. (2008). "The status of subject-object reanalyses in the language comprehension architecture". *Journal of Memory and Language* 59: 54–96.

Heeger, D.J., and Ress, D. (2002). "What does fMRI tell us about neuronal activity?". *Nature Reviews Neuroscience* 3: 142–51.

Helbig, G., and Buscha, L. (1996). *Deutsche Grammatik.* Leipzig: Verlag Enzyklopädie Langenscheid.

Hemforth, B., Konieczny, L., and Scheepers, C. (2000). "Syntactic attachment and anaphor resolution: The two sides of relative clause attachment", in M.W. Crocker, M.J. Pickering, and C. Clifton, Jr. (eds.), *Architectures and mechanisms for language processing.* Cambridge: Cambridge University Press, 259–82.

—— Konieczny, L., and Strube, G. (eds.) (1993). "Incremental syntax processing and parsing strategies", *Proceedings of the 15th Annual Conference of the Cognitive Science Society.* Hillsdale, NJ: Erlbaum, 539–45.

Henderson, J.M., and Ferreira, F. (eds.) (2004). *The interface of language, vision, and action.* New York: Psychology Press.

Henderson, L., Wallis, J., and Knight, K. (1984). "Morphemic structure and lexical access", in H. Bouma, and D. Bouwhuis (eds.), *Attention and performance X: Control of language processes.* Hillsdale, NJ: Erlbaum, 211–26.

Herrmann, C.S., Munk, M.H.J., and Engel, A.K. (2004). "Cognitive functions of gamma-band activity: Memory match and utilization". *Trends in Cognitive Sciences* 8: 347–55.

Hewitt, G. (1979). *Abkhaz*. Amsterdam: North-Holland.

Hirotani, M. (2005). "Constraints on prosodic structures in grammar and parser: Scrambled and unscrambled sentences in Japanese", in S. Kawahara (ed.), *University of Massachusetts Occasional Papers in Linguistics 29: Studies on Prosody*. University of Massachusetts, Amherst: GLSA.

Hoeks, J.C.J., Hendriks, P., Vonk, W., Brown, C., and Hagoort, P. (2006). "Processing the noun phrase versus sentence coordination ambiguity: Thematic information does not completely eliminate processing difficulty". *The Quarterly Journal of Experimental Psychology* 59: 1581–99.

Hoeks, J.C.J., Stowe, L.A., and Doedens, G. (2004). "Seeing words in context: The interaction of lexical and sentence level information during reading". *Cognitive Brain Research* 19: 59–73.

—— Vonk, W., and Schriefers, H. (2002). "Processing coordinated structures in context: The effect of topic-structure on ambiguity resolution". *Journal of Memory and Language* 46: 99–119.

Holcomb, P. (1988). "Automatic and attentional processing: An event-related brain potential analysis of semantic priming". *Brain and Language* 35: 66–85.

—— and Neville, H. (1990). "Auditory and visual semantic priming in lexical decision: A comparison using event-related brain potentials". *Language and Cognitive Processes* 5: 281–312.

Holmberg, A. (1986). *Word order and syntactic features in the Scandinavian languages and English*. Ph.D. thesis, University of Stockholm.

Hopf, J.-M., Bayer, J., Bader, M., and Meng, M. (1998). "Event-related brain potentials and case information in syntactic ambiguities". *Journal of Cognitive Neuroscience* 10: 264–80.

Horn, L. (1997). "Negative polarity and the dynamics of vertical inference", in D. Forget, P. Hirschbühler, F. Martinon, and M.L. Rivero (eds.), *Negation and polarity: Syntax and semantics*. Amsterdam: John Benjamins, 157–82.

Hruska, C., and Alter, K. (2004). "Prosody in dialogues and single sentences: How prosody can influence speech perception", in A. Steube (ed.), *Information structure: Theoretical and empirical aspects*. Berlin: Walter de Gruyter, 211–26.

Hsiao, F., and Gibson, E. (2003). "Processing relative clauses in Chinese". *Cognition* 90: 3–27.

Hyönä, J., and Hujanen, H. (1997). "Effects of case marking and word order on sentence parsing in Finnish: An eye fixation analysis". *Quarterly Journal of Experimental Psychology* 50A: 841–58.

Indefrey, P. (2007). "Brain imaging studies of language production", in M.G. Gaskell (ed.), *The Oxford handbook of psycholinguistics*. Oxford: Oxford University Press, 547–64.

—— Brown, C., Hagoort, P., Herzog, H., Sach, M., and Seitz, R. (1997). "A PET study of cerebral activation patterns induced by verb inflection". *Neuroimage* 5: S548.

Inoue, A., and Fodor, J.D. (1995). "Information-paced parsing of Japanese", in R. Mazuka, and N. Nagai (eds.), *Japanese sentence processing*. Hillsdale, NJ: Lawrence Erlbaum, 9–63.

Inui, T., Ogawa, K., and Ohba, M. (2007). "Role of left inferior frontal gyrus in the processing of particles in Japanese". *Neuroreport* 18: 431–4.

Ischebeck, A.K., Friederici, A.D., and Alter, K. (2008). "Processing prosodic boundaries in natural and hummed speech: An fMRI study". *Cerebral Cortex* 18: 541–52.

Isel, F., Alter, K., and Friederici, A.D. (2005). "Influence of prosodic information on the processing of split particles: ERP evidence from spoken German". *Journal of Cognitive Neuroscience* 17: 154–67.

Ishizuka, T. (2005). "Processing relative clauses in Japanese", in R. Okabe, and K. Okubo (eds.), *UCLA Working Papers in Linguistics, no. 13. Papers in Psycholinguistics 2*. 135–57.

Jackendoff, R. (1972). *Semantic interpretation in generative grammar*. Cambridge, MA: MIT Press.

—— (1997). *The architecture of the language faculty*. Cambridge, MA: MIT Press.

—— (2002). *Foundations of language*. Oxford: Oxford University Press.

Jaeger, J.J., Lockwood, A., Kemmerer, D., Van Valin, R.D., Jr., Murphy, B., and Khalak, H. (1996). "A positron emission tomography study of regular and irregular verb morphology in English". *Language* 72: 451–97.

—— Van Valin, R.D., Jr., and Lockwood, A.H. (1998). "Response to Seidenberg and Hoeffner". *Language* 74: 123–8.

Jahanshahi, M., and Rothwell, J. (2000). "Transcranial magnetic stimulation studies of cognition: An emerging field". *Experimental Brain Research* 131: 1–9.

Janssen, U., Wiese, R., and Schlesewsky, M. (2005). "Electrophysiological responses to violations of morphosyntactic and prosodic features in derived German nouns". *Journal of Neurolinguistics* 19: 466–82.

Jarvella, R., and Meijers, G. (1983). "Recognizing morphemes in spoken words: Some evidence for a stem-organized mental lexicon", in G.B. Flores d'Arcais, and R. Jarvella (eds.), *The process of language understanding*. New York: Wiley, 81–112.

Jezzard, P., Matthews, P.M., and Smith, S.M. (2001). *Functional Magnetic Resonance Imaging: An introduction to the methods*. Oxford: Oxford University Press.

Joanisse, M.F., and Seidenberg, M.S. (1999). "Impairments in verb morphology after brain injury: A connectionist model". *Proceedings of the National Academy of Sciences USA* 96: 7592–7.

—— and —— (2005). "Imaging the past: Neural activation in frontal and temporal regions during regular and irregular past-tense processing". *Cognitive, Affective and Behavioral Neuroscience* 5: 282–96.

Johnson, N.F. (1970). "Chunking and organization in the process of recall", in G.H. Bower (ed.), *The psychology of learning and motivation*. New York: Academic Press.

Johnson, S.M., Breen, M., Clifton, C., Jr., and Morris Florak, J. (2003). "ERP investigations of prosodic and semantic focus". *Journal of Cognitive Neuroscience Supplement*.

Jonides, J., Lewis, R.L., Nee, D.E., Lustig, C.A., Berman, M.G., and Moore, K.S. (2008). "The mind and brain of short-term memory". *Annual Review of Psychology* 59: 193–224.

Jun, S.-A. (2003). "Prosodic phrasing and attachment preferences". *Journal of Psycholinguistic Research* 32: 219–48.

Jurafsky, D. (1996). "A probabilistic model of lexical and syntactic access and disambiguation". *Cognitive Science* 20: 137–94.

—— (2003). "Probabilistic modelling in psycholinguistics: Linguistic comprehension and production", in R. Bod, J. Hay, and S. Jannedy (eds.), *Probablistic Linguistics*. Cambridge, MA: MIT Press, 39–96.

Juranek, K. (2005). *Relationale Aspekte des Sprachverstehens: Die Verarbeitung von Argumenten und Adjunkten [=Relational aspects of language comprehension: The processing of arguments and adjuncts]*. MA thesis, University of Leipzig.

Just, M.A., and Carpenter, P.A. (1992). "A capacity theory of comprehension: Individual differences in working memory". *Psychological Review* 99: 122–49.

—— —— Keller, T.A., Eddy, W.F., and Thulborn, K.R. (1996). "Brain activation modulated by sentence comprehension". *Science* 274: 114–16.

Kaan, E., Harris, A., Gibson, E., and Holcomb, P. (2000). "The P600 as an index of syntactic integration difficulty". *Language and Cognitive Processes* 15: 159–201.

—— and Swaab, T. (2003). "Repair, revision, and complexity in syntactic analysis: An electrophysiological differentiation". *Journal of Cognitive Neuroscience* 15: 98–110.

—— and Swaab, T.Y. (2002). "The brain circuitry of syntactic comprehension". *Trends in Cognitive Sciences* 6: 350–6.

Kaiser, E., and Trueswell, J.C. (2004). "The role of discourse context in the processing of a flexible word-order language". *Cognition* 94: 113–47.

Kamide, Y., and Mitchell, D.C. (1997). "Relative clause attachment: Nondeterminism in Japanese parsing". *Journal of Psycholinguistic Research* 26: 247–54.

—— and —— (1999). "Incremental pre-head attachment in Japanese parsing". *Language and Cognitive Processes* 14: 631–62.

Keenan, E.L. (1976). "Towards a universal definition of 'subject'", in C.N. Li (ed.), *Subject and topic*. New York: Academic Press, 303–33.

—— and Comrie, B. (1977). "Noun phrase accessibility and universal grammar". *Linguistic Inquiry* 8: 63–100.

Kempen, G., and Harbusch, K. (2005). "The relationship between grammaticality ratings and corpus frequencies: A case study into word order variability in the midfield of German clauses", in S. Kepser, and M. Reis (eds.), *Linguistic evidence – Empirical, theoretical, and computational perspectives.* Berlin: Mouton de Gruyter, 329–49.

Kempley, S.T., and Morton, J. (1982). "The effects of priming with regularly and irregularly related words in auditory word recognition". *British Journal of Psychology* 73: 441–54.

Kerkhofs, R., Vonk, W., Schriefers, H., and Chwilla, D.J. (2007). "Discourse, syntax and prosody: The brain reveals an immediate interaction". *Journal of Cognitive Neuroscience* 19: 1421–34.

Kibrik, A.E. (1997). "Beyond subject and object: towards a comprehensive relational typology". *Linguistic Typology* 1: 279–346.

Kim, A., and Osterhout, L. (2005). "The independence of combinatory semantic processing: Evidence from event-related potentials". *Journal of Memory and Language* 52: 205–25.

King, J.W., and Just, M.A. (1991). "Individual differences in syntactic processing: The role of working memory". *Journal of Memory and Language* 30: 580–602.

—— and Kutas, M. (1995). "Bridging the gap: Evidence from ERPs on the processing of unbounded dependencies". *Journal of Cognitive Neuroscience* 5: 196–214.

Kinno, R., Kawamura, M., Shioda, S., and Sakai, K.L. (2008). "Neural correlates of noncanonical syntactic processing revealed by a picture-sentence matching task". *Human Brain Mapping* 29: 1015–27.

Kjelgaard, M.M., and Speer, S.R. (1999). "Prosodic facilitation and interference in the resolution of temporary syntactic closure ambiguity". *Journal of Memory and Language* 40: 153–94.

Kluender, R., and Kutas, M. (1993a). "Bridging the gap: Evidence from ERPs on the processing of unbounded dependencies". *Journal of Cognitive Neuroscience* 5: 196–214.

—— and —— (1993b). "Subjacency as a processing phenomenon". *Language and Cognitive Processes* 8: 573–633.

Knoeferle, P., Crocker, M.W., Scheepers, C., and Pickering, M.J. (2005). "The influence of immediate visual context on incremental thematic role assignment: Evidence from eye-movements in depicted events". *Cognition* 95: 95–127.

—— Habets, B., Crocker, M.W., and Münte, T.F. (2008). "Visual scenes trigger immediate syntactic reanalysis: Evidence from ERPs during situated spoken comprehension". *Cerebral Cortex* 18: 789–95.

Knösche, T.R., Neuhaus, C., Haueisen, J., Alter, K., Maess, B., Witte, O.W., and Friederici, A.D. (2005). "Perception of phrase structure in music". *Human Brain Mapping* 24: 259–73.

Koester, D., Gunter, T.C., and Wagner, S. (2007). "The morphosyntactic decomposition and semantic composition of German compound words investigated by ERPs". *Brain and Language* 102: 64–79.

—— and Schiller, N.O. (2008). "Morphological priming in overt language production: Electrophysiological evidence from Dutch". *NeuroImage* 42: 1622–30.

Koizumi, M. (2005). "Discussion of neurological approaches in linguistic inquiries". *Symposium on neurological approaches in linguistic inquiries, Annual Meeting of the Linguistic Society of Japan.*

Kolk, H.H.J., Chwilla, D.J., van Herten, M., and Oor, P.J. (2003). "Structure and limited capacity in verbal working memory: A study with event-related potentials". *Brain and Language* 85: 1–36.

—— and van Grunsven, M. (1985). "Agrammatism as a variable phenomenon". *Cognitive Neuropsychology* 2: 347–84.

Konieczny, L., Hemforth, B., Scheepers, C., and Strube, G. (1997). "The role of lexical heads in parsing: Evidence from German". *Language and Cognitive Processes* 12: 307–48.

Köpcke, K.-M. (1988). "Schemas in German plural formation". *Lingua* 74: 303–35.

Köster, D. (2004). *Morphology and spoken word comprehension: Electrophysiological investigations of internal compound structure.* Leipzig: Max Planck Series in Human Cognitive and Brain Sciences.

Krifka, M. (1995). "The semantics and pragmatics of polarity items". *Linguistic Analysis* 25: 209–57.

Krott, A., Baayen, R.H., and Hagoort, P. (2006). "The nature of anterior negativities caused by misapplications of morphological rules". *Journal of Cognitive Neuroscience* 18: 1616–30.

Kuczaj, S.A. (1977). "The acquisition of regular and irregular past tense forms". *Journal of Verbal Learning and Verbal Behavior* 16: 589–600.

Kulik, S. (2000). *Syntaktische Funktionsambiguitäten – Der Einfluß intervenierender Information auf die Analyse kasusambiger Nominalphrasen [= Syntactic function ambiguities – The influence of intervening information on the analysis of case ambiguous noun phrases].* MA thesis, University of Potsdam.

—— (2007). *EEG-Untersuchungen zur Informationsstruktur und Verarbeitung koreferenter Nominalphrasen [EEG investigations of information structure and the processing of coreferent noun phrases].* Ph.D. thesis, University of Marburg.

Kuperberg, G.R. (2007). "Neural mechanisms of language comprehension: Challenges to syntax". *Brain Research* 1146: 23–49.

—— Kreher, D.A., Sitnikova, T., Caplan, D.N., and Holcomb, P.J. (2007). "The role of animacy and thematic relationships in processing active

English sentence: Evidence from event-related potentials". *Brain and Language* 100: 223–37.

—— Sitnikova, T., Caplan, D., and Holcomb, P. (2003). "Electrophysiological distinctions in processing conceptual relationships within simple sentences". *Cognitive Brain Research* 17: 117–29.

Kurtzmann, H. (1985). *Studies in syntactic ambiguity resolution.* Ph.D. thesis, MIT.

Kutas, M., and Federmeier, K.D. (2000). "Electrophysiology reveals semantic memory use in language comprehension". *Trends in Cognitive Sciences* 4: 463–9.

—— and Hillyard, S.A. (1980). "Reading senseless sentences: Brain potentials reflect semantic incongruity". *Science* 207: 203–5.

—— and —— (1983). "Event-related brain potentials to grammatical errors and semantic anomalies". *Memory and Cognition* 11: 539–50.

—— and Van Petten, C. (1994). "Psycholinguistics electrified", in M.A. Gernsbacher (ed.), *Handbook of Psycholinguistics.* New York: Academic Press, 83–143.

—— Van Petten, C., and Kluender, R. (2006). "Psycholinguistics electrified II (1994–2005)", in M. Traxler, and M.A. Gernsbacher (eds.), *Handbook of Psycholinguistics.* London: Elsevier, 659–724.

Kwon, N., Polinsky, M., and Kluender, R. (eds.) (2006). "Subject preference in Korean", *Proceedings of the 25th West Coast Conference on Formal Linguistics.* Somerville, MA: Cascadilla Proceedings Project.

Ladefoged, P., and Broadbent, D.E. (1960). "Perception of sequence in auditory events". *Quarterly Journal of Experimental Psychology* 12: 162–70.

Laine, M., Rinne, J.O., Krause, B.J., Teräs, M., and Sipilä, H. (1999). "Left hemisphere activation during processing of morphologically complex word forms in adults". *Neuroscience Letters* 271: 85–8.

Lamers, M.A.J. (2001). *Sentence processing: Using syntactic, semantic and thematic information.* Groningen: Groningen Dissertations in Linguistics.

—— Jansma, B.M., Hammer, A., and Münte, T.F. (2006). "Neural correlates of semantic and syntactic processes in the comprehension of case marked pronouns: Evidence from German and Dutch". *BMC Neuroscience* 7: 23.

Lau, E., Stroud, C., Plesch, S., and Phillips, C. (2006). "The role of structural prediction in rapid syntactic analysis". *Brain and Language* 98: 74–88.

Law, S.-P. (2000). "Structural prominence hypothesis and Chinese aphasic sentence comprehension". *Brain and Language* 74: 260–8.

Lee, M.-W. (2004). "Another look at the role of empty categories in sentence processing (and grammar)". *Journal of Psycholinguistic Research* 33: 51–73.

Lehtonen, M., Cunillera, T., Rodríguez-Fornells, A., Hultén, A., Tuomainen, J., and Laine, M. (2007). "Recognition of morphologically complex words in Finnish: Evidence from event-related potentials". *Brain Research* 1148: 123–37.

Lehtonen, M., Vorobyev, V.A., Hughdal, K., Tuokkola, T., and Laine, M. (2006). "Neural correlates of morphological decomposition in a morphologically rich language: An fMRI study". *Brain and Language* 98: 182–93.

Lenerz, J. (1977). *Zur Abfolge nominaler Satzglieder im Deutschen*. Tübingen: Gunter Narr Verlag.

Leuckefeld, K. (2005). *The development of argument processing mechanisms in German: An electrophysiological investigation with school-aged children and adults*. Leipzig: MPI Series in Human Cognitive and Brain Sciences.

Levin, B., and Rappaport Hovav, M. (2005). *Argument realization*. Cambridge: Cambridge University Press.

Levy, R. (2008). "Expectation-based syntactic comprehension". *Cognition* 106: 1126–77.

Lewis, R.L. (1996). "Interference in short-term memory: The magical number two (or three) in sentence processing". *Journal of Psycholinguistic Research* 25: 93–115.

—— and Vasishth, S. (2005). "An activation-based model of sentence processing as skilled memory retrieval". *Cognitive Science* 29: 1–45.

—— —— and Van Dyke, J.A. (2006). "Computational principles of working memory in sentence comprehension". *Trends in Cognitive Sciences* 10: 447–54.

Lin, C.-J.C., and Bever, T.G. (2006). "Subject preference in the processing of relative clauses in Chinese", in D. Baumer, D. Montero, and M. Scanlon (eds.), *Proceedings of the 25th West Coast Conference on Formal Linguistics*. Somerville, MA: Cascadilla Proceedings Project, 254–60.

Linebarger, M. (1987). "Negative polarity and grammatical representation". *Linguistics and Philosophy* 10: 325–87.

—— Schwartz, M.F., and Saffran, E.M. (1983). "Sensitivity to grammatical structure in so-called agrammatic aphasics". *Cognition* 13: 361–92.

Longe, O., Randall, B., Stamatakis, E.A., and Tyler, L.K. (2007). "Grammatical categories in the brain: The role of morphological structure". *Cerebral Cortex* 17: 1812–20.

Longtin, C.-M., and Meunier, F. (2005). "Morphological decomposition in early visual word processing". *Journal of Memory and Language* 53: 26–41.

Longworth, C.E., Keenan, S.E., Barker, R.A., Marslen-Wilson, W.D., and Tyler, L.K. (2005). "The basal ganglia and rule-governed language use: Evidence from vascular and degenerative conditions". *Brain* 128: 548–96.

Lück, M., Hahne, A., and Clahsen, H. (2006). "Brain potentials to morphologically complex words during listening". *Brain Research* 1077: 144–52.

Lukatela, G., Gligorijevic, B., Kostic, A., and Turvey, M. (1980). "Representation of inflected nouns in the internal lexicon". *Memory and Cognition* 8: 415–23.

MacDonald, M.C., and Christiansen, M.H. (2002). "Reassessing working memory: Comment on Just and Carpenter (1992) and Waters and Caplan (1996)". *Psychological Review* 109: 35–54.

—— Pearlmutter, N.J., and Seidenberg, M.S. (1994). "The lexical nature of syntactic ambiguity resolution". *Psychological Review* 101: 676–703.

MacKay, D.G. (1978). "Derivational rules and the internal lexicon". *Journal of Verbal Learning and Verbal Behavior* 17: 61–71.

MacWhinney, B. (1977). "Starting points". *Language* 53: 152–68.

—— and Pléh, C. (1998). "The processing of restrictive relative clauses in Hungarian". *Cognition* 29: 95–141.

Magne, C., Artésano, C., Lacheret-Dujour, A., Morel, M., Alter, K., and Besson, M. (2005). "On-line processing of 'pop-out' words in spoken French dialogues". *Journal of Cognitive Neuroscience* 17: 740–56.

Mak, W.M., Vonk, W., and Schriefers, H. (2002). "The influence of animacy on relative clause processing". *Journal of Memory and Language* 47: 50–68.

—— —— and —— (2006). "Animacy in processing relative clauses: The hikers that rocks crush". *Journal of Memory and Language* 54: 466–90.

Makeig, S., Debener, S., Onton, J., and Delorme, A. (2004). "Mining event-related brain dynamics". *Trends in Cognitive Sciences* 8: 204–10.

—— Westerfield, M., Jung, T.P., Enghoff, S., Townsend, J., Courchesne, E., and Sejnowski, T.J. (2002). "Dynamic brain sources of visual evoked responses". *Science* 295: 690–4.

Manelis, L., and Tharp, D. (1977). "The processing of affixed words". *Memory and Cognition* 5: 690–5.

Marcus, G., Brinkmann, U., Clahsen, H., Wiese, R., and Pinker, S. (1995). "German inflection: The exception that proves the rule". *Cognitive Science* 15: 173–218.

Marslen-Wilson, W. (1973). "Linguistic structure and speech shadowing at very short latencies". *Nature* 244: 522–33.

—— (2007). "Morphological processes in language comprehension", in M.G. Gaskell (ed.), *The Oxford handbook of psycholinguistics*. Oxford: Oxford University Press, 175–93.

—— and Tyler, L.K. (1980). "The temporal structure of spoken language understanding". *Cognition* 8: 1–71.

—— and —— (1997). "Dissociating types of mental computation". *Nature* 387: 592–4.

—— and —— (2007). "Morphology, language and the brain: The decompositional substrate for language comprehension". *Philosophical Transactions of the Royal Society B* 362: 823–36.

Martin, A.E., and McElree, B. (2008). "A content-addressable pointer mechanism underlies comprehension of verb-phrase ellipsis". *Journal of Memory and Language* 58: 879–906.

Martin, J.H. (1991). "The collective electrical behavior of cortical neurons: The electroencephalogram and the mechanisms of epilepsy", in E.R. Kandel, J.H. Schwartz, and T.M. Jessell (eds.), *Principles of neural science*. London: Prentice Hall, 777–91.

Matzke, M., Mai, H., Nager, W., Rüsseler, J., and Münte, T.F. (2002). "The costs of freedom: an ERP study of non-canonical sentences". *Clinical Neurophysiology* 113: 844–52.

Mauner, G., Fromkin, V.A., and Cornell, T.L. (1993). "Comprehension and acceptability judgments in agrammatism: Disruptions in the syntax of referential dependency". *Brain and Language* 45: 340–70.

McClelland, J.L. (1979). "On the time relations of mental processes: An examination of systems of processes in cascade". *Psychological Review* 86: 287–330.

—— and Patterson, K. (2002a). "'Words or Rules' cannot exploit the regularity in exceptions. Reply to Pinker and Ullman". *Trends in Cognitive Sciences* 6: 464–5.

—— and —— (2002b). "Rules or connections in past-tense inflections: What does the evidence rule out?". *Trends in Cognitive Sciences* 6: 465–72.

McElree, B. (1993). "The locus of lexical preference effects in sentence comprehension". *Journal of Memory and Language* 32: 536–71.

—— Foraker, S., and Dyer, L. (2003). "Memory structures that subserve sentence comprehension". *Journal of Memory and Language* 48: 67–91.

—— and Griffith, T. (1995). "Syntactic and thematic processing in sentence comprehension". *Journal of Experimental Psychology: Learning, Memory and Cognition* 21: 134–57.

—— and —— (1998). "Structural and lexical effects on filling gaps during sentence processing: A time-course analysis". *Journal of Experimental Psychology: Learning, Memory and Cognition* 24: 432–60.

—— and Nordlie, J. (1999). "Literal and figurative interpretations are computed in equal time". *Psychonomic Bulletin & Review* 6: 486–94.

—— Pylkkänen, L., Pickering, M.J., and Traxler, M. (2006). "A time course analysis of enriched composition". *Psychonomic Bulletin & Review* 13: 53–9.

McKinnon, R., Allen, M., and Osterhout, L. (2003). "Morphological decomposition involving non-productive morphemes: ERP evidence". *Neuroreport* 14: 883–6.

—— and Osterhout, L. (1996). "Constraints on movement phenomena in sentence processing: Evidence from event-related brain potentials". *Language and Cognitive Processes* 11: 495–523.

McQueen, J.M. (2007). "Eight questions about spoken word recognition", in M.G. Gaskell (ed.), *The Oxford handbook of psycholinguistics*. Oxford: Oxford University Press, 37–54.

McRae, K., Ferretti, T.R., and Amyote, L. (1997). "Thematic roles as verb-specific concepts". *Language and Cognitive Processes* 12: 137–76.

—— Spivey-Knowlton, M.J., and Tanenhaus, M.K. (1998). "Modeling the influence of thematic fit (and other constraints) in on-line sentence comprehension". *Journal of Memory and Language* 38: 282–312.

Mecklinger, A., Schriefers, H., Steinhauer, K., and Friederici, A.D. (1995). "Processing relative clauses varying on syntactic and semantic dimensions: An analysis with event-related potentials". *Memory and Cognition* 23: 477–94.

Mehler, J. (1963). "Some effects of grammatical transformations on the recall of English sentences". *Journal of Verbal Learning and Verbal Behavior* 2: 346–51.

Meng, M., Bader, M., and Bayer, J. (1999). "Die Verarbeitung von Subjekt-Objekt Ambiguitäten im Kontext" [= The processing of subject-object ambiguities in context], in I. Wachsmuth, and B. Jung (eds.), *Proceedings der 4. Fachtagung der Gesellschaft für Kognitionswissenschaften*. St. Augustin: Infix Verlag,

Miceli, G., Silveri, M., Nocentini, U., and Caramazza, A. (1988). "Patterns of dissociation in comprehension and production of nouns and verbs". *Aphasiology* 2: 351–8.

——— ——— Villa, G., and Caramazza, A. (1984). "On the basis of agrammatics' difficulty in producing main verbs". *Cortex* 20: 207–20.

Miller, G.A. (1962). "Some psychological studies of grammar". *American Psychologist* 17: 748–62.

—— and Chomsky, N. (1963). "Finitary models of language users", in R.D. Luce, R. Bush, and E. Galanter (eds.), *Handbook of mathematical psychology*. New York: Wiley.

—— and Isard, S. (1964). "Free recall of self-embedded English sentences". *Information and Control* 7: 292–303.

Miozzo, M. (2003). "On the processing of regular and irregular forms of verbs and nouns: Evidence from neuropsychology". *Cognition* 87: 101–27.

Mitchell, D.C. (1994). "Sentence parsing", in M.A. Gernsbacher (ed.), *Handbook of Psycholinguistics*. New York: Academic Press, 375–409.

—— and Brysbaert, M. (1998). "Challenges to recent theories of crosslinguistic variation in parsing: Evidence from Dutch", in D. Hillert (ed.), *Syntax and semantics: A crosslinguistic perspective*. San Diego, CA: Academic Press.

—— Cuetos, F., Corley, M.M.B., and Brysbaert, M. (1995). "Exposure-based models of human parsing: Evidence for the use of coarse-grained (non-lexical) statistical records". *Journal of Psycholinguistic Research* 24: 469–88.

Miyamoto, E.T., and Nakamura, M. (2003). "Subject/object asymmetries in the processing of relative clauses in Japanese", in G. Garding, and M. Tsujimura (eds.), *WCCFL 22: Proceedings of the 22nd West Coast Conference on Formal Linguistics*. Somerville, MA: Cascadilla Press, 342–55.

Mohanan, T. (1994). *Argument structure in Hindi*. Stanford, CA: CSLI Publications.

Molfese, D., Burger-Judisch, L.M., Gill, L.A., Golinkoff, R.M., and Hirsch-Pasek, K.A. (1996). "Electrophysiological correlates of noun-verb processing in adults". *Brain and Language* 54: 388–413.

Morris, J., and Holcomb, P. (2005). "Event-related potentials to violations of inflectional verb morphology in English". *Cognitive Brain Research* 25: 963–81.

Muckel, S. (2002). *Wortstellungseffekte beim Satzverstehen: Zur Rolle syntaktische, verbspezifischer und prosodischer Informationen [=Word order effects in sentence comprehension: On the role of syntactic, verb-specific and prosodic information]*. Wiesbaden: Deutscher Universitätsverlag.

Müller, G. (1999). "Optimality, markedness and word order in German". *Linguistics* 37: 777–818.

Müller, H.M., King, J.W., and Kutas, M. (1997). "Event-related potentials elicited by spoken relative clauses". *Cognitive Brain Research* 5: 193–203.

Müller, R.-A., Kleinhans, N., and Courchesne, E. (2003). "Linguistic theory and neuroimaging evidence: an fMRI study of Broca's area in lexical semantics". *Neuropsychologia* 41: 1199–207.

Münte, T.F., Matzke, M., and Johannes, S. (1997). "Brain activity associated with syntactic incongruencies in words and pseudo-words". *Journal of Cognitive Neuroscience* 9: 318–29.

—— Rodriguez-Fornells, A., and Kutas, M. (1999a). "One, two or many mechanisms? The brain's processing of complex words". *Behavioral and Brain Sciences* 22: 131–2.

—— Say, T., Clahsen, H., Schiltz, K., and Kutas, M. (1999c). "Decomposition of morphologically complex words in English: Evidence from event-related brain potentials". *Cognitive Brain Research* 7: 241–53.

—— Schiltz, K., and Kutas, M. (1998). "When temporal terms belie conceptual order". *Nature* 395: 71–3.

Myerson, R., and Goodglass, H. (1972). "Transformational grammar of three agrammatic patients". *Language and Speech* 15: 40–50.

Neville, H.J., Mills, D.L., and Lawson, D.S. (1992). "Fractionating language: Different neural subsystems with different sensitive periods". *Cerebral Cortex* 2: 244–58.

—— Nicol, J., Barss, A., Forster, K., and Garrett, M.F. (1991). "Syntactically based sentence processing classes: Evidence from event-related potentials". *Journal of Cognitive Neuroscience* 6: 233–55.

Nevins, A., Dillon, B., Malhotra, S., and Phillips, C. (2007). "The role of feature-number and feature-type in processing Hindi verb agreement violations". *Brain Research* 1164: 81–94.

Newman, A.J., Ullman, M.T., Pancheva, R., Waligura, D.L., and Neville, H.J. (2007). "An ERP study of regular and irregular English past tense inflection". *Neuroimage* 34: 435–45.

Newman, S.D., Just, M.A., Keller, T.A., Roth, J., and Carpenter, P.A. (2003). "Differential effects of syntactic and semantic processing on the subregions of Broca's area". *Cognitive Brain Research* 16: 297–307.

Nicol, J., and Swinney, D. (1989). "The role of structure in coreference assignment during sentence comprehension". *Journal of Psycholinguistic Research* 18: 5–20.

Nicol, J.L., Forster, K.I., and Veres, C. (1997). "Subject-verb agreement processes in comprehension". *Journal of Memory and Language* 36: 569–87.

Niedermeyer, E., and Lopes da Silva, F. (eds.) (2005). *Electroencephalography. Basic principles, clinical applications, and related fields*. Philadelphia, PA: Lippincott Williams & Wilkins.

Nieuwenhuis, S., Aston-Jones, G., and Cohen, J.D. (2005). "Decision making, the P3, and the locus coerulus-norepinephrine system". *Psychological Bulletin* 131: 510–32.

Nieuwland, M.S., and van Berkum, J.J.A. (2006). "When peanuts fall in love: N400 evidence for the power of discourse". *Journal of Cognitive Neuroscience* 18: 1098–111.

—— Petersson, K.M., and van Berkum, J.J.A. (2007). "On sense and reference: Examining the functional neuroanatomy of referential processing". *Neuroimage* 37: 993–1004.

Nobre, A.C., and McCarthy, G. (1994). "Language-related ERPs: scalp distributions and modulation by word type and semantic priming". *Journal of Cognitive Neuroscience* 6: 233–55.

Noppeney, U., and Price, C.J. (2004). "An fMRI study of syntactic adaption". *Journal of Cognitive Neuroscience* 16: 702–13.

Ogawa, S., Lee, T.M., Kay, A.R., and Tank, D.W. (1990a). "Brain magnetic resonance imaging with contrast dependent on blood oxygenation". *Proceedings of the National Academy of Sciences USA* 87: 9868–72.

—— —— Nayak, A.S., and Glynn, P. (1990b). "Oxygenation sensitive contrast in magnetic resonance image of rodent brain at high magnetic fields". *Magnetic Resonance in Medicine* 14: 68–78.

Opitz, B., and Friederici, A.D. (2003). "Interactions of the hippocampal system and the prefrontal cortex in learning language-like rules". *Neuroimage* 19.

—— and —— (2004). "Brain correlates of language learning: The neuronal dissociation of rule-based versus similarity-based learning". *The Journal of Neuroscience* 24: 8436–40.

Osterhout, L. (1997). "On the brain response to syntactic anomalies: Manipulations of word position and word class reveal individual differences". *Brain and Language* 59: 494–522.

—— Bersick, M., and McLaughlin, J. (1997). "Brain potentials reflext violations of gender stereotypes". *Memory and Cognition* 25: 273–85.

—— and Hagoort, P. (1999). "A superficial resemblance does not necessarily mean you are part of the family: Counterarguments to Coulson, King and Kutas (1998) in the P600/SPS-P300 debate". *Language and Cognitive Processes* 14: 1–14.

Osterhout, L., and Holcomb, P. (1992). "Event-related brain potentials elicited by syntactic anomaly". *Journal of Memory and Language* 31: 785–806.

—— and —— (1993). "Event-related potentials and syntactic anomaly: Evidence of anomaly detection during the perception of continuous speech". *Language and Cognitive Processes* 8: 413–37.

—— —— and Swinney, D. (1994). "Brain potentials elicited by garden path sentences: Evidence of the application of verb information during parsing". *Journal of Experimental Psychology: Learning, Memory and Cognition* 20: 786–803.

—— McKinnon, R., Bersick, M., and Corey, V. (1996). "On the language specificity of the brain response to syntactic anomalies: Is the syntactic positive shift a member of the P300 family?". *Journal of Cognitive Neuroscience* 8: 507–26.

—— and Mobley, L.A. (1995). "Event-related brain potentials elicited by failure to agree". *Journal of Memory and Language* 34: 739–73.

—— and Nicol, J. (1999). "On the distinctiveness, independence, and time course of the brain response to syntactic and semantic anomalies". *Language and Cognitive Processes* 14: 283–317.

Ott, M. (2004). *Verarbeitung von variierenden Animatheitsmerkmalen: Eine Studie zum Animatheitseinfluss bei nicht ambig kasusmarkierten W-Fragen im Deutschen.* MA thesis, University of Potsdam.

Paavilainen, P., Simola, J., Jaramillo, M., Näätänen, R., and Winkler, I. (2001). "Preattentive extraction of abstract feature conjunctions from auditory stimulation as reflected by the mismatch negativity (MMN)". *Psychophysiology* 38: 359–65.

Pannekamp, A., Toepel, U., Alter, K., Hahne, A., and Friederici, A.D. (2005). "Prosody-driven sentence processing: An event-related brain potential study". *Journal of Cognitive Neuroscience* 17: 407–21.

Pascual-Leone, A., Walsh, V., and Rothwell, J. (2000). "Transcranial magnetic stimulation in cognitive neuroscience – virtual lesion, chronometry, and functional connectivity". *Current Opinion in Neurobiology* 10: 232–7.

Patel, A.D., Gibson, E., Ratner, J., Besson, M., and Holcomb, P. (1998). "Processing syntactic relations in language and music: An event-related potential study". *Journal of Cognitive Neuroscience* 10: 717–33.

Pearlmutter, N.J. (2000). "Linear versus hierarchical agreement feature processing in comprehension". *Journal of Psycholinguistic Research* 29: 89–98.

—— Garnsey, S.M., and Bock, K. (1999). "Agreement processes in sentence comprehension". *Journal of Memory and Language* 11: 427–56.

Penke, M., Weyerts, H., Gross, M., Zander, E., Münte, T.F., and Clahsen, H. (1997). "How the brain processes complex words: An event-related potential study of German verb inflections". *Cognitive Brain Research* 6: 37–52.

Penolazzi, B., de Vincenzi, M., Angrilli, A., and Job, R. (2005). "Processing of temporary syntactic ambiguity in Italian 'who'-questions: A study with event-related potentials". *Neuroscience Letters* 377: 91–6.

Perani, D., Cappa, S.F., Schnur, T., Tettamanti, M., Collina, S., Rosa, M., and Fazio, F. (1999). "The neural correlates of verb and noun processing – A PET study". *Brain* 122: 2337–44.

Pesetsky, D. (1994). *Zero syntax*. Cambridge, MA: MIT Press.

Philipp, M., Bornkessel-Schlesewsky, I., Bisang, W., and Schlesewsky, M. (2008). "The role of animacy in the real time comprehension of Mandarin Chinese: Evidence from auditory event-related brain potentials". *Brain and Language* 105: 112–33.

Phillips, C., and Wagers, M. (2007). "Relating structure and time in linguistics and psycholinguistics", in M.G. Gaskell (ed.), *Oxford handbook of psycholinguistics*. Oxford: Oxford University Press, 739–56.

—— Kazanina, N., and Abada, S.H. (2005). "ERP effects of the processing of syntactic long-distance dependencies". *Cognitive Brain Research* 22: 407–28.

Pickering, M.J., and Barry, G. (1991). "Sentence processing without empty categories". *Language and Cognitive Processes* 6: 229–59.

—— Traxler, M., and Crocker, M.W. (2000). "Ambiguity resolution in sentence processing: Evidence against frequency-based accounts". *Journal of Memory and Language* 43: 447–75.

Piñango, M. (2000). "Syntactic displacement in Broca's aphasia comprehension", in R. Bastiaanse, and Y. Grodzinsky (eds.), *Grammatical disorders in aphasia: A neurolinguistic perspective*. London: Whurr, 75–87.

Piñango, M.M. (2006). "Thematic roles as event structure relations", in I. Bornkessel, M. Schlesewsky, B. Comrie, and A.D. Friederici (eds.), *Semantic role universals: Theoretical, typological and psycholinguistic perspectives*. Berlin: Mouton de Gruyter, 303–26.

Pinker, S. (1984). *Language learnability and language development*. Cambridge, MA: Harvard University Press.

—— (1991). "Rules of language". *Science* 253: 530–5.

—— and Prince, A. (1988). "On language and connectionism: Analysis of a parallel distributed processing model of language acquisition". *Cognition* 28: 73–193.

—— and Ullman, M.T. (2002a). "Combination and structure, not gradedness, is the issue. Reply to McClelland and Patterson". *Trends in Cognitive Sciences* 6: 472–4.

—— and —— (2002b). "The past and future of the past tense". *Trends in Cognitive Sciences* 6: 456–63.

Plunkett, K., and Marchman, V. (1993). "From rote learning to system building: Acquiring verb morphology in children and connectionist nets". *Cognition* 48: 21–69.

Poeppel, D. (2003). "The analysis of speech in different temporal integration windows: Cerebral lateralizations as 'asymmetric sampling in time'". *Speech Communication* 41: 245–55.

Polich, J. (1985). "Semantic categorization and event-related potentials". *Brain and Language* 26: 304–21.

—— (2004). "Neuropsychology of the P3a and P3b: A theoretical overview", in C. Moore, and K. Arikan (eds.), *Brainwaves and mind: Recent developments*. Wheaton, IL: Kjelberg Inc, 15–29.

Pollard, C., and Sag, I. (1994). *Head-driven phrase structure grammar*. Chicago: University of Chicago Press.

Prasada, S., and Pinker, S. (1993). "Generalization of regular and irregular morphological patterns". *Language and Cognitive Processes* 8: 1–56.

Preissl, H., Pulvermüller, F., Lutzenberger, W., and Birbaumer, N. (1995). "Evoked potentials distinguish nouns from verbs". *Neuroscience Letters* 197: 81–3.

Primus, B. (1999). *Cases and thematic roles*. Tübingen: Niemeyer.

—— (2006). "Mismatches in semantic-role hierarchies and the dimensions of role semantics", in I. Bornkessel, M. Schlesewsky, B. Comrie, and A.D. Friederici (eds.), *Semantic role universals and argument linking: Theoretical, typological and psycholinguistic approaches*. Berlin: Mouton de Gruyter, 53–87.

Prince, A., and Smolensky, P. (1997). "Optimality: From neural networks to universal grammar". *Science* 275: 1604–10.

Pritchett, B.L. (1988). "Garden path phenomena and the grammatical basis of language processing". *Language* 64: 539–76.

—— (1992). *Grammatical competence and parsing performance*. Chicago: University of Chicago Press.

Pulvermüller, F. (1999). "Words in the brain's language". *Behavioral and Brain Sciences* 22: 253–336.

—— (2005). "Brain mechanisms linking language and action". *Nature Reviews Neuroscience* 6: 576–82.

—— Lutzenberger, W., and Birbaumer, N. (1995). "Electrocortical distinction of vocabulary types". *Electroencephalography and Clinical Neurophysiology* 94: 357–70.

—— —— and Preissl, H. (1999). "Nouns and verbs in the intact brain: Evidence from event-related potentials and high-frequency cortical responses". *Cerebral Cortex* 9: 497–506.

—— Preissl, H., Lutzenberger, W., and Birbaumer, N. (1996). "Brain rhythms of language: Nouns versus verbs". *European Journal of Neuroscience* 8: 937–41.

—— and Shtyrov, Y. (2003). "Automatic processing of grammar in the human brain as revealed by the mismatch negativity". *NeuroImage* 20: 159–72.

—— Shtyrov, Y., Hasting, A.S., and Carlyon, R.P. (2008). "Syntax as a reflex: Neurophysiological evidence for early automaticity of grammatical processing". *Brain and Language* 104: 244–53.

Pustejovsky, J. (1995). *The generative lexicon*. Cambridge, MA: MIT Press.

Pylkkänen, L., and McElree, B. (2006). "The syntax-semantics interface: On-line composition of sentence meaning", in M. Traxler, and M.A. Gernsbacher (eds.), *Handbook of psycholinguistics*. London: Elsevier, 539–80.

—— and —— (2007). "An MEG study of silent meaning". *Journal of Cognitive Neuroscience* 19: 1,905–21.

Rastle, K., Davis, M.H., Marslen-Wilson, W., and Tyler, L.K. (2000). "Morphological and semantic effects in visual word recognition: A time-course study". *Language and Cognitive Processes* 15: 507–37.

Rayner, K. (1998). "Eye movements in reading and information processing: 20 years of research". *Psychological Bulletin* 124: 372–422.

—— Carlson, G., and Frazier, L. (1983). "The interaction of syntax and semantics during sentence processing: Eye movements in the analysis of semantically biased sentences". *Journal of Verbal Learning and Verbal Behavior* 22: 657–73.

Reed, A. (1973). "Speed-accuracy trade-off in recognition memory". *Science* 181: 574–6.

Reichle, E.D., Rayner, K., and Pollatsek, A. (1998). "Toward a model of eye movement control in reading". *Psychological Review* 105: 125–57.

—— —— and —— (2003). "The E-Z Reader model of eye-movement control in reading: Comparisons to other models". *Behavioral and Brain Sciences* 26: 445–526.

Reilly, R., and Radach, R. (2003). "Foundations of an interactive activation model of eye movement control in reading", in J. Hyönä, R. Radach, and H. Deubel (eds.), *The mind's eye: Cognitive and applied aspects of eye movements*.

Reinhart, T. (1983). *Anaphora and semantic interpretation*. London: Croom Helm.

Rizzi, L. (1982). *Issues in Italian syntax*. Dordrecht: Foris.

Rizzolatti, G., and Arbib, M.A. (1998). "Language within our grasp". *Trends in Neurosciences* 21: 188–94.

—— Fogassi, L., and Gallese, V. (2002). "Motor and cognitive functions of the ventral premotor cortex". *Current Opinion in Neurobiology* 12: 149–54.

Röder, B., Stock, O., Neville, H., Bien, S., and Rösler, F. (2002). "Brain activation modulated by the comprehension of normal and pseudo-word sentences of different processing demands: A functional magnetic resonance imaging study". *Neuroimage* 15: 1003–14.

Rodriguez-Fornells, A., Clahsen, H., Lleó, C., Zaake, W., and Münte, T.F. (2001). "Event-related brain responses to morphological violations in Catalan". *Cognitive Brain Research* 11: 47–58.

—— Münte, T.F., and Clahsen, H. (2002). "Morphological priming in Spanish verb forms: An ERP repetition priming study". *Journal of Cognitive Neuroscience* 14: 443–54.

Roehm, D., Bornkessel-Schlesewsky, I., Rösler, F., and Schlesewsky, M. (2007a). "To predict or not to predict: Influences of task and strategy on the processing of semantic relations". *Journal of Cognitive Neuroscience* 19: 1259–74.

Roehm, D., Bornkessel-Schlesewsky, I., and Schlesewsky, M. (2007b). "The internal structure of the N400: Frequency characteristics of a language-related ERP component". *Chaos and Complexity Letters* 2: 365–95.

—— Bornkessel, I., Haider, H., and Schlesewsky, M. (2005). "When case meets agreement: Event-related potential effects for morphology-based conflict resolution in human language comprehension". *Neuroreport* 16: 875–8.

—— Schlesewsky, M., Bornkessel, I., Frisch, S., and Haider, H. (2004). "Fractionating language comprehension via frequency characteristics of the human EEG". *Neuroreport* 15: 409–12.

Roll, M., Horne, M., and Lindgren, M. (2007). "Object-shift and event-related brain potentials". *Journal of Neurolinguistics* 20: 462–81.

Rösler, F., Friederici, A.D., Pütz, P., and Hahne, A. (1993). "Event-related brain potentials while encountering semantic and syntactic constraint violations". *Journal of Cognitive Neuroscience* 5: 345–62.

—— Pechmann, T., Streb, J., Röder, B., and Hennighausen, E. (1998). "Parsing of sentences in a language with varying word order: Word-by-word variations of processing demands are revealed by event-related brain potentials". *Journal of Memory and Language* 38: 150–76.

Ross, J.R. (1967). *Constraints on variables in syntax*. Ph.D. thesis, MIT.

Rossi, S., Gugler, M.F., Hahne, A., and Friederici, A.D. (2005). "When word category information encounters morphosyntax: An ERP study". *Neuroscience Letters* 384: 228–33.

Rubin, G.S., Becker, C.A., and Freeman, R.H. (1979). "Morphological structure and its effects on visual word recognition". *Journal of Verbal Learning and Verbal Behavior* 8: 399–412.

Rugg, M.D. (1985). "The effects of semantic priming and word repetition on event-related potentials". *Psychophysiology* 22: 642–7.

—— (1990). "Event-related brain potentials dissociate repetition effects of high- and low-frequency words". *Memory and Cognition* 18: 367–79.

Rumelhart, D.E., and McClelland, J.L. (1986). "On learning the past tenses of English verbs", in J.L. McClelland, and D.E. Rumelhart (eds.), *Parallel distributed processing (Vol. 2): Psychological and biological models*. Cambridge, MA: MIT Press, 216–71.

Sach, M., Seitz, R., and Indefrey, P. (2004). "Unified inflectional processing of regular and irregular verbs: a PET study". *Neuroreport* 15: 533–7.

Saddy, D., Drenhaus, H., and Frisch, S. (2004). "Processing polarity items: Contrastive licensing costs". *Brain and Language* 90: 495–502.

Sahin, N.T., Pinker, S., and Halgren, E. (2006). "Abstract grammatical processing of nouns and verbs in Broca's area: Evidence from fMRI". *Cortex* 42: 540–62.

Samar, V.J., and Berent, G.P. (1986). "The syntactic priming effect: Evoked response evidence for a prelexical locus". *Brain and Language* 28: 250–72.

Santi, A., and Grodzinsky, Y. (2007a). "Taxing working memory with syntax: Bihemispheric modulations". *Human Brain Mapping* 28: 1,089–97.

—— and —— (2007b). "Working memory and syntax interact in Broca's area". *NeuroImage* 37: 8–17.

Scheepers, C., Hemforth, B., and Konieczny, L. (1998). "Case assignment preferences in processing German object-object ambiguities". *11th Annual CUNY Conference on Human Sentence Processing*.

—— —— and —— (2000). "Linking syntactic functions with thematic roles: Psych-verbs and the resolution of subject-object ambiguity", in B. Hemforth, and L. Konieczny (eds.), *German sentence processing*. Dordrecht: Kluwer, 95–135.

Schlesewsky, M. (1997). *Kasusphänomene in der Sprachverarbeitung. Eine Studie zur Verarbeitung von kasusmarkierten und Relativsatzkonstruktionen im Deutschen*. Ph.D. thesis, University of Potsdam.

—— and Bornkessel, I. (2003). "Ungrammaticality detection and garden path strength: A commentary on Meng and Bader's (2000) evidence for serial parsing". *Language and Cognitive Processes* 18: 299–311.

—— and —— (2004). "On incremental interpretation: Degrees of meaning accessed during sentence comprehension". *Lingua* 114: 1213–34.

—— and —— (2006). "Context-sensitive neural responses to conflict resolution: Electrophysiological evidence from subject-object ambiguities in language comprehension". *Brain Research* 1098: 139–52.

—— —— and Frisch, S. (2003). "The neurophysiological basis of word order variations in German". *Brain and Language* 86: 116–28.

—— —— and Meyer, M. (2002). "Why a 'word order difference' is not always a 'word order' difference: A reply to Weyerts, Penke, Münte, Heinze, and Clahsen". *Journal of Psycholinguistic Research* 31: 437–45.

—— Fanselow, G., Kliegl, R., and Krems, J. (2000). "The subject preference in the processing of locally ambiguous wh-questions in German", in B. Hemforth, and L. Konieczny (eds.), *German sentence processing*. Dordrecht: Kluwer, 65–93.

Schmitt, B.M., Lamers, M.A.J., and Münte, T.F. (2002). "Electrophysiological estimates of biological and syntactic gender violation during pronoun processing". *Cognitive Brain Research* 14: 333–46.

Schriefers, H., Friederici, A.D., and Kühn, K. (1995). "The processing of locally ambiguous relative clauses in German". *Journal of Memory and Language* 34: 499–520.

Schubotz, R.I., and von Cramon, D.Y. (2001). "Interval and ordinal properties of sequences are associated with distinct premotor areas". *Cerebral Cortex* 11: 210–22.

Schütze, C.T. (1996). *The empirical base of linguistics: Grammaticality judgments and linguistic methodology*. Chicago: University of Chicago Press.

—— and Gibson, E. (1999). "Argumenthood and English prepositional phrase attachment". *Journal of Memory and Language* 40: 409–31.

Schwartz, B.D., and Vikner, S. (1996). "The verb always leaves IP in V2 clauses", in A. Belletti, and L. Rizzi (eds.), *Parameters and functional heads. Essays in comparative syntax*. New York/Oxford: Oxford University Press, 11–62.

Seidenberg, M.S., and Arnoldussen, A. (2003). "The brain makes a distinction between hard and easy stimuli: Comments on Beretta et al". *Brain and Language* 85: 527–30.

—— and Gonnerman, L.M. (2000). "Explaining derivational morphology as the convergence of codes". *Trends in Cognitive Sciences* 4: 353–61.

—— and Hoeffner, J.H. (1998). "Evaluating behavioral and neuroimaging data on past tense processing". *Language* 74: 104–22.

Sereno, S.C., and Rayner, K. (2003). "Measuring word recognition in reading: Eye movements and event-related potentials". *Trends in Cognitive Sciences* 7: 489–93.

Shapiro, K., Pascual-Leone, A., Mottaghy, F., Gangitano, M., and Caramazza, A. (2001). "Grammatical distinctions in the left frontal cortex". *Journal of Cognitive Neuroscience* 13: 713–20.

Shapiro, K.A., Moo, L.R., and Caramazza, A. (2006). "Cortical signatures of noun and verb production". *Proceedings of the National Academy of Sciences* 103: 1644–9.

—— Mottaghy, F.M., Schiller, N.O., Poeppel, T.D., Flüß, M.O., Müller, H.-W., and Caramazza, A. (2005). "Dissociating neural correlates for nouns and verbs". *NeuroImage* 24: 1058–67.

Sheldon, A. (1974). "The role of parallel function in the acquisition of relative clauses in English". *Journal of Verbal Learning and Verbal Behavior* 13: 272–81.

Siwierska, A. (1988). *Word order rules*. London: Croom Helm.

Slowiaczek, M.L., and Clifton, C., Jr. (1980). "Subvocalization and reading for meaning". *Journal of Verbal Learning and Verbal Behavior* 19: 573–82.

Spencer, A. (1991). *Morphological theory*. Oxford: Basil Blackwell Ltd.

Squire, L.R., and Zola, S.M. (1996). "Structure and function of declarative and nondeclarative memory systems". *Proceedings of the National Academy of Sciences USA* 93: 13515–22.

Stabler, E. (1994). "The finite connectivity of linguistic structure", in C. Clifton, Jr., L. Frazier, and K. Rayner (eds.), *Perspectives on sentence processing*. Hillsdale: Erlbaum, 303–36.

Stanners, R., Neiser, J., Hernon, W., and Hall, R. (1979). "Memory representation for morphologically related words". *Journal of Verbal Learning and Verbal Behavior* 18: 399–412.

Staub, A., and Rayner, K. (2007). "Eye movements and on-line comprehension processes", in M.G. Gaskell (ed.), *The Oxford handbook of psycholinguistics*. Oxford: Oxford University Press, 327–42.

Steinhauer, K., Alter, K., and Friederici, A.D. (1999). "Brain potentials indicate immediate use of prosodic cues in natural speech processing". *Nature Neuroscience* 2: 191–6.

—— and Friederici, A.D. (2001). "Prosodic boundaris, comma rules, and brain responses: The closure positive shift in ERPs as a universal marker for prosodic phrasing in listeners and readers". *Journal of Psycholinguistic Research* 30: 267–95.

—— Mecklinger, A., Friederici, A.D., and Meyer, M. (1997). "Wahrscheinlichkeit und Strategie: Eine EKP-Studie zur Verarbeitung syntaktischer Anomalien". *Zeitschrift für Experimentelle Psychologie* XLIV: 305–31.

Stemberger, J.P. (1994). "Rule-less morphology at the phonology-lexicon interface", in S.D. Lima, R.L. Corrigan, and G.K. Iverson (eds.), *The reality of linguistic rules*. Amsterdam: John Benjamins, 147–69.

Stevenson, S., and Smolensky, P. (2006). "Optimality in sentence processing", in P. Smolensky, and G. Legendre (eds.), *The harmonic mind: From neural computation to optimality-theoretic grammar. Volume II: Linguistic and philosophical implications*. Cambridge, MA: MIT Press, 307–38.

Stolterfoht, B., and Bader, M. (eds.) (2004). "Focus structure and the processing of word order variations in German", *Information structure: Theoretical and empirical aspects*. Berlin: Walter de Gruyter, 259–75.

—— Friederici, A.D., Alter, K., and Steube, A. (2007). "Processing focus structure and implicit prosody during reading: Differential ERP effects". *Cognition* 104: 565–90.

Stowe, L.A. (1986). "Parsing wh-constructions: Evidence for on-line gap location". *Language and Cognitive Processes* 1: 227–45.

—— Broere, C., Paans, A., Wijers, A., Mulder, G., Vaalburg, W., and Zwarts, F. (1998). "Localising components of a complex task: Sentence processing and working memory". *Neuroreport* 9: 2995–9.

Streb, J., Hennighausen, E., and Rösler, F. (2004). "Differential anaphoric expressions are investigated by event-related brain potentials". *Journal of Psycholinguistic Research* 33: 175–201.

—— Rösler, F., and Hennighausen, E. (1999). "Event-related responses to pronouns and proper name anaphors in parallel and non-parallel discourse structures". *Brain and Language* 70: 273–86.

Strelnikov, K.N., Vorobyev, V.A., Chernigovskaya, T.V., and Medvedev, S.V. (2006). "Prosodic clues to syntactic processing – a PET and ERP study". *Neuroimage* 29: 1127–34.

Stromswold, K., Caplan, D., Alpert, N., and Rauch, S. (1996). "Localization of syntactic comprehension by positron emission tomography". *Brain and Language* 52: 452–73.

Sturt, P., and Crocker, M.W. (1996). "Monotonic syntactic processing: A cross-linguistic study of attachment and reanalysis". *Language and Cognitive Processes* 11: 449–94.

Sutton, S., Baren, M., Zubin, J., and John, E.R. (1965). "Information delivery and the sensory evoked potential". *Science* 150: 1187–8.

Swaab, T.Y., Camblin, C.C., and Gordon, P.C. (2004). "Electrophysiological evidence for reversed lexical repetition effects in language processing". *Journal of Cognitive Neuroscience* 16: 715–26.

Tabor, W., Juliano, C., and Tanenhaus, M.K. (1997). "Parsing in a dynamical system: An attractor-based account of the interaction of lexical and structural constraints in sentence processing". *Language and Cognitive Processes* 12: 211–71.

Taft, M., and Forster, K.I. (1975). "Lexical storage and retrieval of prefixed words". *Journal of Verbal Learning and Verbal Behavior* 14: 638–47.

Tanenhaus, M.K., Boland, J., Garnsey, S.M., and Carlson, G. (1989). "Lexical structure in parsing long-distance dependencies". *Journal of Psycholinguistic Research* 18: 37–50.

—— Spivey-Knowlton, M.J., Eberhard, K.M., and Sedivy, J.C. (1995). "Integration of visual and linguistic information in spoken language comprehension". *Science* 268: 1632–4.

Thompson-Schill, S.L., Bedny, M., and Goldberg, R.F. (2005). "The frontal lobes and the regulation of mental activity". *Current Opinion in Neurobiology* 15: 219–24.

—— D'Esposito, M., Aguirre, G.K., and Farah, M.J. (1997). "Role of left inferior prefrontal cortex in retrieval of semantic knowledge: a reevaluation". *Proceedings of the National Academy of Sciences USA* 94: 14792–7.

Toepel, U., and Alter, K. (2004). "On the independence of information structural processing from prosody", in A. Steube (ed.), *Information structure: Theoretical and empirical aspects*. Berlin: Walter de Gruyter, 227–40.

Travis, L. (1984). *Parameters and effects of word order variation*. Ph.D. thesis, MIT.

Traxler, M., Morris, R.K., and Seely, R.E. (2002). "Processing subject and object relative clauses: Evidence from eye movements". *Journal of Memory and Language* 47: 69–90.

—— and Pickering, M.J. (1996). "Plausibility and the processing of unbounded dependencies: An eye-tracking study". *Journal of Memory and Language* 35: 454–75.

—— —— and Clifton, C., Jr. (1998). "Adjunct attachment is not a form of lexical ambiguity resolution". *Journal of Memory and Language* 39: 558–92.

—— Williams, R.S., Blozis, S.A., and Morris, R.K. (2005). "Working memory, animacy, and verb class in the processing of relative clauses". *Journal of Memory and Language* 53: 204–24.

Trueswell, J.C., and Tanenhaus, M.K. (1994). "Toward a lexicalist framework for constraint-based syntactic ambiguity resolution", in C. Clifton, Jr., L. Frazier, and K. Rayner (eds.), *Perspectives in sentence processing*. Hillsdale, NJ: Erlbaum.

—— —— and Garnsey, S.M. (1994). "Semantic influences on parsing: Use of thematic role information in syntactic disambiguation". *Journal of Memory and Language* 33: 285–318.

—— —— and Kello, C. (1993). "Verb-specific constraints in sentence processing: Separating effects of lexical preference from garden-paths". *Journal of Experimental Psychology: Learning, Memory and Cognition* 19: 528–53.

Tyler, L.K., Bright, P., Fletcher, P., and Stamatakis, E.A. (2004a). "Neural processing of nouns and verbs: The role of inflectional morphology". *Neuropsychologia* 42: 512–23.

—— de Mornay-Davies, P., Anokhina, R., Longworth, C., Randall, B., and Marslen-Wilson, W. (2002a). "Dissociations in processing past tense morphology: Neuropathology and behavioral studies". *Journal of Cognitive Neuroscience* 14: 79–94.

—— Moss, H.E., and Jennings, F. (1995). "Abstract word deficit in aphasia: Evidence from semantic priming". *Neuropsychology* 9: 354–63.

—— Randall, B., and Marslen-Wilson, W.D. (2002b). "Phonology and neuropsychology of the English past tense". *Neuropsychologia* 40: 1154–66.

—— Russell, R., Fadili, J., and Moss, H. (2001). "The neural representation of nouns and verbs: PET studies". *Brain* 124: 1619–34.

—— Stamatakis, E.A., Post, B., Randall, B., and Marslen-Wilson, W. (2005). "Temporal and frontal systems in speech comprehension: An fMRI study of past tense processing". *Neuropsychologia* 43: 1963–74.

—— —— Jones, R.W., Bright, P., Acres, K., and Marslen-Wilson, W. (2004b). "Deficits for semantics and the irregular past tense: A causal relationship?". *Journal of Cognitive Neuroscience* 16: 1159–72.

Ueno, M., and Kluender, R. (2003). "Event-related indices of Japanese scrambling". *Brain and Language* 86: 243–71.

Ullman, M.T. (2001). "A neurocognitive perspective on language: The declarative/procedural model". *Nature Reviews Neuroscience* 2: 717–26.

—— (2004). "Contributions of memory circuits to language: The declarative/procedural model". *Cognition* 92: 231–70.

—— Bergida, R., and O'Craven, K. (1997a). "Distinct fMRI activation patterns for regular and irregular past tense". *Neuroimage* 5: S549.

—— Corkin, S., Coppola, M., Hickok, G., Growdon, J.H., Koroshetz, W.J., and Pinker, S. (1997c). "A neural dissociation within language: Evidence that the mental dictionary is part of declarative memory and that grammatical rules are processed by the procedural system". *Journal of Cognitive Neuroscience* 9: 266–76.

van Berkum, J.J.A., Brown, C.M., and Hagoort, P. (1999). "Early referential context effects in sentence processing: Evidence from event-related brain potentials". *Journal of Memory and Language* 41: 147–82.

van den Brink, D., and Hagoort, P. (2004). "The influence of semantic and syntactic context constraints on lexical selection and integration in spoken-word comprehension as revealed by ERPs". *Journal of Cognitive Neuroscience* 16: 1068–84.

Van Dyke, J.A., and McElree, B. (2006). "Retrieval interference in sentence comprehension". *Journal of Memory and Language* 55: 157–66.

van Gompel, R.P.G., Pickering, M.J., Pearson, J., and Liversedge, S.P. (2005). "Evidence against competition during syntactic ambiguity resolution". *Journal of Memory and Language* 52: 284–307.

—— —— and Traxler, M.J. (2001). "Reanalysis in sentence processing: Evidence against current constraint-based and two-stage models". *Journal of Memory and Language* 45: 225–58.

van Herten, M., Chwilla, D.J., and Kolk, H.H.J. (2006). "When heuristics clash with parsing routines: ERP evidence for conflict monitoring in sentence perception". *Journal of Cognitive Neuroscience* 18: 1181–97.

—— Kolk, H.H.J., and Chwilla, D.J. (2005). "An ERP study of P600 effects elicited by semantic anomalies". *Cognitive Brain Research* 22: 241–55.

Van Petten, C., Kutas, M., Kluender, R., Mitchiner, M., and McIsaac, H. (1991). "Fractionating the word repetition effect with event-related brain potentials". *Journal of Cognitive Neuroscience* 3: 131–50.

Van Valin, R.D., Jr. (1977). *Aspects of Lakhota syntax.* Ph.D. thesis, University of California at Berkeley.

—— (2005). *Exploring the Syntax-Semantics Interface.* Cambridge: Cambridge University Press.

—— (2008). "RPs and the nature of lexical and syntactic categories in RRG", in R.D. Van Valin, Jr. (ed.), *Investigations of the Syntax-Semantics-Pragmatics Interface.* Amsterdam: John Benjamins, 161–78.

Vannest, J., Bertram, R., Järvikivi, J., and Niemi, J. (2002). "Counter-intuitive cross-linguistic difference: More morphological computation on English than in Finnish". *Journal of Psycholinguistic Research* 31: 83–106.

—— and Boland, J. (1999). "Lexical morphology and lexical access". *Brain and Language* 68: 324–32.

—— Polk, T.A., and Lewis, R.L. (2005). "Dual-route processing of complex words: New fMRI evidence from derivational suffixation". *Cognitive, Affective and Behavioral Neuroscience* 5: 67–76.

Vigliocco, G., and Nicol, J. (1998). "Separating hierarchical relations and word order in language production: Is proximity concord syntactic or linear?". *Cognition* 68: B13–B29.

Villardita, C., Grioli, M., and Quattropani, M.C. (1988). "Concreteness/abstractness of stimulus-words and semantic clustering in right brain-damaged patients". *Cortex* 24: 563–71.

Vissers, C.T.W.M., Chwilla, D.J., and Kolk, H.H.J. (2006). "Monitoring in language perception: The effect of misspellings of words in highly constrained sentences". *Brain Research* 1106: 150–63.

—— Kolk, H.H.J., van de Meerendonk, N., and Chwilla, D.J. (2008). "Monitoring in language perception: Evidence from ERPs in a picture-sentence matching task". *Neuropsychologia* 46: 967–82.

Vos, S.H., Gunter, T.C., Schriefers, H., and Friederici, A.D. (2001). "Syntactic parsing and working memory: The effects of syntactic complexity, reading span and concurrent load". *Language and Cognitive Processes* 16: 65–103.

Vosse, T., and Kempen, G.A.M. (2000). "Syntactic assembly in human parsing: A computational model based on competitive inhibition and lexicalist grammar". *Cognition* 75: 105–43.

Walsh, V., and Cowey, A. (2000). "Transcranial magnetic stimulation and cognitive neuroscience". *Nature Reviews Neuroscience* 1: 73–9.

Wanner, E., and Maratsos, M. (1978). "An ATN approach to comprehension", in M. Halle, J. Bresnan, and G.A. Miller (eds.), *Linguistic theory and psychological reality*. Cambridge, MA: MIT Press, 119–61.

Warburton, E., Wise, R., Price, C.J., Weiller, C., Hadar, U., and Ramsay, S. (1996). "Noun and verb retrieval by normal subjects. Studies with PET". *Brain* 119: 159–79.

Warrington, E.K., and McCarthy, R.A. (1987). "Categories of knowledge: Further fractionations and an attempted integration". *Brain* 110: 1273–96.

—— and Shallice, T. (1984). "Category specific semantic impairments". *Brain* 107: 829–53.

Waters, G., and Caplan, D. (1996). "The measurement of verbal working memory capacity and its relation to reading comprehension". *The Quarterly Journal of Experimental Psychology* 49A: 51–79.

—— Caplan, D., Alpert, N., and Stanczak, L. (2003). "Individual differences in rCBF correlates of syntactic processing in sentence comprehension: Effects of working memory and speed of processing". *Neuroimage* 19: 101–12.

Weckerly, J., and Kutas, M. (1999). "An electrophysiological analysis of animacy effects in the processing of object relative sentences". *Psychophysiology* 36: 559–70.

Weyerts, H., Münte, T.F., Smid, H.G.O.M., and Heinze, H.-J. (1996). "Mental representation of morphologically complex words: An event-related potential study with adult humans". *Neuroscience Letters* 206: 125–8.

—— Penke, M., Dohrm, U., Clahsen, H., and Münte, T.F. (1997). "Brain potentials indicate differences between regular and irregular German plurals". *Neuroreport* 8: 957–62.

Wickelgren, W.A. (1977). "Speed-accuracy tradeoff and information process-ing dynamics". *Acta Psychologica* 41: 67–85.

Wiese, R. (1996). *The phonology of German.* Oxford: Oxford University Press.

—— (1999). "On default rules and other rules". *Behavioral and Brain Sciences* 22: 1043–4.

Wolff, S., Schlesewsky, M., and Bornkessel-Schlesewsky, I. (2007). "The inter-action of universal and language-specific properties in the neurocognition of language comprehension: Evidence from the processing of word order permutations in Japanese". *Journal of Cognitive Neuroscience, Supplement.*

—— —— Hirotani, M., and Bornkessel-Schlesewsky, I. (2008). "The neural mechanisms of word order processing revisited: Electrophysiological evi-dence from Japanese". *Brain and Language* 107: 133–57.

Wunderlich, D. (1997). "Cause and the structure of verbs". *Linguistic Inquiry* 28: 27–68.

Ye, Z., Zhan, W., and Zhou, X. (2007). "The semantic processing of syntactic structure in sentence comprehension: An ERP study". *Brain Research* 1142: 135–45.

Zingeser, L., and Berndt, R.S. (1990). "Retrieval of nouns and verbs by agrammatic and anomic aphasics". *Brain and Language* 39: 14–32.

Zurif, E.B. (1995). "Brain regions of relevance to syntactic processing", in L.R. Gleitman, D.N. Osherson, and M. Liberman (eds.), *An invitation to cognitive science: Language.* Cambridge, MA: MIT Press, 381–98.

Zwart, J.-W. (1997). *The morphosyntax of verb movement: A minimalist approach to the syntax of Dutch.* Dordrecht: Kluwer Academic Publishers.

Author Index

Abada 181, 202
Abney 103, 127, 210
Aissen 185
Allen 59, 69
Alpert 194
Alter 238, 240–242, 252–255, 259, 273, 286
Altmann 96, 213, 262
Amayote 140
Arbib 274, 300
Arnoldussen 52, 81
Aston-Jones 227
Augurzky 209, 214, 216–17, 244–5

Baayen 73, 78
Bader 127, 130–1, 163, 169, 177, 270
Bahlmann 151–2, 182, 185
Bai 73
Barber 121, 214
Barber 74
Bard 26
Barry 175
Bartke 59, 64–66, 72, 82
Basar 11
Bates 80
Bayer 163, 169, 177, 207
Becker 79
Bedny 207
beim Graben 167, 192, 298
Ben-Shachar 152–3, 195
Bentin 60, 62, 227
Berent 42
Beretta 49, 51–2, 56
Berger 4, 5
Bergida 50
Berko 48
Berndt 41
Bersick 249
Bertram 78
Berwick 96
Bever 93, 161, 183, 189, 237
Bickel 106
Bierwisch 138, 150
Birbaumer 45
Bird 54

Bisang 45, 182
Blake 129
Blevins 79
Bock 117
Boehm-Jernigan 103, 210
Boland 78, 103, 210
Bornkessel-Schlesewsky 12, 18, 28, 92, 123, 135–136, 140, 151, 153, 155, 156, 159, 168–172, 179, 181, 182, 184–185, 191–193, 205, 207–208, 215, 217, 219, 222, 226, 256–258, 260–265, 270, 273, 285, 288–293, 298, 299
Bossong 185
Bozic 76–78
Bradley 78
Brázdil 21
Bresnan 115, 138, 279
Brett 278
Broadbent 237
Brodmann 18
Brown, C. 10, 120, 122, 212
Brown, R. 48
Brown, W.S. 42
Brysbaert 209
Burani 79
Burkhardt 120, 173, 175, 207, 248, 250
Buscha 179
Bybee 67

Camblin 223, 251
Caplan 18, 41, 149, 188, 194–195, 206
Cappelletti 44
Caramazza 44, 79, 146–7, 197
Carlson 99, 139, 238, 245
Carpenter 188
Carreiras 121, 214–215
Chapman 176
Chappell 182
Chen 194
Chomsky 48, 139, 145, 161, 168, 187, 207, 235, 252
Christiansen 183
Chwilla 224–5
Clahsen 48, 57, 60, 79, 157
Clark 270

Language Index

Subject Index